# Slovenia

## THE BRADT TRAVEL GUIDE

## Robin & Jenny McKelvie

Bradt Travel Guides Ltd, UK
The Globe Pequot Press Inc, USA

**First published May 2005**

Bradt Travel Guides Ltd
23 High Street, Chalfont St Peter, Bucks SL9 9QE, England
www.bradtguides.com
Published in the USA by The Globe Pequot Press Inc, 246 Goose Lane,
PO Box 480, Guilford, Connecticut 06475-0480

ISBN-10: 1 84162 119 6
ISBN-13: 978 1 84162 119 7

**British Library Cataloguing in Publication Data**
A catalogue record for this book is available from the British Library

**Photographs**
*Front cover* Logarska Dolina, Štajerska (Jenny McKelvie)
*Text* Robin and Jenny McKelvie

**Illustrations** Carole Vincer
**Maps** Matt Honour

Typeset from the authors' disc by Wakewing
Printed and bound in Italy by Legoprint SpA, Trento

# Slovenia

## THE BRADT TRAVEL GUIDE

## PUBLISHER'S FOREWORD

The first Bradt travel guide was written in 1974 by George and Hilary Bradt on a river barge floating down a tributary of the Amazon. In the 1980s and '90s the focus shifted away from hiking to broader-based guides covering new destinations – usually the first to be published about these places. In the 21st century Bradt continues to publish such ground-breaking guides, as well as others to established holiday destinations, incorporating in-depth information on culture and natural history with the nuts and bolts of where to stay and what to see.

Bradt authors support responsible travel, and provide advice not only on minimum impact but also on how to give something back through local charities. In this way a true synergy is achieved between the traveller and local communities.

*

After reading Robin and Jenny's evocative manuscript I wondered why on earth I'd never been to Slovenia. It seems to have everything I like: beautiful mountain scenery, a beguiling capital, vineyards and the Adriatic coast. Come to think of it, isn't this what almost everyone likes? I must pay a visit before the rest of the world catches on...

*Hilary Bradt*

Hilary Bradt

23 High Street, Chalfont St Peter, Bucks SL9 9QE, England
Tel: 01753 893444  Fax: 01753 892333
Email: info@bradtguides.com
Web: www.bradtguides.com

# Authors

**Robin McKelvie** has been a full-time travel writer and photographer since 1997 and is a member of both the British Guild of Travel Writers and the Outdoor Writers Guild. He has written about more than 100 European towns and cities – including co-writing *Ljubljana: The Bradt City Guide* – and travelled to over 70 countries worldwide. He first visited Slovenia in 1992, and since then has covered the region extensively, writing on Slovenia, Croatia and Montenegro. His work has been published in over 40 magazines and newspapers around the world including the *Independent on Sunday, Independent Magazine, Sunday Herald, Scotsman, Scotland on Sunday, Guardian, Global Magazine, Wanderlust, CNN Traveller, Trailfinders, TNT, The Australian, Business Traveller, ABTA Travelspirit, Boom Magazine for Millionaires* and *International High Flyer*. Robin is also easyJet's 'Man in Ljubljana', writing destination reports on a monthly basis for their in-flight magazine in conjunction with his wife.

**Jenny McKelvie** has been working as a travel writer since 1998, a job that has taken her to destinations around the world and helped develop her specialist knowledge of central and eastern Europe. Her writing credits include *Highstyle, European Businessman, Classic Travel, People's Friend, Homes Away from Home, Alpha Traveller, TNT, Footloose* and *SX*. She also wrote the *Mintel Emerging Destination Report to Slovenia* and co-wrote *Ljubljana: The Bradt City Guide*. Jenny also helps write monthly updates on Ljubljana for easyJet's in-flight magazine.

## DEDICATION
For Erin

# Contents

Map thumbnails at the opening of each regional chapter relate to this master grid.

# Acknowledgements

In Ljubljana special thanks go to Petra Stušek at the Ljubljana Tourist Office for her unfaltering and invaluable help in the city she helped us love as much as she does, and to her predecessor Petra Čuk, now with Hoteli Bled, who offered her expert knowledge as well as her generous hospitality. Miro Gračanin, formerly of the Slovenian Tourist Board, also enhanced our trips around the country with both practical help and insights into Ljubljana and Slovenia. Our thanks also go out to Mateja Tomin Vučkovič and Jona Senk of the Slovenian Tourist Board, Jan Orsič (who helped guide us around Ljubljana by boat and bike), as well as Nina Turuk, Miha Kovačič, Janis Skok, Janez Fajfar and Eva Ferjan, Matjaž Kos, Štefan Čelan, Marija Lah, Vesna Male, Marko Lenarčič, Boštjan Burger and Studio Breza. Then there are the countless other Slovenes around the country who helped brighten up our research trips with their humour and unerring friendliness.

In the UK we would especially like to thank Angela Rennie at the Slovenian Tourist Board (and Just Slovenia) and Mary Stuart-Miller, the board's UK public relations contact, who both deserve a special mention for their enthusiasm and assistance. Thanks too to Leon Marc at the embassy in Dublin for his thorough feedback on the manuscript.

# Introduction

The first time I (Robin) visited Slovenia back in 1992 it was a country that virtually no-one had heard of. Those who did know it were surprised that I was travelling there as their only experience of Slovenia was from TV news reports of the fighting that had erupted in 1991 during the breakup of Yugoslavia. The reality, though, was that even in 1992 Slovenia was completely safe to visit. Its only direct involvement in the regional conflicts had been a brief ten-day skirmish with the Yugoslav National Army (JNA) a year earlier as it quickly secured its independence.

Since that first visit I have been back to Slovenia a dozen times, Jenny accompanying me on most occasions since we met in 1997, and it still amazes us that the tourist hordes have not yet descended on this unique hideaway sandwiched between Italy, Austria, Hungary and the Balkans. This is a country that more than justifies all the 'Europe in Miniature' clichés. Even though its epic sweep of scenery, everything from Alpine peaks and tumbling rivers in the north to the balmy Adriatic coastline and vineyards in the south, garners increasing praise in the travel pages of magazines and newspapers, the country still remains genuinely 'unspoilt'.

Part of the reason for Slovenia's relative anonymity may lie in the fact that many people, including famously a certain US president, tend to get it confused with Slovakia, once part of Czechoslovakia. True, there is only a slight difference in the spelling and they sound very similar, not to mention the fact that they also have identikit flags, but Slovenia is thoroughly unique. This tiny nation of two million people was not ever behind the Iron Curtain, as many people presume, as it was part of Yugoslavia, an independent socialist state that gave its citizens passports and freedoms that the dissidents of the Prague Spring could only have dreamt of.

In 1992 Slovenia was just starting to emerge from five decades of Yugoslav socialism which, despite its relative freedoms, still kept a tight rein on Slovenia's economy and political set-up as well as suppressing any notion of Slovenian independence. Even then it was an impressive country. Far from fulfilling images of communist deprivations and terminal grey this was a place whose citizens seemed affluent, optimistic and progressive. Then there was the scenery, something that still blows us both away. If you are not a 'mountain person' you may just about manage not to be affected by some of the most dramatic skyscraping peaks in Europe, which rise improbably all around this tiny country, but then surely the Mediterranean light of the coast would beguile you, or maybe just the rolling farmland and trim villages of much of the interior, or perhaps some of Europe's wildest forests where bears and wolves still roam wild.

Fitting into the sweep of landscape are Slovenia's towns and cities, sometimes dwarfed by the scenery, but which each offer something different. The capital, Ljubljana, is a neat and appealing city of around 270,000 inhabitants which manages to pack an incredible amount into a very compact and easily navigable space, but which rarely feels crowded or hectic. Every time we visit there seems to be a new bar, restaurant or café and the place appears to take on even more of a buzz. The same can be said of Maribor, the second city, with its near neighbour Ptuj quite simply one of the most attractive European towns we have ever visited. Then there are Kranj, Piran, Koper and Novo Mesto, or what about Izola, Kropa or Kamnik?

In just over a decade Slovenia has transformed itself from an unwilling appendage of Yugoslavia into a modern and successful European democracy. In 2004 Slovenia joined both NATO and the EU, something no other state in the old federation has yet managed. It is hard not to be impressed by the Slovenes, who seem to have a natural aptitude for just buckling down and getting on with it. Instead of getting immersed in ethnic strife and conflict they have focused on building up their economy, putting their tiny country on the map and infiltrating the previously closed shops of NATO and the EU.

Despite its move towards greater integration with Europe Slovenia still retains a real independent spirit that manifests itself in so many ways, some obvious but others more subtle. In Ljubljana there is the outdoor market right in the heart of the city where, in a defiant stand against the world of supermarket hegemony, old ladies sell their homemade honey and the city's citizens peddle vegetables plucked straight from their gardens. It also comes out in the long lazy lunches and languorous early dinners that many people take, with a nonchalance that is far more Mediterranean than central European. The Slovenes themselves hate being labelled or categorised – they see themselves as independent citizens of their country, not as eastern Europeans, nor central Europeans and certainly not as belonging to the Balkans.

The Slovenia that we are writing about today is a very different one to that which emerged from the breakup of Yugoslavia at the start of the 1990s. Its epic scenic appeal, of course, still entrances, but these days along with the natural attractions tourism is starting to take off with improved transport facilities, better hotels, first-rate restaurants and an attempt to give visitors what they want rather than just relying on the beauty of the mountains and the sea. Any worries that Slovenia will be swamped by mass tourism and the hegemony of the EU do, though, seem a touch unfounded. This is a country that has, after all, managed to survive centuries of domination by the Venetians, Austro–Hungarians and Yugoslav communists, before it recently managed to extricate itself from the biggest armed conflict on the continent since World War II.

Whether it is strolling by the banks of the Ljubljanica River in the capital on an autumnal day as you kick your way through the leaves, heaving yourself up onto the summit of a peak in the Julian Alps and feeling like you are on top of Europe, or simply just relaxing with a chilled glass of Slovenian Chardonnay in a waterfront restaurant by the coast, we have a sneaking suspicion that you may just end up loving Slovenia as much as we do.

Robin and Jenny McKelvie

# Part One

# General Information

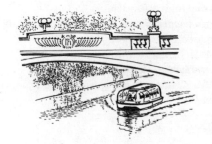

## REPUBLIC OF SLOVENIA AT A GLANCE

**Location** Central Europe sandwiched between Italy, Austria, Hungary and Croatia and with a small stretch of Adriatic coastline

**Area** 20,273 km²

**National parks** Triglav National Park

**Highest peak** Mt Triglav, 2,864m

**Forest** 10,124km²

**Vineyards** 216km²

**Coastline** 46.6km

**Population** 2 million

**Capital** Ljubljana (population 265,900)

**Other major towns and cities** Maribor, Celje, Koper, Kranj, Novo Mesto, Velenje

**Language** Slovene

**Religion** 67.9% Roman Catholic, 23.1% agnostic, 2.3% Serb Orthodox, 1.2% Muslim, 0.7% evangelist, 0.9% other Christian, and 3.9% some 30 other registered religious (2003 survey of public opinion)

**Time zone** Central European (GMT +1 hour)

**International dialling code** +386

**Climate** Average temperature in winter –1°C, spring 10°C, summer 20°C and autumn 10°C

**Currency** Tolar (SIT), 1 tolar = 100 stotins

**Weights and measures** Metric system

**Electricity** 220V, 50Hz, two-pin plug with round prongs

# Background Information

## GEOGRAPHY AND CLIMATE

The Republic of Slovenia is one of Europe's smallest countries, with a territory that covers just 20,273km², making it similar in size to Wales. Located in central Europe Slovenia shares borders with Croatia, Italy, Austria and Hungary. Ljubljana is at the heart of the country and is within a three-hour drive of even the most distant parts of the country. This compact size means that the country's dramatic mountains, thousands of underground caves, forests, Adriatic coast, lakes and rivers are all within easy reach of the capital.

Slovenia has a climate that reflects its diverse landscape. Primorska in the southwest of the country enjoys a Mediterranean climate, with temperatures in the coastal towns of Portorož, Izola, Piran and Koper being especially pleasant. In the summer temperatures hover around the mid-20s and rarely fall below 6°C in the winter.

The rest of Slovenia's lowland, including Ljubljana, has a continental climate with mild and often hot summers, but cold winters. Again July and August are the warmest months, with an average temperature of 20°C and highs hovering around 25°C. Days in May, June and September are often pleasantly warm with average temperatures of 14–17°C, and maximums that can regularly exceed 20°C. April and October, which traditionally mark the beginning and end of the tourist season, are slightly colder with average temperatures of 10°C and highs of 15°C. December, January and February are the coldest months, with an average temperature of –1°C. In January and February the mercury can plummet as low as –5°C and rarely rises above 2°C. Temperatures in Slovenia's Alps are obviously colder and winters here are characterised by frequent snowfalls.

Away from its Adriatic coast, which is drier, Slovenia has high levels of precipitation, with the weather in the spring months particularly changeable; therefore it is wise to bring waterproof clothing or an umbrella at any time of year.

## NATURAL HISTORY AND CONSERVATION

For such a small territory Slovenia has an outstanding geographical- and bio-diversity, with Pannonian plains (a large flat plain extending across central and southeastern Europe, found in the east of Slovenia), Alpine mountains and Dinaric mountains (the term Dinaric is taken from the Dinara mountain range which forms a border between Slovenia and Croatia in the south; it also separates Croatia from Bosnia and Herzegovina) each comprising 30% of the land with the Mediterranean covering the remaining 10%. This diversity brings significant changes in altitude –

## WHEN IS A REGION A REGION?

Trying to delineate Slovenia by region is a difficult and thankless task. Officially there are no regions as such, however, many Slovenes regard the regions that were developed under the Austro-Habsburg Empire as an important part of the history of their country and still talk about the likes of Notranjska (or the Inner Carniola region), Dolenjska (Lower Carniola), Gorenjska (Upper Carniola), Štajerska (Styria) and Koroška (Carinthia). During the Austro-Habsburg era the regions of Štajerska and Koroška extended into modern day Austria, with the greater part of the historical areas of Carinthia and Styria also located there today. Of these historical regions, Lower, Upper and Inner Carnolia (Dolenjska, Notranjska and Gorenjska) are widely considered to be the most 'Slovenian', as the name Carniola was used prior to Habsburg rule, originating from the Latin name for Kranj. The majority of Slovenes will also identify two other regions, Prekmurje and Tržaška (Trieste region), the former, located on the extreme northeast used to be in the Hungarian part of the Austria–Hungary Empire, while Tržaška is now almost entirely in Italy.

This book has been organised in line with these historic regions – areas with many common features and shared histories – with which many Slovenes still identify today. If you want to be a stickler they do not exist and the country must be split up into over 190 municipalities, which makes things a lot more complex. So here we have stuck with the unofficial regions, though of course you will almost certainly come across people who will want to argue the boundaries of Dolenjska or Primorska or subdivide things further still.

from 0m to 2,864m above sea level – and dramatic climate differences (see *Climate*), where annual rainfall is around 3,000mm on the Alps in the west of the country, yet is just 700mm in the east. To cap it all around 54% of Slovenia is forested – making it the third-most forested country in Europe – and this compact nation supports more than 7,000 underground Karst caves. Perhaps unsurprisingly, this incredibly varied landscape is home to an enormous number of animal and plant species.

Slovenia, after gaining independence in 1991, acted swiftly to protect and conserve the country's natural heritage – which had been threatened (and still is) by pollution from industry and increased road traffic, as well as urban and agricultural development – and passed a number of regulatory laws. One of the most important, as far as those visiting the country is concerned, is the Nature Conservation Act (1999) which prohibits removing or harming plants and animals in the wild; the law also protects their habitats and stipulates the need for responsible tourism when visiting Slovenia's fragile natural attractions, such as the Škocjan Caves and Triglav National Park.

Committed to conserving its natural environment the Slovenian government is proactive in the work of UNESCO, the United Nations Environment Programme (UNEP), the Council of Europe and the EU. Although Slovenia has only one national park – Triglav – it also protects a large proportion of its landscape through regional and landscape parks, nature reserves and the official identification of natural monuments. The Slovenian Ministry of the Environment and Spatial Planning (www.sigov.si/cgi-bin/wpl/mop/en/index.htm) is responsible for conservation in Slovenia.

# HISTORY
## A mixed bag
Situated at the heart of Europe on a crossroads between east and west, and providing central Europe's access to the Mediterranean Sea through the Adriatic, Slovenia has long attracted a diverse range of settlers and invaders. You should always, though, take any recent stab at Slovenian history with a pinch of salt as over the last decade the country has been free for the first time to really explore and – as some critics would suggest – rewrite its history and heritage. It is not always wise, though, to challenge the highly subjective version of history you hear from an animated local in this part of the world.

## Humble beginnings
Historical evidence suggests that Slovenia was first inhabited during the Neolithic period – sometime between 4000BC and 3400BC – with human remains, artefacts and dwellings discovered between the Pannonian plains and the Karst. These Stone Age residents were followed by pile dwellers, who lived in stilt-houses built on marshland, including the Ljubljansko Barje (Ljubljana Marshes). Life for the country's earliest settlers was dominated by agriculture and this continued through the Bronze Age into the early Iron Age (8th to 4th century BC), a period that was also characterised by the production of cast-iron objects – remnants of which are proudly displayed at museums throughout the country – and the growth of hilltop settlements such as those in Most na Soči, Rifnik, St Vid, near Stična, and Vače.

## The Celts and the Romans
In the 4th and 3rd centuries BC Celtic tribes from western Europe rumbled into the region and established the state of Noricum. By the beginning of the 2nd century BC, the Noric Celts had established trade links with Rome – a relationship that was to turn sour when the Romans began attacking the territory and finally annexed the state in 10BC. This first Roman era was characterised by the construction of roads and the development of urban settlements that subjugated those in the countryside. It also saw the establishment of the Roman towns of Emona (Ljubljana), Celeia (Celje) and Poetovio (Ptuj), with the last becoming the most important Roman settlement on Slovenian land.

For many of the country's inhabitants everyday life under Roman rule was good, save for the frequent attacks by barbarian Huns and central Asian Avars. The capitulation of the Romans in AD452 saw the country's residents even more exposed to attacks by barbarians and Germanic tribes.

## The Slavs
Historians dispute the timescale of the arrival of the first Slavic settlers in Slovenia; but most sources reckon that Slavs from the north migrated here early in the 6th

century AD. What is certain is that by the 7th century the Slavs had become the dominant people in Slovenia, establishing the first independent Slavic or Slovenian state, Carinthia, in AD746, which later fell under Frankish control. This Frankish period was characterised by a mass conversion to Christianity and the watering down of Slavic identity.

In the 9th century Slovenia was subsumed into the Holy Roman Empire, while the early 10th century saw the writing of the Freising Manuscripts – three religious texts widely believed to be the oldest documentation in the world to be written in a Slavic language – which many in Slovenia regard as the true origin of the nation's distinctive national and cultural identity. Perhaps unsurprisingly their current preservation in the Munich National Library is a bone of contention for many Slovenes.

## Austro-Hungarian dominance

Six hundred years of Austro-Hungarian rule was, arguably, the most defining period in Slovenia's history. In the 14th century the Habsburg dynasty took control of most of Slovenia's territory, with the Counts of Celje holding out until 1456, and they were to remain in power until World War II, with one brief exception when Napoleon usurped their authority. This period of Austro-Hungarian dominance was not without other problems, with Ottoman incursions widespread in the 15th and 16th centuries. Popular uprisings in protest at ineffectual defences against Turkish attacks and against high taxes also resulted in well-supported peasant uprisings in 1572 and 1573, which were violently suppressed.

This general dissatisfaction with Austro-Hungarian rule also asserted itself in more peaceful ways with Protestantism, which rose to the fore in the late 16th century, playing a significant role in shaping the nation's psyche over the next 200 years. A key characteristic of this time was the embracing of the Slovene language and Slovenian traditions. One of the most significant events was the 1550 publication of the first book written entirely in Slovene, Primož Trubar's *Catechismus in Abecedarium*. Around 50 further titles were also published in Slovene including a translation of the Bible by Jurij Dalmatin and Adam Bohorič's book of Slovenian grammar.

This flourishing of Slovene literature was muted by the suppression of Protestantism by the Catholic Church in the early 17th century, something that was happening all over Europe. By the 19th century the picture had turned on its head, with the Catholic Church being the main champion of the preservation of Slovene identity, language and culture. Influential figures in the evolution of Slovenia's cultural, national and literary identity that rose to the fore during this period, include the satirical writer Ivan Cankar (1876–1918) and the romantic poet France Prešeren (1849–1880).

A period of suppression and strict religious direction was replaced with a period of relative freedom as the Enlightenment swept though central Europe under the reign of Emperor Josef II (1765–90). During this time compulsory schooling was established, the Slovene language was introduced into primary schools and the Slovene literati became increasingly active.

## An unlikely champion of Slovenia

The beginning of the 19th century afforded the Slovenian people a brief respite from what was still autocratic Austro-Hungarian rule, when Napoleon made a brief invasion into the Balkans, making Ljubljana the capital of his Illyrian Provinces between 1809 and 1813. During this short-lived period of Napoleonic rule the Slovene language flourished more openly, the taxation system was reformed, Ljubljana was named the capital of the Illyrian Provinces and the distinctive national identity that had been suppressed by the Austro–Hungarians came to the fore. Napoleon's downfall saw the redrawing of the map of Europe and the return of Slovenia to Austro-Hungarian rule at the 1815 Congress of Vienna. It was here that the Habsburg Prince Klemens von Metternich agreed to join the Holy Alliance.

## War clouds and a new nation

World War I heralded the collapse of the Austro-Hungarian Empire and it also saw Slovenia suffer heavy casualties, particularly on the bloody Soča Front (see *The Soča Front* in *Chapter 5*). The fear that the 1915 London Pact would result in the distribution of Slovenian territory among various countries, combined with the rise of the regional pan-Slavic movement which had been growing through the 19th and early 20th centuries, led Slovenes, Croats and Serbs to lobby for a common kingdom in 1917. The plea to Vienna fell on deaf ears, but after the Habsburg monarchy lost the war and disintegrated, Slovenia was in 1918 incorporated into the new Kingdom of Serbs, Croats and Slovenes, which adopted another title, the Kingdom of Yugoslavia, in 1929.

## The dark days of World War II

In 1939 war engulfed Europe once again. After staying on the sidelines for over a year the kingdom entered the fray and was soon swallowed up by the Axis powers, with Germany, Italy and Hungary dividing Slovenia among them. This dark period in Slovenia's history was clouded by massacres, the suppression of Slovenian identity, the collaboration of the Slovenian Home Guard and the murder of thousands of the latter by partisans in the denouement of the war, an event whose full horror only really came to light in the 1970s.

## Tito's Yugoslavia

A dramatically different Slovenia emerged from the rubble of World War II, and in 1945 Ljubljana took its place as one of the six capitals of Tito's new Yugoslavia. The federation's other capitals were Belgrade in Serbia, Zagreb in Croatia, Sarajevo in Bosnia and Herzegovina, Skopje in Macedonia and Titograd (Podgorica) in Montenegro. For almost half a century what was by now known as the People's Republic of Slovenia (which became the Socialist Republic of Slovenia in 1963) found itself under the rigid control of the Yugoslav socialist regime, which was characterised by dictatorial leadership from Serbia and the shared ownership of property.

Slovenia was the most prosperous part of the federation (with per-capita GDP around 2.5 times higher than the other Yugoslav states), but under the socialist system the wealth was redistributed to less-developed regions such as Serbia and Montenegro, a siphoning off of resources that was to turn many Slovenes against the idea of Yugoslavia. This animosity grew amidst recurrent stories of government corruption, nepotism and attempts to suppress Slovenian identity, and was further intensified by Tito's death in 1980. With the man who had welded the disparate parts of Yugoslavia gone the stage was set for the break-up of the federation.

## Independent at last

By the end of the 1980s political parties that opposed the Belgrade-based regime had emerged and gained popular support in Slovenia, with calls for an independent state first officially coming in 1989 under the auspices of the May Declaration. Just over a year later on December 23 1990 an overwhelming majority of voters (88%) asserted their desire to leave the Socialist Federal Republic of Yugoslavia and become an independent country.

After a delay of six months independence was officially declared on June 26 1991, a move that led to a ten-day war with Yugoslav government troops. Mercifully this brief conflict was relatively bloodless. Over 2,000 soldiers from the Yugoslav National Army (JNA) were ordered to seize the country's border stations, but blockades prevented many from leaving their barracks and the well-organised Slovenian domestic forces proved themselves a match for the confused and demoralised JNA troops (some of whom were actually Slovenes), many of whom voluntarily surrendered. After ten days of skirmishes and threats to attack Brnik Airport and Ljubljana itself – a menace that never materialised – the JNA backed down and a ceasefire took effect on July 6 1991.

Slovenia's independence was recognised by the EU on January 15 1992, and by the USA on April 17 1992. The country then set about developing its economy and building political and economic relationships with the rest of the world. Slovenia's integration into the European fold was complete in 2004 when it joined both the EU and NATO. Potential political problems do remain such as the lingering dispute with Croatia over territorial waters in the Adriatic and the fate of the stateless refugees who came north from other parts of Yugoslavia in the 1990s, but for the fledgling nation of Slovenia the future does look as bright as it ever has during any point in its history.

## GOVERNMENT AND POLITICS

The political history of modern-day Slovenia is a relatively short one, which begins with the assertion of independence in 1991 (see *History*). One of the biggest tasks that confronted the newly independent country was the implementation of a new constitution, which materialised in December 1991 under the guidance of the country's first democratically elected prime minister, Lojze Peterle. This new constitution established a democratic parliamentary political system, which clearly delineated the roles of separate judicial, legislative and executive powers. Under this model of government the Državni Zbor (National Assembly), which is the Upper House of the Parliament and has the final say in legislative issues, is the most powerful institution. Slovenia's National Assembly comprises 90 elected officials who are elected through proportional representation and stay in office for four years.

Slovenia's *Državni Svet* (National Council) – which is the Lower House of the Parliament, representing the interests of the city and its workforce – has the power to challenge legislation passed by the National Assembly and can also initiate legislative change, although it rarely does so. The 40 elected officials – 22 of whom represent Slovenia's municipalities, four of whom represent the employers' organisation, four the employees' union, four farmers and craftsmen and six representing education, science, health and similar professions – serve a five-year term. In principle the referendums held by the National Assembly create a transparent political process that directly involves the people. Recent referendums include ballots on membership of the EU and NATO, as well as one on weekend opening hours for retail outlets. Some Slovenes now feel many of these numerous referendums are a waste of money and that state funds could be used more prudently. Others cast aspersions on the authenticity of this process, claiming that the majority of Slovenes did not want to join NATO and yet the result was overwhelmingly in favour of this.

Slovenia's judicial system comprises four different types of court – district, regional, higher and supreme – with the last being the most powerful. District Court judges deal with lesser offences, while those in Regional Courts deal with minors, business law and land registration. Higher Court judges are responsible for repeat offenders and appeals made against the rulings of District and Regional courts. The principle role of the Supreme Court is that of reviewing appeals, settling disputes over jurisdiction and regulating the legal profession. Judges are independent but accountable to the National Assembly, which elected them. Another independent institution, the Bank of Slovenia, is also accountable to the National Assembly.

Slovenia's government holds executive powers, and the country's current government is led by Prime Minister Janez Janša, leader of the Slovenian Democratic Party (SDS), who took up his post in December 2004, two months after the October elections. The other three parties of the Government are New Slovenia Party (NSi), the Slovenian People's Party (SLS) and the Pensioners' Party (DeSUS). In addition to the prime minister the government has 14 cabinet members. Slovenia's other political parties include the Liberal Democratic Party (LDS), the United List of Social Democrats (ZLSDS), the Slovene National Party (SNS), the Slovenian Youth Party (SMS) and the Greens of Slovenia.

Dr Janez Drnovšek, Slovenia's second prime minister, is now the country's president. Elected as Head of State with 56% of the vote in December 2002, Drnovšek resigned his post as prime minister the following day. According to the Slovenian Constitution the president is the country's commander-in-chief and is restricted to a maximum of ten years in office (two five-year terms). Presidential duties include calling elections, nominating a candidate for prime minister and appointing ambassadors and other state officials. Although Drnovšek has held prominent political office since 1992, it has not always been plain sailing for him. In May 2000, while he was still prime minister, a vote of no confidence forced him to resign his post, and Dr Andrej Bajuk of the NSi took over. Six months later parliamentary elections returned the LDS to power and Drnovšek to his role as prime minister.

In recent years the political stage in Slovenia has been dominated by the rapid privatisation of business and preparation for EU membership, which this young country achieved with impressive speed and efficiency on May 1 2004, giving Slovenia access to an internal trade market of over 455 million people. Since 1991 Slovenia has also joined the United Nations, the Council of Europe and NATO, as well as becoming a non-permanent member of the United Nations Security Council.

## ECONOMY

Slovenia has a strong and growing economy, which is set to go from strength to strength as a result of joining the EU in May 2004. Far from being an impoverished new member Slovenia's GNP actually rose above that of more established EU members Portugal and Greece in 2004. The country's GDP has witnessed a steady annual growth since 1991 and inflation has been falling in recent years, standing at 9.1% in 1991 and just 5.5% in 2003. The number of unemployed people in Slovenia has also been declining since the late 1990s, and the country had an unemployment rate of 6.3% in December 2003.

Slovenia's service industry is vital to the country's economy, as it accounts for around 60% of GDP. Manufacturing accounts for 31%, construction 5.8% and agriculture just 3% of GDP. Important service industries include education, health, finance, retail, service industries and tourism. The latter suffered a serious decline as Yugoslavia began to disintegrate in 1991, however, it has been making a steady recovery ever since and is set to boom now that Slovenia is part of the EU. In terms of manufacturing, Slovenia's main products, and exports, include kitchen appliances, Renault cars, car components, electromechanical mechanisms, furniture, pharmaceuticals and transport services. Slovenia is also a world leader when it comes to manufacturing niche products including Elan – one of the world's largest ski producers – and the Seaway yacht. There are some concerns amongst Slovenes that these manufacturing companies will struggle to survive in the open market of the EU.

The agricultural sector is a small and relatively insignificant part of Slovenia's economy, with the main activity here centred on the growth of potatoes, cereal and sugar beet, beef production, dairy farming and fishing. Slovenia's mining industry, which formerly played a vital role in the country's economy, has fallen into decline, with many of the remaining mines set to shut down under a phased closure programme. At one time the mining of coal, zinc, lead and uranium was a mainstay in Slovenia's economy and that of Yugoslavia, however, the country's only uranium mine has been closed for some years. Gas and oil are also drilled near Lendava, but in experimental quantities.

The only clouds on the economic horizon are the structural economic legacies of socialism (such as the power of the trade unions) and the rising domestic costs that have already led some international companies to seek new more cost-effective bases elsewhere in the expanded EU.

## PEOPLE

Trying to tie down who exactly the Slovenes are is a bit tricky given that they have only had their own country since 1991 and that they share land borders

## A SPORTING NATION

With so little acknowledgment of Slovenia on the global political map and with world leaders getting it confused with Slovakia it is perhaps not too surprising that sporting success has become something of an obsession for many Slovenes. The country may not be heralded on TV news programmes around the world, but it has certainly managed to force itself on to the sports bulletins by qualifying for both the European Football Championships in 2000 and the Football World Cup in 2002. The European Championships in 2004, though, proved disastrous as Slovenia narrowly missed out on qualifying in a play-off against arch-rival and neighbour Croatia by a single goal. Then there is Primož Peterka, double ski-jumping World Cup winner, and Davo Karničar, the man who managed the first-ever ski descent of Mount Everest in 2000, a sure sign that Slovenes will go to any length to get noticed. In 2004 Celje also became European handball champions. The country secured Olympic golds at the Sydney 2000 games in the rowing and although no golds were won in Athens in 2004 Slovenia rated fifth on the medal table going by a medals-to-population ratio (the Bahamas with their solitary gold came first!). The Slovenes further demonstrated their sporting prowess in October 2004 by seeing off the mighty Italians in a football qualifying match in Celje for the 2006 World Cup.

with four European countries. Many Slovenes will tell you that they have no idea what exactly constitutes a Slovene. This in a sense is part of the country's attraction as no-one wants to ram down your throat why their nation is the strongest, smartest and most important country in this often volatile part of Europe, something that some of the countries further south could perhaps take a lesson from.

Although it is difficult to pin down what makes someone Slovene, Slovenia is actually one of the most ethnically homogeneous countries in Europe with an overriding majority of people declaring themselves ethnically Slovene. This, though, does not take into account the full picture as many people have at least one parent who is Italian, Hungarian, Croatian or Austrian. Nationalities are fluid in Slovenia, but mercifully not normally a source of conflict.

If you have to generalise about a 'typical Slovene' you could say they have instilled in them a deep sense of the importance of nature, whether or not they live in the countryside. They like nothing better than heading out into the mountains and do so at every opportunity, as you will soon discover with the weekend traffic jams in and out of Ljubljana and Maribor. This back-to-the-earth approach crosses over into their diets as they, unusually for Slavs, enjoy healthy fresh fruit and vegetables and organic produce is much sought after.

In terms of temperament Slovenes have a reputation for being much calmer and more rational than some of their more hotheaded 'Balkan brethren' further south. Having said that, once inflamed they can dig their heels in and be intensely stubborn and once offended they stay offended rather than just laughing things off

### THE LINDEN TREE

One of Slovenia's national symbols is the leaf of the Linden Tree, or *Lipa*, in Slovene. For Slovenes, and other South Slavs, the tree is a symbol of life, therefore villages have traditionally been constructed around now ancient Linden trees. At the geographical centre of a village, the *Lipa* also became the heart of the local communities social life, with villagers meeting at the tree. As well as being planted all over the country, the Linden tree pops up in music and literature, in the form of poems and children's songs. It was also used in a campaign to promote tourism in the former Yugoslavia in the late 1980s.

with the clink of a glass so beware of ruffling their feathers. The oft-quoted 'don't mess with the little guy' line that Slovenes like to trot out has a lot of truth to it.

## LANGUAGE

Slovene is the country's official language, although English is also used widely, especially by the younger generation. In the north German is an important language, as is Hungarian in Prekmurje and Italian in Primorska. In different regions 'foreign' words creep into Slovene depending on the proximity to the borders with Austria, Croatia, Hungary or Italy.

Language is still a very politically charged subject in the former Yugoslavia with the Croats and Serbs for example speaking a very similar language that each passionately claim as their own with steps being taken to 'invent' new words and find differences to separate the two. Slovene, while more different from Serbian and Croatian than they are from each other, is still in the Slavic family of languages and if you have travelled around many of the countries of the 'old east' you will recognise more than a few words and have a major advantage when it comes to pronunciation.

Today Slovene is spoken by most of the two million people in the country with perhaps up to a million of the Slovene diaspora outside its borders able to speak it

### THE NATIONAL FLAG OF SLOVENIA

The Slovenian national flag is a tricolour of white, blue and red, from top to bottom, with a small image of Mt Triglav in the top left-hand corner. It does strongly resemble both the Russian and the Slovakian flags, which has helped cause confusion in the past, especially with 'Slovakia' being so similar in both sound and spelling to 'Slovenia'. There have been calls from some quarters recently for a new national flag to differentiate Slovenia more clearly and ease the confusion, though no consensus has yet emerged on what a new flag would look like. Other unofficial symbols of the country are the ubiquitous *kozolecs* (hay racks) that you will see dotted all over the place, and the traditional bee hive panels that you will also see throughout the countryside, particularly in Gorenjska.

too. Today people speak Slovene with pride, as it was a language that was suppressed for centuries, but neither the Austro–Hungarians, Mussolini nor Tito were able to snuff out this tongue. If you take the effort to learn a few Slovene words it will be amply rewarded with smiles of appreciation, though be aware that your pronunciation will probably be so bad, and your effort so unexpected that you may often just elicit a blank stare as your listener tries to decipher what language you are talking. For an introduction to the basics of Slovene see *Appendix 1.*

## RELIGION

A public opinion survey conducted in 2003 revealed that the majority of Slovenes, 67.9% of the population, consider themselves Roman Catholic, although many do not adhere strictly to the principles of their faith. The next biggest religion in Slovenia is the Serb Orthodox faith (2.3%), followed by Islam (1.2%), other Christian (0.9%) and Evangelist (0.7%). Catholicism and Protestantism (Evangelism) are Slovenia's two domestic religions, and while a small minority of the country's population adhere to the latter faith, historically it played an important role in the development of the Slovene language. Today the Protestant minority live mainly in the region of Prekmurje, an area that fell outside the Roman Catholic influence of the Habsburgs, and in some larger cities. In this same survey 23.1% of respondents reported that they were agnostic. Despite the relative homogeneity of the population, there are a further 30 registered religious societies in Slovenia. Given the divisions, hatred and violence that religion has become synonymous within the Balkans, Slovenes as a rule are pretty tolerant when it comes to religion, though seriously bad publicity was generated thanks to a recent bid to block the construction of Ljubljana's first mosque.

## EDUCATION

Education is very important to most Slovenes and the country has one of Europe's highest adult (over-15) literacy rates at 99.6% (based on 2001 figures). The main language of education is Slovene. Nine years of elementary school education is compulsory and free from the ages of six to 15. All children between the ages of one and six are entitled to attend pre-school. At the end of their compulsory schooling students in Slovenia have a variety of choices, including continuing their general secondary education until age 18 or 19 or completing vocational training for up to three years. In terms of universities the University of Ljubljana is the oldest in the country, established in 1919. It has since been joined by the University of Maribor and, the newest arrival, the University of Primorska in Koper. Students generally begin university when they are 19 years old and spend three to six years studying. A system of post-graduate education also operates within the country, with most students starting this at the age of 23. For more information see the Slovenian Ministry for Education website, www.mszs.si.

14

Invigorate
your body

Find more invigorating
information about
Slovenia, a new
EU-member, at:
**Slovenian Tourist Board:**
Dunajska 156
SI-1000 Ljubljana
tel.: +386 1 589 18 40
fax: +386 1 589 18 41

www.slovenia.info

 **Slovenia**
INVIGORATES

*Julian Alps, golden eagle/aquila chrysaetos/in flight*

# Practical Information

## WHEN TO VISIT

There really is no bad time to visit Slovenia. In early May, when the spring showers have largely ceased and the temperature often rises above 20°C, blossoming trees, blooming flowers and fresh green leaves give the country's dramatic landscape an ethereal beauty. From spring through to October you can indulge in the diverse range of outdoor activities on offer, from white-water rafting on grade-5 rapids, hang-gliding and canyoning through to hill walking and mountain climbing. At this time of year the country also offers al-fresco living with cafés, bars and restaurants exploding on to the streets in a flurry of tables.

In autumn when the country's bountiful trees start to change colour and shed their leaves Slovenia is an incredibly romantic place to be as you kick your way through the leaves by the Ljubljanica River or take a bracing stroll through some of the most stunning landscapes in Europe. Many of Slovenia's pavement cafés keep their tables out, giving you the best of the summer without the humidity of July and August. September vies with May for being the best month to visit many parts of the country, as the chill of winter still seems a long way off.

Winter is the season that tends to put off many would-be visitors, worried

---

### SUGGESTED ITINERARIES
**A long weekend** Ljubljana and day trip to Bled and/or Bohinj.
**One week** Start in Ljubljana, loop up to Bled, Bohinj, Kranjska Gora and over the Vršic Pass to Primorska, coming back north via Idrija to Ljubljana.
**Two weeks** Same as one week but continue south to the coast and explore Piran and Koper before heading back to Ljubljana via Lake Cerknica and either the Postojna or the Škocjan Caves. Side trips to Slovenia's second city, Maribor, or one of the oldest towns in Slovenia, Ptuj, are also highly recommended.
**One month** Same as two weeks, but head east through the Kočevski Rog to Novo Mesto. Explore Bela Krajina before striking north for Maribor, Ptuj and Prekmurje. Then head back west through Slovenj Gradec to Logarska Dolina before dropping down through Kamnik to Ljubljana.

On the longer trips there is plenty of time for stopping off at a *terme*, seeking out a rural *gostilna* or indulging in adventure sports.

that they will be frozen by the ravages of a continental European winter. True, the mercury can plummet, but the weather can also be glorious with clear blue skies accompanying walks across the crisp fresh snow. October to late April are also great months for winter-sports enthusiasts, with ski resorts in the north and west offering exhilarating runs that are largely undiscovered by the rest of Europe. Myriad winter sports on offer at this time include ice-climbing, snow trekking, tobogganing, tubing and snowboarding, as well as both downhill and cross-country skiing.

Slovenia's historic cities, towns and villages are enjoyable places to visit at this time of year, with a host of winter festivals livening up the atmosphere. In the run-up to Christmas seasonal markets spill into the streets and if you follow the locals and wrap up warm, bring a brolly and pepper your visit with plenty of glasses of warming mulled wine, then you will really get into the festive spirit. At New Year, Ljubljana is engulfed by a giant street party.

Slovenia's lively cultural and artistic scene also ensures that there is always plenty to do, with a string of events and festivals taking place year-round (see *Public Holidays and Festivals*).

## HIGHLIGHTS

The 'Europe in Miniature' eulogies of the tourist office and many travel writers do for once really ring true. You could quite easily spend a month in Slovenia and only touch the surface – to be honest you could spend a month just in Primorska or Gorenjska and not cover everything. When planning a trip to Slovenia it is essential not to underestimate how much there is to see and do and then to let its compact size and good transport infrastructure work with you to get the best out of your trip.

Ljubljana is a must-do, and a holiday that uses the city only as a brief entry and exit point will be all the poorer for it. Allow at least two or three days here, more if you can, especially from May to September when the days are long and the pavement café tables are out.

Then there are the rest of the country's towns and cities. Maribor is well worth a visit for its culture and Old Town, while Ptuj is remarkably attractive. Celje and Novo Mesto may not be as aesthetically cohesive, but have their charms and plenty to see and do, while the list of worthwhile historic towns would not be complete without mentioning Kamnik, Radovljica, Slovenj Gradec and, of course, the superlative Venetian town of Piran on the coast.

It is the countryside that many people come for and there is much more on offer than a quick day trip to Bled hints at. The Julian Alps and Triglav National Park are the blockbusters and simply must not be missed, with the famous lake at Bled and the equally impressive alpine stretch of water at Bohinj. Also try venturing into the Kamniške–Savinje Alps, down the Soča Valley and through the wild expanse of the Kočevski Rog, one of Europe's wildest forests. Then there is Logarska Dolina, a superlative-defying alpine valley that you will simply never forget, while the Adriatic coastline offers another world altogether.

Admiring the scenery is one thing but make sure, if you are fit and able, to hurl yourself into it: scale the peaks, ride the rapids, fling yourself off a bungee jump or tumble down a mountain on two wheels. Slovenia is an adventure-lover's paradise with Bovec, Kranjska Gora and Kobarid all good bases for adrenaline junkies.

It may be small in size, but below ground the country delves on and on with over 7,000 caves. The Postojna Caves are well and truly on the tourist map and deservedly so, but the Škocjan Caves are if anything more stunning, a Tolkienesque netherworld that delights and intrigues in equal measure. Many of the smaller caves around Slovenia lie virtually untouched by tourists.

Culture vultures will not be disappointed by the first-class museums in all of Slovenia's major cities, with Ljubljana being the obvious highlight. You will also find ancient monasteries, rural churches with stunning Gothic frescos and unusual museums (like the beekeeping museum in Radovljica) sprinkled around the country. Slovenes love their music, literature and art; this is after all a country with a holiday dedicated to the national poet France Prešeren, so there is plenty of intellectual stimulus on offer too.

Then there are the castles, with hundreds scattered around the country acting as a constant reminder of Slovenia's rich and chequered history. Highlights include the sturdy fortress in Ljubljana and the picturesque ramparts high above Bled, not to mention the chance to actually spend the night in your very own castle at Mokrice or Otočec. When all the sightseeing gets too much then there are always the countless spas, or *terme*. Here bubbling hot water gushes from the earth and you can join Slovenes frolicking around in the regenerative waters, maybe popping off for a massage afterwards. This is a country where spas are no mere fad.

After a dip in the spa an Epicurean treat awaits. This is one of Europe's most underrated wine-producing countries and you can savour a wide range of quality reds and whites, not to mention some good sparkling wines and some fiery *digestifs*. On the plate there is the bountiful seafood of the Adriatic, the *pršut* (air-dried ham) of the Karst and the tempting desserts of Prekmurje. Once you have travelled around and tried Slovenia's myriad attractions, you may just want to pop back for another visit, as there is always something to see in a corner of Europe that manages to cram so much in, making it hard to believe its small size.

## TOUR OPERATORS

The Slovenian Tourist Board can provide a full list of tour operators based in your country of residence. Contact details for your closest office can be found at www.slovenia-tourism.si.

Kompas are a Slovenian company with representatives at various offices around the globe.

## UK

A large number of UK travel agents offer package holidays and city breaks in Slovenia. They can also assist with independent travel arrangements. In the UK flights commonly leave from Gatwick, Heathrow or Manchester, although some serve other regional airports and Dublin.

**Balkan Holidays** Sofia House, 19 Conduit St, London W1S 2BH; tel: 0845 130 1114; email: res@balkanholidays.co.uk; www.balkanholidays.co.uk

**Crystal Holidays** Kings Pl, Wood St, Kingston upon Thames KT1 1JY; tel: 0870 848 7015; email: travel@crystalholidays.co.uk; www.crystalholidays.co.uk

**Exodus Travels** Grange Mills, Weir Rd, London SW12 0NE; tel: 0870 240 5550; email: sales@exodus.co.uk; www.exodus.co.uk

**Holiday Options** 3rd floor, 49 The Martlets, Burgess Hill, West Sussex RH15 9NJ; tel: 01444 244499; email: sales@holidayoptions.co.uk; www.holidayoptions.co.uk

**Inghams Travel** 10–18 Putney Hill, London SW15 6AX; tel: 020 8780 4400; email: info@inghams.co.uk; www.inghams.co.uk

**Just Slovenia** The Barns, Woodlands End, Mells, Frome, Somerset BA11 3QD; tel: 01373 814230; fax: 01373 813444; email: justslovenia@planos.co.uk; www.justslovenia.co.uk

**Kompas London Ltd** 2 Canfield Pl, London NW6 3BT; tel: 020 7372 3844; fax: 020 7372 3763; email: kompas.london@virgin.net; www.kompas.net

**Major Travel Plc** Fortress Grove, London NW5 2HB; tel: 0870 330 7315; email: sales@majortravel.co.uk; www.majortravel.co.uk

**Regent Holidays** 15 John St, Bristol BS1 2HR; tel: 0117 921 1711; fax: 0117 925 4866; email: regent@regent-holidays.co.uk; www.regent-holidays.co.uk

**Shearings Holidays** Miry Lane, Wigan, Lancs WN3 4AG; tel: 01942 244246; email: reservations@shearingsholidays.co.uk; www.shearingsholidays.com

**Solo's Holidays** 54–58 High St, Edgware HA8 7EJ; tel: 0870 499 8800; email: travel@solosholidays.co.uk; www.solosholidays.co.uk

**Thermalia Travel** 1a Stanmore Hill, Stanmore, Middx HA7 4BL; tel: 0870 165 9420; email: sales@thermalia.co.uk; www.thermalia.co.uk

**Vamos Travel** Fernwood House, Brindley Brae, Kinver, West Midlands DY7 6LR; tel: 01384 878 125; fax: 0870 762 1016; email: info@vamostravel.com; www.vamostravel.com

## Ireland

**Crystal Holidays** 18–19 Duke St, Dublin 2; tel: +353 01 433 1043; fax: +353 01 670 8910; email: info@crystalholidays.ie; www.crystalholidays.ie

**Falcon Holiday** Block 5, Westland Sq, Pearse St, Dublin 2; tel: +353 01850 453 545; www.falconholidays.ie

**Harry Cahill Tours and Travel** 1st Floor, 6th Suite, Morrison Chambers, 32 Nassau St, Dublin 2; tel: +353 01 670 5123; fax: +353 01 670 5126; email: harry.cahill@harry-cahill-travel.ie; www.harry-cahill-travel.ie

**Topflight** Jervis House, 3rd Floor, Jervis St, Dublin 1; tel: +353 01 240 1700, fax: +353 01 2401 707; email: info@topflight.ie; www.topflight.ie

## USA

**Kompas Holidays International** 2929 E Commercial Bd, Suite 201, Ft Lauderdale, FL 33308; tel: +1 954 771 9200 or toll-free +1 800 233 6422; fax: +1 954 771 9841; email: kompas@kompas.net; www.kompas.net

## Canada

**Kompas Tours International** PO Box 474 'Westmount Station', Montreal, Quebec, Canada H3Z 2T6; tel: +1 514 938 4041; fax: +1 514 938 4039; email: kompas.canada@primus.ca; www.kompas.net

## Austria

**Kompas Touristik Reiseveranstaltung GesemBH** Siebensterngasse 21, 1070 Vienna; tel: +43 01 402 2042; fax: +43 01 402 2825; email: kompasvie@via.at; www.kompas.net

## Benelux

**Kompas Holidays International BV** Benthuizerstraat 29 ben, 3036 CB Rotterdam, Netherlands; tel: +31 010 465 7431; fax: +31 010 46575 14; email: kompasnl@euronet.nl; www.kompas.net

## France

**Kompas France International SA** 14, rue de la Source, 75016 Paris; tel: +33 01 53 92 27 80; fax: +33 01 42 15 20 52; email: parkompas@wanadoo.fr; www.kompas.net

## Germany

**Kompas International Reisen GmbH** Mainluststrasse 6/6, 60329 Frankfurt am Main; tel: +49 069 233 024; fax: +49 069 236 945; email: info.fra@kompas.de; www.kompas.net

**Kompas International Reisen GmbH** Hochbruckenstrasse 10, 80331 Munchen; tel: +49 089 904 6355; fax: +49 089 904 6253; email: info@kompas-muc.de; www.kompas.net

**Kompas International Reisen GmbH** Glienickerstrasse 40, 14109 Berlin; tel: +49 030 8060 2780; fax: +49 030 805 9037; email: kir@kompas-berlin.de; www.kompas.net

## Italy

**Kompas SRL** S Marco 1497, 30124 Venice; tel: +39 041 240 5600; fax: +39 041 520 6184; email: kompas.venice@kompas.it; www.kompas.net

**Kompas SRL** Piazza dell'Esquilino 8/G, 00185 Rome; tel: +39 06 4782 4267; fax: +39 06 4891 6042; email: kompas.rome@kompas.it; www.kompas.net

## Russia

**Kompas Representative Office** ul 3ya Tverskaja-Yamskaya 24/1, 125047 Moscow; tel: +70 095 251 3236; fax: +70 095 251 6795; email: kompas@cityline.ru; www.kompas.net

## Scandinavia

**Kompas Scandinavia** Enhojsparken 1, 3450 Allerod, Denmark; tel: +45 048 141 997; fax: +45 048 161 997; email: kompas.scandinavia@wanadoo.dk; www.kompas.net

## Spain

**Kompas Touristik Espana SA** Calle Valencia 494, Esc Dcha-A, 1°-2a, 08013 Barcelona; tel: +34 093 246 6777/5295; fax: +34 093 245 4188; email: incoming@kompas-spain.com; www.kompas.net

## Switzerland

**Kompas Travel Tour Operating** Alpenstrasse 1, 6004 Lucerne; tel: +41 041 418 8030; fax: +41 041 418 8036; www.kompas.net

# RED TAPE

Although Slovenia joined the European Union on May 1 2004 it does not currently have Schengen border regulations. While the country is preparing for this, it will not be eligible to join the Schengen zone until at least 2007. For most visitors Slovenia's border formalities are nominal and the majority simply need a valid passport for stays of less than three months. Citizens from EU countries and those from Croatia and Switzerland can enter Slovenia for up to 30 days with a national identity card.

Visa requirements for those travelling to Slovenia from a country that has not signed the Schengen agreement vary. At present those from Australia, New Zealand, Canada and the USA can stay for up to 90 days without a visa, while South Africans need a visa to enter Slovenia. Visa requirements are subject to change and non-EU citizens are advised to check with the Slovenian Ministry of Foreign Affairs (www.sigov.si/mzz).

In accordance with EU regulations, citizens from EU member states can freely bring tobacco and alcohol into Slovenia for personal use. For non-EU members duty-free rules still apply. These restrict the import of tobacco to 200 cigarettes or 250g of tobacco, or 50 cigars; 2l of wine, 1l of spirits, 50g of perfume and 250ml of eau de toilette can also be imported. Anyone entering Slovenia with more than 3,000,000SIT in cash or personal possessions needs to declare this on entry.

## SLOVENIAN EMBASSIES OVERSEAS

**Australia** Level 6, Advance Bank Centre, 60 Marcus Clarke St, Canberra, ACT 2601; tel: +61 02 6243 4830; fax: +61 02 6243 4827

**Austria** Nibelungengasse 13, A-1010 Vienna; tel: +43 01 586 1309; fax: +43 01 586 1265; email: VDU@mzz-dkp.gov.si

**Belgium** Av Louise 179, B-1050 Brussels; tel: +32 02 646 9099; fax: +32 02 646 3667

**Canada** 150 Metcalfe St, Suite 2101, Ottawa, Ontario K2P 1P1; tel: +1 613 565 5781/2; fax: +1 613 565 5783; email: vot@mzz-dkp.gov.si

**Denmark** Amaliegade 6, 2nd floor, 1256 Copenhagen; tel: +45 33 730 120; fax: +45 33 150 607

**France** 28 rue Bois-le-Vent, 75116 Paris; tel: +33 01 44 96 50 66; fax: +33 01 45 24 67 05

**Germany** Hausvogteiplatz 3–4, D-10117 Berlin; tel: +49 030 206 145/0; fax: +49 030 206 145/70; email: VBO@mzz-dkp.gov.si

**Ireland** Morrison Chambers, 2nd floor, Nassau St, Dublin 2; tel: +353 01 670 5240; fax: +353 01 670 5243; www.gov.si/mzz/dkp/vdb

**Italy** Via Leonardo Pisano 10, I-00197 Rome; tel: +39 06 8091 4310; fax: +39 06 8081 471; email: VRI@mzz-dkp.gov.si

**New Zealand** PO Box 30247, Lower Hutt, Wellington; tel: +64 04 567 0027; fax: + 64 04 567 0024

**Russia** ul Mala Dimitrovka (Čehova) 14/1, 103006 Moscow; tel: +75 03 737 3398; fax: +70 095 200 1568

**Spain** Hermanos Becquer 7–2, 28006 Madrid; tel: +34 091 411 6893; fax: +34 091 564 6057

**Switzerland** Schwanengasse 9/II, CH-3011 Bern; tel: +41 031 311 4421; fax: +41 031 312 4414; email: VBE@mzz-dkp.gov.si

**UK** 10 Little College St, London SW1P 3SJ; tel: +44 020 7222 5400; fax: +44 020 7222 5277; email: VLO@mzz-dkp.gov.si; www.slovenia.embassyhomepage.com
**USA** 1525 New Hampshire Av NW, Washington, DC 20036, tel: +1 202 667 5363; fax: +1 202 667 4563; email: slovenia@embassy.org; www.embassy.org/slovenia

## OVERSEAS EMBASSIES AND CONSULATES IN SLOVENIA

All of the embassies and consulates listed below are located in Ljubljana.

**Australian Consulate** Trg Republike 3/XII; tel: 01 425 4252; fax: 01 426 4721
**Austrian Embassy** Prešernova 23; tel: 01 479 0700; fax: 01 252 1717; email: austroamb@austrianembassy.si; www.austriantrade.si
**Belgian Embassy** Trg Republike 3/IX; tel: 01 200 6010
**Canadian Consulate** Miklošičeva 19; tel: 01 430 3570; fax: 01 430 3575
**Danish Embassy** Eurocentre, Tivolski 48; tel: 01 438 0800
**EU** Trg Republike 3/XI; tel: 01 425 1303
**French Embassy** Barjanska 1; tel: 01 479 0400
**German Embassy** Prešernova 27; tel: 01 479 0300; fax: 01 425 0899
**Irish Embassy** Palača Kapitelj, Poljanski nasip 6; tel: 01 300 8970; fax: 01 282 1096; email: irish.embassy@siol.net
**Italian Embassy** Snežniška 8; tel: 01 426 2194; fax: 01 425 3302; email: amblubiana@siol.net
**New Zealand Consulate** Verovškova 57; tel: 01 580 3055; fax: 01 568 3526; email: janja.bratos@lek.si
**Russian Embassy** Tomišičeva 9; tel: 01 425 6875
**South African Consulate** Pražakova 4; tel: 01 200 6300; fax: 01 200 6434
**Spanish Embassy** Trnovski pristan 24; tel: 01 425 6875
**Swiss Embassy** Trg Republike 3/VI; tel: 01 200 8640
**UK Embassy** Trg Republike 3/IV; tel: 01 200 3910; fax: 01 425 0174; email: info@british-embassy.sil; www.british-embassy.si
**USA Embassy** Prešernova 31; tel: 01 200 5500; fax: 01 200 5555; email: email@usembassy.si; www.usembassy.si

## GETTING THERE AND AWAY
### By air

Ljubljana's Brnik Airport, located 23km northwest of the city centre, is small by European standards. Facilities in the departures hall are better than those in arrivals (where annoyingly there is not even an ATM), with an ATM, car rental, currency exchange, bar, telephone-operated hotel booking system, restaurants, telephones, toilets and shops. The airport terminal is well served by taxis and bus services. Six scheduled airlines fly to Brnik providing the city with direct connections to more than 20 destinations worldwide including Amsterdam, Belgrade, Berlin, Brussels, Budapest, Copenhagen, Dublin, Frankfurt, Istanbul, London (Stansted and Gatwick), Manchester, Moscow, Munich, Ohrid, Paris, Podgorica, Prague, Pristina, Sarajevo, Skopje, Split, Tel Aviv, Tirana, Vienna and Zürich. Charter flights also serve Slovenia's Portorož and Maribor airports as well as the capital.

**Ljubljana Brnik Airport** Tel: 04 206 1981; fax: 04 206 1109; email: info@lju-airport.si; www.lju-airport.si
**Maribor Airport** Letališka 10, Orehova Vas; tel: 02 629 1175; fax: 02 629 1253; email: info@maribor-airport.si; www.maribor-airport.si
**Portorož Airport** Sečovlje 19, Sečovlje; tel: 05 672 2525; fax: 05 672 2530; email: info@portoroz-airport.si
**Adria Airways** Tel: 04 2594 245; www.adria-airways.com
**Austrian Airlines** Tel: 01 2391 900; www.aua-si.com
**Czech Airlines** Tel: 04 2061 750; www.czechairlines.com
**easyJet** Tel: 04 2061 677; www.easyJet.com
**JAT Airways** Tel: 04 2061 780; www.jat.com
**Malév** Tel: 04 2061 676; www.malev.hu

The introduction of easyJet flights from London Stansted to Ljubljana in April 2004 provided the city with its first low-cost carrier. easyJet added a direct Berlin connection later in 2004 and a Basel–Ljubljana route in 2005. Adria Airways operates twice weekly direct flights from Dublin to Ljubljana during the summer season. Those who are seeking to keep costs down might also consider flying with Ryanair to Trieste, 110km from Ljubljana, or to Klagenfurt, 79km away. If you are planning to do this it is essential to consider the cost of onward travel from these destinations. Rumours persist of a new Ryanair London to Maribor route but at the time of writing nothing was concrete.

**Ronchi dei Legionari Trieste Airport** Via Aquileia 46, 34077 Ronchi dei Legionari, Italy; tel: +39 0481 773 224; fax: +39 0481 474 150; email: info@aeroporto.fvg.it; www.aeroporto.fvg.it. Airport transfers with Atlas Express in Portorož (tel: 05 674 6772; fax: 05 674 8820; email: atlas.portoroz@siol.net) to anywhere on Slovenia's Adriatic coast cost €60 for 3 passengers and €110 for 4–8 passengers.
**Klagenfurt** Flughafenstraße 60–66, A-9020 Klagenfurt, Austria; tel: +43 0463 41500; email: info@klagenfurt-airport.at; www.klagenfurt-airport.com
**Ryanair** Tel: +353 01 249 7851 (those making reservations from outside Ireland are charged at the applicable international rate); www.ryanair.com

## By train

Slovenske Železnice (Slovenian Railways; tel: 01 291 3332; email: potnik.info@slo-zeleznice.si; www.slo-zeleznice.si), whose network connects the country to the rest of Europe via Germany, Italy, Austria, Switzerland, Hungary and Greece, as well as countries that were formerly part of Yugoslavia, operate Slovenia's train services. Key international services include the Mimara (Munich–Zagreb via Salzburg, Villach, Jesenice and Ljubljana), the Emona (Vienna–Ljubljana via Graz), the Simplon Express (Geneva–Zagreb via Ljubljana), the Citadella (Budapest–Ljubljana), the Drava Express (Budapest–Venice via Ljubljana) and the Pohorje (Graz–Ljubljana). The new high-speed Casanova travels between Ljubljana and Venice (Mestre and Santa Lucia) once daily, missing out the Trieste switchback and cutting journey times by 90 minutes to four hours. There are also frequent rail services to Slovenia from Belgrade, Karlovac, Milan, Pula, Rijeka, Rome, Skopje, Thessaloniki, Trieste and Zürich.

Slovenske Železnice has invested heavily in their rolling stock in recent years and the majority of their trains are comfortable and modern, with sleeping berths available on some overnight services. Buying a ticket within Slovenia should be straightforward as many sales agents speak English. However, one way to avoid confusion is to note departure time and the train number listed on the timetable before buying your ticket or making a reservation.

### Rail passes/ticket discounts

Standard rail tickets for international services to and from Slovenia are not as expensive as those in many western European countries, but are still not cheap. They are more expensive than the bus, when you consider the distance travelled. A direct train from Ljubljana to Zagreb costs around 2,800SIT ($2^1/_2$ hours), Ljubljana to Munich 15,000SIT ($6^1/_2$ hours) and Ljubljana to Budapest 11,300SIT (8 hours).

Slovenia is included in Zone G of the Inter-Rail Pass. This zone also covers Italy, Greece and Turkey. Passes are available for one zone (valid for 16 days), two zones (valid for 22 days) or all eight zones (valid for one month). Standard fees charged in the UK are £155, £215 and £295 respectively for the under 26s, although older travellers can purchase a 26+ card for 35% more, and discounted tickets are available for children. In order to qualify for an Inter-Rail ticket you must purchase it in your country of origin and have been resident there for six months. Euro Domino passes valid for three to eight days of travel in a one-month period are also available with adult, youth (under-26), child and senior fares. For further information contact **Rail Europe** (tel: +44 08705 848 848; email: reservations@raileurope.co.uk; www.raileurope.co.uk/inter-rail, or www.raileurope.com for the USA and Canada).

Those under 26 years of age can also purchase discounted tickets for travel to and from some European destinations; these are available at Wasteels offices (there is one in Ljubljana train station; www.wasteels.com) and cost around 70% of the standard fare.

## By bus

Ljubljana's *avtobusna postaja* (bus station; Trg Osvobodilne fronte 4; tel: 090 4230; email: avtobusna.postaja@ap-ljubljana.si; www.ap-ljubljana.si. Open: daily 05.30–21.00) is served by an extensive number of national and international services, with connections to destinations all over Slovenia and neighbouring Croatia. There are also a large number of routes operating from the other states in the former Yugoslavia – Bosnia and Herzegovina, Macedonia, Serbia and Montenegro. International services also link the Slovenian capital to Austria, Hungary, Denmark, Sweden, Germany, France, Belgium and Italy.

Croatia and Slovenia are particularly well connected with coaches from Rijeka, Pula, Rovinj and Poreč in Croatian Istria running to Koper, Piran and Portorož on Slovenia's Adriatic coast, these services being more frequent during the summer months. A more limited number of international services also operate between other destinations in Slovenia and Croatia; these include services to and from Varaždin, in Croatia, from Celje and Ptuj. The Croatian capital, Zagreb, is also accessible by bus from Ptuj and Maribor.

Bus fares are reasonably priced, but not cheap: a $2^1/_2$-hour journey to Zagreb from Ljubljana costs approximately 3,200SIT and a 2¹/₂-hour journey to Trieste from Ljubljana 2,200SIT, while an eight-hour journey to Belgrade from the Slovenian capital will set you back around 9,000SIT.

## By car

Slovenia is easily accessible by car from much of mainland Europe. The key routes from Austria include the E651 which links Ljubljana to Villach, the E652/E61 from Klagenfurt and the E57/E59 from Graz. From Italy the E61/E70 connects Trieste to Ljubljana, while the E70 serves Zagreb in neighbouring Croatia and the E57/E71 extends to Budapest in Hungary. Since Slovenia became part of the EU in May 2004 procedures at its borders with Italy, Austria and Hungry have become more relaxed, although you still need to make sure that you have a valid passport or national identity card, the correct papers for your car and international vehicle insurance (meaning that those with cars registered outside of the EU need to purchase a Green Card, which costs around €45 for a fortnight or €65 for a month, at the Slovenian border). If you are planning to travel to Slovenia from Great Britain you will obviously have to cross either the North Sea or the English Channel, with the former providing the most direct route.

Some typical road distances from Ljubljana include: Klagenfurt 79km, Trieste 110km, Zagreb 135km, Graz 202km, Venice 249km, Salzburg 290km, Vienna 395km, Munich 430km, Budapest 491km and Belgrade 507km.

## By sea

Marinas in Portorož (Cesta Solinarjev 8, 6320 Portorož; tel: 05 676 1100; fax: 05 676 1210; email: marina.portoroz@marinap.si; www.marinap.si), Izola (Tomažičeva 10, 6310 Izola; tel: 05 640 0250; fax: 05 641 8346; email: info@marinaizola.com; www.marinaizola.com) and Koper (Kopališko nabrežje 5, 6000 Koper; tel: 05 662 6100; fax: 05 662 6161; email: info@marina-koper.si; www.marina-koper.si) have facilities for yachts. During the tourist season two passenger catamaran services, Prince of Venice and Venezia Lines, run between Venice and the Slovenian coast.

**Prince of Venice** (PE Portorož, Obala 41, 6320 Portorož; tel: 05 617 8000; fax: 05 674 7258; email: portoroz@kompas.si; www.kompas-holy.si) services operate from March to October, shuttling passengers between Venice and Izola (approximate journey time 2¹/₂ hours; prices 9,800–15,500SIT). Ticket prices for this service include a guided tour of Venice and can be purchased from Kompas travel agents in Slovenia.

The **Venezia Lines** (tel: +39 041 520 5473; fax: +39 041 277 8335; email: info@venezialines.com; www.venezialines.com) service from Venice docks at Piran. Tickets for this service can be purchased from Atlas Express travel agents and cost around 10,800SIT for a single ticket and 19,200SIT return.

If you arrive in Slovenia at either Izola or Piran you can take a local bus to Koper from where regular train and bus services connect the coast to Ljubljana.

## HEALTH

It is safe to drink tap water throughout Slovenia and visitors do not need any special inoculations. However, it is advisable to ensure that your tetanus and diphtheria vaccinations are up to date and that you have been inoculated against polio. Vaccination against typhoid and hepatitis A are also recommended, although there have been no recorded cases of typhoid in modern times. Every large town or city in Slovenia has a health centre, generally open Monday–Friday 07.00–19.00, and a pharmacy (*lekarna*) open Monday–Friday 07.00–20.00, Saturday 08.00–13.00. If you urgently require medication the prescribing doctor should be able to help you find a reasonably close 24-hour pharmacy.

Emergency medical care for EU citizens is free upon the production of a valid E111 form (European Health Insurance Cards are being phased in to replace the E111 forms, a process that started on June 1 2004) or other appropriate documentation. For UK citizens a passport is sufficient, as long as treatment is given in a state-funded hospital or health centre. Other non-emergency treatment or consultations and medicine must be paid for. Citizens from Croatia, Romania and Bulgaria are also entitled to free emergency medical care in Slovenia.

Visitors from countries that do not have a reciprocal healthcare agreement with Slovenia must pay for all of their medical treatment, including emergency care. Your national health ministry can tell you if any mutual agreements exist. Regardless of any health agreements that may be in place, all international visitors to Slovenia should take out travel insurance with an adequate level of medical cover before travelling to the country. This is important in case you need emergency repatriation.

A few simple precautions before you leave for Slovenia will help you safeguard your health during your trip. If you take prescribed medication make sure you pack it and keep a separate note of the drug's generic name and not just its brand. This will make replacement easier. Those who are travelling for a long time should consider going for a dental check-up. Taking an adequate supply of contact lenses or a spare pair of glasses is also advisable.

In Slovenia itself one of the biggest risks to your health is the sun. It can get surprisingly hot in the cities and along the coast during the summer months, making it essential to pack light clothing that allows your skin to breathe, sunglasses that provide protection against UV rays, a sunhat and plenty of suntan lotion. If you forget any of these items you will be able to buy them in any town or city.

Those who are intending to travel in the countryside, particularly in forested areas, need to consider the following health risks.

## Tick-borne encephalitis

Tick-borne encephalitis is a viral infection, transmitted by ticks found in densely forested parts of Slovenia, which affects the central nervous system. It is possible to vaccinate against the disease, though this is not generally recommended for those at low risk, such as day-trippers. If you are planning on spending a prolonged time in forested areas you should seek appropriate medical advice before leaving. Other precautionary measures include avoiding tick-infested areas from April to August when the risk of infection is at its highest, wearing clothing that covers your skin (including tucking trousers into boots and wearing a hat) and wearing an insect repellent containing DEET (N, N diethyl-m-toluamide). *Permethrin*-based insect repellents can also be applied to your clothing and camping gear, although this should never be put on to your skin. These repellent agents are also effective against Slovenian mosquitoes, which can give you painful bites but do not carry malaria. You can also get tick-borne encephalitis from unpasteurised dairy products and these should be avoided.

## Lyme disease

Lyme disease is a bacterial infection transmitted by ticks that have fed on an infected host animal. Again the risk of infection is at its highest in forested areas between April and August. Symptoms associated with Lyme disease include a red abrasion at the site where the tick bit, which can be up to 7.5cm in diameter and is often clear in the centre. Fever, headaches, a stiff neck, muscle pain, inflamed joints and extreme lethargy are also amongst the symptoms.

## Hepatitis A

The Hepatitis A virus attacks the human liver and, while it is rare, can affect anyone. After an incubation period of three to five weeks, infected individuals display flu-like symptoms and experience fever, abdominal pains, nausea, lack of appetite, physical exhaustion and jaundice. The length of illness and convalescence varies and can be prolonged, but the majority of patients make a complete recovery. The disease is transmitted through food or water contaminated with human faeces, so it is essential to maintain a high level of personal hygiene when travelling. Restaurants in Slovenia conform to high standards, so visitors do not normally need to worry about what they are eating or drinking. Hikers or climbers intending to drink water from streams should either boil it or treat it with purifying tablets. If you have any doubts about the quality of the water that you are drinking opt for bottled mineral water. Vaccination against hepatitis A is usually recommended for those who travel frequently. Injections are administered in two stages with the second dose being given at least six months after the first. Those who have already suffered with hepatitis A are immune to the disease.

## Rabies

Rabies is a viral disease transmitted in the saliva of an infected animal via a bite or a lick on an open wound. Although it is extremely rare, rabies does occur in Slovenia. Untreated rabies is always fatal. The best defence against rabies is prevention, making it essential to avoid handling wild or stray animals. If you are bitten, scratched or licked over an open wound by any warm-blooded animal that is not known to be a domestic pet, wash the wound immediately with soap and water and apply an antiseptic. Go immediately for medical help to get post-exposure treatment.

## Travel clinics and health information

A full list of current travel clinic websites worldwide is available from the International Society of Travel Medicine on www.istm.org. For other journey preparation information, consult www.tripprep.com. Information about various medications may be found on www.emedicine.com.

## SAFETY

Slovenia is a safe country. Crime rates in its urban and rural areas are low, especially when compared to those in most European countries, and violent crimes are rare. Travellers should take sensible precautions to safeguard their valuables, as tourists occasionally fall prey to pickpockets and handbag snatchers. Simple and effective deterrents against crime include not leaving valuables unattended, keeping purses and wallets in inside pockets, and carrying any bags securely while holding them so that they are not facing the road. Anyone unfortunate enough to become a victim of crime must report it to the police immediately; this is especially important if you intend to make a travel insurance claim when you return home. National embassies or consulates can also provide useful help and information.

Slovenia is a small country and all generations are used to foreign visitors. Although some older people may think that it is strange for women to travel alone they will always be treated politely and with respect. Female travellers should not experience any specific difficulties, but sensible precautions should be taken to avoid potentially dangerous situations, eg: not meeting strange men in secluded places. The usual precautions should also be taken against sexually transmitted diseases.

## WHAT TO TAKE

Slovenia is a modern and prosperous country where you can buy almost anything that you might need. Therefore your only essentials are a valid passport or acceptable national identity card, a visa (if necessary), transport tickets, travel insurance documents, money (debit or credit cards, travellers' cheques or Slovenian tolars), E111 or other documentation showing an entitlement to healthcare, driving licence (national or international depending on country-specific requirements) and, if appropriate, student discount cards and a Hostelling International (international youth hostel) card. It is also a good idea to keep photocopies of important documents such as passports, visas and travel insurance policies in case they need to be replaced.

It is advisable to pack for the weather, sticking to light clothes that let your skin breathe in the summer, with sunscreen, sunglasses and a hat all essential items. In the winter you will need a warm and waterproof coat, and a lighter jacket in the spring and autumn. It is also sensible to take a light waterproof raincoat or an umbrella at any time of year. Ljubljana, Maribor and the Adriatic coast have a buzzing nightlife scene, so you might want to pack your favourite clubbing gear. Anyone intending to dine out in some of the country's more expensive restaurants should pack smart casual clothes, though formal wear is not normally required except for specific business functions.

Plug sockets in Slovenia are of the two-pin, round-pronged European variety; if you are travelling with electrical items you may want to take an adapter with you. While you will be able to buy them at your departure airport, they are hard to come by once in Slovenia.

## MONEY MATTERS
### Currency

The official currency of Slovenia is the delightfully colourful Slovenian tolar (SIT). The tolar is a decimal currency and there are 100 stotins in a tolar, although stotins are no longer produced. Tolar notes, brightly bedecked with images of great Slovene painters, writers and thinkers rather than monarchs and politicians – a refreshing change – come in denominations of 5,000, 1,000, 500, 200, 100, 50 and 20SIT. There are also one, two, five, ten, 20 and 50SIT coins. With large figures representing small amounts of money you can end up with a substantial wad of notes in your pocket, so be careful when pulling them out. Many prices in Slovenia are also quoted in euros and this currency is accepted in many hotels.

### Exchange rates
Exchange rates at the time of going to press included:

€1 = 240SIT
£1 = 350SIT
US$1 = 200SIT
A$1 = 140SIT
C$1 = 155SIT
NZ$1 = 130SIT

## Banks
Most towns and cities in Slovenia have at least one centrally located bank. Most open Monday–Friday 08.30–12.30 and 14.00–17.00 and many open on Saturdays

### HINTS ON PHOTOGRAPHY
Nick Garbutt and John Jones
All sorts of photographic opportunities present themselves in Slovenia. For the best results, give some thought to the following tips.

- As a general rule, if it doesn't look good through the viewfinder, it will never look good as a picture. Don't take photographs for the sake of taking them; be patient and wait until the image looks right.
- Photographing people is never easy and more often than not it requires a fair share of luck. If you want to take a portrait shot of a stranger, it is always best to ask first. Focus on the eyes of your subject since they are the most powerful ingredient of any portrait, and be prepared for the unexpected.
- Look at the surroundings – there is nothing worse than a distracting twig or highlighted leaf lurking in the background. Getting this right is often the difference between a mediocre and a memorable image.
- A powerful flashgun adds the option of punching in extra light to transform an otherwise dreary picture. Artificial light is no substitute for natural light, though, so use it judiciously.
- Getting close to the subject correspondingly reduces the depth of field. At camera-to-subject distances of less than a metre, apertures between f16 and f32 are necessary to ensure adequate depth of field. This means using flash

08.30–12.00. In bigger towns and cities some remain open during the lunch period. Most banks exchange foreign currency and travellers' cheques.

## ATMs

Banks with ATMs (automated teller machines) that accept Maestro, Cirrus, Visa and MasterCard can be found in any of Slovenia's larger villages, towns and cities. This is the easiest way to get money in the country and banks generally give a good exchange rate, although it is worth checking how much your bank will charge for each transaction that you make when you are in Slovenia.

## Currency exchange

Cash can be exchanged in banks, many post offices, exchange offices, higher-grade hotels, some petrol stations, tourist agencies and even supermarkets; however the same outlets will not necessarily accept travellers' cheques. The euro is the most easily converted currency, though sterling and US dollars are also relatively easy to exchange.

## Credit cards and debit cards

American Express, Diners Club, MasterCard/Eurocard and Visa credit cards and Visa, Electron, Plus, Maestro and Cirrus debit cards are accepted in most shops, restaurants and hotels. It is also possible to withdraw cash from most ATMs using your credit or debit card, as long as you have a valid PIN number. With the majority of cards you can also withdraw money inside the bank if you don't know

to provide enough light. If possible, use one or two small flashguns to illuminate the subject from the side.

**Landscapes** are forever changing, even on a daily basis. Good landscape photography is all about good light and capturing mood. Generally the first and last two hours of daylight are best, or when peculiar climatic conditions add drama or emphasise distinctive features. Never place the horizon in the centre – in your mind's eye divide the frame into thirds and either exaggerate the land or the sky.

### Film

If you're using conventional film (as against a digital camera), select the right film for your needs. Film speed (ISO number) indicates the sensitivity of the film to light. The lower the number, the less sensitive the film, but the better quality the final image. For general print film, ISO 100 or 200 fit the bill perfectly. If you are using transparencies for home use or for lectures, then again ISO 100 or 200 film is fine. However, if you want to get your work published, the superior quality of ISO 25 to 100 film is best.

- Try to keep your film cool. Never leave it in direct sunlight.
- Don't allow fast film (ISO 800 and above) to pass through X-ray machines.
- Under weak light conditions use a faster film (ISO 200 or 400).

your PIN or the ATM is broken. Cash withdrawal fees and exchange rates vary between banks and credit card companies, so check these before you leave home. Credit and debit card transaction charges can be kept down by withdrawing larger sums of money, although there will be an upper limit on the amount you can extract.

If you are travelling with credit cards it is sensible to keep a record of the issuer's international telephone number for reporting lost or stolen cards. In the case of loss or theft your credit card company should help you arrange emergency cash if necessary. You can also get assistance with damaged, lost or stolen cards in Ljubljana.

**American Express** Trubarjeva 50; tel: 01 433 2024
**Diners Club** WTC, Dunajska 156; tel: 01 589 6111
**MasterCard/Eurocard** Nova Ljubljanska Banka, Trg republike 2; tel: 01 425 0155, or SKB Banka, Ajdovščina 4; tel: 01 433 2132
**Visa** A Banka, Slovenska 58; tel: 01 431 1031

## Travellers' cheques
Travellers' cheques are much safer than carrying cash. Euro or US dollar travellers' cheques can be exchanged at banks, exchange offices, travel agencies and some post offices. Banks offer the best rate with commissions ranging from zero to 1%. Remember that you will need a valid passport or identity card to cash your cheques.

## Wiring money
If you need emergency cash this can be wired via Western Union (www.westernunion.com) agents. These agents are Nova Ljubljanska Banka (head office tel: 01 425 0155; www.nlb.si) and Nova Kreditna Banka Maribor (head office tel: 02 229 2290; www.nkbm.si), each with branches in towns and cities throughout Slovenia.

## BUDGETING
Slovenia is more affordable than many western European countries, although any notions of a poverty-stricken eastern European nation with rock-bottom prices will soon be dispelled. However, there are options to suit all budgets with hostel accommodation and camping typically costing under 2,840SIT (€12) per person, while private accommodation costs 4,560–7,200SIT (€14–20) for a double room. Meanwhile a double room in a mid-range hotel would typically cost 12,000–16,800SIT (€50–70), with luxurious four- and five-star accommodation coming in at 32,000–56,000SIT (€133–233). Restaurants likewise cater to a broad range of budgets. Regardless of your budget there are a couple of things to bear in mind: prices in the capital and the country's popular tourist resorts, like Lake Bled, will be more expensive than in other areas. Accommodation costs can also be significantly reduced if you are travelling with a partner or friends, as splitting the cost of double, triple or quadruple rooms works out cheaper.

## Rock bottom
You can get by on 5,000–6,000SIT a day if you camp or stay in a youth hostel dormitory and buy food from a market or fast-food stands. This budget will also allow you to eat one meal in a pizzeria or student eatery and to buy drinks from a supermarket. If you are planning to travel on a tight budget it is essential that you book your accommodation in advance.

## Modest
Being savvy about where you stay will allow you to eat two meals in modestly priced but good-quality restaurants and enjoy four or five drinks in cafés and bars for 10,000–15,000SIT a day. Again if you want to keep your accommodation costs down then it is advisable to book a hostel or private room in advance.

## Fun
For 20,000–25,000SIT a day you can afford single occupancy in a mid-range hotel, eat two reasonably priced meals and not have to worry about what you drink.

## Indulgent
Spend 35,000–45,000SIT a day and stay in good three- or four-star hotels and eat out twice, choosing from the majority of Slovenia's restaurants. You will also be able to pay entrance fees to the sights of your choice and enjoy a night out.

## Extravagant
From 45,000SIT a day upwards you will be able to stay in four- or five-star hotels, eat in Slovenia's most exclusive restaurants and spend the day as you choose, eg: relaxing in cafés, drinking in bars or sightseeing. Again a budget of this size means that you can go out at night without having to watch the tolars.

# GETTING AROUND
## By car
Slovenia's compact size and its good network of roads lend themselves to exploration by car. Driving also gives you easy access to Slovenia's more remote villages and dramatic rural scenery. Car hire costs from around 48,000SIT a week for a budget model, and a litre of unleaded petrol costs 190–200SIT. To hire a car you must be over 21 years old (those under 25 have to pay additional insurance premiums of around 1,200SIT a day) and have held a clean driving licence for at least a year. You also need your national driving licence, passport, a valid credit card and nerves of steel.

Many Slovenes have a fairly haphazard attitude to driving and almost everyone, from compact cars to articulated lorries, seems to drive above the mandatory speed limit. Speed is not the only problem, though, as many drivers assume that they always have the right of way, while others pull out from side streets and then look to see if there is anything coming. One favourite pastime is zig-zagging in and out of the traffic to either undertake or overtake. At night the roads take on additional perils, as many of the best bars and restaurants are located in rural areas and drinking and driving is an accepted part of the culture.

## RULES OF THE ROAD

Traffic in Slovenia drives on the right. Mandatory speed limits are usually 130km/h on motorways, 100km/h on main highways, 90km/h on regional roads outside residential areas and 50km/h in built-up areas. You will often see signs for 70km/h, 60km/h and even 40km/h – these are usually on very winding sections of road, or when workmen are at the side of the road. Many Slovenes do not stick to the speed limits, but you should as the police are vigilant and issue fines and penalty points to speeding drivers. It is illegal to overtake a school bus, seat belt use is compulsory and dipped headlights should be kept on at all times while driving. The last is a fairly new law so the police may just remind drivers to turn their lights on, although they can issue a fine. The legal alcohol blood level is 0.05% or 0.5g/kg, but it is much safer to avoid alcohol when driving.

For more information on driving in Slovenia contact the country's national automobile club, Auto-Moto Zveza Slovenije (AMZS; Dunajska 128, 1000 Ljubljana; tel: 061 530 5300; fax: 01 568 5317; email: info.center@amzs.si; www.amzs.si). Their emergency roadside number is tel: 1987.

However, traffic outside of urban centres is light, making driving in the countryside a straightforward and pleasant experience.

## By bus

Slovenia has a good bus network and it is possible to travel by bus to most of the country's towns and cities from its capital city, although smaller villages are less accessible and usually require local connections. Slovenes like their cars so the frequency of services varies greatly between destinations. Vehicles that service national routes are generally modern, with air conditioning. In addition they often represent the most straightforward and direct way of reaching some destinations such as Bled, the Julian Alps and the regions of Notranjska, Dolenjska and Koroška.

Fares are calculated by the distance covered, allowing you to travel 25km for 600–700SIT, 50km for 1,300SIT, 100km for 2,000SIT and 200km for 3,700SIT. With short distances between destinations the fare will never be that high (see road distances from Ljubljana below). You can buy bus tickets from any *avobusna postaja* (bus station), or just turn up and pay as you board the bus. Seat reservations can be made a day in advance for 130SIT.

Some typical road distances from Ljubljana include: Kranj 26km, Bled and Postojna 53km, Novo Mesto 73km, Celje 77km, Črnomelj 91km, Koper 117km, Bovec 125km, Maribor 133km, Ptuj 136km and Kranjska Gora 221km.

### Bus timetables

*Vozni red* (timetables) are usually displayed in bus stations, but can be difficult to understand. Some are colour coded; as a rule of thumb a black or white text indicates that the service is daily, blue indicates Monday–Friday, green and orange are for daily excluding Sundays, yellow means during school hours and red is for on Sundays and holidays. Those that have letters to indicate the frequency of service are coded as follows:

V – daily
D – Monday–Friday
D+ – daily excluding Sundays
N – Sundays
NP – Sundays and holidays
ŠP – during school hours

Those that run only on certain days of the week take the first two letters of the spelling for the day, eg: Torek (Tuesday) is To. For the Slovene words for all the days of the week, see *Time* in *Appendix 1*.

Staff at the information window or ticket office will also help you decipher complex timetables.

## By train

Slovenia's rail network extends over 1,200km of track operated by Slovenske Železnice (Slovenian Railways; tel: 01 291 3332; email: potnik.info@slo-zeleznice.si; www.slo-zeleznice.si), and both track and rolling stock are in good condition. Travelling by train in Slovenia can be frustrating, though, as one enduring legacy of socialist Yugoslavia is few direct routes between towns and cities, with most journeys requiring connections through Ljubljana; for example it is quicker to travel from Maribor to Novo Mesto (which is almost due south) via Ljubljana in the west of the country. Lengthy journeys and the need to backtrack probably explain why it is cheap in terms of price per km to travel by rail, with a 100km journey costing around 1,300SIT.

Understanding some of the codes on train timetables makes it easier to navigate the system. A boxed R indicates that an advance reservation is needed in order to board the train, while an R that is not boxed simply indicates that reservations are available. The abbreviation IC denotes a faster but more expensive Inter-City route, although the supplement is small at 350SIT. When there is no reservation required it is possible to simply board the train and pay the conductor, although this costs an additional 500SIT per person.

## By boat

During the main tourist season (April–October) it is possible to travel by passenger boat along the Slovenian coast, with the **Big Red** (tel: 05 641 8310; www.slo-istra.com/aquamarine) operating services between Piran, Bernardin, Strunjan, Portorož, Izola, Koper and Ankaran. The one-way fare ranges from 400 to 2,300SIT depending on your start and finish points.

## ACCOMMODATION
### Hotels

Slovenia has a total accommodation capacity of almost 81,000 beds, of which around 27,000 are in over 160 hotels. Hotels are classified from one to five stars, with the former meeting basic standards and the latter being the most luxurious accommodation. The majority of the country's accommodation is in three-star properties, although the number of good-quality four-and five-star hotels is growing slowly. Hotels in Slovenia are not as cheap as you might expect – especially during high season – with singles/doubles costing around 7,000/10,000SIT in one-star properties, 9,500/15,000SIT in two-star properties, 11,000/17,000SIT in three-star hotels, 20,000/26,000SIT in four-star hotels and 25,000/40,000SIT in hotels that have been awarded five stars. Increasingly, good-value deals are available through the internet. Many hotels offer beds in triple and quadruple rooms, which reduces the cost further.

## Thermal spas

*Terme* (thermal spas) are one of Slovenia's most appealing features and a large component of its tourism industry. At present 15 *terme* across the country offer curative and preventative health programmes, recreational facilities constructed around natural thermal spas, gyms, beauty parlours and aqua-parks. These resorts also have their own hotel accommodation. The quality of the facilities and accommodation varies greatly, with some being ultra-modern and others throwbacks from Slovenia's socialist era. A large amount of money is being invested in upgrading *terme* throughout the country and at the time of writing the new Rimska Čarda resort was being built and the **Laško Health Resort** (Zdraviliška 4; tel: 03 734 5122; email: info@zdravilisce-lasko.si; www.zdravilisce-lasko.si) was being renovated. Two of Slovenia's best thermal spas are **Terme 3000** (tel: 02 512 2200; email: info@terme3000.si; www.terme3000.si) and **Terme Čatez** (tel: 07 49 36 700; email: info@terme-catez.si; www.terme-catez.si).

## Private rooms

Privately owned rooms and apartments are available throughout Slovenia, although capacity in Ljubljana is limited. You can go directly to the owner, who will be displaying a *sobe* (rooms) sign, usually with a picture of a bed. In more tourist-orientated areas these may be accompanied by signs in other languages, with the German *zimmer frei* being the most common. Alternatively tourist offices and tourist agencies can help you book private accommodation. Like hotels, private accommodation is graded and a one- to four-star classification system is used. Properties with one star are basic and often have shared facilities, while a four-star property is the most luxurious and will be en suite. Charges vary according to location and classification with single rooms costing 2,500–9,500SIT (average 4,000SIT), double rooms 4,400–14,000SIT (average 7,000SIT) and apartments sleeping two to six people 7,500–25,000SIT). Many enterprising landlords have a presence on the internet, enabling you to book accommodation directly with them before you leave for Slovenia. Some owners will not take guests who want to stay for less than three days, while others might levy a surcharge of up to 30% per night for this.

### Private accommodation websites

www.istratourist.com
www.sloveniaholidays.com

www.bled-holiday.com
www.kranjska-gora.si

## Youth hostels

The Maribor-based Hostelling International Slovenia (PZS; Gosposvetska 84, 2000 Maribor; tel: 02 234 2137; fax: 02 234 2136; email: info@youth-hostel.si; www.gaudeamus.si/hostelling) has 19 HI-affiliated hostels, concentrated in the northeast and northwest of the country, with the exception of Ljubljana and those in Piran and Koper on Slovenia's southwest Adriatic coast. The majority of these hostels open year-round and nightly rates range from 2,800 to 4,500SIT. June–August and December are busy months for Slovenia's hostels and you are advised to make advanced bookings during these months.

## Camping

Around 50 official *kamps* (campsites) are registered with the Slovenian Tourist Board. Located at or close to some of the country's main attractions these offer cost-effective accommodation. Most campsites are seasonal and open April–October. Visitors without tents may find that they can rent either a tent or a bungalow. Facilities on offer in each campsite vary, although many offer recreational activities and, perhaps more importantly for those spending a long time in Slovenia, self-service laundries. As a guide camping costs 1,500–2,000SIT per person.

## Tourist farms

Around 270 farms in rural areas of Slovenia offer accommodation; endearingly these are called 'Tourist Farms' which conjures up quite an unusual image. To really get away from it all and experience traditional Slovenian hospitality these can be a good option. Tourist farms can be viewed and booked through the Slovenian Tourist Board website, www.slovenia.info. There is also a small network of traditional houses – *Hiše s tradicijo* (Houses of Tradition) – that have been renovated in order to attract tourists, web: www.hisestradicijo.com.

## EATING AND DRINKING
### Food

Forget any anachronistic images that you may harbour of communist-era culinary deprivations as Slovenia is fast developing into something of an eating and drinking oasis. It is difficult to say exactly what constitutes definitive Slovenian cuisine as the country wholeheartedly embraces Austrian, Hungarian, Croatian and Italian influences, then tops them all off with a generous helping of genuine Slovenian hospitality.

In the hinterland, particularly the mountains, hearty meat dishes and a wide variety of grilled sausages and black pudding dominate the menu. Here sweet doughnuts and dumplings are also traditional. Fresh seafood is prevalent on the Adriatic coast, while freshwater fish, especially trout, are typically found on menus in areas close to rivers and lakes, particularly in Gorenjska. Each region of Slovenia has its own distinctive dishes. From Prekmurje there is goulash and the *gibanica* – pastry filled with poppy seeds, walnuts, apple and cottage cheese then topped with

**TEN GREAT RESTAURANTS**
Špazja Ljubljana (see page 64)
Pri Vitezu Ljubljana (see page 63)
Smrekarjev Hram Ljubljana (see page 63)
Neptun Piran (see page 169)
Plesnik Logarska Dolina (see page 228)
Gostilna Pri Lojzetu Zemono Dvorec, Vipava Valley (see page 153)
Kendov Dvorec Spodnja Idrija (see page 148)
Restaurant Topli Val Kobarid (see page 142)
Kotlar Kobarid (see page 142)
Ribič Ptuj (see page 232)

cream – the country's favourite sugary treat. Then there are sour soups from Pohorje and potato- and bean-based soups from Gorenjska and Primorska. Influences seep from the Balkans with the fast food *burek*, an artery-clogging pastry with meat or cottage cheese.

One constant in Slovenia's restaurants is the quality of the ingredients. Fresh produce is paramount and the daily specials that are recommended by waiters are usually the preferred option of local diners. This is a country where the 'slow food' movement and organic food reign supreme, and where sitting down to a good meal is regarded as a God-given right rather than a luxury.

Venues are very loosely divided between *gostilnas*, *gostiš* and *restavracijas*. In practice these definitions are very blurred, but generally a *gostilna* is an inn that serves drinks and traditional food. The *gostišče* is very similar and also specialises in Slovenian-style dishes, while a *restavracija* tends to be a more formal set-up with a more innovative, modern or international menu. In recent years it has become quite trendy to call your new restaurant a *gostilna* or *gostišče* as diners are seeking to re-explore traditional food, further blurring the lines. One constant is a lack of formality and there are few places in Slovenia where you will feel out of place in casual dress. Handily almost all eating venues have English-language menus and multi-lingual staff.

Over the last few years a number of more exotic cuisines have been sneaking into Slovenia with the likes of Mexican, Japanese and Chinese all now in the mix. In the days before independence in 1991 tucking into a bowl of *sushi* would have been unimaginable, but today Ljubljana's first *sushi* restaurant is one of its most fashionable spots. The most established 'foreign' cuisine is Italian, with pizza a staple of many Slovenian diets, and the country's myriad pizzerias offer excellent pizza that would not be out of place in Naples.

For most locals the day starts with a light breakfast, increasingly taken on the move with a quick coffee and pastry. Lunch is usually quite a low-key affair except on weekends when it can go on all afternoon and even extend into the evening, especially if you are at a *gostilna* or *gostišče* out in the countryside. Dinner is the main meal of the day and if you are meeting friends you should not plan to do much else afterwards. Slovenes like to take their time over dinner and snake their way through a large number of courses, so if you are lucky enough to snare an invite to dine with a Slovene, settle in for a long haul and remember to wish all of your dining companions 'dober tek' (bon appétit).

Slovenia offers exceptionally good value when it comes to eating out, though prices do vary markedly from the cheap and cheerful places through to the increasing array of top-end options.

## Wine

People have been making wine here for almost 2,500 years and Slovenia has more than 200km² of vineyards with an estimated annual production of around 80 million litres. This wine is grown in three main regions: Podravje, Posavje and Primorska. Popular wines include a semi-dry white Sauvignon Blanc with a straw colour, and Cviček, a blend of red and white wines that is not quite a rosé, and whose acidity renders it an acquired taste. Modra Frankinja meanwhile is a full-bodied red wine with a deep colour and a harsh taste. On the other end of the scale Laški Rizling is a sweet white. Other good whites include Chardonnay, always a safe option, and Beli Bizeljčan, a full-flavoured dry wine with a flowery taste, which locals often mix with sparkling mineral water to make a spritzer. Slovenia also has its own brand of sparkling wine, with good brands on a par with champagne. Slovenes are divided about which brand of sparkling wine is the most superior, with some rooting for Zlata Radgonska Penina and others going for those produced by the Istenič family. Many of Slovenia's wine areas have dedicated wine routes where you can drive or cycle between the different producers – see the individual regional chapters in this book or ask at local tourist offices.

## Prices
### Food
You can pick up a pastry and a hot drink for around 700SIT. In terms of price there is little to differentiate lunch and dinner when ordering à la carte, although a growing number of cafés and restaurants offer fixed price menus that start at around 1,200SIT and rarely sneak above 4,000SIT. Price guidelines for a three course evening meal excluding wine are: top-end, over 6,000SIT; mid-range, 2,000–6,000SIT; budget, under 2,000SIT.

### Drinks
Soft drinks, mineral water and beer (both on draught and in bottles) come in at around 350–450SIT per drink, while tea and coffee is generally a little cheaper at 250–300SIT. A 10cl glass of wine starts at around 300–400SIT per measure, although in practice most wine drinkers order double measures. If you order a full bottle of wine, this will usually cost upwards of 3,000SIT.

## PUBLIC HOLIDAYS AND FESTIVALS
### Public holidays

| | |
|---|---|
| January 1 and 2 | New Year Holiday |
| February 8 | Prešeren Day or Slovene Day of Culture |

Easter Monday
April 27          Day of Uprising Against the Occupation (World War II)
May 1 and 2      Labour Day Holiday
Pentecost
June 25           Slovenia Day
August 15        Feast of the Assumption
October 31       Reformation Day
November 1       All Saints' Day
December 25     Christmas Day
December 26     Independence Day

## Festivals and special events
### Spring
**Slovenian Musical Days** Organised by Festival Ljubljana (www.festival-lj.si), showcasing contemporary music by Slovenian and European composers. Ljubljana, April.

**Izola Theatre and Dance Marathon** Izola, April.

**Exodos** This festival of contemporary performing arts (www.exodos-festival.si) has been an annual event in Ljubljana for over a decade. Past performers have included Japanese drummers, Vietnamese puppet theatre and a performance of *Thumbelina*. Main venue Cankarjev Dom. Ljubljana, May.

**Internautica** Five-day international boat show. Portorož, May.

**Druga Godba** The outdoor Križanke theatre is the main venue for a five-day festival (email: info@drugagodba.si) of alternative and ethnic concerts by international performers. Founded in 1985 and a local favourite, the name literally means 'alternative bands'. The diverse music on offer ranges from modern jazz and ethno-electronic to folk music and African beats. Ljubljana, May–June.

### Summer
**Summer Night of Museums** An open-door event that gives access to museums, exhibitions and galleries in Ljubljana. Free workshops, tours, concerts, film screenings, performances, lectures and presentations also take place on this day. Ljubljana, June.

**Lent Festival** A 17-day annual summer fair with theatrical performances, concerts and firework displays. Maribor. June–July.

**Summer in Ljubljana Old Town** A series of free concerts staged in the Old Town's streets, squares, churches and courtyards. Ljubljana, June–August.

**Ljubljana Jazz Festival** This event, which has been running for almost half a century, spans three evenings with performances from Slovene and international musicians. Ljubljana, July.

**Trnfest Festival** Five-day celebration of alternative culture in the Ljubljana suburb or Trnovo, including video, dance, music, theatre, exhibitions and events for children. Ljubljana, July.

**International Folklore Festival** Maribor, July.

**Bled Days & Bled Nights** Lighting displays and fireworks come to this beautiful setting. Bled, July.

**Ljubljana Summer Festival** The capital's biggest festival is organised by Festival Ljubljana (www.festival-lj.si) and dates back to 1953. The city's stages fill with performers from around the world and its population swells to over 300,000, as 50,000 visitors flock to the festival. Musical, theatrical and dance performances take place in the Slovenian Philharmonic Hall, Cankarjev Dom, Križanke Summer Theatre, Ljubljana Castle and the Cultural and Congress Centre. Ljubljana. July–August.

**Mini Summer Festival** This children's festival with its puppet shows and children's theatre is a perfect compliment to the Ljubljana Summer Festival. Ljubljana, July–September.

**Summer in Piran** Pop concerts, classical performances and fashion shows come to Piran under the guise of the Summer Beats of Piran (Thursdays) and Musical Evenings of Piran (Fridays) amongst other events. Events for the forthcoming week are read out by the mayor on Saturdays in Tartini Square. Piran, July–August.

**Mediterranean Festival** and **Fisherman's Festival** Izola, August.

## Autumn

**Ljubljana Marathon** This annual sporting event caters to varying abilities, with a full marathon, half-marathon and fun run. Ljubljana, October.

**Medieval Day** Reviving life in the Slovene capital during the Middle Ages, with Ljubljana Castle as a spectacular venue. The length and month of this festival is subject to change. Ljubljana, October.

**Borštnik Festival** The second city's stages fill with first-rate theatre performances for a two-week period. Maribor, mid–late October.

**Peace Festival** and **United Nations Day** Celebrating the town's role as a 'Peace Messenger City'. Slovenj Gradec, October.

**Ljubljana International Wine Festival** A chance to taste more than 300 wines including those produced in Slovenia. The date and venue are subject to change. Ljubljana, November.

**Ljubljana International Film Festival** (www.ljubljanafilmfestival.org) More than 100 films from around the world including South Korea and Japan are screened at Cankarjev Dom, Komuna Cinema, Vic Cinema and the Slovenska Kinoteka. Ljubljana, November.

## Winter

**Ljubljana Gay and Lesbian Film Festival** Ljubljana, November–December.

**Festive December** Festival Ljubljana (www.festival-lj.si) presents a series of Christmas and New Year concerts. Ljubljana, December.

**December in Ljubljana** Seasonal festivities throughout the city. Ljubljana, December.

**Christmas and New Year Fairs** Seasonal gifts and food. All main towns and cities, December–January.

**Ski World Cup Women's Slalom Races** Maribor, January.

**Dog Sled Race** Kranjska Gora, January.

**Ski World Cup Men's Slalom Races** Kranjska Gora, February.

**Kurentovanje Festival** Traditional festival designed to fend off evil winter spirits and welcome spring, where the town's young men dress up in extravagant costumes and masks to chase out the devils. Ptuj, February–March.

**World Military Winter Games** Bled, March.

**World Championship Ski Flying and Ski Jumping** Planica, March.

## SHOPPING

Lace, basketry, wooden utensils, pottery and ceramics, crystal cut glass, gold jewellery, beeswax, Slovenian wine, wrought iron and woodcarvings are all good souvenirs. The majority of shops open Monday–Friday 08.00–19.00 and Saturdays 08.00–12.00, although opening and closing times may vary by an hour or two between stores. Department stores in big cities may also open on Saturday afternoons, with the enormous BTC City shopping and entertainment complex in Ljubljana opening 09.00–20.00 on Saturdays and until 13.00 on Sundays.

## ARTS AND ENTERTAINMENT
### Art

Much of Slovenia's early art was brought to the region by the various civilisations that breezed through, with the Romans leaving their early traces. There is a wealth of Gothic treasures, such as Hrastovlje's *Dance of Death* murals and the frescos in the Church of St John the Baptist in Bohinj. The big names of Slovenian painting emerged in the 19th century with the Romantic works of Matevž Langus and Josip Tominc. As the 19th century moved into the 20th century a new phase of Impressionism took over with Rihard Jakopič and Ivan Gohar at the forefront. Even within the confines of Yugoslav socialism Slovenian art produced some very good work with the sculptors Jakob Savinšek and Lojze Dolinar excelling. After Tito's death the avant-garde strain that had always been evident throughout the history of Slovenian art rose up in the Neue Slowenische Kunst (NSK or New Slovenian Art) movement, where it was a case of the more challenging and thought-provoking the better. Today you can delve into this period in the Modern Art Gallery in Ljubljana.

Zoran Mušič, Jože Plečnik (whose work is covered in more detail in the Ljubljana chapter of this book), Boris Podrecca and Marko Ivan Rupnik are amongst Slovenia's most famous 20th-century artists. Zoran Mušič was born in Slovenia in 1909, but spent most of his life in France, where he still lives today.

### JANEZ VAJKARD VALVASOR

In his own way Valvasor was every bit as influential as France Prešeren, certainly in terms of shaping the way we look at Slovenia's history, landscape, flora and fauna. Born in Ljubljana in 1641 Valvasor was, for a man of his time, quite an accomplished traveller, having spent time in many European countries as well as making forays into Africa. His seminal work was *The Glory of the Duchy of Carniola*, an impressively detailed multi-volume account of the country around him. Like Prešeren, Valvasor died (in 1693) with little real idea of the esteem in which he would be held one day and in tragic circumstances as by then he was virtually penniless. He was recognised to some extent in his lifetime for his explanation of the until-then unfathomable, intermittent Lake Cerknica in Notranjska. Today Valvasor is eulogised as the man who wrote perhaps the greatest-ever study of Slovenia; he is also a member of the British Royal Society.

Many Slovenes regard the painter and graphic artist as the greatest Slovene artist alive today. Boris Podrecca, who was born in Belgrade in 1940, but whose family came from the Primorska region of Slovenia, another of Slovenia's great artists, is heralded as one of the greatest contemporary Slovenian architects, adopting a style that is heavily influenced by Plečnik.

The Slovene artist Marko Ivan Rupnik came to the attention of art lovers around the world when he was commissioned, in 1999, to decorate the walls of the Pope's Chapel of the Saviour's Mother in Vatican City. He rose to the challenge with a contemporary mosaic.

## Handicrafts

Until the 19th century the majority of Slovenes were country folk, with few attending institutes of higher education or coming into contact with the higher art forms, therefore it is perhaps no surprise that Slovenian handicrafts have flourished as an art form over the centuries. Woodwork is the strongest medium with the brightly painted beehive panels, mainly associated with the Gorenjska region, a fine example of expressive handicrafts. Today throughout the country at local markets you can pick up unique wooden souvenirs, whether it be miniature beehive panels or simple ladles, usually with excellent workmanship and quality wood. If you want to delve further into the history of the beehive panels head for the dedicated beekeeping museum in Radovljica.

## Literature

The history of Slovenian literature can be traced back as far as the 10th century with the publication of the three Freising Manuscripts, though a Slavic oral tradition is said to have predated this first Slovene Slavic text. The first book entirely in Slovene was published in 1550 – Primož Trubar's *Catechismus in Abecedarium*. Some 50 other titles were also published in Slovene around this time, including a translation of the Bible by Jurij Dalmatin and Adam Bohorič's book of Slovenian grammar. Slovene as a literary language still struggled and the most comprehensive series of books on the country written before the 20th century (perhaps ever), Janez Vajkard Valvasor's *The Glory of the Duchy of Carniola*, was not even written in Slovene.

Under the Austro–Hungarians the poet Valentin Vodnik and the playwright Anton Tomaž Linhart rose to the fore, with the former publishing the country's first newspaper between 1797 and 1800 and the latter writing a history of the Slovenes. However, Vodnik and Linhart pale into insignificance compared to Slovenia's most famous writer, poet France Prešeren, who emerged in the 19th century (see box under *Kranj* in the *Gorenjska* chapter). His 1847 publication *Poezije* was especially influential. Slovenia's increasing taste for the avant garde grew in the 20th century with the poet Oton Župančič and novelist–playwright Ivan Cankar, whom many Slovenes rate as the greatest-ever writer in the Slovene language. The post-World War II years witnessed, on the one hand, socialist realism in service to the regime, but, on the other, existentialism. One particularly notable dissident voice was Edvard Kocbek, who fought the Germans as a partisan but turned against the regime in his later work.

### VLADIMIR BARTOL

Vladimir Bartol's *Alamut* is arguably the most famous Slovenian book in the world today. Published in the late 1930s, the book is set in Iran during the Midldle Ages and focuses on the subjugation of the minority Shiite population by Seljuk Sunni Turkish leaders, and in particular the character of Hasan. As Hasan's ambition grows, he stoops to new lows in his degradation of and efforts to control those beneath him, including the use of drugs to command and manipulate his own private army. Many modern analyses of the book cast the main character in the role of an Islamic terrorist and regard it as a prediction of the type of fundamentalist terrorism that has risen to the fore in the 21st century. When it was first released, however, many interpreted it as an allusion to totalitarian domination in Europe, with characters in the book being likened to Hitler, Stalin and members of the SS. The casting of Hasan as an out of control megalomaniac has seen his character most strongly associated with Benito Mussolini, with suggestions that Bartol originally wanted to dedicate the book to the Italian fascist dictator, but was prevented from doing so. *Alamut* has been translated into Spanish, French and most recently English (see *Further Reading*).

Slovenia's most important and most translated contemporary writer, Drago Jančar (b1948), is celebrated for his analysis of modern society and illuminating essays about Central Europe and Slovenian society. For Slovenes his work is as significant as that of the Czech writer Milan Kundera, with his book titled *Mocking Desire* (see *Further Reading*) in English held in particularly high esteem. The Trieste-based writer, Boris Pahor, is another influential Slovene writer, and he has had his works widely translated into French and Italian.

## Music

Much of Slovenia's early musical heritage dates back to the ecclesiastical style practised in the country's churches and monasteries during the 15th century, a style that remained popular for around 300 years. One of the most famous composers of this style of music was the Cistercian Monk Jakob Gallus (1550–91), often referred to as Jacob Handl. Gallus's most famous piece, *Opus Musicum*, is still performed by choirs around the world. The Ljubljana-based Academia Philharmonicorum Labacensium (which became the Filharmonija in 1794) was established in 1701 at a time when secular music had fallen out of fashion, and while choir singing remained an intrinsic component the focus was shifting to orchestra-led performances. Jakob Zupan (1734–1810) broke with tradition when he penned the first opera written by a Slovene in 1780. Throughout the 19th century the classical music scene in Slovenia was dominated by a Romantic school of composers such as Benjamin Ipavec (1829–1908), whose work includes the *Serenade for Strings*, with Blaž Arnič (1901–70), who wrote nine symphonies during his lifetime, continuing this legacy.

*Ljudska glasba* (folk music) has always been a popular facet of music in Slovenia. Most of what you hear will be accordion-laden reels and jigs piped out of speakers on Sunday afternoons at *gostilnas* across the land, but you may chance upon the real thing. Bela Krajina has a reputation as a hotbed of traditional music so if you are interested venture there and enquire at the tourist office in Metlika about what is on. Alternatively there are often concerts on in Ljubljana and Maribor so check with their tourist offices. Traditional instruments include the *frajtonarica* (accordion), *okarina* (flute) and *trstenke* (reed pipes). Among Slovenia's most influential folk musicians are the Avsenik brothers (www.avsenik-sp.si) who hail from Begunje. Other big names to look out for these days include Katice, an excellent female vocal group, and Terra Folk, a cross-genre ensemble that utilises a variety of instruments and incorporates musical styles from gypsy songs to Balkan pop.

Slovenia produced some interesting punk bands in the 1970s in the form of Pankrti and Laibach (the Austrian name for Ljubljana), whose lead singer later committed suicide. For a time Laibach were huge in Yugoslavia and behind the Iron Curtain. What little pop and rock music is produced domestically today tends to be heavily influenced by American and British bands, though some of the groups belting out at powerful gigs at the Metelkova squat in Ljubljana are more original. One growing field of music is dance, with Slovene DJs hitting the decks in Ljubljana, Novo Mesto and along the coast alongside big European names, garnering valuable experience and in the process getting some much-needed exposure for a musical genre that is the choice of today's teenagers and young adults.

During the 20th century a number of Slovenes achieved international acclaim in the field of classical music and opera, including the mezzo-sopranos Marjana Lipovšek (b1946) and Bernarda Fink (b1955) and pianist Dubravka Tomšič-Srebotnjak (b1940). The voice of Ljubljana-born Marjana Lipovšek, daughter of composer Marjan Lipovšek, has been appreciated by opera-goers around the world, as she has taken the leading role in venues like Vienna, Hamburg, Munich and Paris, won various awards for her singing and worked alongside various orchestras. Born in Buenos Aires, Argentina, to Slovene parents, Bernarda Fink has enjoyed the same kind of success in her career as Marjan Lipovšek, performing with internationally

## ACCORDION OOMPAH

The Slovene kings of Accordion Oompah are the four Avsenik brothers – Slavko, Vinko, Janez and Majda – who formed the Avsenik Brothers Quintet in 1936, when Slavko the youngest was just seven years old. In a career that spans more than half a century, they have recorded more than 50 albums and sold over 31 million records. The folk music crafted by the Avsenik brothers is particularly popular in Upper Carniola (Gorenjska) and therefore appeals to Slovenes, Austrians and Germans from this historic region. The Avsenik Brothers have achieved acclaim on an international stage, playing to an audience of 80,000 at a stadium in western Berlin back in 1961, and touring North America in the same year. Their impressive collection of awards includes 31 Gold, two Diamond and one Platinum disc.

acclaimed orchestras and at classical music festivals around the world. The repertoire of Dubravka Tomšič-Srebotnjak, who performs with internationally renowned orchestras at prestigious venues around the world, is also remarkable.

## MEDIA AND COMMUNICATIONS
### Press

Slovenia has four daily newspapers, printed in Slovene and available on the internet: the Ljubljana-based *Delo* (Work; www.delo.si), *Dnevnik* (Daily; www.dnevnik.si) and *Ljubljanske Novice*, and the Maribor-based *Večer* (Evening; www.vecer.si). There is also a diverse range of weekly, fortnightly and monthly newspapers and magazines on sale.

English-language publications include the weekly *Slovenia News* (http://www.slonews.sta.si), the monthly *Slovenia Times* (www.sloveniatimes.com), the quarterly *Ljubljana Life* whose website www.geocities.com/ljubljanalife contains the *Slovenia Bulletin*, a weekly review of the stories in Slovenia's mainstream press, and the quarterly *Slovenija Magazine* (www.zdruzenje-sim.si). Sources of business news include the quarterly *Slovenian Business Report* (Slovene language; www.gvrevija.com) and the online *Slovenia Business Week* (English language; www.gzs.si). In addition the government's *Public Relations and Media Office* (www.uvi.si/eng) is an official source of English-language news.

*The Guardian International*, *International Herald Tribune*, *USA Today* and *The Financial Times* are also widely available in hotels, bookshops and at kiosks throughout Ljubljana. Higher-class hotels and thermal resorts frequently have a limited supply of foreign-language publications.

### Radio

Radiotelevizija Slovenija (RTV Slovenia; www.rtvslo.si) transmits three national radio channels, regional radio channels that include tourist broadcasts in foreign languages and one radio channel each for the country's Italian and Hungarian minorities. Around 100 stations in Slovenia also transmit commercial and non-commercial programmes. Turistični Radio (Tourist Radio) is available on 87.6MHz, 89.2MHz, 91.1MHz, 102.4MHz and 102.8MHz.

You can also access English-language broadcasts of the BBC World Service (www.bbc.co.uk/worldservice) and Voice of America (www.voa.gov).

### Television

RTV Slovenia transmits two national television channels and two regional channels – Koper-Capodistia in Koper and another in Maribor. Pro Plus operates the commercial channels Kanal A and Pop TV, which air a mixture of domestic and international programmes, while TV3 has a mixed Croatian–Slovenian ownership. Most of Ljubljana's better hotels have CNN, BBC World and other satellite channels such as Discovery, MTV and Eurosport.

### Internet cafés

Home internet use is widespread in Slovenia so few locals need internet cafés, but there are still a sprinkling of places to get online, concentrated in urban centres.

Many hotels and hostels provide internet points for guests. Where internet access is available the fee charged ranges from free to 600SIT an hour.

## Post offices

Every city and town has at least one post office, as do most villages. Post offices are easily identifiable by the black horn against a yellow background and the word *Pošta*. You can buy stamps, phonecards and postcards, bank your money and exchange currency in most post offices. Those located in tourist areas often sell a range of souvenirs. Opening hours are generally Monday–Friday 08.00–19.00 and Saturday 08.00–12.00, although smaller offices may close earlier. The postal service in Slovenia is comparable to any western European service with next-day delivery on internal first-class mail, and a quick airmail service to other destinations. Expect letters or cards sent to the UK to take around four to five days to arrive.

## Telephones

Telekom Slovenije (www.telekom.si) operates the country's telephone network and has a useful online directory available in Slovene and English. Only magnetic phonecards (*telekartica*) can be used in public phones; these cost 700–3,500SIT and are sold at post offices and some newspaper kiosks.

### Dialling

To call Slovenia from outside the country dial the exit code of the country you are in, followed by Slovenia's country code, 386. When calling from overseas the first 0 of the regional code needs to be omitted before dialling the rest of the number eg: instead of 01 for Ljubljana you just dial 1. When making international calls from Slovenia the exit code is 00. GSM networks cover the whole country, so as long as you have an international roaming agreement with your mobile telephone company you should have no problems using your handset. Remember to dial the city code in full. Mobile networks include SIMobil (Vodafone), Vega and Mobitel. If you call a mobile number from inside Slovenia make sure you dial all of the digits. Dialling codes for Slovenian cellphones often begin with 041.

### Useful telephone numbers

**Police** 113
**Fire** 112
**Medical emergency** 112
**Automobile Association of Slovenia (AMZS ) roadside assistance** 1987
**Directory enquiries** 1188
**International directory enquiries** 1180
**International operator** 115
**General information** 090 93 9881
**Alarm call** 198 10

## BUSINESS

Since becoming independent in 1991 Slovenia has quickly established itself as an efficient and stable democracy. As such business enterprises in Slovenia operate to the same high standards as other Western countries. Its recent accession to the EU is expected to open up trade links with other member states and to attract more international investors to the country. Key benefits for prospective investors include a highly skilled workforce, the majority of which is proficient in English, and a central European location.

For those conducting business in Slovenia a few common courtesies will ensure that everything runs smoothly. These include wearing smart business dress, making an appointment to see people and arriving on time for meetings. You will be expected to exchange business cards, so make sure that you have an ample supply. The majority of businesspeople in Ljubljana will have a high level of fluency in English or German, whilst those close to the Italian border are also likely to speak Italian. Business may be conducted in the office or over lunch or dinner. Office hours are generally Monday–Friday from 08.00 to 16.00 or 17.00. You should expect a meeting that includes a meal to last longer, as Slovenes like to take time over their meals and will not want to appear rude by rushing you.

Slovenia is a good venue for meetings, incentives, congress and exhibition (MICE) events. In Ljubljana many of the city's four- and five-star hotels provide conference and business facilities. For larger groups the Cankarjev Dom Congress and Cultural Centre (www.cd-cc.si) has ten halls which can accommodate a maximum of 1,400 delegates; it also has four additional conference rooms. The five-star Habakuk Hotel in Maribor, hotels and conference centres in Bled, and thermal spas are also excellent MICE venues. Meanwhile activities on offer in resorts like Kranjska Gora, Bovec, the Phorje and Logarska Dolina are great for team-building events. The Slovenian Chamber of Commerce and Industry (www.gzs.si), the website InvestSlovenia–Tipo (www.investslovenia.org), Slovenia Business Week (www.gzs.si/eng/news/sbw) and commercial advisors at foreign embassies in Slovenia can all provide useful information for prospective investors.

## CULTURAL DOS AND DON'TS
### Dos

Slovenes consider it polite to shake hands, especially when meeting for the first time. Those on business are also expected to exchange business cards. In restaurants and hotels it is usual to leave a 10% tip, unless the service has been really poor. Taxi drivers will also expect a tip. When clinking glasses and toasting say '*Na zdravje*' (pronounced noz-drav-yee and meaning 'cheers'), make sure you look everyone in the group in the eye and then take a sip before returning your glass to the table.

### Don'ts

Slovenes expect the same standards of behaviour in public as most other western European countries. It is also illegal to smoke in cinemas, theatres and waiting rooms, or on public transport. Be polite and considerate to cyclists as cycling is part of the culture; you will seldom win an argument with anyone on two wheels even if they have just tried to cut you in half on a pedestrian crossing.

## GAY AND LESBIAN TRAVELLERS

The gay and lesbian scene in Slovenia is not as prominent as in many European countries but there is one, and while attitudes towards homosexuality amongst the older generation are often far from enlightened, being gay or lesbian is becoming more socially acceptable. Although attitudes are improving, especially in the big cities, public displays of affection between gay or lesbian partners are still not the norm.

The first Ljubljana Gay and Lesbian Pride Parade was staged in 2000, and this annual event has been credited with changing attitudes in the city. The gay and lesbian communities in Ljubljana showed that they were not willing to be pushed around during the so-called 'water protest' a few years ago when the new owner of Galerija decided to axe it as a gay bar. For months the gay community showed its resolve by occupying the money-spinning outdoor tables and ordering only water. This defiant face of gay and lesbian culture has been given a very visible face by Sestre (Sister), the transvestite trio who won the contest to represent their country at the 2002 Eurovision Song Contest, much to the chagrin of more conservative elements of Slovenian society.

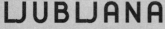

# KEY TO STANDARD SYMBOLS

**Bradt**

| | | | | |
|---|---|---|---|---|
| —·—·— | International boundary | $ | Bank |
| ------ | District boundary | | Statue, monument |
| - - - - - | National park boundary | •• | Archaeological or historic site |
| | Railway | | Historic building |
| ■ | Railway station | | Castle, fortress |
| ---------- | Footpath | | Town wall |
| ✈ | Airport | ✝ | Church, cathedral |
| | Helicopter service | | Ski centre, skiing |
| | Petrol station, garage | ▶ | Golf course |
| P | Car park | | Stadium |
| ::::::::::: | Tunnel (Ljubljana) | △ | Boundary beacon |
| | Passenger ferry | ▲ | Summit |
| | Bus station etc | ✕—✕ | Border post |
| → | One-way street | | Cave |
| M | Underground station | ☐—o—☐ | Cable car, funicular |
| | Hotel, inn etc | | Mountain pass |
| | Ski hut | ◉ | Outpost |
| Λ | Campsite | ✳ | Scenic viewpoint |
| ☆ | Nightclub | | Botanical site |
| ♀ | Bar, café-bar | | Specific woodland feature |
| ✕ | Restaurant, café | | Lighthouse |
| ⊠ | Post office | | Marsh |
| ( | Telephone | | National park |
| e | Internet café | | Bird reserve |
| ✚ | Hospital, clinic etc | ∭ | Waterfall |
| ✚ | Pharmacy | ✲ | Source of river |
| | Museum, gallery | | Spa |
| i | Tourist information | | Scuba diving |
| | Zoo | | Beach |

*Other map symbols may be shown on individual maps*

# Part Two

# The Guide

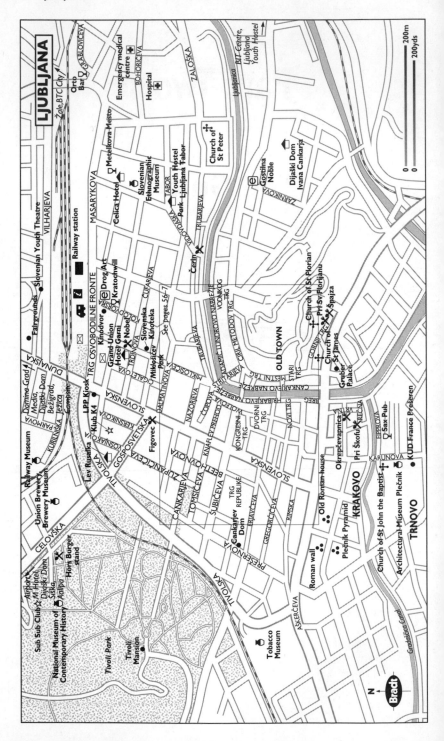

# Ljubljana

Recent years have seen Ljubljana increasingly hailed as the 'new Prague', but comparisons like these do not do the Slovenian capital justice. Perhaps the tendency to compare the city comes from the fact that it is not as widely known as big city-break players like Prague, Paris and London, but it may also be because it does take some of the most attractive features from other cities and weaves them into a truly unique mix. At times walking around Ljubljana does feel a bit like Prague or Vienna, but also Amsterdam, Riga or Salzburg, making Ljubljana a sort of 'greatest hits' of European architecture and city planning.

No introduction to Ljubljana would be complete without an immediate mention of the man responsible for much of the way the city looks and is ordered today: Jože Plečnik (see page 52). Perhaps it should be 'Prague, the new Ljubljana' as the seminal Slovene architect honed his skills in Ljubljana before heading off to work on Prague Castle. His work in the Slovenian capital is perhaps even more impressive as he remoulded much of the city, bringing in the Triple Bridge across the Ljubljanica, giving the river new banks as it travelled through the centre of the city, adding the colonnades by the Central Market and turning Tivoli Park into a landscaped park in the grand European tradition. Everywhere you look in Ljubljana the hand of Plečnik can be seen.

While Plečnik shaped the core of the city, Ljubljana has also been heavily influenced by the other nations and ideologies which have rumbled through this strategic hub over the centuries. In Ljubljana an Italianate church rests comfortably beside a functional socialist-era office block and a lavish art nouveau façade sidles up to a sharp new steel and glass hotel. The Hungarians, Austrians and Italians are amongst those who have left their indelible marks. Other older civilisations have also left their stamp with the remnants of the old Roman walls sneaking out as a permanent reminder of the city's days as Emona. These eclectic influences permeate many aspects of city life such as its food and drink so that enjoying an Italian-style ice-cream by the river is as much part of the Ljubljana experience as savouring hearty Hungarian goulash or quaffing a hoppy pilsner in a beer cellar.

For all its myriad influences Ljubljana is also very Slovenian – a neat, tidy and organised city, with green spaces never far away. Ljubljana was always a cultural hub in the former Yugoslavia, with an aggressively avant-garde reputation, and this vivacity still ripples through the city today with its artistically literate population and

## JOŽE PLEČNIK

The Slovene architect Jože Plečnik is to Ljubljana what Haussmann was to Paris. He had an even greater influence on his city as his touch is almost everywhere. Born in 1872 Plečnik had a grand vision for Ljubljana, which he wanted to be the Slovenian Athens, a spiritual home for a people who were in the process of discovering and developing their national identity. He honed his considerable talents in Graz and at the Vienna Academy of Fine Arts, later lecturing at the Prague Academy and working right up until his death in 1957. A modest and religious man, he took on a multitude of projects, many of them on an epic scale. He dared to use unfashionable materials like concrete, often out of economic necessity, but still managed to infuse all his work with a quiet dignity and a human dimension. For those with plenty of time in the city a day spent exploring his legacy is fascinating. There is his landmark Triple Bridge, the nearby Cobbler's Bridge, his remodelling of the banks of the Ljubljanica, the Križanke theatre complex, his bridge in Trnovo and, of course, the National and University Library, which many Ljubljančani rate as Plečnik's masterpiece. Then there is his work adding the colonnades to the Central Market, the entrance to the Žale Cemetery and in Tivoli Park; the list is as extensive as it is impressive in its unfaltering quality.

a large and active student community. One-off cultural performances and various 'happenings' are all the rage and you are as likely to hear local students talking through the latest experimental theatre as you are their favourite cutting-edge DJs.

## HISTORY

According to local legend, Ljubljana's first inhabitants came straight from the pages of Greek mythology when, after being tricked into stealing a golden fleece that belonged to King Aeetes, Jason and his Argonauts fled from Colchis. The *Argo* then transported the ancient warriors on their epic adventure from the Black Sea to the Danube, onward to the Sava River and finally into the Ljubljanica. Having successfully escaped the wrath of Aeetes, the Argonauts were confronted by a formidable fire-breathing dragon which, during a fierce battle, the brave Jason managed to slay. In commemoration of this courageous act the city's coat of arms bears a picture of the beast. The Ljubljana dragon can also be found throughout the city, on the castle's tower, the town hall and railings along the banks of the Ljubljanica, as well as standing proud on the eponymous bridge and, of course, on a wealth of tourist souvenirs.

While it may not be full of colourful characters from Greek mythology, Ljubljana's recorded history is no less intoxicating. Historical evidence suggests that Ljubljana's first inhabitants were pile dwellers from the Copper Age, who lived in stilt-houses built on marshland. Next came the Illyrians, who settled near Ljubljana in the late Bronze Age. Cave paintings near the capital depict members of this ancient tribe engaged in battle and sporting events, enjoying great feasts and conducting ritual sacrifices. Around the 3rd century BC Celtic tribes rumbled into the region.

The arrival of the Romans in the 1st century BC saw Ljubljana's status elevated from a rough tribal settlement to a military base and later to a city. Under the Romans Ljubljana was called Emona and remnants of the Roman settlement can still be found on the left bank of the Ljubljanica, including reconstructed sections of the Roman walls. For its residents life in Emona was good save the frequent attacks by the barbarian Huns and the central Asian Avars, but the Romans finally capitulated in AD452.

By the 7th century the Slavs had become the dominant people in Slovenia, establishing the first independent Slavic or Slovenian state, Carinthia. In AD746 Carinthia fell under the auspices of the Bavarian Dukes. Ljubljana next emerged as a significant city in medieval times, with its Austrian name Laibach (a name that it kept until 1918) first appearing in written documents in 1144. In 1335, under the Austro–Hungarians, Ljubljana became the capital of the province of Carniola, and the Austro-Hungarians remained the dominant force in the city until the end of World War I.

In 1511 a devastating earthquake felled much of Ljubljana. While reconstruction after the earthquake helped shape the city's physical appearance, Protestantism, which rose to the fore in the late 16th century, played a significant role in shaping the city's psyche over the next two hundred years. By the 19th century, however, the Catholic church had become an influential force in the shaping of Ljubljana's (and Slovenia's) cultural and linguistic identity. Today Primož Trubar, Ivan Cankar and France Prešeren remain writ large on the national consciousness of modern Ljubljana. More than 150 years after his death in 1849, a looming statue of Prešeren still watches protectively over Ljubljana's residents.

At the beginning of the 19th century Napoleon made a brief incursion into the region, which left Ljubljana as the capital of the French emperor's Illyrian Provinces from 1809 to 1813. With Austro-Hungarian rule restored by the 1814–15 Congress of Vienna, the other defining events in Ljubljana's history were the construction of the Vienna–Trieste railway, which was completed in 1857 and brought new cultural influences to the Slovenian capital, and a second devastating earthquake in 1895. The rebuilding of the city in the late 19th and early 20th centuries gave rise to the stunning art nouveau (or secessionist) buildings found on Ljubljana's historic left bank.

World War I heralded the end of four decades of peace in Europe and the collapse of the Austro-Hungarian Empire. In 1918 Slovenia became part of the Kingdom of Serbs, Croats and Slovenes. The inter-war years saw the city take on much of its iconic architecture under the guiding hand of Jože Plečnik. At this time the biggest skyscraper in Yugoslavia, the Nebotičnik, was constructed. Currently closed due to a legal wrangle brought on by the process of denationalisation, the skyscraper still stands on Slovenska as an enduring testimony to the grand ambitions of this newly independent pan-Slavic country.

A dramatically different Slovenia emerged from the rubble of World War II, and in 1945 Ljubljana took its place as one of the six capitals of Tito's new Yugoslavia. For almost half a century the Slovenian capital found itself under the rigid control of a socialist regime, characterised by dictatorial leadership and the shared ownership of property, which was ended by the declaration of Slovenian independence on June 26 1991.

In the period since independence Ljubljana has come of age as a capital city. In 2004 Slovenia joined both NATO and the European Union, heralding in a new phase for Slovenia and Ljubljana. The physical appearance as well as the political importance of the city is changing too, as new office buildings and houses spring up and older buildings are given much-needed refurbishment. Ljubljana today is a dynamic and rapidly evolving city that is becoming increasingly popular with both business people and tourists from the rest of the EU and beyond.

# GETTING THERE
## By air
Located 23km northwest of Ljubljana's city centre, Ljubljana Brnik Airport (tel: 04 206 1981; fax: 04 206 1109; email: info@lju-airport.si; www.lju-airport.si) is well served by taxis and bus services.

### Airport transfers
Buses (tel: 090 4230) leave Brnik for Ljubljana city centre on the hour between 05.00 and 20.00 Monday–Friday, and every two hours from 10.00–20.00 at the weekend, with an additional service at 07.00. Buses leave the main bus station for the airport at 05.20 and then at ten minutes past the hour from 06.10–20.10 Monday–Friday. At weekends they leave at 06.10 and then every two hours from 09.10 to 19.10. Journey time is 45 minutes; one-way fare is 740SIT.

Markun (tel: 04 252 1016) operate a private bus service between the airport and Ljubljana bus station. These depart Brnik airport daily at 07.30, 09.55, 11.30, 13.45, 15.00, 16.00, 18.10, 21.50, 23.00 and midnight. Buses for the airport leave Ljubljana at 05.20, 06.15, 10.25, 12.15, 14.10, 15.30, 17.00 and 22.30. Journey time is 30 minutes; fare is 1,000SIT. Taxis to and from the city centre cost around 7,000SIT.

## By bus
Ljubljana bus station (Trg Osvobodilne fronte 4; tel: 090 4230; email: avtobusna.postaja@ap-ljubljana.si; www.ap-ljubljana.si. Open 05.30–21.00) is easily accessible by bus from towns and cities across Slovenia including: Kamnik (35 minutes), Škofja Loka (40 minutes), Kranj (40 minutes), Postojna (1 hour), Novo Mesto (1 hour 10 minutes), Idrija ($1^1/4$ hours), Bled (1 hour 20 minutes), Celje (1 hour 35 minutes), Ribčez Laz for Lake Bohinj (2 hours), Kranjska Gora (2 hours), Koper (2 hours 20 minutes), Nova Gorica ($2^1/2$ hours), Piran (2 hours 40 minutes), Maribor ($2^3/4$ hours) and Murska Sobota (4 hours).

## By rail
Regular train services link the capital railway station (Trg Osvobodilne fronte 6; tel: 01 291 3332; email: info@slo-zeleznice.si; www.slo-zeleznice.si) to the rest of Slovenia; services tend to be less frequent and a little slower than buses. Available routes include: Kamnik (50 minutes), Postojna (1 hour), Novo Mesto (1 hour 40 minutes), Maribor ($2^1/4$ hours), Črnomelj ($2^1/2$ hours), Koper ($2^1/2$ hours), Metlika ($2^3/4$ hours) and Ptuj ($2^3/4$ hours).

# GETTING AROUND
## Bicycle hire
From May to October free bicycle hire is available from Prešernov trg, Plečnikov trg, Trg Osvobodilne fronte (outside the railway station) and the Slovenian Tourist Information Centre on Krekov trg. You need photo ID and a refundable deposit of 1,000SIT. The city also has commercial hire outlets and many hotels offer bicycle hire to guests.

**Tours** Kongresni trg 13; tel: 01 426 9441
**Café Maček** (see *Entertainment and Nightlife*) Krojaška 5; tel: 01 425 3791

## By bus
The city bus service run by Ljubljanski Potniški Promet (LPP) is useful if you are staying outside the city centre. Most of the 21 routes operate from 05.00 to 22.30, although some run from 03.15 until midnight. You can pay with cash (300SIT) or *žetoni* (metal tokens), which are available for 190SIT from newsstands, kiosks and anywhere displaying a *žetoni* sign. Tokens and daily or weekly passes can also be purchased at the bus station or directly from LPP.

**LPP Information Centre** (also lost and found) Celovška 160; tel: 01 582 2420/421/422; email: mail@lpp.si; www.lpp.si
**LPP Information Centre** Trdinova 3; tel: 01 434 3248/249
**LPP Kiosk** Slovenska 55

## By taxi
Taxi ranks are located near the Ljubljana TIC on Stritarjeva, outside the Slon Hotel on Slovenska, at the railway station and near Mestni trg. At night taxis also wait on Prešernov trg. Dialling 9700, 9701, 9702, 9703, 9704, 9707 or 9709 will connect you to one of seven taxi firms.

## By rail
Ljubljana has a limited local route, which includes services north to Ježica, Črnuče and Vižmarje, east to Polje and southeast to Rakovnik.

## Car hire
Car hire is available at the airport, in central Ljubljana and at some of the city's hotels. Central locations include:

**Avis** Čufarjeva 2; tel: 01 430 8010; fax: 01 430 8014; email: lji@avis.si; www.avis-alpe.si
**Avis** Hotel Lev, Vošnjakova 1; tel: 01 438 3250; fax: 01 438 3255; email: lj3@avis.si; www.avis-alpe.si
**Budget** Grand Hotel Union, Miklošičeva 3; tel: 01 421 7340; fax: 01 421 7344; email: budget.car@siol.net
**Europcar** Hotel City Turist, Dalmatinova 15; tel: 01 507 6127; fax: 01 519 9876
**Hertz** Ljubljana Bus Station, Trg Osvobodilne fronte 5; tel: 01 234 4646; fax: 01 234 4647; email: info@hertz.si; www.hertz.si

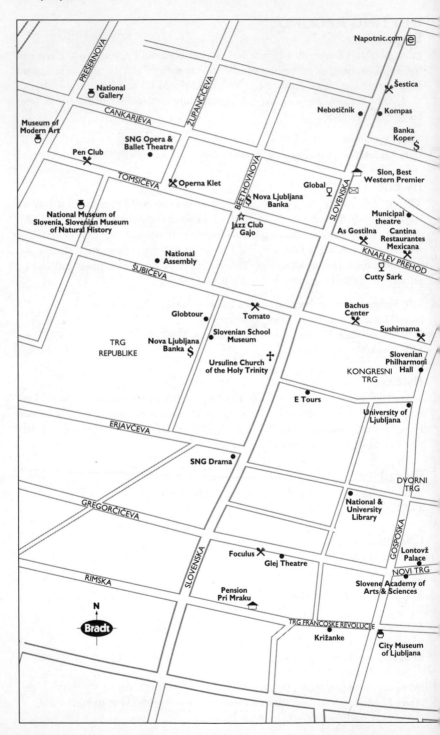

Napotnic.com

PREŠERNOVA

National Gallery

Museum of Modern Art

CANKARJEVA

ŽUPANČIČEVA

Šestica

Nebotičnik

Kompas

Banka Koper

SNG Opera & Ballet Theatre

Pen Club

TOMSIČEVA

Operna Klet

BEETHOVNOVA

Nova Ljubljana Banka

Global

SLOVENSKA

Slon, Best Western Premier

National Museum of Slovenia, Slovenian Museum of Natural History

Jazz Club Gajo

Municipal theatre

As Gostilna

Cantina Restaurantes Mexicana

KNAFLEV PREHOD

National Assembly

ŠUBIČEVA

Cutty Sark

Globtour

Tomato

Bachus Center

Sushimama

TRG REPUBLIKE

Nova Ljubljana Banka

Slovenian School Museum

Ursuline Church of the Holy Trinity

Slovenian Philharmoni Hall

KONGRESNI TRG

E Tours

University of Ljubljana

ERJAVČEVA

SNG Drama

DVORNI TRG

National & University Library

GREGORČIČEVA

GOSPOSKA

Lontovž Palace

NOVI TRG

Foculus

Glej Theatre

Slovene Academy of Arts & Sciences

RIMSKA

SLOVENSKA

Pension Pri Mraku

N

Bradt

TRG FRANCOSKE REVOLUCIJE

Križanke

City Museum of Ljubljana

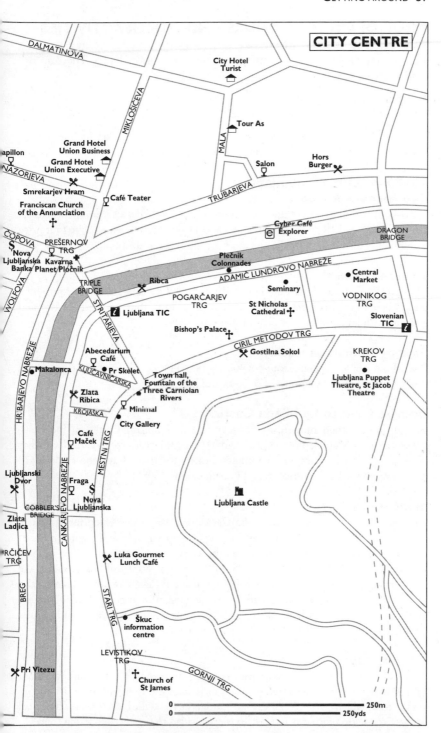

**CITY CENTRE**

DALMATINOVA

City Hotel Turist

MIKLOŠIČEVA

MALA

Tour As

Grand Hotel
Union Business

apillon

NAZORJEVA

Grand Hotel
Union Executive

Salon

Hors
Burger

TRUBARJEVA

Smrekarjev Hram

Café Teater

Franciscan Church
of the Annunciation

Cyber Café
Explorer

DRAGON
BRIDGE

ČOPOVA

PREŠERNOV
TRG

Nova
Ljubljanska
Banka

Kavarna
Planet Pločnik

Plečnik
Colonnades

ADAMIČ LUNDROVO NABREŽE

Central
Market

WOLFOVA

TRIPLE
BRIDGE

Ribca

POGARČARJEV
TRG

Seminary

St Nicholas
Cathedral

VODNIKOG
TRG

Slovenian
TIC

STRITARJEVA

Ljubljana TIC

Bishop's Palace

CIRIL METODOV TRG

KREKOV
TRG

Abecedarium
Café

Gostilna Sokol

HRIBARJEVO NABREŽIE

Makalonca

KLJUČAVNIČARSKA

Pr Skelet

Town hall,
Fountain of the
Three Carniolan
Rivers

Ljubljana Puppet
Theatre, St Jacob
Theatre

Zlata
Ribica

KROJAŠKA

Minimal

City Gallery

Café
Maček

MESTNI TRG

CANKARJEVO NABREŽIE

Ljubljanski
Dvor

Fraga

COBBLER'S
BRIDGE

Nova
Ljubljanska

Zlata
Ladjica

Ljubljana Castle

RČIČEV
TRG

BREG

Luka Gourmet
Lunch Café

STARI TRG

Škuc
information
centre

LEVIŠTIKOV
TRG

Pri Vitezu

GORNJI TRG

Church of
St James

0 ——————————— 250m
0 ——————————— 250yds

## TOUR OPERATORS, TOURS AND OTHER ACTIVITIES
### Full service tourist agencies
Kompas and Globtour offer a variety of excursions from Ljubljana. They can also help you to arrange accommodation and onward travel.

**Kompas** Slovenska 36; tel: 01 200 6222; www.kompas.net
**Globtour** Trg Republike 1; tel: 01 244 1320; www.globtour.si

A range of city tours and excursions can be booked at the Tourist Information Centres. Most areas of the country are accessible on day trips.

### Walking tours of Ljubljana
*Two-hour walking tours*
Two-hour walking tours of the Old Town and the castle depart from the town hall daily at 10.00 and 18.00 May–September and 11.00 October–April. The tour price (1,500SIT, concessions 700SIT) includes a trip on the tourist train.

*Ljubljana by night*
This two-hour tour of the Old Town (daily 20.30 July–August, 20.00 April–June and September; price: 2,000SIT) combines a walking-tour with a boat trip and finishes with an ice-cream or glass of sparkling wine.

### Sightseeing tours on request
Two-hour guided walking tours (8,400–24,000SIT) are available in 16 languages and can be booked by groups of 5–50 throughout the year.

### Tourist train to Ljubljana Castle
A daily tourist train runs from Prešernov trg to Ljubljana Castle on the hour, 09.00–21.00 May–September and 10.00–19.00 October–April (weather dependent). It takes around 15 minutes and return trains leave the castle at 20 minutes past each hour. Price: 600SIT, concessions 400SIT.

### Boat tours
One-hour boat tours depart from the Cankarjevo nabrežje pier during the main tourist season. The boat doesn't travel far, with Trnovo and the Dragon Bridge its extremities, but it makes a change to get this close to the Ljubljanica. You can pay on board (1,500SIT, concessions 700SIT), but might want to book ahead at the TIC during peak season. A candlelit and commentary-less 'Romantic Tour' is also available and includes a glass of sparkling wine. Departure times and frequency are subject to weather and demand so check the timetable pinned on the ship's mast by the pier or at the TIC.

### Cycling tours
From May to October the Slovenian Tourist Information Centre runs two-hour guided bike tours for three to ten people. For insurance reasons only over-16s can go on the tour, which costs 3,000SIT. On Saturdays at 10.00 the bicycle tour is free. Staff at the Krekov trg office can also usually be persuaded to organise off-season tours.

## General excursions

The Tourist Information Centres provide information about, and can make bookings for, various excursions outside Ljubljana, including to Šmarna Gora, the historic town of Škofja Loka, the stunning Vintgar Gorge and the Kamniške Savinje Alps.

## Skok Sport Centre

Located just 7km outside the city centre on the banks of the Ljubljanica River, the Skok Sport Centre (Marinovseva 8; tel: 01 512 4402 or 040 218 000; email: info@skok-sport.si; www.skok-sport.si) offers kayaking (ten-hour course; 25,000–31,200SIT), rafting trip (3,600–6,240SIT), mountain-biking and beach volleyball. The flexible family team headed by Janez Skok can cater activities to suit all age groups and levels of experience. Rafting on Slovenia's Soča River is a real highlight and costs around 6,240SIT per person. You can also hire rafting, kayaking and mountain-bike gear (mountain-bike hire 1,200–14,400SIT for two hours–one week) from the centre.

## Hot-air ballooning

A unique way to see Ljubljana is from the air aboard a hot-air balloon. **Balonarski Centre Barje** (Flandrova 1; tel: 01 512 9220; email: balon@siol.net) organise flights out across the Ljubljana marshes with unforgettable views of the city and surrounding mountains.

# WHERE TO STAY
## City centre

**Celica Hostel** (29 rooms) Metelkova 9; tel/fax: 01 430 1890; email: info@souhostel.si; www.souhostel.si. Just five minutes' walk from the bus and train stations, this bright and funky hostel offers 92 beds in two–14-person rooms, and is one of the most colourful places to stay in Ljubljana. Housed in a former prison that once served as the military barracks of the Yugoslav Army, the best rooms are the 20 renovated prison cells that sleep two or three people. Each of these individual and local-artist-designed cells retains its original window and cell bars. If you stay in a cell then bathroom facilities are shared, although the hostel's nine other rooms have private bathrooms. Celica also has a room for disabled guests, a bar, café, gallery, internet access, prayer room, self-service laundry and kitchen. Celica's unique style and cheap prices mean that it is often full, so it is essential to book in advance. Under 35s 3,500–5,250SIT per person, over 35s 4,950–5,750SIT per person.
**City Hotel Turist** (123 rooms) Dalmatinova 15; tel: 01 234 9130; fax: 01 234 9140; email: info@hotelturist.si; www.hotelturist.si. Very centrally located three-star business hotel with en-suite, air-conditioned rooms. On-street parking, half- and full-board rates and bicycle hire (for guests only) are also available. The hotel has its own restaurant, bar, soft-drinks dispenser and public internet terminal in the lobby. Singles 13,680–22,320SIT, doubles 23,760–33,360SIT, triples 28,320–36,000SIT, business suite 30,240–37,920SIT.
**Grand Hotel Union Business** (139 rooms) Miklošičeva 3; tel: 01 308 1170; fax: 01 308 1914; email: hotel.business@gh-union.si; www.gh-union.si. Formerly a Holiday Inn, the modern wing of the Grand Hotel Union has an unattractive exterior compared to its

illustrious relation next door. However, guestrooms are furnished to the same high standards as rooms in the Executive and guests have access to all of the facilities detailed in the listing below. There is a modest gym and a small swimming pool that offers sweeping views of the skyline. Singles 32,400–44,800SIT, doubles 42,200–54,000SIT.

**Grand Hotel Union Executive** (191 rooms) Miklošičeva 1; tel: 01 308 1270; fax: 01 308 1015; email: hotel.union@gh-union.si; www.gh-union.si. Housed in a stunning art nouveau building dating from 1905, Ljubljana's most attractive hotel is just a minute's stroll from Prešernov trg and the river, as well as the main entertainment area. Classically decorated rooms feature satellite TV, minibars and, that Ljubljana rarity, fluffy bathrobes and slippers. Meeting and conference facilities, good-quality restaurants and garage parking are also on offer. Guests can use the leisure facilities at the hotel's Business sibling. Singles 32,400–44,800SIT, doubles 42,200–54,000SIT.

**Grand Hotel Union Garni** (74 rooms) Miklošičeva 9; tel: 01 308 4300; fax: 01 230 1181. Renovated in 1999 and bought by the Grand Union in 2004 this hotel attracts a mainly business crowd. Large guestrooms are comfortable and equipped with all the amenities that you would expect to find in a four-star hotel. The hotel also has its own restaurant, bar, relaxation centre with sauna, conference facilities and a hard-to-beat location, just a few minutes' walk from the main bus and railway stations and 500m from the Old Town. Singles 25,600–28,000SIT, doubles 33,600SIT.

**Lev** (189 rooms) Vošnjakova 1; tel: 01 433 2155; fax: 01 230 2578; email: info@hotel-lev.si; www.hotel-lev.si. This is Ljubljana's only five-star hotel, a place aimed firmly at businesspeople, though there are often good deals at weekends to attract leisure travellers as well. Rooms are spacious, classically styled and comfortable. En-suite bathrooms have a shower and bath. The hotel also has rooms for disabled guests, a restaurant, bar, small gym, internet point and beauty parlour. Some of the city-side rooms on the higher levels have castle views and others overlook Tivoli Park. Singles 46,600–51,300SIT, doubles 56,000–58,300SIT, suite 69,900SIT.

**Park** (122 rooms) Tabor 9; tel: 01 433 1306; fax: 01 433 0546; email: hotel.park@siol.net; www.hotelpark.si. The Park is located 800m from the main bus and railway stations and is one of the few budget hotels in Ljubljana. It is a good alternative for those who cannot get a bed in the nearby Celica Hostel. Housed in an uninviting concrete tower block it has clean and basic single and double rooms with en-suite facilities, and as few frills as you would expect. Singles 10,800–11,760SIT, doubles 13,920–15,120SIT.

**Pension Pri Mraku** (30 rooms) Rimska 4; tel: 01 421 9600; fax: 01 421 9655; email: daj-dam@daj-dam.si; www.daj-dam.si. This guesthouse has a good location on an attractive street near the Križanke theatre, so if you are here for a concert or for the summer festival this is the place to stay. Despite their Old-World feel guestrooms are fairly large and have modern facilities including internet access and cable TV. Singles 13,560–16,800SIT, doubles 21,360–25,200SIT, triples 26,160–28,800SIT, 1–4 person suites 36,000–43,000SIT.

**Slon Best Western Premier** (176 rooms) Slovenska 34; tel: 01 470 1100; fax: 01 251 7164; email: sales@hotelslon.com; www.hotelslon.com or www.bestwestern.com. The Slon has one of the best locations in the city, with shops to one side and the city's historic attractions rambling away on the other, not to mention Tivoli Park, which is only a short walk away. In addition to comfortable air-conditioned rooms, the Slon offers internet access in the lobby and a ground-floor deli, café and restaurant. Good rates are often available through the Best Western website. Singles 20,640–28,320SIT, doubles 28,760–39,840SIT, triples 43,920SIT, suites (1–4 people) 42,720–87,840SIT.

**Tour As** Mala ulica 8; tel: 01 434 2660; fax: 01 434 2664; email: info@apartmaji.si; www.apartmaji.si. Agency co-ordinating stays in apartments. All properties are fully furnished, have telephones, satellite TV and internet connections. Ensure that you know the exact location of your apartment before booking if you want to avoid long walks or buses into town; a handy map on the company's website will help you do this. Prices range from 14,290–25,000SIT per day depending on location and the number of people that the apartment will sleep.

**Youth Hostel Ljubljana Tabor** (59 beds) Vidovdanska 7; tel: 01 234 8840; fax: 01 234 8855; email: ssljddta1s@guest.arnes.si; www.youth-hostel.si. From late June to late August these centrally located student dorms offer accommodation in single, twin, triple and four-bedded rooms which are basic but clean. There are also an onsite café-bar and a car park, as well as handball, volleyball and basketball courts. Price 3,600–4,800SIT per person.

## Outside the city centre

**AA Lipa** Celovška 264; tel: 01 507 4590; fax: 01 507 4960; email: aa-lipa@siol.net; www.aa-lipa.si. Bus 1 direction Vižmarje, bus 15 direction Medvode or bus 16 direction Gameljne to Dravlje stop. Located on busy Celovška not far from the M Hotel (about 3km out of town), the AA Lipa offers basic motel-style accommodation in an unappealing tower block. Handy if you are in a hurry to get to the airport, but otherwise there is little, other than the price, to recommend this pension. Singles 8,940SIT, doubles 11,930SIT.

**Bit Centre** (37 rooms) Litijska 57; tel: 01 548 0055; fax: 01 548 0056; email: hotel@bit-centre.net; www.bit-center.net. Bus 5 or 9 direction Štepansko naselje and bus 13 direction Sostro to Emona stop. On the same site as the Ljubljana Youth Hostel this budget hotel is a step up from dormitory accommodation. Rooms are basic and small with satellite TV and private bathrooms with shower. Guests get a 50% reduction on the facilities offered at the adjoining sports centre and can use the outdoor pool free of charge in the summer. Singles 6,790SIT, doubles 9,590SIT.

**Dijaški Dom Bežigrad** (70 rooms) Kardeljeva ploščad 28; tel: 01 534 0061; fax: 01 534 2864; email: dd.lj-bezigrad@guest.arnes.si. Bus 6 direction Črnuče, bus 8 direction Ježica or bus 21 direction Beričevo to Mercator stop. Those struggling to find affordable accommodation in Ljubljana could do worse than turn to the student dormitories in Bežigrad, open in July and August. A total of 240 budget-priced beds are offered in basic student rooms with one, two or three beds. Price 2,880–4,320SIT per person.

**Dijaški Dom Ivana Cankarja** (180 rooms) Poljanska 26; tel: 01 474 8600; fax: 01 432 0369; email: dd.lj-ic@guest.arnes.si; www.dic-lj.com. Bus 5 direction Štepansko naselje or bus 13 direction Sostro to Roška stop. The student dorms are just ten minutes' walk from central Ljubljana, close to Castle Hill. This part-time hostel has 480 beds in single, double and triple rooms from mid-June until the end of August. The residence also has its own parking spaces, sports stadium, football pitch and basketball courts. Price 2,640–3,840SIT per person.

**Dijaški Dom Šiška** (50 beds) Aljaževa 32; tel: 01 500 7802; fax: 01 500 7820; email: ddsiska@email.si; www.ddsiska.com. Bus 1 direction Vižmarje, bus 3 direction Litostroj, bus 5 direction Podutik, bus 8 direction Brod, bus 15 direction Medvode or bus 16 direction Gameljne to Stara Cerkev stop. Student dormitory located in Šiška, open from the beginning of June to the end of August. Accommodation takes the form of simply furnished twin rooms. This seasonal hostel also has a television room, café-bar, currency-exchange facilities and a car park. Price 2,640–3,600SIT per person.

**Domina Grand Media Ljubljana** (213 rooms) Dunajska 160; tel: 01 569 1192; fax: 01 569 1193; email: grandmedia.ljubljana@domina.it; www.dominahotels.it. Bus 6 direction Črnuče, bus 8 direction Ježica or bus 21 direction Beričevo. Opened in summer 2004, one of Ljubljana's newest hotels claims to be the 'Most Hi-Tech Hotel in the World'. Comfortable doubles and junior suites offer broadband internet connections, free email, pay TV and computer games. In many rooms huge plasma television screens also provide on-screen newspapers, books, films and even virtual sightseeing tours of Ljubljana. Additional facilities include an indoor pool, sauna, gym, casino, restaurants, bars, convention centre, meeting rooms and video conferencing. The only bugbear is that the hotel is located 3km out of the city centre, which means you will need to catch the hotel's shuttle bus, a taxi or municipal bus to and from town. Good rates are often available on the internet. From 19,200SIT.

**Ježica Campsite and Bungalows** Dunajska 270; tel: 01 568 3913; fax: 01 568 3912; email: ac.jezica@gpl.si; www.gpl.si. Bus 6 direction Črnuče or bus 8 direction Ježica to Ježica stop. Located 3km from the city centre Ježica has electricity points, hot water, showers, laundry and dishwashing facilities, as well as its own recently refurbished restaurant and a snack bar. There is the option of renting a bungalow equipped with a telephone and television. Onsite facilities include a skittle alley, gym, sauna, games courts and three swimming pools. Camping 1,730–2,100SIT per person. Bungalows: singles 12,000SIT, doubles 15,000SIT, triples 19,000SIT.

**Ljubljana Youth Hostel** Litijska 57; tel: 01 548 0055; fax: 01 548 0056; email: hotel@bit-centre.net; www.yh-ljubljana.com. Bus 5 or 9 direction Štepansko naselje or bus 13 direction Sostro to Emona stop. Affiliated with HI and providing accommodating in two-, three- and ten-bedded rooms. The rooms are bright and modern and guests get a 50% discount on sporting facilities and free usage of the outdoor pool in summer. The hostel also has a car park and a summer terrace bar. Shared bathrooms. Price 2,700SIT per person.

**M Hotel** (157 rooms) Derčeva 4; tel: 01 513 7000; fax: 01 519 3048; email: info@m-hotel.si; www.m-hotel.si. Bus 1 direction Vižmarje, bus 5 direction Podutik, bus 8 direction Brod, bus 15 direction Medvode or bus 16 direction Gameljne to Šiška stop. Don't let your first glimpse of the Mercator-owned M Hotel put you off. The hotel is not, as it may at first appear, totally immersed in a jungle of concrete high-rises and busy roads. Rooms at the front of the hotel overlook a quiet tree-lined street and Tivoli Park. With friendly staff and modern rooms the M Hotel is arguably Ljubljana's best three-star property. Singles 13,450–18,800SIT, doubles 19,580–23,600SIT, extra bed 47,200SIT, suite 38,940SIT.

**Mons Hotel** (114 rooms) Pot za Brdom; tel: 01 470 2700; email: info@hotel.mons.si. Opened in September 2004, this stylish design hotel – a box-like green and glass structure that was designed by the famous Slovenian-born architect Boris Podrecca – is Ljubljana's newest accommodation. Rooms are comfortable and high-tech. The hotel also has a wine bar, fitness centre, snooker room, two restaurants and a conference centre making this a perfect hotel for business travellers. For leisure guests, however, this new hotel is yet another out-of-town establishment, necessitating a taxi journey to get there. The hotel does run a free shuttle bus to Kongresni trg. Singles 18,950–23,800SIT, doubles 25,500–29,950SIT, suites 35,950–52,800SIT.

**Vila Minka** Kogovškova 10; tel: 01 583 0080; fax: 01 507 4691; email: minka@vilaminka.si; www.vilaminka.si. Bus 5 direction Podutik or bus 22 direction Kamna Gorica stop Koseze. Located 3km from the city centre in the suburb of Koseze, just north of Tivoli Park, Vila Minka has spacious rooms and apartments. Facilities include satellite TV, internet access and car parking. Apartments also have small private kitchens, while those staying in single or double rooms can use the communal cooking area. Car and bicycle hire is also offered. Singles 10,000SIT, doubles 13,000SIT, apartments 17,000–30,000SIT (1–6 people). A surcharge of 10–30% is applied for stays of less than three days.

# WHERE TO EAT
Forget any anachronistic images that you may harbour of communist-era culinary deprivations as Ljubljana is fast developing into something of an eating and drinking oasis, a compact city with a smorgasbord of bars, cafés and restaurants. Over the last few years a number of more exotic cuisines have been sneaking into the Slovenian capital with the likes of Mexican, Japanese and Chinese all now in the mix.

## Top-end dining
**As Gostilna** Knaflev prehod 5a; tel: 01 425 8822. This is the place for a meal amongst Ljubljana's cognoscenti with top-quality cuisine and fine wine, but make sure to dress up smart. The main building has an Old-World atmosphere with candles and oil paintings, making it the perfect venue for impressing that special companion. The outdoor covered terrace has more of a buzz and is less formal. Both venues concentrate on excellent seafood with a shared Adriatic platter to die for, as well as some creative options presented with lashings of flair.

**Pri Sv Florijanu** Gornji trg 20; tel: 01 251 2214. One of Ljubljana's oldest upscale restaurants has recently been revamped and its intimate and rustic interior has taken on a new chic edge. The menu upstairs expertly fuses Slovenian and French cuisine with treats like steak laced with a truffle and cream sauce, and sea bass infused with celery and caviar. Downstairs is a much cosier space called Moro that serves a rich Moroccan menu in suitably Arabic surrounds with a shisha pipe also on hand for that touch of Arab authenticity. The 1,890SIT lunch and 2,700SIT menus are a complete steal.

**Pri Vitezu** Breg 20; tel: 01 426 6058. This fashionable and classy riverside brasserie and wine bar fuses Italian and Slovenian cuisine, and is a great place to try more adventurous fish dishes and Slovenian roast meats. The Old-World décor with oil paintings and vaulted wooden ceilings conjures up the traditional cosiness of the Karst region in the south of the country, making it a great favourite for locals looking to take someone out for a traditional treat.

**Smrekarjev Hram** Nazorjeva 2; tel: 01 251 6810. The signature restaurant at the Grand Union Hotel has been at the top of the tree for years, but these days it has a decent set of rivals. With an ambience and appearance more reminiscent of a grand 1920s ocean liner than a Ljubljana hotel, Smrekarjev Hram still delivers on the plate, with the likes of pasta with truffles or *pršut* ham to start and grilled sole or venison with maraschino cherries amongst the mains.

**Špajza** Gornji trg 28; tel: 01 425 3094. Špajza reopened following a change of management and refurbishment in summer 2004, but already it is back to its best. This is the archetypal Slovenian upmarket restaurant, managing to conjure up first-class cooking, fresh ingredients and a cosy, informal ambience where jeans are perfectly acceptable.

## Mid-range

**Figovec** Gosposvetska 1; tel: 01 446 4210. One of the oldest coaching inns in the city serves up a menu that will have vegetarians diving for cover. Horsemeat comes in various permutations and there are the likes of pigs' trotters for the adventurous. More mainstream Slovenian dishes include grilled Adriatic squid and Prekmurje-style goulash.

**Gostilna Sokol** Ciril Metodov trg 18; tel: 01 439 6855. A bustlingly popular *gostilna* close to the central market serving lashings of hearty traditional food including goulash, wild boar, Slovenian blood sausage and chunky vegetable broth, all washed down with generous carafes of wine.

**Operna Klet** Župančičeva 2; tel: 01 252 7003. Hiding away in a small cellar by the Opera House is one of Ljubljana's best seafood restaurants, with the likes of crab croquettes and tartar sauce and grilled squid with garlic to start. Grilled fresh fish is the highlight of the main menu. In summer there is also an outdoor terrace upstairs.

**Pen Club** Tomsičeva 12; tel: 01 251 4160. Traditionally the meeting place for the Slovene literati, this intimate venue has a menu that changes daily. With décor that has a discernible 1970s edge the Pen Club manages to be pleasingly kitsch without even trying. There are no English menus, but the staff is more than happy to explain a menu that includes starters such as pasta laced with white truffles and homemade ravioli stuffed with spinach. The fish dishes are the standouts amongst the mains.

**Rusalka** Vosnjakova 1; tel: 01 433 2155. The Lev Hotel's ground-floor restaurant styles itself as 'international', but the highlights are often the excellent Slovenian dishes. The venison with cracked pepper and cranberries is melt-in-the-mouth sublime, though the dandelion (yes, really) salad takes a bit of getting used to, as well as a lot of chewing.

**Zlata Ribica** Cankarjevo nabrežje 5; tel: 01 241 0690. This refurbished riverside restaurant in the heart of the Old Town serves a mix of hearty Slovenian meat dishes, Italian-influenced cuisine and vegetarian meals. Its waterside terrace has good views and makes a pleasant dining space on warmer days. Not as cheap as it was before its revamp, but still reasonable value, with the likes of baked sea bass laced with shrimps coming in at around 4,000SIT.

## Budget

**Luka Gourmet Lunch Café** Stari trg 9. Run by the people behind Pri Vitezu you can sample the same quality ingredients here that make the restaurant such a success. On sunny days the tables outside are the perfect place to enjoy the ridiculously good-value 1,200SIT set menus, which include soup to start followed by a green salad and a main course which could be prawn and dill pasta, or grilled beef with hand-cut chips and tomato.

**Pri Škofu** Rečna 8; tel: 01 426 4508. There is no menu as such with bright, young waitresses gaily recanting the day's offerings, usually a choice of soup to start, including a heart-pumping ginger concoction, before a main course of seafood risotto, roasted turkey or the house speciality, plump beefsteak cooked with a peppercorn crust.

**Ribca** Tržnica Jožeta Plečnika. For budget seafood Ribca is hard to beat. Located beneath Plečnik's colonnades just by the fish market, the fish could not be much fresher or better value. The terrace is pretty no-frills with plastic chairs, but there are views out over the river and back towards Prešernov trg. Take the steps that descend from the shops beneath the colonnades.

**Šestica** Slovenska 40; tel: 01 242 0850. Huge portions and cheap prices have punters still piling into one of the city's oldest *gostilnas* after all these years. The building dates to 1670, with the first inn opened on the site in 1776. Back then it was at No 6 (hence the name) and these days it is on the map thanks to its hearty soups, spicy goulash and chunky risotto.

**Tomato** Šubičeva 1; tel: 01 252 7555. Fresh and healthy food is on offer at this massively popular take-away restaurant. They make sandwiches for many of the city's cafés and it is easy to see why, with fresh, inventive toppings and generous portions. There are over 30 sandwich permutations and also plenty of scope for choosing your own.

**Vegedrom** Vodnikova 35; tel: 01 519 3901. A real gem, this homely oasis serves tempting soups, sandwiches, vegetarian plates for two, tofu, gnocchi and risotto. Equally tempting are deserts like *gibanica* – the traditional Prekmurje pastry cake. If you have been struggling to eat your five daily portions of fruit and vegetables, there is also a self-service salad bar.

## Other national cuisines (all mid-range)

**Cantina Restaurantes Mexicana** Knaflev prehod; tel: 01 426 9325. Ousting a busy bar from this central location may not have been a popular move, but the Cantina is trying to make amends by offering passable *fajitas* and *burritos* in pleasant surrounds. The candlelit terrace is the place to be in summer, while the well-thought-out interior also looks the part.

**Okrepčevapnica** Vrtna 8; tel: 041 843106. 'Welcome to Sarajevo' reads the sign as you enter and this new grill restaurant really does offer a slice of Bosnia in a thoughtfully refurbished house in Krakovo. The simple menu offers *čevapčiči* (meat balls), *pleskavica* (meat pattie) and *sudukice* (thin sausages), served with fluffy Balkan bread, crispy onions and creamy *kajmak* cheese. Gloriously politically incorrect Turkish coffees come served with a cigarette.

**Sushimama** Wolfova 12; tel: 01 426 9125. Styling itself as 'modern Japanese cooking', this funky central restaurant is the first in the city to serve up fresh sushi and it does not disappoint. The menu also features cooked dishes such as beef teriyaki and Japanese beer too, though steer clear of the saki if you want to emerge walking in a straight line.

## Pizza

**Čerin** Trubarjeva 52; tel: 01 232 0990. Dependable and centrally located pizzeria serving thin-crust pizzas. Flexible staff allow you to design your own topping and free internet access keeps you busy while you wait.

**Foculus** Gregorčičeva 3; tel: 01 421 9295. 'Probably the most popular pizzeria in Slovenia' scream the flyers and its large and bustling interior, with big tables and ceiling paintings, is certainly a bit of a surprise on this sleepy street. The pizza list is extensive with over 50 choices that include all the usual suspects, while at weekends families rule as kids are brought along for a treat.

**Ljubljanski Dvor** Dvorni trg 1; tel: 01 251 6555. A spacious outdoor terrace, with unrivalled views back across the river to Ljubljana's Old Town, make this restaurant and pizzeria an enduring favourite with visitors and locals alike. The toppings are seemingly endless, though pepperoni with added jalapeno peppers seems to be the local favourite. The pizzas are enormous – do not even contemplate ordering anything bigger than the gigantic *classico*. The back of the restaurant on Kongresni trg serves up take-away pizza and ice-cream, while upstairs is a 'proper' restaurant serving an extensive menu of international dishes where the good-value set lunch menu costs around 3,500SIT.

## Fast food (all budgets)

**Tržnica Central Market** The sprawling market offers a range of affordable culinary goodies every day bar Sunday. There are vans dispensing fresh Adriatic seafood as well as a network of stalls offering fresh fruit and vegetables. Amidst the colonnades is a sprinkling of more permanent shops that sell excellent bread, meats, pastries and *burek*.

**Hot Horse** Just as it sounds, this particular local 'treat' consists of a huge burger bun stuffed with horsemeat, various relishes and vegetables. Ljubljana's late-night drinking set insist you have not been on a real night out until you have topped it off with a horseburger from the stand at the northern side of Tivoli Park across from the Lev Hotel. The Hot Horse take-away at Trubarjeva 31 is more central, but for the real authentic experience Tivoli is the place to go.

**Burek** This southern Balkan staple is an instantly filling and very popular snack. It basically consists of a wrap of moist pastry that is stuffed with either meat or soft cheese, with a worryingly high fat and calorie content. Arguably the best place to try *burek* is at the central Nobel take-away at Miklošičeva 30, but as long as it is piping hot and has not been sitting around *burek* is the sort of comfort food that you cannot go too wrong with anywhere.

## ENTERTAINMENT AND NIGHTLIFE

For a small city, Ljubljana has a decent supply of theatre venues – with high-quality acting and vivid productions often transcending the language barrier. Throughout the year it bustles with the arts, ranging from small-scale street theatre and outdoor concerts, right through to grand opera performances, classical music recitals and the granddaddy of them all, the Ljubljana Summer Festival. Then there are the cafés, bars and nightclubs.

Ljubljana's café and bar scene is becoming increasingly sophisticated. Alongside the Old-World cafés and grungy bars are an array of bright new drinking venues, complete with guest DJs, funky décor and waiting staff who would not look out of place in a glossy fashion magazine. Closing times are often the only thing that really differentiates cafés from bars. The majority of the cafés wind down before midnight during the week, while bars generally stay open until 01.00, some as late as 03.00. New places arise and shut down with alarming regularity and the best advice is to tap a local to find out where the newest hip venue is. At weekends the key is to start late and build up gradually with the action not really getting going until after 21.00.

Whatever your taste there is something to suit everyone. All of Ljubljana's tourist offices hand out the free monthly *Where To* leaflet, with a good listings rundown, as well as a free sheet detailing events on a weekly basis. For more alternative and small-scale events and happenings ask in trendy bars like Café Maček or Fraga. *Major Events in Ljubljana* is an annual publication that allows for a bit of advance planning if you can get hold of it.

## Theatre

**Slovensko Narodno Gledališče Drama (SNG Drama)** Erjačeva 1; tel: 01 252 1511; www.sngdrama-lj.si. Slovenia's national theatre company is enviably housed in this lavish art nouveau building.

**Café Teater** Miklošičeva 2; tel: 01 252 7108; www.café-teater.si. Staging musicals and comedy productions, with some performances in the Križanke theatre.

**Cankarjev Dom** Prešernova 10; tel: 01 241 7299; www.cd-cc.si. One of Slovenia's largest venues, covering everything from theatre to classical music, dance and opera. Booking office is open Mon–Sat 11.00–13.00, Mon–Fri 15.00–20.00 and for one hour before performances start.

**Gledališče Glej (Glej Theatre)** Gregorčičeva 3l; tel: 01 421 9240. This is renowned as an avant-garde venue with a daring programme geared towards more experimental material. Closed July and August.

**Križanke** Trg Francoske Revolucije 1; tel: 01 252 6544. This wonderful outdoor arena in a sculpture-laden old monastery is at the crux of the Ljubljana Summer Festival. The Križanke complex dates back to the 13th century, with church and monastery buildings from that era still standing today. Outside of the festival, performances continue to take place in the outdoor arena, the Knights Hall and the anteroom.

**Lutkovno Gledališče Ljubljana (Ljubljana Puppet Theatre)** Krekov trg 2; tel: 01 300 0970 or 01 080 2004 (ticket office); www.lgl.si. Not just for children, the theatre's ambitious programmes range from *Winnie the Pooh* to Shakespeare. Also hosts Ljubljana's biennial International Puppet Theatre Festival.

**Mini Teater Ljubljana** Ljubljanski Grad; tel: 01 434 3620; www.mini-teater.si. Ljubljana Castle provides an unusual and romantic setting for theatrical performances. The Mini Theatre also organises the city's Medieval Day with Renaissance music, puppet shows, battle re-enactments and plays.

**Mestno Gledališče (Municipal Theatre)** Čopova 14; tel: 01 251 0852; www.mgl.si. The spectrum of performances on offer at the city's theatre includes satirical plays, comedies and modern theatre productions.

**Šentjakobsko Gledališče (St Jacob Theatre)** Krekov trg 2; tel: 01 231 2860; www.sentjakobsko-gledalisce.si. The performance list of this alternative theatre group includes Monty Python's *Life of Brian*, Jules Verne's *20,000 Leagues Under the Sea* as well as the work of Ivan Cankar.

**Slovensko Mladinsko Gledališče (Slovenian Youth Theatre)** Vilharjeva 11; tel: 01 231 0610; www.mladinsko-gl.si. The Slovenian Youth Theatre prides itself on its eclectic range of mainstream and experimental productions. Past performances include works by Chekhov, Dostoyevsky, Lewis Carroll and T S Eliot.

**KUD Teater 55** Dunajska 113; tel: 041 555 555; www.teater55.com. Small comic theatre group performing at the Festivalna Dvorana Ljubljana and the Kulturni Dom Mengeš.

**Teater Komedija (Comedy Theatre)** Šmartinska 152; tel: 01 585 1432; www.btc.si. By night the BTC City Convention Hall takes on a new ambience as it plays host to comic productions.

## Cinema

Ljubljana's cinemas generally screen films in their original language with Slovene subtitles, and mainstream cinemas show the predictable range of Hollywood films, though the local appetite for all things alternative spills over at the Slovenska Kinoteka and the Kinodvor. In November each year the city plays host to the Ljubljana International Film Festival (LIFFE; http://www.liffe.spletnastran.com) and the Ljubljana Gay and Lesbian Film Festival.

**Kolosej** Šmartinska 152; tel: 01 520 5500; www.btc.si. Part of the suburban BTC City complex, Slovenia's first multiplex cinema has 12 screens, a bar, restaurant and confectioner.
**Slovenska Kinoteka** Miklošičeva 38; tel: 01 434 2500; www.kinoteka.si. This cinema specialising in art-house productions closed towards the end of 2004, but the tourist board assured us that it would reopen after a refurbishment in time to celebrate 100 years of Slovenian film later in 2005.
**Kinodvor** Kolodvorska 13; tel: 01 434 2544; www.kinodvor.si. Shows contemporary art-house films that have received wide critical acclaim such as Sue Brooks's *Japanese Story*. During the summer the cinema also screens Slovene-language films with English subtitles.

## Music

Ljubljana's music venues are as diverse as the concerts held in them and include the Centralni Stadion (Central Stadium), Križanke, the Slovenian National Opera and Ballet Theatre and the Slovenian Philharmonic Hall, as well as a range of nightclubs. Big one-off events include the Ljubljana Summer Festival, Ljubljana Jazz Festival and the Druga Godba festival (see *Public Holidays and Festivals* in *Chapter 2*). Tickets can be purchased from venue box offices and, increasingly, over the internet. The ŠKUC Information Centre (Stari trg 21; tel: 01 121 3142) also sells tickets for pop and rock concerts.

### Classical and opera venues

**Slovensko Narodno Gledališče Opera in Balet (SNG Opera and Ballet Theatre)** Cankarjeva 11; tel: 01 241 1740; www.operainbalet-lj.si. Traditional and contemporary opera and ballet productions grace the stage of this Old-World theatre.
**Slovenska Filharmonija (Slovenian Philharmonic Hall)** Kongresni trg 10; tel: 01 241 0800; www.filharmonija.si. One of the most atmospheric venues in the country is home to the Slovenian Philharmonic Orchestra and the Slovenian Philharmonic Choir.

### Rock, pop and jazz venues

**Sax Pub** Eipprova 7; tel: 01 283 9009. This Trnovo mainstay serves up a solid menu of live jazz every Thursday evening. The cosy interior feels more like a music lover's bedroom than a pub. Arrive early if you want a seat when there is music. At other times this is a relaxed place for a drink among a slightly older crowd.
**Centralni Stadion** (Central Stadium) Dunajska. This tatty suburban football stadium is a decent venue for larger concerts – Lenny Kravitz played here in 2004.
**Jazz Club Gajo** Beethovnova 8; tel: 01 425 3206; www.jazzclubgajo.com. This centrally located jazz club has regular live performances and weekly informal jam sessions, with the latter generally held on Monday evenings. Check the monthly schedule online.

## LJUBLJANA SUMMER FESTIVAL

The Ljubljana Summer Festival has been going strong since 1952 and now embraces most of the city's performance spaces in a cultural extravaganza that rumbles through July and August. The key venue is the Križanke, but Ljubljana Castle, Cankarjev Dom and the Slovene Philharmonic Hall all come into play with myriad events. In 2004 guests included the London Symphony Orchestra, the NHK Tokyo Symphony Orchestra and the Moscow Soloists Chamber Orchestra. Neighbouring countries are also embraced with 2004 bringing in the Croatian National Theatre as well as the National Theatre of Belgrade. The latter's choice of *Dr Jekyll and Mr Hyde* seemed strangely apposite to many locals who have lived through the Yugoslav wars of the 1990s and Serbia's recent struggle to change from a hardline Slobodan-Miloševic-run state to a modern democracy.

**KUD France Prešeren** Karunova 14; tel: 01 283 2288; www.kud-fp.si. This popular youth venue prides itself on promoting alternative culture, with the calendar dominated by music performances, theatre and art that veer away from the mainstream.

**Metelkova Mesto** (see *Clubs* later in this chapter). Everything from banghra and African tribal groups, through to nu-metal and rap. Multiple venues in the squat itself, combined with the concerts at the Gala Hala in Tivoli Park, means that there is always something happening.

**Orto Bar** Grabloviceva 1; tel: 01 232 1674; www.orto-bar.com. Hosting everything from blues and jazz to punk and trash. The bar's signature red velvet lounge may be characterful, but it can also get very smoky.

## Cafés and bars

**Abecedarium Café** Ribji trg; tel: 01 426 9514. This café lays dual claims to being located in the oldest house in the city and the former home of Primož Trubar. Just a stone's throw from the river it has a good choice of coffees and beers and some decent snacks and light meals too.

**Kavarna Planet Pločnik** Prešernov trg. When the sun shines this is the place to be, in the shadow of the statue of France Prešeren right at the heart of the city by the river. A sprinkling of tables and chairs wrap around a brightly lit bar and black-clad staff keep the coffee and stronger drinks flowing. Powerful heat lamps ensure that the people-watching stretches on late into the night with sandwiches, ice-cream and *kremna rezina*, a deliciously tempting cream cake, on hand to ensure you don't have to surrender your prized ringside seat. In summer there is regular live music right in front of the café.

**AS Lounge** Knaflev prehod 5a. On busy nights this subterranean retreat buzzes with energy as students and the pre-club set work themselves up for a big night. The restaurant above is one of the city's most expensive and formal, but there are no airs and graces about this party venue. When there are live DJs the bar area can become a throbbing mass of dancing bodies.

**Café Galerija** Mestni trg 5. One of the city's most chic drinking dens would not look out of place in a spread for a fashion magazine. Delve through the modest foyer, itself

## BEER BATTLES

The main brewers in Slovenia are Union in Ljubljana and Laško from the eponymous town in the east of the country. Traditionally *Ljubljančani* have stayed loyal to Union (www.pivo-union.si), whose gigantic brewery is unmissable on the edge of the city centre by Tivoli Park, while Laško (www.pivo-lasko.si) has increasingly come to dominate outside of the capital and expanded into other countries in the region, including Croatia and Montenegro. The picture has been muddied recently with a tussle over ownership of Union, which has seen Laško locking horns with international brewery giant Interbrew. After an interminable struggle Laško has taken a 54% stake with Interbrew ending up with 41.3%. This situation is not ideal as it still leaves many questions hanging over the future of Union. Worries amongst loyal Union drinkers that the flavour and even the brand may disappear have so far proved unfounded.

Both Union and Laško have a variety of different tipples to suit all tastes. The main Union product is simply called Union and comes in a trademark red can or bottle. It is backed up by Union 1964 lager, a dark beer (Črni Baron) and a Pilsner. A newer product is Smile, a beer with lemon that is very popular with the younger inhabitants of the city and is sold in many clubs and bars. There are tours of the brewery (see the later *What to see* section).

Lasko's most famous product is Zlatorog, a refreshing beer, usually in 50cl bottles. They also do a dark beer (Temno), a low-alcohol beer (Gren) and an ever-increasing range of other brews. In parallel with Union, the newest product is Roler, a beer with a twist of lemon.

used for various happenings, art exhibitions and catwalk-style shows, and you enter a world of candlelit glamour, awash with mirrors, bountiful sofas and Ottoman décor.

**Café Maček** Krojaška 5. For years this has been *the* place to be down on the riverside. 'Meet me at Maček' is still an often-heard refrain as everyone seems to end up here at some point over a weekend. When the weather allows the main action is outside where rampant people-watching and river breezes are perfect company for a cold glass of Union or Laško or a heart-starting *macchiato*. When Maček is too busy in summer just pop next door to **Boheme**, which has a similar terrace set-up.

**Cutty Sark** Knaflev prehod; tel: 01 425 8822. Within easy staggering distance of Prešernov trg, Cutty Sark seems to have a magnetic hold for Ljubljana's expat community. All the home comforts are here in a decent stab at a British pub with a big bar area, bar service and a range of beers and ales including Guinness and Kilkenny.

**Kratochwill** Kolodvorska 14; tel: 01 433 3114. Now that Katacombe on Stari trg has become the Konoba and no longer produces its own beer, Kratochwill is the city's only micro-brewery pub. The *svetlo* and *temno* (light and dark beers), available in 20cl, 30cl, 50cl and huge one-litre glasses, may not suit all tastes as they are both decidedly sour.

**Fraga** Mestni trg 15. This new minimalist bar in the Old Town is bedecked with intriguing modern art and attracts a suitably pretentious but still friendly crowd. Sit on a sofa or cram into a funky plastic chair, admire the artwork and enjoy the literary nights and various events.

**Makalonca** Hribarjevo nabrežje. In summer this is the place amongst the colonnades on the right bank of the river. Follow the candles down the stairs by the wooden footbridge from where Ljubljana's only tour boat is berthed and you will enter a busy bar space. There are two main seating areas, with candlelit outdoor tables the perfect setting for relaxing and congratulating yourself on finding this great spot. Inside, the small bar area is perfect for those not enjoying the river breezes.

**Minimal** Mestni trg 4. As minimal as the name suggests the interior is practically polar with white, white and more white. Do not let the beautiful staff and artsy ambience put you off, though, as this is a relaxed venue for a coffee in the afternoon or something stronger at night when the posing brigade ships in en masse.

**Pr Skelet** Ključavničarska 5; tel: 01 252 7799. Delve below street level in the Old Town and you will soon be surrounded by an army of skulls and skeletons in this cellar bar. Once you get over the novelty of the horror theme it is not too disturbing and during the colder months this is a cosy retreat for a glass of mulled wine.

**Salon** Trubarjeva 23; tel: 01 433 2006. One of the trendiest venues in the city underwent a touch-up recently and it is now looking great. One expat that we spoke to described it as 'lounge bar meets camp hairdressing salon', a remarkably apt summation.

**Zlata Ladjica** Jurčičev trg 1; tel: 01 241 0695. This popular bar by the Cobbler's Bridge suffers from schizophrenia – by day it is a mellow outdoor café, but at night the action moves inside to a maritime-themed bar that is often one of the most raucous in the city – no wonder with Tennents Super, the lethal-strength Scottish beer, on draught.

## Clubs

**Bachus Centre** Kongresni trg 3; tel: 01 241 8244; www.Bachus-center.com. Central and well-designed complex with a café, bars, restaurant and even a pool hall, as well as a basement dance floor. On a good night Bachus buzzes, but on busy weekends it can seem to be full of underage drinkers and big egos clad in ill-fitting R'n'B clobber.

**Discoteka Fun Factory** Industrijska zona Rudnik, Jurčkova 224; tel: 01 428 9690; www.discoteka-funfactory.com. Bus 19 direction Livada. Ljubljana's biggest club is located south of the city centre in Rudnik. Here you will find all the things you expect in a large venue, such as chill-out rooms, multiple bars and separate dance floors.

**Global** Tomšičeva 1; tel: 01 426 9017; www.global.si. Take the elevator from street level at the Nama department store and less than a minute later you will be in this modern nightlife oasis with sweeping views of the city centre and the castle. The terrace is open during the day as a café/restaurant, but the real action is inside at night on the single dance floor. The music policy is a bit hit-and-miss, so check ahead if you don't want to find yourself at a weird and wacky theme night.

**Klub K4** Kersnikova 4; tel: 01 431 7010; www.klubk4.org. K4 was pumping out cutting-edge sounds when Global and Bachus were only pipe dreams and it is still going strong well over a decade since it first opened its doors. The dingy and grungy rooms echo the nefarious hideouts of East Berlin and the music is similarly alternative with indie rock and metal ruling. Sunday is K4's gay night, transforming the grungy student venue into the 'Roza Klub'.

**Papillon** Nazorjeva 6; tel: 01 426 2126. Techno dominates Papillon's music scene at the weekend, while retro nights are in order during the week. This idiosyncratic venue is styled like a French colonial prison and its namesake film is played on a continuous loop. **Metelkova Mesto** Metelkova cesta; tel: 01 432 3378; www.metelkova.org. This independent and unique cultural centre can easily keep visitors occupied on a night out. A predominantly young and alternative Slovene crowd is drawn to the clubs and bars that inject life into this former military barracks and squat. Venues include Klub Gromka with live music and international DJs, and Klub Channel Zero where heavy metal, punk, hardcore and trance reign supreme. The squat also has a gay nightlife scene – Klub Tiffany is a gay café-bar cum club and Klub Monkel is a lesbian nightclub that shares its premises with Tiffany's.

**Latino Klub Cuba** Celovška 54; tel: 01 434 3158. Bus 1 direction Vižmarje, bus 5 direction Podutik, bus 8 direction Brod, bus 15 direction Medvode or bus 16 direction Gameljne. This multi-level venue has been paying homage to Hemingway for years, but still it has a sparkle. Choose from the à la carte restaurant, Key West pub or Latino Klub Cuba. Latino beats, salsa music and free-flowing cocktails are all winning ingredients in the last.

**Sub Sub Club** Celovška 25; tel: 01 515 3575. Part of the Hala Tivoli, this centrally located club is popular with the dance music crowd. Opening times vary so it is wise to look out for flyers and posters advertising upcoming events.

**Klub Central** Dalmatinova 15; tel: 01 200 8740. This once-popular club that pumped out cheesy disco to a youthful crowd of locals and tourists has re-emerged after a refit as a fairly pricey gentleman's club.

## SHOPPING

Ljubljana's compact size means that dedicated shoppers can cover the entire city centre on foot. Slovenska, which bisects the city centre, is one popular shopping boulevard with its big-name shops and the Nama department store. However, a far more pleasant experience is on offer in the Old Town squares of Stari trg, Mestni trg and Gornji trg, where medieval and baroque buildings house eclectic boutiques selling everything from jewellery, perfume, shoes and clothes to traditional crafts and designer gear made in studios behind the stores. The right and left banks of the Ljubljanica River are also increasingly brimming with boutique stores and small art galleries. Gosposvetska cesta, near the Lev Hotel, also has some boutiques.

### Arts and crafts

**Ruby and Sapphire Lanka** Gornji trg 10; tel: 01 425 1462. Elegant boutique selling traditional and contemporary jewellery from Sri Lanka.

**Kodre Zlatarstvo** Cankarjevo nabrežje 27; tel: 01 422 5110. Chunky rings and bracelets, dangling pendants and oversized looped earrings are just some of the individual pieces by Slovene designers guaranteed to get you noticed.

**Kamen** Stari trg 32; tel: 01 426 9975. Modern chunky pieces made with stones, beads, metal and silver. Kamen also has a small selection of unusual gifts including clocks.

**Pletilni Studio Draž** Gornji trg 9; tel: 01 426 6041. Stunning viscose and cotton dresses are made in the studio behind the shop.

**Katarina Silk** Gornji trg 5; tel: 01 425 0010. Stylish silk scarves and other items are handcrafted on the premises.

**Artglass Atelje** Dvorni trg 2; tel: 01 426 3104. Stylish studio selling beautiful glassware products made by Slovene designer Tomaž Miletič.

**Ažbe Galerija** Mestni trg 18/II; tel: 01 425 1337; www.galerija-azbe.si. A wonderful collection of paintings, antiques, glass, silverware and bric-a-brac, displayed in traditional glass-fronted cabinets.

**Skrina Galerija** Breg 8; tel: 01 425 5161; www.skrina.si. Charming riverside gallery selling crafts from all over Slovenia including Idrija lace, Prekmurje pottery, Rogaška glass and beehive panels. It is cheaper to pay by cash than by credit card.

**Galerija Idrijske Čipke** Gornji trg; tel: 01 425 0051. Small gallery selling a wide selection of handmade lace from Idrija.

**Rustika Gallery** Ljubljanska Grad. Ljubljana Castle's gallery has high-quality souvenirs with prices to match. Highlights include Idrija lace, ceramics, glassware and woodwork.

**Dom** Mestni trg 24; tel: 01 241 8300. Large souvenir shop housed in a municipal building with wicker, wood, pottery and woollen crafts on sale, alongside alcohol and a wide range of Ljubljana-labelled souvenirs.

## Food and drink

**Vinoteka Bradeško** Fairgrounds/Gospodarsko razstavišče-Paviljon Jurček, Dunajska 18; tel: 01 431 5015. Under the expert guidance of owner Simon Bradeško staff here really know their wine. The huge variety of Slovenian wines on sale and the opportunity to dine in the fantastic cellar restaurant make the short journey to this Ljubljana institution well worthwhile.

**Vinoteka Movia** Mestni trg 2; tel: 01 425 5448; www.movia.si. Trendy wine bar and shop owned by the well-known Movia wine producer. The wines are stacked high up the wall behind the bar and many of them are available to taste before you buy including the excellent 1997 Cabernet Sauvignon at 6,000SIT a bottle.

**Čajna Hiša** Stari trg 3. Ljubljana's only dedicated teahouse also has a great shop selling speciality teas, mugs and tea paraphernalia. The city's supermarkets cannot even begin to match the myriad teas on sale in this charming oasis.

**Plečnik colonnades** Adamič–Lundrovo nabrežje. The small shops selling bread, cheese, wine, ham and fish are a great place to stock up on fresh Slovenian produce. This is also a good place to buy honey as a gift to take home.

**Mercator** has centrally located branches at Kongresni trg 9 and Stritarjeva 9. The former is open on Sundays.

## Department stores and shopping centres

**Nama** Tomišičeva 1; tel: 01 425 8300. The large United Colours of Benetton outlet on the ground floor is one of the department store's biggest attractions.

**BTC City** Šmartinska 152; tel: 01 585 1100; www.btc-city.com. Open: Mon–Sat 09.00–20.00, Sun 09.00–13.00. Bus 17 direction Letališka to BTC Uprava stop. This enormous shopping mall boasts over 400 shops including Top Shop, Top Man, Miss Selfridge, Levis, Marks & Spencer, H&M and Benetton. It also has myriad sports facilities including tennis, badminton, go-karting and a swimming pool, plus restaurants, multiplex cinema and a comedy theatre.

**BTC Emporium** Letališka 3; tel: 01 585 4800; www.emporium.si. Bus 17 direction Letališka to BTC Emporium stop. This shopping centre is a haven for those who love buying clothes. High-street shops like Dorothy Perkins and Levis sell their wares alongside Hugo Boss, Lacoste and Fred Perry.

**Maximarket** Trg Republike 1; web: www.maxi.si. Don't be put off by its grungy appearance, this city centre department store is regarded by most of the Ljubljančani to be the most prestigious department store in town. In addition to your usual department store fare it also has a decent deli and a health store.

## Markets

**Tržnica (Central Market)** Vodnikov trg and Pogačarjev trg. Open daily except Sunday this is a great place to pick up cheap produce, flowers, clothes and even a small selection of souvenirs including wooden crafts and honey.

**Flea Market** Cankarjevo nabrežje. This Sunday morning market lines the Ljubljanica between the Triple Bridge and the Cobbler's Bridge.

**Ljubljana Monmarte** Cankarjevo nabrežje. On Saturdays from June to September the banks of the Ljubljanica are once again transformed into a market. This time arts and crafts are on sale between 10.00 and 15.00. A highlight for younger visitors are the many creative workshops that are held as part of the market.

## Outdoor and sports

**ProMontana** Poljanski nasip; tel: 280 0590; www.promontana.si. This travel agency specialising in outdoor activities has a retail outlet that sells and rents equipment and clothing for various outdoor pursuits.

## Books

**Mladinska Knjiga** Slovenska 29; tel: 01 241 0651. Often referred to as 'Knjigarna Konzorcij'.

**Mladinska Knjiga** Nazorjeva 1; tel: 01 241 4700

**Knjigarna Novak** Wolfova 8; tel: 01 422 3410

**Geonavtik** Kongresni trg; tel: 01 252 7027

## PRACTICALITIES
## Tourist information

**Ljubljana Tourist Information Centre** Stritarjeva; tel: 01 306 1215; email: info@ljubljana-tourism.si; www.ljubljana-tourism.si. Open: daily 08.00–21.00 Jun–Sep and 08.00–19.00 Oct–May.

### TOURIST DISCOUNTS
The **Ljubljana Tourist Card** gives free or reduced entrance to the city's museums, galleries and some special events. It also gives the holder free city-bus travel and discounts on guided tours and some souvenirs. Some of Ljubljana's hotels, restaurants, bars and clubs also give Tourist Card holders a discount, as do some taxi companies, car rental firms and shops. Valid for 72 hours from the time of purchase, the Ljubljana Tourist Card is available for 3,000SIT at TICs and some hotels.

WHAT TO SEE AND DO

**Tourist Information Centre at the railway station** Trg Osvobodilne fronte 6, železniška postaja; tel: 01 433 9475; email: ticzp@ljubljana-tourism.si; www.ljubljana-tourism.si. Open: daily 08.00–22.00 Jun–Sep and 08.00–19.00 Oct–May.
**Slovenian Tourist Information Centre** Krekov trg 10; tel: 01 306 4575/76; fax: 01 306 4580; email: stic@ljubljana-tourism.si; www.slovenia-tourism.si. Open: daily 08.00–09.00 Jun–Sep, 08.00–19.00 Oct–May.

## Communications
### Post offices
Slovenska 32. Open: Mon–Fri 07.00–20.00, Sat 08.00–13.00.
Trg Osvobodilne fronte 5. Open: Mon–Fri 07.00–midnight, Sat 07.00–18.00, Sun 09.00–12.00.
Cigaletova 5. Open 24 hours.

### Internet cafés
**Napotnic.com** Trg Ajdoušcina 1; tel: 01 431 1016; www.napotnica.com. Access 500SIT per hour.
**Cyber Café Xplorer** Petkovškovo nabrežje 23; tel: 01 430 1991; www.sisky.com. Five minutes 110SIT, 1 hour 860SIT.
**Čerin** Trubarjeva 52; tel: 01 232 0990. Pizzeria (see *Where to eat*) with free internet.
**DrogArt** Kolodvorska 20; tel: 01 439 7270. Log on for 15 minutes free, 1 hour 400SIT.
**Gostilna Nobile** Zarnikova 3; tel: 01 439 7040. Suburban eatery with two terminals.

## Banks
You won't have to walk far to find a bank or ATM in the centre of Ljubljana.

**Banka Koper** Nazorjeva 6
**Nova Ljubljanska Banka** Branches include Trg Republike 2, Beethovnova 7, Dalmatinova 4, Čopova 3 and Mestni trg 16.

## Medical facilities
**Klinični Centre Ljubljana (Hospital)** Zaloška 2; tel: 01 552 5050
**Urgenca Klinični Centre (Emergency Medical Centre)** Bohoričcva 4, tel: 01 552 8408
**Dentist** Kotnikova 36; tel: 01 425 4061
**Central pharmacies** Lekarna Miklošič, Miklošičeva 24; tel: 01 231 4558 and Prešernov Trg.

## WHAT TO SEE AND DO
### The unmissables
#### Prešernov trg (Prešeren Square)
Prešernov trg is at the physical, historical and spiritual heart of the city. This is where *Ljubljančani* come to meet their friends, watch the world go by from pavement cafés and stroll by the river. The square boasts three river crossings, plus the landmark **Frančiškanska Cerkev Marijinega Oznanjenja** (Franciscan Church of the Annunciation – see *Churches and cathedrals*) and a **statue** of **France Prešeren**. Ivan Zajec's and Maks Fabiani's dramatic monument to the man

trumpeted as Slovenia's greatest bard dates from 1905. Despite his bravado and his swirling muse the tortured writer is forced to gaze across his namesake square at a bust of Julija Primic, the love of his life. Julija may be peering back at Prešeren, but in real life she never returned his love, and many see her presence as a cruel and constant reminder of this most tragic of tragic Romantic poets and his unrequited love. Julija aside, the steps of this giant statue make a great place to relax with an ice-cream or to meet some new friends.

As well as being the most popular meeting spot in the city, Prešernov trg boasts some of Ljubljana's finest examples of art nouveau architecture. The large white building standing proudly behind Prešeren is the **oldest pharmacy in Ljubljana** (refurbished in 2004), while the city's first department store – the Centromerkur – sits to its left. On the opposite side of the square is the Hauptman House, now also owned by Centromerkur. Look out for the bronze model of the city, which has been at the bottom of Čopova since June 1991 when Slovenian independence was declared.

Ljubljana's most vibrant square also sees the coming together of France Prešeren and another of Slovenia's most famous sons, Jože Plečnik, with the designs of the latter giving the square its modern-day appearance. One of Plečnik's most famous works, the **Tromostovje** (Triple Bridge), was completed in 1931 with the addition of two straddling walkways to the main 19th-century span. Plečnik wanted to mimic the bridges that traverse Venice's canals, incorporating ornate Renaissance balustrades and a string of street lamps into his flamboyant design.

## Ljubljanski Grad (Ljubljana Castle)

Ljubljana Castle (tel: 01 232 9994; www.festival-lj.si/virtualnimuzej) hangs omnipresent above the city, vaulting into view when you turn many a street corner. If you are feeling lazy there is a tourist train up to here from Prešernov trg (see *Tour operators* earlier in this chapter), but a better option is to walk up the steep slopes and see the view start to unravel below. Recent excavations have shown signs of settlement as far back as the 12th century BC, but the castle was first fortified by the Celts and the Illyrians. Later the Romans also capitalised on the highly strategic location, with sweeping vistas right out over the whole city and up towards the Julian and Kamniške Savinje Alps.

In many ways the medieval fortress is most impressive from the outside, as once inside the central courtyard the shamble of buildings date from different periods, with a truly hideous 1960s functional section that has already aged badly. The 15th-century remnants are more appealing and there is a flurry of things to keep you occupied including a café, a well-stocked gift shop with souvenirs from all over the country, a tower with a great view and a multimedia exhibit. The last runs visitors through a 3D history of the city, tracing its development vividly from its Roman days as Emona, right through its grand baroque era to the 1980s. The 20-minute show is well timed to avoid boredom setting in. The castle is also home to a string of cultural and religious events, including Sunday masses in summer, Ljubljana Summer Festival events and New Year fireworks. From June to September the castle's history is brought to life by knowledgeable guides who lead visitors through various halls, the chapel and the dungeon.

*Open: daily 10.00–21.00 Oct–Apr, daily 09.00–22.00 May–Sep. Free. Tours: 10.00 and 16.00 Jun–mid-Sep or by arrangement. Virtual museum and viewing tower open daily 10.00–21.00 Oct–Apr, daily 09.00–21.00 May–Sep. 700SIT, concessions 400SIT, family ticket 900SIT.*

## Mestni trg, Stari trg and Gornji trg

These connecting squares, which hug the base of Castle Hill, ripple through the heart of the Old Town in a flurry of appealing baroque and medieval buildings. Many of the city's most popular cafés, bars and restaurants are located in or around these long squares, which buzz with life. Even the advent of supermarket chains and out-of-town malls has failed to kill off the impressive array of boutique shops and small businesses that help keep the area alive.

### Ljubljanica

The Ljubljanica may not be as impressive and grand as some of Europe's great rivers, but what is often little more than a sleepy stream can churn into quite a lively rush of water after heavy rain or snowmelt. Boat tours of the river with guided commentary leave just across from Prešernov trg on the Old Town side. Strolling along the riverbanks is equally rewarding with a constantly changing view of the city. If you follow the banks south from Prešernov trg you will reach the **Trnovo district** (see *Krakovo and Trnovo*). This is a great place to relax on a balmy summer's day or to work off the cobwebs on a crisp winter's afternoon. From here you can cross to the Prule district and meander back up the river to the Old Town on the tree-shrouded lanes.

As well as being central to the social lives of *Ljubljančani*, the attractive banks of the Ljubljanica also harbour some of the city's most impressive sights. The concrete riverbanks themselves are the work of Ljubljana's most influential architect, with Jože Plečnik having altered the river's course to prevent flooding. The steep concrete banks that predominate in the heart of the city are brightened up with trees, flowers, well-planned street lighting and even temporary art exhibitions. Plečnik also constructed the **Čevljarski Most** (Cobbler's Bridge) – so named because it was the location where cobblers once sold their wares – with its balustrades and tall lampposts. The medieval and baroque dwellings that line the river reveal ornate coving, wrought-iron balconies and arched doorways, as well as colourful though often faded façades. Heading east along the river beyond the market brings you to the **Zmajski Most** (Dragon Bridge; see *Other sites and monuments*).

## Museums/galleries
### Moderna Galerija (Museum of Modern Art)

The Museum of Modern Art (Tomšičeva 14; tel: 01 241 6800; fax: 01 251 4120; email: info@mg-lj.si; www.mg-lj.si) is one of Ljubljana's true joys, and lovers of avant-garde art should make a beeline for this gallery and allow plenty of time. Even if your tastes are more traditional it is well worth looking around for some interesting domestic artists and a variety of temporary exhibits and, as the Museum of Modern Art is only a stone's throw from the National Gallery, you can combine both in a contrasting visit.

Edvard Ravnikas's building, which was completed in 1939 as war erupted across Europe, looks quite foreboding from the outside, with definite Plečnik influences clearly discernible. Inside it is spacious and flexible with an exhibition space on the ground floor as well as additional galleries in the basement. The main focus of the permanent collection is on Slovenian art from the 20th century, but the temporary exhibits draw on both domestic and international talents. Other activities include art workshops, discussion groups and publications on Slovenian art. The gallery also owns the **Mala Galerija** (Small Gallery) and exhibition space at Metelkova 22.
*Open: Tue–Sun 12.00–20.00 Jul–Aug, Tue–Sun 10.00–18.00 Sep–Jun. 800SIT, concessions 600SIT, free Sat.*

### Narodni Muzej Slovenije (National Museum of Slovenia)
The National Museum (Muzejska 1; tel: 01 241 4404; fax: 01 241 4422; email: info@narmuz-lj.si; www.narmuz-lj.si), housed in a stunning neo-Renaissance palace, has an impressive façade, a striking vestibule with ornate frescos and an attractive stone-and-marble staircase with banisters adorned with white statues. Considering the size of the building the museum exhibits are surprisingly small. The permanent collection on the ground floor is displayed in corridors around a central courtyard, and consists mainly of stone relics and reliefs from Slovenia's Roman period. Descriptions of the artefacts are in both Slovene and English. As you travel through the exhibits you will also encounter an attractive Roman mosaic and a handful of Egyptian artefacts including a mummy, reputedly the only one in Slovenia.

The remaining exhibits are upstairs – take the right branch of the staircase when it splits, a spot marked by a bust of Prešeren. The left staircase will take you to the Natural History Museum, which shares the same building (see following listing). When we last visited there were two galleries open, one of which had an engaging display of prehistoric glass and amber from different regions of Slovenia. Large and informative boards in both Slovene and English provide information about the objects, their origins and the regions where they were found. Although temporary the exhibition showed what could be made of this space.
*Open: Tue, Wed and Fri–Sun 10.00–18.00, Thu 10.00–20.00. 700SIT, concessions 500SIT, children 400SIT, free 1st Sun of month. Combination ticket with the Slovenian Museum of Natural History 1,000SIT, concessions 700SIT.*

### Prirodoslovni Muzej Slovenije (Slovenian Museum of Natural History)
The Natural History Museum (Prešernova 20, entrance Muzejska 1; tel: 01 241 0940; fax: 01 241 0953; email: uprava@pms-lj.si; www.2pms-lj.si) is a taxidermist's dream, brimming with stuffed mammals and amphibians. It also has a large collection of skeletons and a visually striking photographic exhibition of Slovenia's fauna and flora. It may be old fashioned, but children love it. Highlights for younger visitors include more than 300 different varieties of birds – including a griffon vulture, golden eagle and white-tailed eagle – huge bears, stags and a wild boar. There is also a sizeable display of stuffed fish, including a shark and an

enormous salmon. Not all of the exhibits have been conserved by taxidermy, with poisonous snakes pickling in preservative jars. A gruesome display of bones, including a human skeleton, the skeleton of a dog and the skulls of a gorilla and an antelope, and the skeletal reconstruction of an enormous woolly mammoth, also fascinate children visiting the museum.

The stunning pictures of Triglav National Park, which form part of the display on Slovenia's natural environment, are a highlight for older visitors. In other galleries myriad varieties of rocks and minerals hint at the country's diverse geology. *Open: Fri–Wed 10.00–18.00 and Thu 10.00–20.00. 500SIT, concessions 400SIT, free 1st Sun of month. Combination ticket with National Museum of Slovenia 1,000SIT, concessions 700SIT.*

## Mestni Muzej (City Museum of Ljubljana)

Until it closed for renovation in 2000 the City Museum (Gosposka 15; tel: 01 252 2930; email: info@mm-lj.si; www.mm-lj.si) was one of Ljubljana's most popular museums. It reopened to much fanfare in 2004, but its permanent collection wasn't expected to return until the summer of 2005. Until then visitors can admire the sheer beauty of the building and its brilliant refurbishment, walk amongst Roman ruins including a section of old Roman road, and watch projections of the planned permanent exhibitions. In addition there are regular temporary shows, some of them delving into the history of the city as the museum did before the revamp. The Auersperg Palace, in which the City Museum is housed, is multi-functional with children's workshops, adult classes, a congress hall and a relaxed café. When the permanent collection is installed it will follow the evolution of the city, the Auersperg family and the *Ljubljančani*.
*Open: Tue–Sun 10.00–18.00. Free.*

## Slovenska Kinoteka

Part cinema and part museum, the Kinoteka (Miklošičeva 28; tel: 01 434 2520; fax: 01 434 2521; email: kinoteka@kinoteka.si; www.kinoteka.si) when fully functioning, exhibits artefacts and documents from cinematic history and has a regular schedule of retro and art-house cinema from Slovenia and around the globe. It is also a venue for the Ljubljana Film Festival, the annual Lesbian and Gay Film Festival (see *Public Holidays and Festivals*) and other events. Local sources say the Kinoteka, closed for renovation in September 2004, is set to reopen in 2005 to celebrate the 100th anniversary of Slovenian film-making.

## Arhitekturni Muzej Plečnik (Architectural Museum Plečnik Collection)

Plečnik devotees must make the pilgrimage to the architect's beloved Trnovo home, which is located near the Church of St John the Baptist in Trnovo. The building, which Plečnik made his home for 40 years, now comes under the auspices of the Architectural Museum (Karunova 4; tel: 01 280 1600; email: pz@aml.si; www.arhmuz.com). Most of the house, including his bedroom, drawing room and studio, is open to visitors. The Winter Garden is currently used for Plečnik study groups.
*Open: Tue and Thu 10.00–14.00. 600SIT, concessions 300SIT.*

## Slovenski Šolski Muzej (Slovenian School Museum)

Reopened in September 2004 after a renovation, this museum (Plečnikov trg 1; tel: 01 251 3024; email: solski.muzej@guest.arnes.si; www.ssolski-muzej.si) is primarily of interest to Slovene speakers and education enthusiasts. This specialised collection essentially looks at the history of teaching in Slovenia, teaching methods and aids, the evolution of schools and classroom furniture. Photographs of Slovenian schools through the centuries are also part of the collection, as are over 55,000 educational titles, which are kept in the museum's library.
*Open: Mon–Fri 09.00–13.00. Free.*

## Pivovarski Muzej (Brewery Museum)

If your interest in Union, Ljubljana's home-grown beer, is insatiable and you can round up a group then you will be able to go on an organised tour at the Union Brewery, where there is a small museum (Pivovarniska 2; tel: 01 471 7340; email: pivovarski.muzej@pivo-union.si; www.pivo-union.si) dedicated to the hallowed brew. If you want to visit the brewery call ahead.
*Open: by appointment, first Tue of month 08.00–13.00. Free.*

## Tobačna Muzej (Tobacco Museum)

Visual exhibits in this museum (Tobačna 5; tel: 01 477 7344; fax: 01 477 7155; email: tobacna@tobacna.si; www.tobacna.si) trace the history of tobacco production from the time the tobacco plant was first discovered in America through to its export to Europe and Slovenia. Even in the absence of English translations visitors can learn a surprising amount about the development of the Ljubljana Tobacco Company, where the museum is housed. Ornate snuffboxes, cigarette holders and pipes are also on display.
*Open: 10.00–18.00 every 1st Wed and 3rd Thu of the month or by appointment. Free.*

## Slovenski Etnografski Muzej (Slovenian Ethnographic Museum)

Since 2002 activity at the Ethnographic Museum (Metelkova 2; tel: 01 432 5403; email: etnomuz@etno-muzej.si; www.etno-muzej.si) has been restricted to occasional exhibitions and events, due to the construction of a new museum building. Scheduled to reopen fully in 2005, exhibitions in the new building will give an insight into traditional Slovenian life through folk art, artefacts from rural life, folk craft and displays based around trade, textiles, home furnishings and architecture. The Ethnographic Museum will also have a collection of artefacts from around the world, with a focus on North America and Africa.
*Open: Mon–Wed, Fri–Sun 10.00–18.00, Thu 10.00–20.00. Free.*

## Muzej Novejše Zgodovine (National Museum of Modern History)

A range of audio-visual effects, photographs and artefacts take you on a journey through Slovenia's modern history, from the beginning of World War I to the country's declaration of independence in 1991. The collection (Celovška 23; tel: 01 300 9610; fax: 01 433 8244; www.muzej-nz.si) resides in the attractively restored 18th-century Cekin Mansion on the outskirts of Tivoli Park. The

remains of a Yugoslav Army helicopter shot down over the city vividly evoke the 1991 war.
*Open: Tue–Sun 10.00–18.00. 500SIT, concessions 300SIT, free first Sun of month.*

## Železniški Muzej (Railway Museum)

In a country whose railways have a fascinating history, rail buffs will not want to miss the Railway Museum (Parmova 35 and Kurilniška 3; tel: 01 291 2641). As well as old photos of the network, largely put together by the Austro–Hungarians when they governed Slovenia, there are also hulking great train engines and accompanying wagons. For such a small country and city the array of over 60 locomotives is pretty impressive. Note that the museum is spread across two sites which are within walking distance of each other.
*Open: Mon–Thu 10.00–13.00. Free.*

## Arhitekturni Muzej (Architectural Museum)

The main collection of the Architectural Museum (Fužine Castle, Pot na Fužine 2; tel: 01 540 9798; email: aml@aml.si; www.arhmuz.com) is dramatically housed in a Renaissance mansion. Given the significant focus on Jože Plečnik it is tempting to think of this as a Plečnik museum, but in fact the work of many other modern Slovenian architects is covered including Ivo Spinčič, France Tomažič, Ivo Medved and Vinko Glanz. The various departments of the Architectural Museum encompass industrial design, visual and electronic media and photography, with explorations also into the history of Fužine Castle itself as well as regular temporary exhibitions. Town planners or architects wanting to spend an afternoon on a busman's holiday may wish to delve into the comprehensive library, though much of the material is in Slovene. The permanent Plečnik collection is an edited version of the large exhibition staged at the Pompidou Centre in Paris in 1986, which covers all his main periods from his days in Vienna and Prague, through to his seminal work in Slovenia. Some of the most interesting exhibits are plans by the prolific architect for further additions to his beloved Ljubljana.
*Open: Tue–Sun 11.00–19.00. 300SIT, concessions 150SIT.*

## Narodna Galerija (National Gallery)

Designed by the Czech Škrabout and constructed a year after the 1895 earthquake as the National House, Slovenia's biggest art gallery (Prešernova 24; tel: 01 241 5434; fax: 01 241 5403; email: info@ng-slo.si; www.ng-slo.si) boasts an impressive collection of sculpture and paintings from the Middle Ages through to the late 19th century. It also has an interesting photographic collection that gives a pictorial history of Slovenia. The gallery has recently been expanded, and a new wing has added a collection of works by European masters to those of well-known Slovene artists like Jakopič, Kobilca and Metzinger.
*Open: Tue–Sun 10.00–18.00. 800SIT, concessions 600SIT.*

## Mestna Galerija (City Gallery)

Not content with one location the City Gallery manages to spread its eclectic wings across four sites, two of them in the heart of the city and two in the suburb of

Bežigrad. In the original three-level building (**Mestna 1**; Mestni trg 5; tel: 01 241 1770; email: mestna.galerija-lj@siol.net; www.mestna-galerija.si) is a gallery with around a dozen temporary exhibitions a year. Nearby is the gallery's permanent collection (**Mestna 2**; Cankarjevo nabrežje 11/I; tel: 01 2411 790; www.mestna-galerija.si), which houses nearly 200 works of art by both Slovene and international artists. There are two further galleries in Bežigrad, each with its own temporary exhibitions. The first (**Bežigrad 1**; Dunajska 31; tel: 01 436 6957; www.mestna-galerija.si) was brought under the wing of the City Gallery in 1996 and like its patron holds around a dozen exhibitions a year. Many exhibits tend to focus on installations, 'concrete poetry' and other multimedia projects. Although founded in 1976 the second Bežigrad branch (**Bežigrad 2**; Vodnova 3; tel: 01 436 4057; www.mestna-galerija.si) also came on board in 1996 with a similar emphasis in its exhibitions. *Open: Tue–Fri 10.00–18.00, Sat 10.00–13.00 Sep–Jun, Tue–Sat 10.00–14.00 and 17.00–20.00, Sun 10.00–13.00 Jul–Aug. Free.*

### Other galleries

**Tivoli Gallery/International Centre of Graphic Art** Grad Tivoli, Pod turnom 3; tel: 01 241 3800; www.mglc-lj.si. Open: Wed–Sun 11.00–18.00. Free.

**Mala Galerija (Small Gallery)** Slovenska 35; tel: 01 251 4106. Open: Tue–Sat 10.00–18.00, Sun 10.00–13.00. Free.

**ŠKUC Galerija** Stari trg 21; tel/fax: 01 421 3140; email: galerija.skuc@guest.arnes.si; www.galerija.skuc-drustvo.si. Open: Tue–Sun 10.00–20.00. Free.

**DESSA Architectural Gallery** Židovska steza 4; tel: 01 251 6010; fax: 01 421 7975; email: ljdessa1@guest.arnes.si. Open: Mon–Fri 10.00–15.00. Free.

**Luwigana** Gornji trg 19; tel: 01 252 7369. Open: Mon–Fri 11.00–19.00, Sat 10.00–13.00. Free.

**Galerija Hest** Židovska 8; tel: 01 422 0000; www.galerijahest-sp.si. Open: Mon–Fri 10.00–14.00 and 15.30–20.00, Sat 10.00–13.00. Free.

**Galerija Hest 35** Novi trg 6; tel: 01 426 2168; www.galerijahest-sp.si. Open: Mon–Fri 10.00–14.00 and 15.30–20.00, Sat 10.00–13.00. Free.

## Other sites and monuments
### Nebotičnik (Skyscraper)
Ljubljana's original skyscraper, located at Slovenska 37, was the tallest building in the region when it was constructed in 1933. A café once tempted at the top of the building offering stunning views of the city's skyline. For now visitors have to content themselves with a street-level exploration as a debate centred around denationalisation has led to its closure and there is little to suggest it will reopen soon. If you head a little further south down Slovenska to the Nama department store at Tomšičeva 1, and take the lift to the Global Café and Nightclub on the fifth floor, you can get a similar view.

### Miklošičeva and Miklošičev Park
In the streets immediately north of Prešernov trg visitors will discover a profusion of historically and culturally significant buildings that were constructed after the earthquake that devastated the city in 1895. Josip Vancaš's great art nouveau

structure, the **Grand Union Hotel Executive**, at Miklošičeva 1, was opened in 1905 after having taken just 18 months to complete. In addition to its striking exterior the hotel boasts etched-glass windowpanes and an elegant interior that retains many period features. Opposite the hotel at Miklošičeva 4 is the **Slovenska Zadružna Kmetijska Banka** (People's Loan Bank), with its intricate decorations, symbols, blue tiles and attractive figures, two of whom sit on the roof. The MaxMara clothing store (Miklošičeva 6) features intricate detail below the roof and understated tiles that frame its arched windows.

More immediately striking is the former **Nekdanja Zadružna Gospodarska Banka** (Commercial Co-operative Bank) created by Ivan Vurnik – which is located opposite the hotel at No 8. Vurnik's wife, Helen, gave him a helping hand and is credited with painting it from head to toe in a vibrant pink, with its doors and windows framed by elaborate rusty red, yellow, blue and white geometric patterns. Ljubljana's most colourful building is especially impressive on a bright sunny day. One question, though, continues to perplex those who come to admire it: just how do you fit the whole building into your camera viewfinder?

Other impressive buildings on this side are the **Bambergova Hiša** (Bamberg House) at Miklošičeva 16 – look out for the ceramic reliefs of some of Slovenia's most renowned painters – the **Krisperjeva Hiša** (Krisper House) at Miklošičeva 20 and **Regali Hiša** (Regali House) at Miklošičeva 18. The first two secessionist structures are the masterpieces of Maks Fabiani who was commissioned to rebuild the area around Miklošičev Park, or Slovenska trg (Slovene Square) as it was formerly known, in the early 20th century. Fran Berneker is the architect behind Regali House. The former workers' chamber – notable for the seven marble figures, sculpted by Lojze Dolinar, that adorn the roof – is at Miklošičeva 28, the present-day location of the Slovenska Kinoteka (see *Museums/galleries*).

On the western side of Miklošičev Park you can see two more examples of art nouveau architecture. Sadly the green façade of the **Čudnova Hiša** (Chuden House) is looking slightly the worse for wear. Presiding over the park from Tavčarjeva 9 is Ljubljana's **court building**. Notable features of this expansive neo-classical structure include the four columns that stand tall over the main entrance, its balconied windows and the intricate geometric brickwork. Look out for the clock on the right gatepost that still tells the correct time.

Immediately opposite the courthouse you will see a statue of Franc Miklošič himself. The story of how the Slovene professor of Slavic studies came to be there is perhaps more interesting than the somewhat incongruous statue. The statue's pedestal was originally home to the Austro-Hungarian Emperor Franz Josef, who was later replaced by figureheads from the Socialist Federal Republic of Yugoslavia. Tired of constantly replacing the heads of state that resided here, the city authorities decided that the effigy should be neutral.

## Tržnica (City Market)

This is worth visiting for Plečnik's dramatic colonnades alone – the riverside arcade of columns built in 1939–40 which follow the gentle curve of the Ljubljanica. The best time to visit the market, which fills Vodnikov trg and the smaller Podgačarjev trg, is on Saturday, when it seems like the whole city has turned out and brightly coloured and strongly scented flowers abound. On Podgačarjev trg you will also find the **Stolna Cerkev Sv Nikolaja** (St Nicholas's Cathedral – see *Churches and cathedrals*) and the **Škofijski Dvorec** (Bishop's Palace). Constructed in 1512 the latter is one of Ljubljana's oldest buildings. In the five centuries since its construction it has played host to eminent Europeans, with Napoleon Bonaparte and the Russian Tsar Alexander I rumoured to be amongst them.

The square is also home to the **Semenišče** (Seminary) that dates from the beginning of the 18th century. Two hulking stone giants, carved by sculptor Angelo Pozzo, guard the Seminary's south portal. The real beauty of this theological college, though, lies in its library – an impressive combination of Giulio Quaglio's breathtaking frescos and its baroque furnishings. Viewing of the library is by appointment only, as the academy is still used today; this can be arranged at the Ljubljana TIC.

## Zmajski Most (Dragon Bridge)

The first concrete and iron bridge to cross the Ljubljanica is located at the northern end of Plečnik's colonnades and was erected in 1888 to commemorate the 40th anniversary of Austro-Hungarian Emperor Franz Josef's accession to the throne. Designed in secessionist style by Juriji Zaninovič, a Croatian architect who studied at the Wagner School in Vienna, and constructed in 1900–01, the bridge's chief attraction is the four large green dragons that sit in each corner of the bridge and the smaller dragons that guard the bridge's lights. Local legend claims that the dragons will wag their tails when a virgin crosses the bridge; others have somewhat cruelly nicknamed this impressive structure the 'mother-in-law' due to its fiery nature.

## Mestni trg

Perhaps the smartest of Ljubljana's three Old Town squares, Mestni trg, owes much of its contemporary appearance to the baroque period of the late 17th and 18th centuries. Here amongst the beautiful façades and courtyards of ancient palaces and middle-class houses you will find the seat of the city council, a smattering of expensive shops and some of the city's most refined bars and restaurants. As you walk down the street remember to look up to really appreciate the intricacies of the square's ornate façades – particularly noteworthy is the **Souvanova Hiša** (Souvan House) at No 24.

## Rotovž (town hall)

There have been buildings on this site as far back as the 15th century, but most of today's baroque structure was conjured up by Gregor Maček in 1718. Although the town hall (Mestni trg 1; tel: 01 306 3000) still functions as a seat of power, tourists can flit amongst some of its most interesting parts. Key features to look out for are the external balcony, pentagonal clocktower, interior courtyard, Gothic entrance hall, the patterned arches of the baroque arcade, the auditorium and the Hercules and Narcissus Fountain, the work of Robba's workshop.
*Atrium open: Mon–Fri 09.00–19.00. Free.*

### Robba's Fountain
Another of Robba's attractive fountains – the Fountain of the Three Carniolan Rivers – stands resplendent outside the town hall. Having recently been brought back to its best with a comprehensive renovation, this vaulting masterpiece depicts the three great rivers of Carniola: the Krka, the Ljubljanica and the sweeping Sava. Each of the rivers has been personified by a mighty triton pouring out water from large jugs. A number of visitors have suggested that Robba got his idea for the 1751 masterpiece from Italian artist Gian Lorenzo Bernini, who created the Fountain of the Four Rivers in Rome's Piazza Navona. Plans have been mooted to relocate the fountain to Prešernova, outside the National Gallery.

### Stari trg
The main attractions on Stari trg are its bountiful cafés, restaurants, bars and shops, but if you can drag yourself away there are a number of buildings worth exploring. Look out for the beautiful wrought-iron balcony, the bust of Slovene poet Lili Novy and the particularly impressive baroque frontage on the **Schwieger Hiša** (Schwieger House) at No 11a.

### Levstikov trg
The focal point of this attractive square, which received a Plečnik makeover in the early 1930s, is the **Cerkev Sv Jakob** (Church of St James – see *Churches and cathedrals*). Outside the church is the Shrine to Mary, which was placed here in 1681 as a thank-you to God when the Turks bypassed Ljubljana. Across traffic-clogged Karlovška is the **Gruberjeva Palača** (Gruber Palace), which is widely regarded as one of Ljubljana's most impressive examples of late baroque architecture. Constructed by Gabriel Gruber between 1773 and 1781 the building boasts a dome-capped oval stucco staircase, and its own chapel complete with frescos by Kremser Schmidt depicting scenes from the life of the Virgin Mary.

### Gornji trg
A raft of baroque and medieval dwellings climb gently eastward away from Stari trg and Levstikov trg on what is arguably Ljubljana's most attractive street, Gornji trg. Only a few of the houses retain their original medieval style; these can be identified by three windows running across the width of each building, while those with more windows have been combined and given a later baroque style. Walking up the street, immerse yourself in window-shopping with myriad handmade gifts, antiques and ornate jewellery amongst the offerings. Just beyond the midway point the highlight is the **Cerkev Sv Florijana** (Church of St Florian – see *Churches and cathedrals*).

### Kongresni trg
This grand square was constructed in 1821 to commemorate the formation of the Holy Alliance, although it was later restyled by Plečnik. Just one block back from the Ljubljanica, it is a place where locals gather for free concerts and special events, yet curiously it does not flourish with pavement cafés and definitely plays second

fiddle to Prešernov trg. Its highlights include the views back towards the castle and the flurry of impressive buildings that crowd all around it, including the university headquarters, the **Slovenska Filharmonija** (Slovene Philharmonic Hall), the **Uršulinska Cerkev Sv Trojice** (Ursuline Church of the Holy Trinity – *see Churches and cathedrals*) and the **Kazina** – a stunning classical construction. In the centre is a network of paths which form a star shape, and myriad benches that make good venues for enjoying a slice of pizza from the Ljubljanksi Dvor take-away on the square's east side.

## Univerza v Ljubljani (University of Ljubljana)

Josip Hudetz's epic neo-Renaissance building dominates the southern corner of Kongresni trg. Complete with attractive baroque towers this impressive mansion was built shortly after the devastating 1895 earthquake. Note the 15 gilded coats of arms, which represent the Carniolan state and Carniolan towns. The fountain in the front courtyard is called Europa and was commissioned to commemorate the EU's recognition of an independent Republic of Slovenia in 1992. A major refurbishment should be completed by summer 2005.

## Slovenska Filharmonija (Slovene Philharmonic Hall)

Slovenia proudly boasts one of the oldest philharmonic orchestras in the world, established in 1701 as the **Academia Philharmonicorum Labacensium** and becoming the Philharmonic Society in 1794. Today's hall (see *Music*) is the building's third incarnation, as it was destroyed first by fire in 1887 and then by the earthquake in 1895. This impressive structure is very different to the wooden construction that originally stood on the spot. Be sure to look at the wave-like shape of the rear of the hall, which backs onto the Ljubljanica. Stunning as it is from the outside the best way to really enjoy the Slovene Philharmonic Hall is to catch a performance by Slovenia's Philharmonic Orchestra or the Chamber Choir who are based in the same building.

## Trg Republike

Ljubljana's biggest square, the centre of socialist-era Slovenia, is dominated by two hulking towers and the Cankarjev Dom Cultural and Congress Centre (see *Theatre*), all imposing leftovers from the 1980s. The reliefs on the façade of the Slovenian **Državni Zabor** (National Assembly) on the north side of the square are worth looking at. Sculpted by Zdenko Kalin and Karel Putrih, they depict heroic socialist scenes. You can also seek out the small memorial in the adjacent park, the work of Edo Mihevc and Boris Kalin, a tribute to Slovenia's national heroes.

## Slovensko Narodno Gledališče Drama (SNG Drama; Slovene National Theatre)

Designed by Alexander Graf and completed in 1911, the SNG Drama (see *Theatre*) took two years to construct and has an impressive façade. As you pass, pop into the entrance hall where you will find the busts of four of the country's most famous classical actors – Počkaj, Linhart, Levstik and Župančič.

*Above* Julian Alps from Kranjska Gora, Gorenjska
*Below* Novo Mesto, Dolenjska

*Above* Shutters on a house in Izola on the Slovenian coast

*Right* Typical Štajerska/Prekmurje food

*Below* Typical farmstay, Gorenjska

## Narodna in Univerzitena Knjižnica (NUK; National and University Library)

Jože Plečnik was the man behind this deeply impressive library, widely regarded as his finest work. The futuristic and textured red-brick-and- stone exterior is constructed entirely from local materials; even the beautifully sculpted doors are striking, but it is the interior that really stands out. Visitors are allowed to climb the grand and austere black marble staircase, flanked by 32 dark marble columns, which leads to the reading room. Unless you are a member or prospective member this is as far as your exploration can go. Much of the lighting, layout and many of the fixtures and fittings inside also originate from Plečnik's studio. The library was built on the site of an old palace that was destroyed in the 1895 earthquake, taking five years to reach completion in 1940 as war broke out across Europe. Local legend has it that Slovene-language literature was secretly tucked away in the depths of the library when the city was occupied from 1941 to 1945.

While you may not be able to delve into Plečnik's stunning reading rooms you can at least pop down to the basement café/canteen designed by the great artist himself. Neat lines, funky tables and top-class *bela kava* are the order of the day and this is a good option for those looking to laze around with local students leafing through a newspaper or trying to strike up a conversation with your guidebook on show.

## Slovenska Akademija Znanosti in Umetnosti (Slovene Academy of Arts and Sciences)

The Lontovž Palača (Lontovž Palace; Novi trg 3; tel: 01 425 6068) – a stunning baroque mansion – has been the institution's nerve centre for almost 70 years and is of major cultural significance to the *Ljubljančani*. For visitors the building's ornate façade, which was designed by Jožef Schemerl and completed between 1786 and 1790, the busts of the academy's former presidents in the entrance hall, and Neptune's Fountain in the courtyard are all of interest. Looking across Novi trg to No 5 you will find another of the academy's imposing properties, complete with heavy wooden doors and elaborate decoration below the windows.

## Trg Francoske Revolucije

This square is home to the only statue of Napoleon outside of France, known as the Illyrian Monument. It was yet another work of Jože Plečnik, though perhaps not one of his finest with a rather frightening, garland-shrouded bust of France's finest perched precariously above the square. Zdenko Kalin's outsized bust of Simon Gregorčič also stands in the square as a memorial to the Slovene poet.

## Križanke

This former monastic complex, which dates back to the 13th century, was transformed by Jože Plečnik in the 1950s. Today the Križanke (see *Theatre*) is regarded as one of the city's premier performance venues. Even when there is no show on it is possible to visit the modest Church of St Mary and the baroque Knights Hall, or admire the ornate arcades, busts and sculptures in the grounds; you will find an incarnation of Plečnik himself in the atrium. During the warmer months the Križanke courtyard is a great place to enjoy a coffee from the theatre's small café.

## Krakovo and Trnovo

Just a short stroll south along the left bank of the Ljubljanica will take you to the twin suburbs of Krakovo and Trnovo, commonly regarded as the oldest and most historic part of the city.

Krakovo is notable for its compact medieval housing, the produce grown in its allotments or market garden and sold at the daily market on Vodnikov trg, and the visible remains of the city's Roman era. On Mirje you find the city's best-preserved stretch of **Roman wall**, complete with Plečnik modifications. According to locals the Emperor Augustus laid the first stone of the wall in AD14. The slightly incongruous pyramid at the eastern end of the wall stands 6m tall and shows you the minimum height that the Roman wall would have been originally. Other remnants of Emona are part of an open-air archaeological museum at Mirje 4 where you can see the ruins of an old Roman house. The building's second claim to fame arises from the fact that it was once home to the Slovene painter Rihard Jakopič.

The lively suburb of Trnovo, separated from Krakovo by the Gradaščica Canal, boasts a string of waterfront bars, cafés and restaurants on Eipprova ulica, as well as the **Cerkev Sv Janeza Krstnika** (Church of St John the Baptist – see *Churches and cathedrals*), and the former home of Jože Plečnik at Karunova 4. Today the architect's house forms part of the **Arhitekturni Muzej** (Architectural Museum – see *Museums/galleries*). Plečnik invested a lot of time and energy in landscaping his beloved Trnovo and Krakovo, and his influence can be seen in the gentle sloping embankment of the canal, tree-lined promenades, the **Trnovski Pristan** (Trnovo Pier) and the **Trnovski Most** (Trnovo Bridge) which traverses the Gradaščica. The latter is made of iron and concrete and incorporates a distinctive pyramid at each corner, and an obelisk.

## Slovensko Narodno Gledališče Opera in Balet (SNG Opera; Slovenian National Opera and Ballet Theatre)

The Opera and Ballet Theatre (see *Music*), one of Ljubljana's most attractive buildings, sits proudly in the centre of a square brimming with impressive architecture. The ornate neo-Renaissance design was the brainchild of Czech architects J V Hráský and A J Hrubý, and came into being in 1882. The ornate figures that shelter in niches and adorn the tympanum above the main entrance are the work of sculptor Alojz Grand.

## Žale

Ljubljana's main burial place (bus 2 direction Zelena jama) takes its name from the old Slavic word for cemetery. Opened in 1906 and still used today, Žale is laced with grand architecture and layers of history. Graves include those of both Italian and Slovene soldiers killed in World War I. The tombs and headstones of Slovenia's famous personalities are intricate works by some of the country's most reputable artists. Legendary Slovenian architect Jože Plečnik has also stamped his distinctive mark on the cemetery, including its dramatic colonnaded entrance

(1938–40), the Farewell Park, a small chapel and the *Tomb of Blumauer* (1942). Other notable features include Zdenko Kalin's *Fountain of Life*, a hexagonal pond flanked by six frolicking figures, Kralj's *Tomb of the Menardi Family* (1930), Dolina's tombstone of J E Krek (1920) and an ossuary containing the bones of Slovene soldiers who died in World War I and, in the new part of the cemetery, a memorial commemorating the victims of the ten-day war for independence in 1991.

## Churches and cathedrals

### Stolna Cerkev Sv Nikolaja (Cathedral of St Nicholas)

The dedication to the patron saint of fishermen and sailors is fitting for this cathedral (Dolničarjeva 1; tel: 01 234 2690. Open: daily 06.00–12.00 and 15.00–18.00) located near the Ljubljanica. The original probably stood on the site as far back as the 13th century, but most of today's incarnation is the result of work carried out at the beginning of the 18th century, with the main architect, the Italian Andrea Pozzo, completing work on the city's most important spiritual building in 1706. The cupola was added by Gregor Maček, who took over the construction of the cathedral in the later years. The Cathedral of St Nicholas has two entrances and it is worth exploring both. The weighty bronze portal on the south side of the church is known locally as the City Door and is composed of the busts of various bishops of the city, the work of local sculptor Mirsad Begič. Another local artist, Tone Demšar, added an impressive relief to the main, or Slovenian, door in preparation for the Pope's triumphal 1996 visit. The image that now adorns this western portal depicts 1,250 years of Christianity.

Equally noteworthy are the frescos that adorn both the exterior and the interior. On the southern façade you can see Giulio Quaglio's depiction of the Annunciation, while his image of Jesus Christ in Jordan can be found on the northern wall. Quaglio was also the master behind the ceiling frescos in the nave, which are currently being renovated with work scheduled to continue until 2006. Janez Wolf's painting *The Angel's Proclamation of Zahriah Wolf* on the cathedral's eastern façade, Langus's altar painting, Plečnik's bishop's throne and Robba's cherubs, which adorn the Altar of Corpus Christi, are also worth seeking out.

### Frančiškanska Cerkev Marijinega Oznanjenja (Franciscan Church of the Annunciation)

Franciscan monks commissioned this attractive pink-coloured church (Prešernov trg; tel: 01 425 3001), one of the symbols of the city, in the middle of the 17th century. Numerous renovations have seen the building alter considerably over time and today's church dates largely from the 18th century. The inspiration for the structure's attractive façade came from a late-Renaissance church in Florence, Santa Maria Novella. Internally, the oldest building on the square (it survived the 1895 earthquake) is less impressive with the most distinguished feature being an altar designed by Francesco Robba. Also look out for Matevž Langus's frescos near the windows, and those added to the nave by Matej Sternen in 1935–36. The adjoining monastery didn't fare so well in the earthquake, with the majority of it needing to be rebuilt. Today it boasts a library housing more than 10,000 books and manuscripts.

## Cerkev Sv Janeza Krstnika (Church of St John the Baptist)

Fabled as the place where the Romantic Slovene poet France Prešeren first spotted Julija Primic – his great unrequited love – the church (Kolezijska 1; tel: 01 283 5060) is usually referred to as the Trnovo Church. The church was originally constructed in the middle of the 18th century and underwent various renovations and reconstructions that altered its appearance. Today's neo-Romanesque incarnation dates from the early 20th century when it was rebuilt after the 1895 earthquake that devastated much of Ljubljana. Internally the church's most noteworthy aspects are Metzinger's baroque masterpiece – a stunning altar painting of the church's patron St John the Baptist – the frescos designed by Sternen and Goršič and a mid-19th century organ.

## Cerkev Sv Florijana (Church of St Florian)

This Old Town church (Gornji trg 18; tel: 01 252 1727) was built in 1672 after a devastating fire engulfed this part of the city. Seventeenth-century locals hoped that dedicating the church to the patron saint of fires and firemen, St Florian, would protect it against any future blazes. Plečnik stamped his indelible mark on the church in the 1930s when he moved the main portal, bricking up the original and placing Robba's statue of St John Nepomuk in front of it. Another of Robba's works, a dramatic depiction of St John being tossed into Prague's Vlatva River from the Czech capital's Charles Bridge, is also located inside. The church is at its most atmospheric during services and regular classical concerts.

## Cerkev Sv Jakob (Church of St James)

Built by Jesuits in 1613 to complement their monastery, this imposing Old Town church (Levstikov trg; tel: 01 252 1727) boasts the highest belltower in the city, an attractive baroque interior and a Jesuit chapel with intricate stucco work and an unusual octagonal shape. Before the 1895 earthquake the church actually had two belltowers. The sacristy was also added after the earthquake. Francesco Robba, who lived on Levstikov Square, designed the church's high altar, which was added in 1732. When Plečnik was commissioned to redesign the square in 1933–34 some say he planted a row of poplar trees to hide the church's façade, which he disliked intensely.

## Uršulinska Cerkev Sv Trojice (Ursuline Church of the Holy Trinity)

Located on the western side of regal Kongresni trg, this central church (Slovenska 21; tel: 01 252 4862) boasts an attractive baroque façade and conceals an enormous multicoloured altar constructed with African marble, and altar paintings by Valentin Metzinger. Built in 1726 in Venetian style, the church's most striking external features are the six columns that flank its entrance and a balustrade staircase designed by Jože Plečnik.

A copy of the Column of the Holy Trinity stands outside. The original – widely believed to be the work of Mislej and Robba and erected back in 1693 as the *Ljubljančani* gave thanks for those who survived the plague – is in the safe hands of the City Museum.

### Cerkev Šempetrska (Church of St Peter)
Designed by Italian artist Giovanni Fusconi, the church (Trubarjeva 80) was constructed between 1729 and 1733. Its somewhat bland exterior is brightened up by Ivan and Helen Vurnik's (of the Co-operative Bank fame, see Miklošičeva and Miklošičev Park paragraphs) attractive mosaics. St Peter sits proudly above the main entrance. The interior is also adorned with stunning frescos painted by Franc Jelovšek, a local Slovene artist.

### Srbska Pravoslavna Cerkev (Serbian Orthodox Church)
Partially hidden behind trees on Prešernova the church has an attractive façade and a brightly decorated Orthodox interior. With a statue of Primož Trubar standing outside this is a place for Ljubljana's other faiths, Protestants and Orthodox Christians, in a country dominated by Roman Catholicism.

### Cerkev Sv Frančiška Asiškega (Church of St Francis of Assisi)
One of Plečnik's most striking and unique churches (Černetova 20. Bus 22 direction Kamna Gorica to Drenikova stop) can be found in the suburb of Šišak. The Church of St Francis of Assisi features a square ground plan, 20 magnificent internal pillars and a futuristic belltower. Internally the church takes the shape of a covered square complete with colonnades, a flat wooden ceiling and highly individual altars and furnishings.

### Cerkev Sv Mihaela (Church of St Michael)
Another of Plečnik's creations, the Church of St Michael (bus 19 direction Barje) at the heart of the Ljubljansko Barje (Ljubljana Marshes), was built in the periods 1920–28 and 1937–40 around ten pillars. This fortress-like wooden church was constructed on a very tight budget and innovative ways of cutting costs reputedly included using sewage pipes rather than concrete for the pillars.

## Parks and escapes
### Tivoli Garden
Just a small part of Ljubljana's green lung, this immaculately landscaped garden hangs tantalisingly on the edge of the city centre. Its walkways, trees, fountains and benches are the perfect venue for relaxing away from what big- city bustle Ljubljana can muster. This garden also boasts a children's playground, cafés, fountains and a recreation centre with a pool, roller-skating, tennis and bowling. There is also a large glass greenhouse near the southern entrance to the park.

### Krajinski Park Tivoli (The Landscape Park of Tivoli)
Tivolski Vrh, Šišenski, Debeli and Rožnik hills, Rkovnik and Mostec collectively make up the largest part of Ljubljana's green lung. The most visited area is Rožnik hill where visitors find the charming Church of St Mary, the Ivan Cankar Memorial Room and restaurants that feel more like countryside inns. Myriad walking, running and mountain-biking trails weave their way through the park's densely forested hills. Maps and waymarks help keep walkers on the right track, although vandals have damaged some of the signposts. If you are feeling really

energetic you can flex your muscles and test your aerobic stamina on a variety of fitness tracks that offer al-fresco circuit training.

### Živalski Vrt (Ljubljana Zoo)

The city's zoo (Večna pot 70; tel: 01 244 2188; email: info@zoo-ljubljana.si; www.zoo-ljubljana.si) has an agreeable forest location, and is home to over 500 animal species. Younger visitors coo over the farm animals, beavers, deer and mouflon sheep, while older visitors are more appreciative of the zoo's Siberian tiger, giraffes, zebras and leopards. A café, hands-on activities, children's playground and archaeological collection help keep everyone happy. *Open: daily 09.00–19.00 Apr–Sep, 09.00–18.00 Mar and Oct and 09.00–17.00 Nov–Feb. Admission 800SIT.*

### Ljubljansko Barje (Ljubljana Marshes)

This peaty marshland 3km from the centre of town (bus 19 direction Barje) is real throwback to life in Ljubljana when marsh dwellers lived in houses built on stilts in 2000BC. Today the houses have gone but this boggy land, which is believed to be around two million years old, is still home to around 70 animal species and is visited by more than 250 species of birds each year, making it something of an ornithologist's paradise. Plečnik's **Cerkev Sv Mihaela** (Church of St Michael – see *Churches and cathedrals*) is also here. It is also possible to take a hot-air balloon trip over the marshes (see *Tour operators*).

### Šmarna Gora

There is no doubting the city's most popular hill. Šmarna Gora, 10km northwest of the city centre (bus 8 direction Brod), is awash at weekends with *Ljubljančani* fleeing the city. Once a fortress against the Ottomans, today the 669m-high hill is invaded by day trippers seeking a bit of exercise and sweeping views back towards the city. For any reasonably fit adult the trip to the top can be tackled in under an hour. Look out also for the Church of the Holy Mother, with its frescos by Matevž Langus.

# Gorenjska

If it is mountains you have come to Slovenia to see then this is the region for you. Everywhere you look in Gorenjska voluminous peaks rise improbably from sweeping river valleys and the skyline dances with ridges and sky-scraping peaks, many of which retain a liberal dusting of snow for much of the year. Quite simply Gorenjska boasts some of the finest alpine scenery anywhere in the world. In the famous resort at Cake of Bled they are well aware of this gift and tourism these days is an increasingly slick affair, though there is always somewhere to escape the crowds even at the height of summer. Then there is the Cake at Bohinj, much larger and if anything even more impressive and with far fewer tourists. If the weather is good and you have time the best plan is to just get out into the hills for a gentle hike on the lower slopes or for a serious climb, if you have the gear and experience, up the likes of Mount Triglav, a peak with mythical status for many Slovenes. After a hard day in the outdoors cosy *gostilnas* await with sublime Bohinj trout a speciality, with perhaps a wickedly creamy *kremna rezina*, another Gorenjska speciality, for dessert.

## KAMNIK

Just a half-hour drive north of Ljubljana is the pretty medieval town of Kamnik, a quiet and relaxed place that is perfect for a minimum-effort day trip or a stopover en route to Logarska Dolina even further north (see the *Štajerska* chapter). The spectacular Kamniške Savinje Alps loom behind the compact old centre, though there is not too much to do bar floating around the sprinkling of cafés, bars and churches and admiring the view. Kamnik is not a big place so the best plan is just to stroll down the main street, Glavni trg, and on to Šutna taking in the attractions as you go.

### Getting there

Frequent buses and trains leave Ljubljana for Kamnik. The bus is generally a little quicker and takes 25–30 minutes, although some services take almost an hour, while the trains take around 50 minutes.

### Where to stay

**Pension Kamrica** (5 rooms) Trg Svobode 2; tel: 01 831 7707. Located on a quiet street just behind Šutna this small pension has good-sized rooms and private parking. 6,000SIT per person.

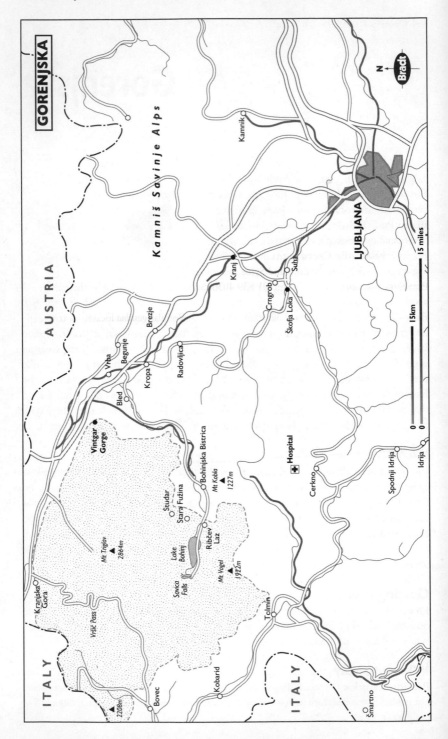

**Pri Cesarju** (10 rooms) Tunjiška 1; tel: 01 839 2917. This pension just north of Glavni trg has decent rooms and some triples. Singles 8,500SIT, doubles 12,000SIT.
**Prenočišca Špenko** (12 rooms) Prešernova 14c; tel: 01 831 7330. Less appealing than Kamnik's other centrally located pensions the rooms here are still an option. 6,000SIT per person.
**Kamp Resnik** Maistrova 32; tel: 01 831 7314. Small campsite on the banks of the Nevljica River. 500SIT per person.

## Where to eat
**Pivnica Pri Podkvi** Trg Svobode 1; tel: 041 961 559. This tavern has a quiet and pleasant back-street location. Its set menu at 700SIT is excellent value.
**Kavarna Veronika** Glavni trg 6; tel: 01 839 1143. Pleasant café with terrace located beneath the castle, serving cakes, sandwiches and ice-cream.
**Bistro Pod Gradom** Sadinkarjeva 1a. Popular eatery inside a wooden hut with a shady terrace and overlooked by the castle.
**Okrepčevalnica de Cecco** Šutna 68; tel: 01 831 7447. Busy spaghetteria at the end of Šutna with decent pasta options and Swiss specialities like fondue.
**Pizzerija Korobač Šutna** 76; tel: 01 839 4030. Solid pizzeria located near the railway station.
**Gostilna Pod Skalo** Maistrova 32; tel: 01 839 1233. Popular *gostilna* located next to Kamp Resnik, with fish and meat grills.

Self-catering options include:

**Vele supermarket** Trg talcev 8
**Delikate Sa** Glavni trg 2
**Mini Market** Šutna 28

## Practicalities
**Tourist Information Centre** Tomšičeva 23; tel: 01 839 1470; fax: 01 831 8192; email: infocentre.kamnik@siol.net; http://www.turizem.kamnik.si. Open: Mon–Fri 08.00–16.00, Sat 08.00–12.00.
**Post office** Glavni trg 27. Open: Mon–Fri 08.00–19.00, Sat 08.00–12.00.
**Ljubljanska Banka** Glavni trg 10. Open: Mon–Fri 08.00–12.00 and 15.00–17.00.
**SKB Banka** Glavni trg 13. Open: Mon–Fri 08.00–12.00 and 15.00–17.00.

## What to see
### Cerkev Sv Jakoba (Church of St Jacob)
Ljubljana's main man Jože Plečnik ventured north to give the town one of his trademark designs with his impressive altar, though most of the rest of the church, on Frančiškanski trg, is baroque.

### Frančiškanski Samostan (Franciscan Monastery)
This 15th-century creation (Frančiškanski trg; tel: 01 831 8030. By appointment) is nothing special, but its claim to fame is that it holds the first translation of the Bible into the Slovene language, written by Jurij Dalmatin, a Protestant minister.

### Galerija Miha Maleš (Miha Maleš Gallery)

This gallery (Glavni trg 2; tel: 01 839 1616. Open: Tue–Sat 08.00–13.00 and 16.00–19.00. 500SIT, concessions 300SIT) celebrates the life and work of local boy-made-good Miha Maleš, who was born in the town at the start of the 20th century. Today the collection has expanded to include an ever-changing range of temporary exhibits.

### Terme Snovik

This new spa complex (Molkova pot 5; tel: 01 830 8631; fax: 01 830 8620; email: terme.snovik@zarja-kovis.si) has thermal pools with temperatures of up to 31°C, whirlpools, massage and sports facilities, an enormous indoor pool and a modern sauna centre with a range of wet- and dry-heat treatments.

## LJUBLJANA TO BLED – ON THE TOURIST TRAIL

Many time-starved visitors rush straight through on the fast road to Bled from Ljubljana, but if you follow suit you will miss out on a flurry of historical towns and villages. If you really are desperate to get to Bled then consider staying by the lake and making a couple of trips back to these gems.

## ŠKOFJA LOKA

On a balmy summer night with Loka Castle twinkling floodlit above and the Old Town rambling down the hillside below Škofja Loka takes on an ethereal beauty that Disney can only dream of. The town may be blighted by a handful of apartment blocks on its outskirts and a faceless new town, but the surrounding countryside offers plenty of hiking and cycling opportunities, as well as a brace of remarkable churches. Much of the protected Old Town may need more than a lick of paint, but the local authorities have invested in English-language information plaques on buildings and have made a real effort in recently revamping the castle's museum.

### History

Škofja Loka (Bishop's Meadow) is swathed in tales of German emperors and Freising bishops dating back more than 1,000 years. It also enjoyed a golden age as a trading hub on the route from Bavaria to the Adriatic, though this trade was decimated in the 15th century when the natural disaster of an earthquake combined with sacking at the hands of both the Ottomans and the Counts of Celje. Fortunately most of the destroyed Old Town buildings were reconstructed centuries ago and prosperity returned to the town under the Austro–Hungarians. These days the sprinkling of industry in the suburbs is in decline and tourism is emerging as Škofja Loka's welcome new breadwinner.

### Getting there

Škofja Loka is a 30-minute drive from Ljubljana. Regular buses from Kranj (20 minutes), Ljubljana (40 minutes) and Cerkno (45 minutes) also stop here, as do trains from Kranj (10 minutes), Ljubljana (25 minutes), Radovljica (30 minutes) and Lesce–Bled (35 minutes). The **bus station** is on Kapucinski trg 13 (tel: 04 517

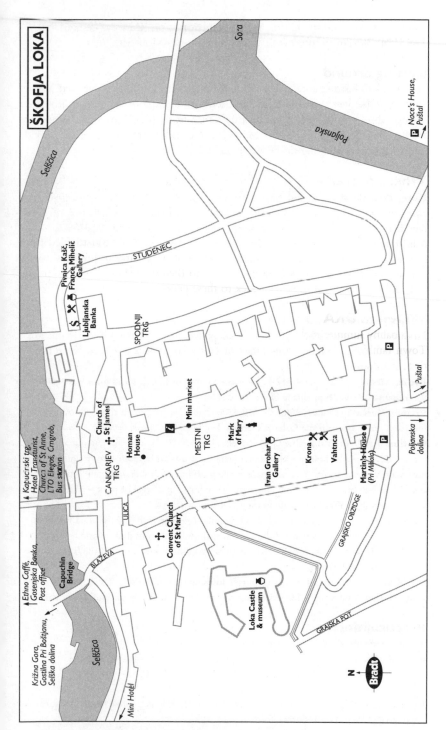

0300; www.alpetour.si), and the **railway station** is on Kidričeva cesta 61 (tel: 04 294 4174) 3km from town with an hourly bus link (Mon–Sat).

## Getting around

Škofja Loka's historic core can easily be explored on foot. Bicycle hire will also let you really discover the town's beautiful setting and explore the verdant Poljanska Valley. More serious cyclists can pick up a map from the Blegoš tourist office (see *Practicalities*) detailing 12 cycle routes in the Loka area. They also provide information about hiking in the Škofja Loka hills.

## Where to stay

**Hotel Transturist** (47 rooms) Kapucinski trg 9; tel: 04 512 4026; fax: 04 512 4096; email: info@transturist.com; www.transturist.com. Škofja Loka's only hotel is situated just outside the historic core. Singles 12,240SIT, doubles 17,520SIT, triples 22,320SIT.

**Mini Hotel** (8 rooms) Vincarje 47; tel: 04 515 0540; fax: 04 515 0542; email: metka@minihotelzorka-sp.si; www.minihotelzorka-sp.si. This well-equipped hotel 2km from the Old Town also has a sports centre with an outdoor pool, games courts, sauna and fitness studio. Singles 8,880SIT, doubles 12,720SIT, triples 15,840SIT.

## Where to eat and drink

**Homan** Mestni trg 2; tel: 04 512 3047. Café, pizzeria and restaurant rolled into one in a historic building right at the heart of the Old Town. Locals flock to Homan for its tasty cakes and pastries.

**Krona** Mestni trg 32; tel: 04 512 7910. More salubrious than it looks from the outside, this restaurant serves homemade Slovenian dishes.

**Pivnica Kašča** Spodni trg 2; tel: 04 512 4300. Basement restaurant serving Slovenian food and pizzas beneath the Galerija Franceta Miheliča (see *A walking tour*).

**Gostilna Pri Boštjanu** Križna Gora 8a; tel: 04 510 3320. Bawdy and raucous at weekends and public holidays, this large restaurant boasts an outdoor terrace with stunning mountain views as well as a cosier space inside with lots of timber and traditional ovens. If you are feeling hungry call ahead and arrange a whole leg of veal or pork served with various garnishes. Well worth the journey out of town.

**Vahtnca** Mestni trg 31; tel: 04 512 3380. Popular café-bar with slightly faded furniture, an upper level and clocks that tell the time in various cities around the world.

**Ethno Caffè** Kapucinski trg 15. The bar's large windows offer views of the Selščica River and the Old Town.

**Pri Miholu** Mestni trg 24. Bar with terrace forming part of the Old Town walls.

**Mini Market** Mestni trg 9. Identifiable only by the small display of groceries in the window.

## Practicalities

**Tourist Information Centre** Mestni trg 7; tel/fax: 04 512 0268; email: td-skofja.loka@siol.net; www.skofjaloka.si. Open: Mon–Fri 08.30–19.30, Sat–Sun 08.30–12.30 and 17.00–19.30 Jun–Aug, Mon–Fri 09.00–19.00, Sat–Sun 08.30–12.30 Sep–May.

**Blegoš** Kidričeva 1a; tel: 04 517 0600; fax: 04 517 0605; email: info@lto-blegos.si; www.lto-blegos.si. Local tourist office.

**Ljubljanska Banka** Spodnji trg 1
**Gorenjska Banka** Kapucinski trg 8. Open: Mon–Fri 08.00–18.00, Sat 08.00–12.00.
**Post office** Kapucinski trg 9. Open: Mon–Fri 07.00–19.00, Sat 07.00–12.00.

## What to see
### A walking tour

The logical place to begin a walking tour of Škofja Loka's Old Town is at **Loka Grad**, the castle (Grajska pot 13; tel: 04 517 0400. Open: Tue–Sun 09.00–18.00 Apr–Sep, Sat–Sun 09.00–17.00 Nov–Mar. 500SIT). Follow the path that runs up the hill adjacent to the town's medieval walls. In the castle's courtyard you will notice the coats of arms adorning the walls, all of which feature a black king. Local legend puts this down to bygone days when the black servant of a wealthy landlord saved him from a bear, and the king promised that his heroic deed would be remembered forever.

A lot of effort went into the renovation of the **castle museum** and now there is a welcome English-language leaflet as well as information notes for many of the artefacts. Some of the more interesting exhibits are a scale model of the castle showing the original 25m-high central tower, a relief map of the town and a slightly fusty but illuminating natural history section with wildlife from the surrounding countryside. Unfortunately one of the most interesting sections, about the German occupation of the region and subsequent partisan resistance, is in Slovene only, though many of the graphic photographs speak for themselves.

Back down the hill **Martinova Hiša** (Martin's House), part of a 14th-century defensive extension of the city walls and home to the Pri Miholu bar (see *Where to eat and drink*), stands beside the Poljanska Dolina gate, which leads to Mestni trg. Elegant houses dating from the 16th and 17th centuries flank this long pedestrianised square. You can visit the **Galerija Ivana Groharja** (Ivan Grohar Gallery; Mestni trg 37; tel: 04 512 2692), named after the craftsman whose work is on display in the castle museum. To your right notice the column with three statues, the Mark of Mary erected in 1751 to give thanks for protection against fire and the plague, and the 19th-century fountain displaying Škofja Loka's coat of arms. The **Homanova Hiša** (Homan House) at No 2, with its ornate frescos, is another highlight. Continue on to the **Cerkev Sv Jakob** (Church of St James), which dates back to 1471, with an interior restyled by Jože Plečnik; it is on Cankarjev trg at the end of Mestni trg.

At the end of the street cross the Selščica River, a branch of the Sora, pass the bus station and turn left once you have passed the post office, and you will come to the small **Cerkev Sv Ane** (Church of St Anne) that is worth popping into. From here cross back over the river on the 15th-century **Kapucinski Most** (Capuchin Bridge). Ironically it was commissioned by Bishop Leopold, who met his fate when he tumbled from his horse and fell to his death in the waters below.

Back across the river you will soon come to the **Nunska Cerkev** (the Nun's Church or the Convent Church of St Mary) on Blaževa. Its current baroque design was the result of a 17th-century fire. From here go behind the Church of St James to Spodnji trg. Marred by fast-moving traffic Spodnji trg does have a handful of interesting buildings, those that the authorities consider to be cultural monuments are indicated with a plaque that gives their name and a brief description in both English and Slovene. The most interesting building on the square is the **Galerija Franceta Miheliča** (France Mihelič Gallery; Spodnji trg 1; tel: 04 517 0400. Open: Tue–Sun 12.00–17.00), where paintings by the Slovene artist France Mihelič, who died in 1998, are exhibited in a former granary.

## Nacetova Hiša (Nace's House)

This stone and timber house (Pruštal 74; tel: 04 029 5916. Open: by appointment – ask at the TIC. 400SIT), which once served as an inn, offers a real insight into local living down the ages, through both its original 16th-century elements and sections that were added in the 18th century. Highlights include the black kitchen (so-called because it is thick with the soot that did not have a chimney to escape through), a workshop brimming with old tools and a room where aggressive or drunk guests were locked away until they calmed down. Call ahead and the granddaughter of the last resident who lived here until 1977, opera singer Polde Polenec, may even show you around herself. From the expansive garden there are good views back across the river towards the castle and Old Town so bring your camera.

# AROUND ŠKOFJA LOKA
## Crngrob

If you have your own wheels or fancy getting your walking shoes on, head for two fascinating churches outside Škofja Loka. The village of Crngrob, which translates ominously as 'black grave', is accessible on the ramshackle road from town, but a better option is to take the main road north towards Kranj and turn down the sealed road from there. The **Cerkev Marijino Oznanjenje** (Church of the Annunciation), which dominates from a grassy redoubt, is massively out of proportion with the small hamlet below, but it has always been a church of pilgrimage rather than just serving the local parishioners. Today's structure evolved over more than four centuries, with the original single-nave church constructed in the 17th century. By 1853 it had three naves, a beautiful rib-vaulted ceiling, presbytery, belfry and neo-Gothic portico.

Make sure you have a good look at the large fresco outside of **St Christopher** – local folklore has it that you will not die on the same day that you see it, though the locals we asked were unclear whether taking a photo would work, or whether having a peek at it every day would grant one immortality. Venture beneath the portico and you will come across frescos on either side of another door. To the left is *The Passion of Christ*, while to the right are warnings on activities banned on the Lord's Day, with a vivid depiction of what happens if you disobey – a dragon awaits to snatch sinners to a fiery new home in hell.

Highlights inside the church include the largest gilt altar in Gorenjska, dating from 1652, ornate frescos, and ceiling joints above the altar which are actually the coats of arms of various donors including Bavarian families – a legacy of the region's past. More intriguing is the large rib that hangs from a timber beam. This commemorates a local legend about a girl who was so big that she could stand with one foot on the hill of Šmarjetna Gora, near Kranj, and the other foot on Šmarna

Gora, near Ljubljana. As she stood astride the valley the giant girl gathered from the River Sava the stones used to construct the church.

If you are feeling brave head through the door to the right of the altar where you can ascend to the choir stalls and then head up what has to be Slovenia's narrowest stone staircase to the rafters, where the wooden construction of the roof reveals itself – not for the faint-hearted or less than sure-footed. There is a daily mass at 16.00; when it is closed pick up the key at house No 10.

### Practicalities

**Pri Marku** Crngrob 5; tel: 04 513 1626; fax: 04 513 9790; email: kt.pri.marku-porenta@siol.net. This pleasant farm accommodation was in the process of increasing its capacity from four to 14 rooms at the time of our last visit in 2004. Cosy and homely with wonderful home-baked rolls for breakfast. Singles 3,360SIT, doubles 6,720SIT.
**Gostišče Crngrob** Crngrob 13; tel: 04 513 1601. Offers hearty Slovenian meat dishes and views of the valley and mountains.

## Suha

The roadside **Cerkev Sv Janez Krstnik** (Church of St John the Baptist) in Suha, 2.5km from Škofja Loka, may not be as immediately striking as those in Crngrob, but its interior frescos are perhaps more impressive and cover the entire rib-vaulted ceiling of the presbytery. Vivid images include the *Last Judgement*, scenes from Christ's life and illustrations of disciples and angels. The **Španova domačija** (Špan's Home), with its external baroque frescos and 18th-century shrine, is also worth visiting. If you don't make it to Suha the museum in Škofja Loka's castle has a scale model of the house and copies of the church frescos. You can usually get the key from No 32 near the church.

## KRANJ

Only 10km from Škofja Loka, Slovenia's fourth-largest city may be blighted by a swathe of factories on its outskirts, but its ethnically diverse citizens – thanks to workers brought in from other parts of Yugoslavia in the 1970s and 1980s – are justifiably proud of a charming Old Town that rests spectacularly on a rocky bluff surrounded by the Sava and Kokra rivers, with the lofty peaks of the Kamniške–Savinje Alps framing the background. With a couple of accommodation options, numerous bars and a choice of restaurants Kranj invites an overnight stay and is a good base for exploring the rest of this part of Gorenjska. Kranj is an essential stop for fans of the great Slovene writer France Prešeren as he lived here for the final years of his life and died in the Old Town in a house that is now a dedicated museum.

### History

Archaeological finds in the area date back as far as the 8th century BC, although Kranj didn't really rise to the fore until the 13th century AD when it became a city and important trading centre. In the 19th century Kranj was very much at the heart of industrial development, with factories springing up on the banks of the Sava. Kranj has also enjoyed brief periods as the informal capital of the Slovenian lands,

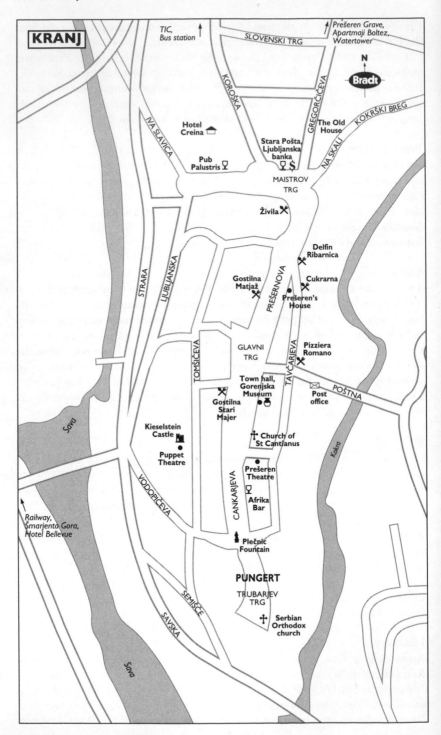

surpassing the importance of Ljubljana prior to the construction of the Vienna–Trieste railway (which elevated the status of the present-day capital) in the 1850s. Kranj also flourished in the late 19th and early 20th centuries, at a time when Ljubljana was suffering from the effects of the devastating 1895 earthquake. Today tourism is rapidly becoming the city's main industry as its traditional manufacturing industries wane and its role as a convention and fair venue evaporates, with a shopping mall now occupying the island that used to be the main venue.

## Getting there
Just 10km from Škofja Loka, Kranj is within easy cycling and driving distance. Regular buses also serve the **bus station** (Stošičeva; tel: 04 201 3210) from Škofja Loka (20 minutes), Radovljica (30 minutes), Bled (40 minutes) and Ljubljana (40 minutes). Kranj's railway station (tel: 04 294 4133; 10 minutes' walk from the Old Town) is served by trains from Škofja Loka (10 minutes), Radovljica (20 minutes), Lesce-Bled (25 minutes) and Ljubljana (35 minutes).

A word of warning: the city was known locally as 'Kranjsterdam' in the 1990s as it had a serious hard-drug problem. This seems to have eased in recent years, but exercise caution especially around the bus and railway stations after dark. By no means is this London or New York, but be just a touch more careful than you would be elsewhere in Slovenia.

## Where to stay
**Apartmaji Boltez** (10 rooms) Oldhamska 10a; tel: 04 201 4070; fax: 04 201 4071; email: apartmaji@boltez.si; www.boltez.si/apartmaji. Modern apartments next to the water tower, catering to a business crowd, with refrigerators and free broadband internet access in all rooms and apartments. Singles 10,000–14,000SIT, doubles 14,000–19,000SIT, triples 23,000SIT, quads 25,000–33,000SIT.
**Hotel Creina** (89 rooms) Koroška 5; tel: 04 202 4550; fax: 04 202 2483; email: info@hotel-creina.si; www.hotel-creina.si. Kranj's only central hotel is housed in an ugly socialist-era building with equally uninspiring rooms, and caters largely for a business clientele. Singles 11,500SIT, doubles 16,000SIT and triples 20,400SIT.
**Hotel Bellevue** (18 rooms) Šmarjetna Gora 6; tel: 04 270 0000; fax: 04 270 0020; email: bellevue@bellevue.si; www.bellevue.si. Hilltop hotel 2km from Kranj's Old Town with stunning panoramic views. The most expensive rooms have water beds. Singles 7,050–11,050SIT, doubles 13,000–17,800SIT.

## Where to eat
**Gostilna Matjaž** Prešernova 16; tel: 04 202 5690. Simple but delicious Slovenian cuisine.
**Delfin Ribarnica** Tavčarjeva 1; tel: 04 202 2909. Fishmonger and restaurant serving good-quality fresh fish.
**Pizzeria Romano** Tavčarjeva 31; tel: 04 236 3900. Cheap pizzeria with an outdoor terrace with great mountain views.
**Gostilna Stari Majer** Glavni trg; tel: 04 236 4550. The 2004 renovation has improved this centrally located restaurant which serves Slovenian dishes.
**Živila** Maistrov trg 11. Supermarket in the heart of the Old Town.

## FRANCE PREŠEREN

No-one more vividly and emotively captures the emotions of the Slovenes than national bard France Prešeren. It is fitting that Prešeren's verse, *A Toast*, is used today as the national anthem and that it is his figure that stands grandly overlooking the square dedicated to him in central Ljubljana. Prešeren was born in 1800 in Vrba, a village near the capital, but the most romantic and tragic phase of his life began at a service in the Cerkev Sv Janeza Krstnika (Church of St John the Baptist) in Trnovo where he fell madly in love with the teenage Julija Primic. She was from a wealthy family and her parents were less than impressed with the poet-lawyer's prospects. The two were destined never to be together. A lonely and heartbroken Prešeren died prematurely in 1849 in Kranj, and much of his best verse was inspired by his feelings for Primic. Many visitors take the semi-naked muse (the subject of much controversy when it was revealed in 1905) above his figure in Prešernov trg in Ljubljana to be Julija, but the young woman is actually depicted in a bust on the front of a building on adjacent Wolfova, with some locals rather unkindly suggesting she is there to eternally mock him.

## Entertainment and nightlife

Kranj has a large number of bars, which the locals claim date back to the days when there was no running water so everyone drank wine instead – it seems that a taste for alcohol persists. You can drink anywhere in the Old Town without worrying about the handful of drunks who loiter around the bus station.

**Cukrarna** Tavčarjeva 9; tel: 04 281 8290. Bright and hip café with a children's area and terrace with mountain views to the rear. It also sells mouth-watering cakes and ice-creams.

**Stara Pošta** Koroška 2; tel: 04 202 6075. Trendy 4th-floor bar with good views from its small outdoor terrace.

**Afrika Bar** Cankarjeva 5. Hidden behind a hairdressers, with African artefacts and a small inner courtyard.

**Pub Palustris** Reginčeva 4. Cross between an Irish pub and an Australian bar, with Kilkenny and Guinness on draught, a crocodile skin on the ceiling and raised outdoor terrace.

**The Old House** Na Skali 5. Café-bar with a lively outdoor terrace.

## Practicalities

**Tourist Information Centre** Koroška 29; tel: 04 236 3030; fax: 04 236 3031; email: td.kranj@siol.net; www.turisticnodrustvo-kranj.si. Open: Mon–Fri 08.00–19.00, Sat 08.00–12.00. Internet access.

**Post office** Poštna ulica 4. Open: Mon–Fri 07.00–15.00.

**Banks** There is a cluster of banks on Koroška near the entrance to the Old Town including Ljubljanska Banka at No 2.

## What to see
### A walking tour

The compact Old Town is the place to base all your sightseeing, though consider starting your exploration at the imposing **Water Tower**, located at the junction of Oldhamska, Kokrskega odreda and Partizanska street, from where the short walk south to the Old Town takes you through a green and appealing residential district. Keeping the Kokra River on your left you will come across France Prešeren's last resting place, **Prešernov Gaj** (Prešeren Grave) in a small cemetery. His tomb was paid for with local donations and it is the most impressive in the cemetery, which also features the graves of rich local families and various Kranj luminaries.

Continue south down Gregoričiceva and after five minutes you will come to **Maistrov trg**, the divide between Kranj's dodgy socialist-era architecture and its more appealing Old Town. You are now on the promontory that proved a successful natural protective ring for the city for centuries, with the Kokra River running to your left and the Sava to your right. The confluence of the rivers marks the furthest extremity of the Old Town, and is just a short walk south at Pungert.

The **Prešernova Hiša** (Prešeren's House; tel: 04 201 3950. Open: Tue–Fri 10.00–12.00 and 17.00–19.00, Sat–Sun 10.00–12.00 May–Sep, Tue–Fri 10.00–12.00 and 16.00–18.00, Sat–Sun 10.00–12.00 Oct–Apr. 500SIT) is at Prešernov 7. In 2002 the bard's former residence reopened after a much-needed revamp and now it has English-language information boards to help guide visitors through. This is no fusty old museum and the ground level and late-Gothic cellar are given over to temporary exhibitions by innovative domestic artists. The exhibits dedicated to Prešeren himself are on the first floor and spread through various rooms occupied by the poet during his tenure here from late 1846 to February 1849, when he served as the city's first independent lawyer.

The museum's text – displayed on boards that are not attached to the walls due to a preservation order that bans any changes to the house – chronicle Prešeren's life, from his school years through to his death and also, of course, his infatuation with Julija Primic. Slightly unnerving sounds of hollering and coughing, which are supposed to convey the writer's anguish, add to the atmosphere. Exhibits include Prešeren's bed, desk, diaries and even the original entry of his birth in the city's register. The museum staff hope to open up the attic as an extra display area, but they say their hands are tied by a legal wrangle over rights to what is currently a defunct space.

Continue south and you will soon come to Glavni trg with its jumble of Gothic and Renaissance buildings. The standout is perhaps the **Mestna Hiša/Gorenjski Muzej** (Town Hall/Gorenjska Museum) (Glavni trg 4; tel: 04 201 3950. Open: Tue–Fri 10.00–12.00 and 17.00–1900, Sat–Sun 10.00–12.00 May–Sep, Tue–Fri 10.00–12.00 and 16.00–18.00, Sat–Sun 10.00–12.00 Oct–Apr. 500SIT), which, like Prešeren's house, was originally two buildings and now performs twin functions as a civic space for weddings and other events and as the **Gorenjska Museum**. There are two floors of exhibition space with a rather dated series of displays on the evolution of man in the Kranj area (though it does have some interesting artefacts), as well as an exhibit on iron production in the region. The small room used for weddings has a stunning baroque wooden ceiling and two

Renaissance porches. Look out also for the early Slavic graves that are visible through transparent panels in the floor of the vestibule and which date back as far as the 9th century.

The next building of note is the **Cerkev Sv Kancijan** (Church of St Cantianus) just a short distance further along Glavni trg. The first church on the site dates back to the 6th century, but today's incarnation is based upon a Gothic model that has been added to down the centuries. The central design, with its nave and aisles of equal height, was taken up as a template in Cerknica, Radlovljica and Škofja Loka. Also look out for 15th-century frescos depicting angelic musicians, and an organ whose chest dates back to the mid-19th century and which was refurbished in 2002. If your visit to the town hall did not satiate your interest in Slavic bones then below the northern flank of the church is an ossuary. It is officially closed, but if you ask nicely at the town hall or tourist office they may be able to arrange a brief visit. Plans have been mooted to reopen the small ossuary with a more modern display, but nothing definite has been agreed upon.

Take a minute to look at the two statues on the south side of the church. Beside the church itself you will see a priest being dragged into the Sava by an octopus as a distraught woman stands at the side. The towering Tito-like figure that looms outside the **Prešeren Theatre** is supposed to be Prešeren.

There is also a story behind the fountain that marks the beginning of Glavni trg. Erected in 1998 to replace a fountain that had been standing on the spot since 1836, today's incarnation is the work of local designer and eccentric Marko Pogacnik. According to Pogacnik the fountain stands on a spot where supernatural powers infuse Kranj with positive energy, and the artist believed that this energy had the power to 'heal the earth'. This seems to raise a wry smile from the locals, who evidently don't share Pogacnik's off-the-wall optimism. The two streams of water spurting from the fountain represent the Kokra and Sava rivers.

As you continue down the street it becomes Cankarjeva and then merges with Tavčarjeva where the Old Town comes to an abrupt end at Pungert. Here there is a small park and a viewing platform that looks out on to the Kokra River. More noteworthy though is the city's old defence tower, the crumbling remains of Kranj's Old Town wall and the **Srbska Pravoslavna Cerkev** (Serbian Orthodox Church). The building itself dates back to the 15th century, but it didn't become a centre of the Serbian faith until the 20th century when the Serbian Orthodox Church was established.

Retracing your steps bear left at the Plečnik Fountain on to Tomšičeva. To the left, behind a wrought-iron gate, you will find the **Kieselstein Grad** (Kieselstein Castle), more a manor house than a castle. Sections of the Old Town wall can be found in Kieselstein's courtyard and it is a venue for many of the city's cultural events as well as the permanent home of Kranj's **Puppet Theatre**. There are also outdoor cultural events here in the summer months.

## RADOVLJICA

Radovljica enjoys an enviable location just east of the confluence of the two main forks of the Sava River, with its Old Town perched on what was once the terminal moraine for the Bohinj glacier and the Julian Alps rising dramatically to the west on a clear day. Written mentions of Radovljica can be traced as far back as the 11th century and its golden age came before the arrival of the Austro–Hungarians, when it flourished as a major market town and trading hub in the 15th and 16th centuries. The Old Town is the most interesting district, basically consisting of one main square with a liberal sprinkling of fine baroque, Gothic and Renaissance architecture. If you are en route to Bled, Radovljica is worth at least half a day of your time.

## Getting there

Radovljica **railway station** (Cesta Svobode) can be reached by train from Lesce-Bled (5 minutes), Kranj (20 minutes), Škofja Loka (35 minutes) and Ljubljana (55 minutes). Buses run to the **bus station** on Kranjska from Bled (15 minutes), Kropa (20 minutes), Ljubljana (1¼ hours), Kranjska Gora (1 hour 25 minutes), Ribčev Laz for Lake Bohinj (45 minutes).

## Where to stay

**Hotel Grajski Dvor** Krajinska 2; tel: 04 531 5585; fax: 04 531 5878; email: info@hotel-grajski-dvor.si; www.hotel-grajski-dvor.si. Many of the hotel's rooms are recently renovated and upgraded so ask for one of these. Singles 7,900–8,900SIT, doubles 11,800–13,800SIT.
**Gostilna Kunstelj** Gorenjska 9; tel: 04 531 5178; fax: 04 530 4151; email: kunstelj@siol.net; www.kunstelj.com. Friendly and welcoming *gostilna* on the edge of the Old Town with decent food options and comfortable rooms.
**Camping Radovljica** Kopališka 9; tel/fax: 04 531 5770; email: pkrad@plavalniklub-radovljica.si. This small campsite enjoys a pleasant forest location and guests can use the adjacent 50m outdoor swimming pool. 1,400SIT per person.
**Camping Šobec** Šobečeva 25; tel: 04 535 3700; fax: 04 535 3701; email: sobec@siol.net; www.sobec.si. Large and pleasantly located campsite in Lesce, just 2.5km from Radovljica, offering myriad activities. Wooden bungalows sleeping up to 6 can be rented for a minimum of 7 days. Camping 2,100–2,400SIT per person, bungalows 19,600–29,400SIT per week.
**Grad Podvin** Mošnje 1; tel: 04 532 5200; fax: 04 532 5250; www.robas.si/grad-podvin. The castle, 4km from Radovljica, offers compact and functional rather than luxurious rooms. It also has indoor and outdoor tennis courts and an open-air swimming pool. Singles 11,000–12,000SIT, doubles 14,000–15,000SIT, suites 18,000–20,000SIT (cheaper if you stay for at least 3 days).

## Where to eat

**Grajska Gostilnica** Kranjska 2; tel: 04 531 4445. The tempting menu at the Hotel Grajski Dvor's stylish new restaurant fuses Italian and Slovenian cuisine.
**Pivnica Avgustin** Linhartov trg 15; tel: 04 531 4163. Serving good-value and hearty Slovenian food. Make sure you go through to the restaurant or terrace at the back with its views over the gorge.
**Gostilna Lectar** Linhartov trg 2; tel: 04 537 4800. At the heart of the Old Town but without the spectacular views of Avgustin. A local favourite.

## Shopping

**Vinoteka Sodček** Linhartov trg 8; tel: 04 531 5071. Wine shop selling a wide selection of Slovenian wines.

**Kulturnica Blaž Kumerdej** Linhartov trg 3; tel: 04 531 5100. Sells Slovenian wines, spirits, liqueurs – including the famous pear brandy produced by monks at the Pleterje Monastery – vinegars, honey and cheese.

## Practicalities

**Tourist Information Centre** Gorenjska 1; tel: 04 531 5300; email: tdradovljica@siol.net. Open: Mon–Fri 08.00–18.00, Sat 08.00–12.00.
**Post office** Kranjska 1. Open: Mon–Fri 07.00–19.00, Sat 07.00–12.00.

## What to see

In 2003 the local authorities finally got around to banning parking in the rectangular Linhartov trg, named after Radovljica's greatest son (18th-century Slovene dramatist Anton Tomaž Linhart), greatly enhancing the appeal of one of the most attractive historic quarters in Slovenia. On the right-hand side of the square is the **Šivčeva Hiša** (Šivec House; No 22) with its 17th-century mural on the façade exterior, late-Gothic entrance hall and vaulted ceiling – all features that were typical of Gorenjska at this time. Šivec these days has been given a new lease of life as a gallery, which is home to an eclectic range of temporary exhibitions. Other notable buildings include the **Vidičeva Hiša** (Vidič House), also with a mural façade and this time with a fountain as well, and the **Linhartov Hiša** (Linhart House), with a plaque noting that this was the writer's birthplace. At the furthest end of Linhartov trg is the rather shabby **Cerkev Sv Petra** (Church of St Peter), which was originally Romanesque though it was given a late-Gothic makeover. The sculptures by Angelo Pozzo on the baroque high altar and the fresco of St Christopher are also worth popping inside for.

Back around the corner on Linhartov trg, to the right is Radovljica's main tourist attraction, the **Čebelarski Muzej** (Beekeeping Museum; Linhartov trg 1; tel: 04 532 0520. Closed Jan–Feb. Open: Tue–Sun 10.00–12.00 and 15.00-17.00 Mar–Dec), which is housed in a baroque manor house. While spending an hour or so studying bees may not seem too alluring this really is a first-class museum and few leave disappointed. Although you can learn everything you never knew you wanted to know about bees and their lives, especially the local Carniolan Grey Bee, perhaps the most interesting sections are those displaying the traditional painted beehives, mainly from the golden age of beekeeping in the 18th and 19th centuries, which are artworks in themselves. Handily most exhibits are labelled in English.

## KROPA

From the 14th to the 20th centuries this picturesque village, whose name translates as 'boiling water', was awake with the sound of clanging and hammering as one of Slovenia's leading iron-forging centres. Furnaces blazed day and night as the river Koprarca was diverted to power no fewer than 50 water wheels and the local forests harvested to fire the smelters. Kropa's fame extended beyond Slovenia and its 100-plus varieties of nails and myriad other items were in demand all over

Europe. By the mid-18th century Kropa's only real industry was firmly in decline as domestic iron-ore deposits dried up and increasing competition put the remote village out of touch. The Plamen factory, which you can still see in the village today, staggered on until 1997 when it switched to automobile-parts production. Today Kropa's new industry is tourism, which has helped keep some of the craftsmen in employment and ensured that Kropa's heritage is not forgotten altogether.

## Getting there

Kropa is just 10km from Radovljica on a winding, tree-lined narrow road – head in the direction of Lesce and then turn left at the sign and you will come to it after a ramble of countryside. If you are travelling by bus the journey takes around 20 minutes.

## What to see

The main square, the *Plac*, is a good place to start exploring and there is space to park just downhill. If you are really keen to delve into Kropa's forging history make the effort to head up the hillside to the **Slovenian Smelting Furnace**, which dates back to the 14th century when it was capable of producing 100kg of iron for forging in ten hours with the help of 800kg of charcoal. You can see iron wherever you look in Kropa – look out in particular for the trademark dragons, which were said to ward off evil spirits outside many of the village's houses.

From here cross the bridge by the waterfall slightly upstream and descend to **Gostilna Pr' Kovač**, a good place to stop for a drink and try to conjure up Kropa's old days – most of the clanging may be gone, but the rushing waters of the river and its diverted channels still echo all around. As you pass the Plac you will see the sturdy Resistance Monument, which was forged in the village in 1965 as a tribute to the local people who were heavily involved in fighting Axis forces in World War II. Stick to the right bank of the river as you tumble down the hillside and watch out for traffic whose sound the water tends to drown out. After decades of decline many of Kropa's charming houses are now being touched up and returned to their original bright selves with strong Renaissance and baroque touches.

Soon you will come across the **Kovaški Muzej** (Blacksmith's Museum; Kropa 10; tel: 04 533 6717. Open: Tue–Sun 10,00–13.00 and 15.00–18.00. 300SIT) on the right, which is housed in the attractive **Klinar Hiša** (Klinar House). Inside are models of a working forge as well as a scale model of Kropa in the early 19th century. The museum gives an idea of the scope of the village's production – everything from tiny tacks for snow boots right through to hulking industrial spikes for hammering sections of concrete together. A real highlight is the exhibition of works by Joža Bertoncelj, one of Kropa's most renowned iron sculptors. Guided tours of the museum are available in advance and if you call ahead they may even consider opening the museum up especially for you.

Across the road is the **Umetniško Kovaštvo** (UKO Forger's Workshop; Kropa 7b and 7a; tel: 04 533 7300) and a store where today's craftsmen sell their work. In the visitors' book are some complaints about the expense, but prices for those unique souvenirs are reasonable when you consider that this is niche not mass production and you are buying a piece of history. Similar souvenirs on sale elsewhere in Slovenia generally cost 30–50% more.

## BREZJE

The hamlet of Brezje, the 'National Shrine of Slovenia', whose population is only around 500, is worth visiting principally to see the **Marija Pomagaj** (Basilica of the Virgin Mary). Today's church has been evolving since the 15th century, with the latest and most significant addition being the Chapel of the Virgin Mary in 1880. Inside the chapel you will find Layer's *Madonna and Child*, which Slovenes believe has miraculous powers, making this one of the country's biggest places of pilgrimage for over 100 years.

### Getting there

Brezje can be reached by bus from Bled and Ljubljana.

## BLED

Despite the best efforts of the gaggle of socialist-era hotels that litter its banks there is no denying the ethereal beauty of Lake Bled, which national Slovene bard France Prešeren once eulogised as 'this second Eden, full of charm and grace'. Early in the morning as the mists clear and the bells ring out from the famous island church in the middle of the lake there are few better places to be in Europe, with hulking alpine peaks rising all around and birds joining in the celebration of the new day. Throughout the day *pletna* (gondolas) ferry tourists to the church while Bled's wash of restaurants and bars switch on to the needs of the increasing number of foreign visitors. Somehow Bled is never spoiled and there is always an escape, whether it be setting off for a stroll around the lake, finding a quiet spot to lean against a tree and listen to the lapping of the water, or taking a rowing boat out on Slovenia's most famous stretch of water and one of Europe's most picturesque lakes.

### History

In 2004 Bled celebrated its millennium – the first written mention of the settlement came in 1004 when it was awarded to the bishop of Brixen. Over the following centuries pilgrims flocked to Bled, ensuring that the town had a constant stream of income. In the late 19th and early 20th centuries Bled re-emerged as a popular spa resort: the moneyed classes of the Austro-Hungarian Empire were attracted by its climate and the lake's waters, which are said to have curative and restorative properties. The success was largely due to new railways from Italy and Austria and the efforts of one Dr Arnold Rikli, who built a bathing area here and spent the best part of half a century extolling the virtues of Bled. After World War II the new regime in the region held Bled in such high esteem that Tito chose it as the site of his summer retreat, a place to relax and the perfect venue for entertaining his illustrious guests. These days Bled owes much of its continued success to the fact that it is an easy drive from Ljubljana and the Italian and Austrian borders. Bled has been part of the Triglav National Park since the latter's inception in 1906 and further development in the area is now carefully controlled.

> ### THE BAPTISM ON THE SAVICA
> The action in France Prešeren's masterpiece *The Baptism on the Savica* takes place in Bohinj and Bled. The poem vividly depicts the battle between the Germanic-Christian army and an early Slovene pagan army at a fortress where Bled Castle stands today. After the fighting comes the baptism at the Slap Savica (Savica Waterfalls) in Bohinj. The subtext of the writing is the notion that while the Slovenes accepted the Christian faith they rejected Germanic rule, when Prešeren wrote this, Slovenia was under Habsburg rule, therefore this clearly had political connotations at the time. At various places within the poem the reader's attention is also drawn to the beauty of Lake Bled, which Prešeren refers to as 'paradise serene.'

## Getting there
Regular buses serve Bled from Ljubljana (1¼ hours), Ribčev Laz/Lake Bohinj (40 minutes) and Radovljica (15 minutes). Trains from Ljubljana (45 minutes–1 hour), which go via Škofja Loka (35 minutes), Kranj (25 minutes) and Radovljica (5 minutes) also stop at Lesce-Bled. Lesce-Bled station is around 4km from the centre of Bled; buses that connect the two run every 30 minutes and take 10–15 minutes. The closest railway station to the centre of Bled is Bled Jezero (1.5km out of town), which is served by trains from Bohinj (20 minutes).

**Lesce-Bled Train Station** Zelezniska 12, Lesce; tel: 04 531 8384
**Bus station** Cesta Svobode 4; tel: 04 574 1114
**Bled Jezero Train Station** Koldovorska 50; tel: 04 294 2363

## Getting around
**Taxi** Tel: 031 205 6111
**Tourist train** Tacky and not cheap, this train circles Lake Bled during the tourist season. Running from 09.00 until almost 21.00, it does provide access to the restaurants and bars around town if you are staying somewhere more remote. Fare 550SIT.

## Tour operators
**ProMontana** Ljubljanska 1; tel: 04 574 2605; fax: 04 201 4878; email: bled@promontana.si; www.promontana.si. Outdoor specialist offering hiking, trekking, climbing, caving, canyoning, kayaking, rafting and mountain-biking from Bled and Bohinj.
**Kompas Bled** Ljubljanska 4; tel: 04 574 1515; fax: 04 574 1518; email: info@kompas-bled.si; www.kompas-bled.si. Accommodation and excursions.
**M Tours** Prešernova 3; tel: 04 575 3300; fax: 04 575 3311; email: mtours@mtours.net. Full tourist service.
**Triglav National Park** Kidričeva 2; tel: 04 574 1188; fax: 04 574 3568; email: triglavski-narodni-park@tnp.gov.si; www.sigov.si/tnp. Day trips and overnight guided tours.

## Where to stay
**Grand Hotel Toplice** (87 rooms) Cesta Svobode 12; tel: 04 579 1000; fax: 04 574 1841; email: info@hotel-toplice.com; www.hotel-toplice.com. Bled's only five-star

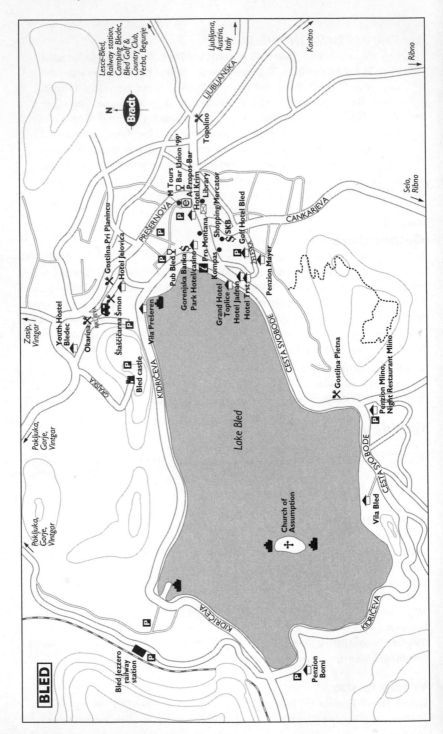

hotel, with a thermal pool, sauna, steam room and Turkish bath, is surprisingly good value for money. Make sure you book a lake-view room. Even if you are not staying come to the lounge for a coffee and a *kremna rezina* and just take in the view. Singles 24,000–28,800SIT, lake-view singles 31,200–40,800SIT, doubles 31,200SIT–36,000SIT, lake-view doubles 38,400–48,000SIT, suites 50,400–60,000SIT.

**Vila Bled** (30 rooms) Cesta Svobode 26; tel: 04 579 1500; fax: 04 574 1320; email: hotel@vila-bled.com; www.vila-bled.com. Tito's ghost still haunts this palatial lakeside villa, which was once his favourite retreat. You can even send emails from his old desk. The hotel was recently impressively refurbished with the addition of the health spa in the basement, though a severe storm in summer 2004 put things back a bit. An unforgettable place to stay. Singles 28,800–33,600SIT, doubles 38,400–43,200SIT, suites 43,200–57,600SIT, Presidential suite 96,000SIT

**Hotel Jadran** (45 rooms) Cesta Svobode 12; tel: 04 579 1000; fax: 04 574 1841; email: info@hotel-toplice.com; www.hotel-toplice.com. Pleasant three-star hotel in the centre of town with balconied rooms. Singles 10,800–13,200SIT, lake-view singles 15,600–18,000SIT, doubles 14,400–16,800SIT, lake-view doubles 19,200–21,600SIT.

**Park Hotel** (217 rooms) Cesta Svobode 15; tel: 04 579 3000; fax: 04 574 1505; email: recpark@gp-hoteli-bled.si; www.hotel-park-bled-com. Enormous hotel with a thermal pool, small fitness centre, sauna and solarium. Rooms are modern and comfortable and many have views of the lake. Singles 17,100–21,200SIT, lake-view singles 18,600–22,600SIT, doubles 23,200–27,600SIT, lake-view doubles 25,600–30,000SIT.

**Hotel Trst** (32 rooms) Cesta Svobode 19; tel: 04 579 1000; fax: 04 574 1841; info@hotel-toplice.com; www.hotel-toplice.com. Ask for a lake-view room with a balcony. Singles 10,800–13,200SIT, lake-view singles 15,600 18,000SIT, doubles 14,400–16,800SIT, lake-view doubles 19,200–21,600SIT.

**Penzion Mayer** Želeška 7; tel: 04 574 1059; fax: 04 576 5741; email: pension@mayer-sp.si; www.mayer-sp.si. Four-star pension with pleasant en-suite rooms. Singles 9,600SIT, doubles 14,400–18,000SIT.

**Penzion Mlino** (29 rooms) Cesta Svobode 45; tel: 04 574 1404; fax: 04 574 1506; email: mlino@mlino.si; www.mlino.si. Guesthouse in a more secluded location close to Vila Bled with good food and simple rooms. Singles 7,650 8,850SIT, doubles 12,000–14,400SIT.

**Penzion Bomi** (7 rooms) Kidriceva 12; tel: 04 574 3594; email: bomi@siol.net. Pleasant alpine-style guesthouse in an elevated position at the southwestern extremity of Lake Bled. All rooms have their own balconies and three have lake views.

**Youth Hostel Bledec** (13 rooms) Grajska 17; tel: 04 574 5250; fax: 04 574 5251; email: bledec@mlino.si; www.mlino.si. Light and clean accommodation in mainly three- or four-bed rooms, with doubles/twins and bunks. A great location, its own restaurant, bar and internet access led one traveller to eulogise in the guestbook: 'This is the best hostel I have ever stayed at.' 3,600–4,800SIT per person.

**Camping Bledec** Kidričeva 10c; tel: 04 575 2000; fax: 04 575 2020; email: info@camping.bled.si; www.camping.bled.si. Campsite 2km from Bled town with restaurant, grocery store and bungalows to rent. Guests can use the internet connection in the camp's reception and rent bikes and sports equipment. 1,580–2,320SIT per person, bungalows 13,300–15,300SIT.

**Vila Prešeren** Kidričeva 1; tel: 04 578 0800; fax: 04 578 0810; email: vila.preseren@siol.net; www.vila.preseren.s5.net. Upscale guesthouse with lakeside location and a good fish restaurant. The suite is a real step above the rest of the rooms with a Jacuzzi bath and private balcony overlooking Lake Bled. Singles 12,000–13,200SIT, lake-view singles 13,920–16,320SIT, doubles 16,080–17,280SIT, lakeview doubles 18,720–21,120SIT, suite 26,880–36,940SIT.

**Golf Hotel Bled** (150 rooms) Cankarjeva 4; tel: 04 579 2000; fax: 04 574 1768; email: recgolf@gp-hoteli-bled.si; www.gp-hoteli-bled.si. Renovated in 2003 the hotel has large guest rooms with balconies. The Golf also has thermal pools, a sauna and a golf course. Singles 18,500–22,600SIT, lake-view singles 19,500–23,600SIT, doubles 25,600–30,000SIT, lake-view doubles 27,200–31,400SIT, suites 33,200–52,400SIT.

**Hotel Krim** (115 rooms) Ljubljanska 7; tel: 04 579 7000; fax: 04 574 3729; email: prodaja@hotel-krim.si; www.hotel-krim.si. Package hotel located 100m from the lake with light and pleasant enough rooms. Singles 8,880–12,700SIT, doubles 12,960–20,600SIT.

**Hotel Jelovica** (100 rooms) Cesta Svobode 8; tel: 04 579 6000; fax: 04 574 1550; email: jelovica@hotel-jelovica.si; www.hotel-jelovica.si. Separated from the lake by a park the hotel has decent rooms and good facilities including a health centre with swimming pool, a bar and a restaurant. Singles 9,360–12,960SIT, doubles 12,960–20,160SIT.

## Where to eat

**Night Restaurant Mlino** Cesta Svobode 45; tel: 04 574 1404. Late-night eatery serving tasty traditional food.

**Kings Club House** Kidričeva 10c; tel: 04 537 8300; email: clubhouse@golf.bled.si; www.golf.bled.si. Recently revamped restaurant with a terrace overlooking the golf course. A Mediterranean-influenced menu with generous and tasty portions. There are also 9 luxurious rooms and suites.

**Vila Prešeren** (see *Where to stay*). On warm summer evenings this is the place to come for romantic views of the lake. Dining inside is not nearly as pleasant, as the service can be a bit hit-and-miss. Trout with garlic and herb sauce is a good bet.

**Gostilna Pri Planincu** Grajska 8; tel: 04 574 1613. Homely pub-style set-up with more tables through the back and an outdoor terrace. Although it has no views this eatery, serving hearty local food, is popular with locals and tourists.

**Okarina** Riklijeva 9; tel: 04 574 1458. Serving a mixture of Indian and Slovenian dishes in pleasant surrounds and with separate dining rooms for smokers and non-smokers, and a candlelit terrace to the rear. Fresh chilli sauces add extra spice to tikka and masala dishes cooked for Slovenian palates.

**Topolino** Ljubljanska 26; tel: 04 574 1781. Highly recommended by the locals, serving a good-quality mix of Hungarian- and Italian-influenced Slovenian food.

**Park Hotel** (see *Where to stay*). The menu at the hotel's funky new restaurant fuses Slovene and Mediterranean flavours with starters like rocket with beef fillet and seafood risotto. Fresh fish dishes and grilled meat comprise the mains and the *kremna rezina* is divine.

**Penzion Mayer** (see *Where to stay*). Platters of Slovenian cheese and *pršut* and excellent boiled trout have helped this restaurant earn its well-deserved reputation for good food.

**Gostilna Pletna** Cesta Svobode 37; tel: 04 574 3702. Cheap and cheerful *gostilna* in Mlino serving pizzas and grills.

**Mercator** Ljubljanska 4. Supermarket in the shopping centre.
**Šlaščičarna Šmon** Grajska 3 and Ljubljanska 11. Many Slovenes will tell you that this pastry shop sells the best *kremna rezina* in the country.

## Entertainment and nightlife
**Gostilna Pri Planincu** (see *Where to eat*). Old-Worldy pub with bags of atmosphere, especially popular with backpackers.
**Grand Hotel Toplice Café** Cesta Svobode 12a; tel: 04 579 1000. Great views of the lake and a refined atmosphere, all very regal. Great place for a *kremna rezina* cream cake.
**Bled Shopping Centre** Unsightly shopping complex with a few rowdy bars; Café Latino is slightly more appealing than the rest. Opposite Park Hotel.
**Casino Bled** Cesta Svobode 15; tel: 04 574 1811; www.casino-bled.si. This is the place to come if you're feeling lucky or fancy a big night out. Open: daily 15.00–05.00.
**Pub Bled** Cesta Svobode 19a; tel: 04 574 2622. Popular pub with live music, DJs, cocktails and friendly staff.

## Practicalities
### Tourist information
**Tourist Information Centre** Cesta Svobode 15; tel: 04 574 1122; fax: 04 574 1555; email: td-bled@g-kabel.si; www.bled.si. Open: Mon–Sat 08.00–21.00, Sun 10.00–21.00 Jul–Aug, Mon–Sat 08.00–19.00, Sun 11.00–18.00 Jun and Sep, Mon–Sat 09.00–21.00, Sun 11.00–16.00 Oct and Mar–May, Mon–Sat 09.00–17.00, Sun 12.00–16.00 Nov–Feb.

### Communications
The post office (Ljubljanska 10; tel: 04 578 0900) is open Monday–Friday 07.00–19.00, and Saturday 07.00–12.00.

### Internet access
**Bled Library** Ljubljanska 10
**Hotel Jelovica** Cesta Svobode 8; tel: 04 579 6000
**Hotel Kompas** Cankarjeva 2; tel: 04 578 2100
**Hotel Astoria** Prešernova 44; tel: 04 574 1144
**Hotel Krim** Ljubljanska 7; tel: 04 579 7000
**A Propos Bar** Ljubljanska 4; tel: 04 574 4044
**Bar Union '99** Ljubljanska 9; tel: 04 578 0119

### Banks
**Gorenjska Banka** Cesta Svobode 15; tel: 04 574 1300. Open: Mon–Fri 09.00–11.30 and 14.00–17.00, Sat 08.00–11.00. In Park Hotel shopping arcade.
**SKB Banka** Ljubljanska 4. Open: Mon–Fri 08.30–12.00 and 14.00–17.00. In Bled Shopping Centre.

## What to see
### Cerkev Marijinega Vnebovzetja (Church of the Assumption)
The tiny Church of the Assumption, set adrift on the small island in the middle of the lake, is perhaps Bled's best-known and most alluring sight. Today's structure dates

back to the late 17th century, but evidence suggests that there has been a church on Bled Island since the 9th century, and that before this the picture-postcard island was a Stone-Age burial ground. Look out for the remnants of the 15th-century frescos and a wooden statue of the Madonna dating from the same period.

To reach the church take a gondola from Mlino or from the jetties near the Grand Hotel Toplice on the eastern shore. From the quay on the island you then have to climb the 99 steps to the top. If you are staying at Vila Bled a more romantic way to visit the island is to get up early and row over to the island yourself, using one of the hotel's own boats. An early-morning visit will also save you from the clamour to ring the bell in the 15th-century belfry, which is supposed to help your wishes come true. The church is a favourite wedding spot for foreigners as well as Slovenians (contact Bled Catholic Parish for details; Riklijeva 26; tel: 04 574 4046).

### Blejski Grad (Bled Castle)

Presiding majestically from a rocky outcrop 139m above the lake is one of Slovenia's most impressive castles (Grajska 25; tel: 04 574 1230). There are tourist trains up here in summer as well as car-parking space, but if you are feeling energetic take on the heart-pumping trek. Even before the bishop of Brixen arrived in the area there was already said to have been a fortification on the strategically important site, though today's incarnation is largely the result of a 20th-century revamp. Romanesque elements can still be found in the walls, and late-Gothic in the chapel. The **museum** illuminates the eclectic history of both the castle and the Bled region in general, while visitors can pick up a hand-pressed certificate to say they have been to Bled Castle. On a sunny day relaxing in the café with the mountains and lake spreading out into the distance is the real pleasure. Classical music concerts are also held at the castle on summer nights.

*Open: 08.00–20.00 May–Sep and 09.00–17.00 Oct–Apr. 800SIT, concessions 500SIT.*

### Walk around the lake

There is no better way to appreciate Lake Bled than to stroll along the easy path that hugs its banks. A good place to start is at the Grand Hotel Toplice so that in moments of tiredness you can dream of returning here at the end for coffee and a *kremna rezina*, the delicious vanilla-and-fresh-cream cake that they serve in their opulent waterfront café. As you head west you spend a short section by the main road, which is not too pleasant with tour buses rattling by in summer, but as you pass the hamlet of Mlino the path heads back down to the lake and then on to the grounds of the recently refurbished Vila Bled, Tito's old summer home. Soon after the Vila the path becomes a wooden walkway with the lake lapping against it and beech and chestnut trees overhanging the water. Looking back east is the church on the island – this is a good place for photographs as sunset approaches.

Continuing clockwise the path passes a small watersports centre and campground before coming across Slovenia's only rowing club at Zaka (www.vesl-klub-bled.si), which was the base for Slovenia's two gold-medal rowers at the Sydney 2000 Olympics. As you circle back round, the view changes again and Bled town starts to get lost behind the trees as the path meanders past the grand holiday homes of Slovenia's rich and famous. In summer the final approach to Bled town is awash with the clamour from the bathing area below the path – if you want to escape take the path to the right that is signposted 'Grad 1' and which leads up in a steep ascent to the castle. Coming back into town the hustle and bustle of the resort soon engulfs you before the respite of a neatly laid-out park by the eastern shores of the lake. Take a pew here to appreciate the effort of the serious rowers who hammer up and down the marker lanes in the centre of the lake. By now you should have worked up enough of an appetite to fully appreciate a *kremna rezina* so head into the café of the Grand Hotel Toplice (no muddy boots or beachwear allowed) and savour this wonderfully sugary treat as you admire the views.

### Blejski Vintgar (Vintgar Gorge)

The trek to Vintgar Gorge, located just 4km from Bled, is an easy and rewarding one. If you are stuck for time however you might want to drive to the car park, or time your visit to coincide with one of the local buses. The gorge runs for over 1.5km and cuts deep into the rock. It is, of course, at its best after heavy rain, though it can be slippery at these times and extra care should be taken. A series of walkways guide visitors and the path is easy to follow.
*Open: daily 08.00–19.00 mid-Apr–Mar. 600SIT, concessions 300SIT.*

# BOHINJ

A pleasant 26km drive south of Lake Bled, following the path of the Sava Bohinjska River, is glacial Lake Bohinj. Slovenia's largest lake (5km wide by 10km long) is if anything even more dramatic than Lake Bled: a wider, longer and wilder expanse of alpine water that snakes away towards the looming hulk of Triglav. While the most accessible end of Lake Bohinj has a straggle of tourist developments and is plied by lake cruises, development is on a much less obvious scale and this is the place to come for a get-away-from-it-all break, without all the frills of Bled.

## History

The area around the lake, encompassing half a dozen small villages and the tourist base of Ribčev Laz, is known as Bohinj. Human habitation here can be traced as far back as the Iron Age. The first written mention of Bohinj came later than Bled in 1070 when Germanic settlers arrived. The prevalence of iron ore boosted the local economy by the 16th century and when it started to wane in the 19th century tourism was already emerging in an embryonic form with Viennese tourists visiting here from health retreats in Bled.

## Getting there

Lake Bohinj is 26km from Bled and the lake and nearby villages are an easy 20-minute drive away. Buses connect Ribčev Laz to Stara Fužina (10 minutes), Studor (10 minutes), Bohinjska Bistrica (15 minutes), Bled (40 minutes) and Ljubljana (1¾ hours). Trains from Bled Jezero (20 minutes) and Nova Gorica (1 hour 20 minutes) stop at Bohinjska Bistrica. There is also a car-train service (tel: 041 320 973) between Bohinjska Bistrica and Most na Soči, via Podbrdo, which cuts through the mountains between the Gorenjska and Primorska regions.

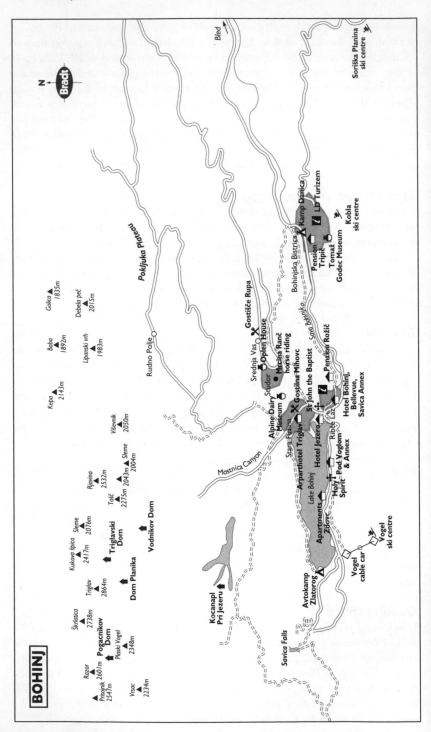

BOHINJ

*Bled*

Soriška Planina
ski centre

Kamp Danica

LD Turizem

Kobla
ski centre

Pension
Triplč
Tomaž
Godec Museum

Bohinjska Bistrica

Gostišče Rupa

Srednja Vas
Oplen House

Mrcina Ranč
horse riding

Studor

Penzion Rožič

Gostilna Mihovc

St John the Baptist

Alpine Dairy
Museum

Hotel Bohinj,
Bellevue,
Savica Annex

Stara Fužina

Arparthotel Triglav

Ribče

Hotel Jezero

Mostnica Canyon

Pod Voglom
& Annex

Holy
Spirit

Apartments

Zlatorog

Lake Bohinj

Vogel
cable car

Vogel
ski centre

Artokamp
Zlatorog

Kocanapl
Pri Jezeru

Savica Falls

Pokljuka Plateau

Rudno Polje

*Golica*
1835m

*Debela peč*
2015m

*Baba*
1892m

*Lipanski vrh*
1983m

*Kepa*
2143m

*Viševnik*
2050m

*Rjavina*
2532m

*Tosč*
2275m  2043m *Sleme*
2004m

Vodnikov Dom

*Kukova špica*
2417m  *Sleme*
2076m

Triglavski
Dom

*Triglav*
2864m

Dom Planika

*Škrlatica*
2738m

*Plaski Vogel*
2348m

Pogacnikov
Dom

*Razor*
2601m

*Prisojnik*
2547m

*Vrsac*
2234m

## Getting around
### By bus
During high season (June–September) buses run from Bohinjska Bistrica to the Savica Waterfall, picking up at the Hotel Jezero in Ribčev Laz on the way. A bus service also runs from Stara Fužina to the falls via the Hotel Jezero.

### Bicycle hire
This is a great way to get around if you don't have your own transport. Various tour operators in Bohinj rent out bicycles and mountain-bikes.

### Tour operators
**Alpinum** Ribčev Laz 50; tel: 04 577 8000; fax: 04 572 3446; email: info@alpinum.net; www.alpinum.net. Tourist agency offering camping and hotel accommodation alongside an extensive list of summer and winter sports, including mountain-biking, paragliding, hiking, skiing and ice-climbing.
**Pac Sports** Ribčev Laz 50; tel: 041 698 523; email: info@pac-sports.com; www.pac-sports.com. Offering paragliding, rafting, canyoning, hydrospeed, mountain-biking and kayaking amongst other sports. They also rent out mountain-bikes, kayaks, canoes and rafts.
**Alpinsport** Ribčev Laz 53; tel/fax: 04 572 3468; email: alpinsport@siol.net; www.alpinsport.si. Organising accommodation and a wide range of winter and summer sports.

## Where to stay
The tourist information centre in Ribčev Laz (see *Practicalities*) can arrange private accommodation for around 2,500SIT per person. A surcharge is generally applied for stays of less than three days, for single occupancy and for breakfast, although the last charge is nominal.

**Aparthotel Triglav** (27 apartments) Stara Fužina 23; tel/fax: 04 572 3371; www.alpinum.net. Modern apartments with balconies sleeping 2–5 people, with access to a fitness centre, sauna, table tennis and bike hire. 7,200–19,800SIT.
**Hotel Bohinj** (20 rooms) Ribčev Laz 45; tel: 04 572 6000; fax: 04 572 3446; www.alpinum.net. Alpine-style hotel located opposite the tourist information centre. Some of the modern rooms have their own balconies or terraces. The hotel also has a fitness centre and tennis courts, and offers bike hire to guests. Singles 12,480–15,600SIT, doubles 20,160–26,400SIT.
**Hotel Jezero** (63 rooms) Ribčev Laz 51; tel/fax: 04 572 3375; email: hotel.jezero@cc-line.si. Modern lakeside hotel with an indoor pool, sauna, solarium, fitness centre and restaurant. Ask for a room with a balcony. Singles 10,800–15,120SIT, doubles 13,440–31,200SIT.
**Hotel Bellevue & Savica Annex** (57 rooms) Ribčev Laz 65; tel: 04 572 3331; fax: 04 572 3684; www.alpinum.net. Located on a hill above the lake with a restaurant and tennis courts. Balconied rooms are worth the extra cost. Singles 10,300–14,400SIT, doubles 14,000–21,400SIT.
**Hotel Pod Voglom & Annex** (27 rooms) Ribčev Laz 60; tel: 04 572 3461; fax: 04 572 3073; www.alpinum.net. Good-value two-star hotel on the shores of Lake Bohinj. Bike hire is available to guests. Singles 5,760–9,600SIT, doubles 11,500–16,800SIT.

**Penzion Rožič** (30 beds) Ribčev Laz 42; tel: 04 572 3393; fax: 04 574 6111; email: rozic@siol.net; www.penzion-rozic.som. The pension has decent en-suite rooms and offers bicycle and boat rental. Singles 3,800–4,500SIT, doubles 7,600–9,000SIT.

**Apartments Zdovc** (10 apartments) Ribčev Laz 138; tel: 04 572 3594; fax: 04 574 6420; email: zdovc@amis.net; www.bohinj.si/zdovc. New apartments sleeping 4–6 people, with private kitchens on the outskirts of the village. Guests can use a shared Jacuzzi, sauna and small fitness centre. Supplements are charged for stays of less than three days, for breakfast and for use of leisure facilities. 8,000–20,500SIT.

**Pension Tripič** (13 rooms) Triglavska 13, Bohinjska Bistrica; tel/fax: 04 572 1282; email: pension.tripic@bohinj.si; www.bohinj.si/tripic. Good-sized rooms sleeping 2–5 people. The pension, in the centre of town, also has a meeting room, restaurant, sauna and solarium. Singles 8,880–12,680SIT, doubles 12,960–20,560SIT.

**Avtokamp Zlatorog** Ukanc 2; tel/fax: 04 572 3482; www.alpinum.net. Well-equipped campsite with space for 180 tents and access to an indoor pool and tennis courts. Bike hire is also available. 1,800–2,300SIT.

**Kamp Danica** Triglavska 60, Bohinjska Bistrica; tel: 04 572 1055. Large campsite with sporting and entertainment facilities. Reservations can be made at the tourist office in Ribčev Laz. 1,300–1,800SIT per person.

## Where to eat
Many accommodation establishments in Bohinj offer half- and full-board options.

**Gostišče Rupa** Srednja Vas 87; tel: 04 572 3401. Restaurant in the shadow of the Julian Alps with an outdoor terrace, home cooking, first-rate trout and staff wearing traditional folk costumes.

**Penzion Rožič** (see *Where to stay*). Serving good Slovenian food in a homely restaurant or on a covered outdoor terrace.

**Gostilna Mihovc** Stara Fužina; tel: 04 572 3390. With hearty Slovenian cooking and homemade brandy.

**MK Pizzeria** Ribčev Laz 48. Decent pizzas and grills in a central location by the tourist information centre.

**Mercator** Ribčev Laz 49. Handily located supermarket next to the tourist information centre.

## Practicalities
**Tourist Information Centre** Ribčev Laz 48; tel: 04 574 6010; fax: 04 572 3330; email: tdbohinj@bohinj.si; www.bohinj.si. The TIC provides information and souvenirs. Staff can arrange accommodation and there is also a currency exchange. It also sells the Bohinj Guest Card which gives discounts on accommodation, parking, restaurants, activities and entrance to museums.

**LD Turizem** Letoviška 2, Bohinjska Bistrica; tel: 04 574 7600; fax: 04 574 7601; email: darja.lazar.net. Tourist agency providing information, private accommodation, bicycle rental and outdoor activities.

**Post office** Ribčev Laz 47. Open: Mon–Fri 08.00–09.30, 10.00–15.30 and 16.00–18.00, Sat 08.00–12.00. Also has a handily located ATM.

## What to see
### Lake Bohinj
In high season there are myriad ways to explore the lake's relatively balmy waters with tourist craft, rowing boats and canoes to choose from. Another option is simply to follow the trail around the lake, but note that this takes at least three hours at a brisk pace and it can be miserable if you get caught in a downpour and have to trudge around soaked. An easier choice is to take a bus from Ribčev Lav to the Hotel Zlatorog and then walk back from there. From May to October you can join one of six daily cruises on the lake (tel: 041 434 986) with departure points at Ribčev Laz and Camp Zlatorog. Out-of-season trips run subject to demand and weather.

### Mt Vogel Cable Car
The recently modernised cable car up Mt Vogel (Ukanc 6; tel: 04 572 4236. provides spectacular views over the lake and Julian Alps in both summer and winter. On a clear day you can even see Triglav. The station at the Ski Hotel is a lofty 1,537m high. If you are feeling energetic two hiking routes – one from Ribčev Laz and one from Ukanc – also take you to the top.
*Open: daily 07.00/08.00–18.00/19.00. Single 1,400SIT, return 2,000SIT, concessions single 1,000SIT, return 1,400SIT.*

### Slap Savica (Savica Falls)
Continue around the banks of Lake Bohinj away from Ribčev Laz and the road delves into verdant alpine forests which hide a couple of hotels and the access to the cable car up the slopes of Mt Vogel (see above). Further on, the old gravel track has thankfully been sealed and driving up to the Savica Falls, perhaps the most dramatic waterfall in Slovenia, is no longer a struggle except when there are tour buses vying for road space in the summer. The best time to appreciate Savica is in spring when the snow is melting and the water thumps its way 78m down from the rocky heights above and smacks into the pool below. The steep path is well marked, although it can be slippery, but it is no longer possible to get right up to the base of the waterfall as a padlocked gate now blocks access. There is, however, a small gazebo which provides a good vantage point and also gives a bit of cover when alpine rains move in for the day. Look for the plaque that commemorates the 19th- century visit of Archduke Johann of Austria. Access to the Savica path is 400SIT (concessions 200SIT). There is supposed to be a charge for parking, though this is not always applied.

### Churches
#### Cerkev Sv Janez Krstnik (Church of St John the Baptist)
Located opposite the small stone bridge in Ribčev Laz Cerkev Sv Janez Krstnik offers stunning views of Lake Bohinj. This church, which has its origins in the 13th century, is the most interesting building around Bohinj. It has undergone various revamps throughout its history and now features a baroque belltower as well as 17th-century altars, but it still boasts a wealth of preserved 14th-century frescos and its façade is decorated, typically for Gorenjska, with a depiction of St Christopher.
*Open: 09.00–12.00 and 17.00–20.00 Jul–Aug. 100SIT. Out of season ask at the TIC.*

## Cerkev Sv Duh (Church of the Holy Spirit)

The highlight of this baroque church is Matija Koželj's fresco of St Christopher.

## Museums

### Muzej Tomaž Godec (Tomaž Godec Museum)

Quite bizarrely every tenth entrance ticket to this museum (Zoisova 15; tel: 04 572 1763) dedicated to a communist Slovene war hero, is free. Renowned as a championship skier before the outbreak of fighting, Godec was instrumental in the 1941 uprising against the Germans, though he paid the ultimate price for his heroics when he was captured and executed by the Germans a year later. The building was the venue for the setting up of the Central Committee of the Yugoslav Communist Party in 1939, a meeting where Tito himself was present.
*Open: Tue–Sun 10.00–12.00 and 14.00–16.00 May–Oct, Wed, Sat and Sun 10.00–12.00 and 14.00–16.00 Jan–Apr. 400SIT, concessions 300SIT.*

### Planšarksi Muzej (Alpine Dairy Museum)

This museum (Stara Fužina 181; tel: 04 572 3095) steps back to the time when Bohinj was at the centre of alpine dairy farming in Slovenia, an industry that was gradually 'killed off' by modern methods and by the opening of a new dairy in Srednja Vas in 1971. Reconstructed alpine huts and dairy exhibits form the crux of the collection.
*Open: Tue–Sun 10.00–12.00 and 16.00–18.00 Jan–Jun, Sep and Oct, Tue–Sun 11.00–19.00 Jul–Aug. 400SIT, concessions 300SIT.*

### Oplenova Hiša (Oplen House)

Oplen House (Studor 16; tel: 04 572 3522) is a traditional farmhouse constructed in the 19th century from stone and wood, in a longhouse style that combines living and farming space. Today visitors can explore the preserved living room, bedroom, attic, cellar and black kitchen. In the barn there is a display of traditional farming tools.
*Open: Tue–Sun 10.00–12.00 and 16.00–18.00 Jan–Jun, Sep and Oct, Tue–Sun 11.00–19.00 Jul–Aug. 400SIT, concessions 300SIT.*

## ACTIVITIES AROUND BLED AND BOHINJ

There are a seemingly endless swathe of activities on offer in and around Bled and Bohinj, with operators providing a pick-up service from both resorts. Summer pursuits include mountain-biking, hiking and fishing, while adrenaline junkies can try their hand at climbing, tandem paragliding, canyoning, kayaking, rafting, canoeing or hydrospeed. When the mercury drops these are replaced by downhill and cross-country skiing, ski tours and ice-skating. In the depths of winter it is also possible to climb both the Julian Alps and frozen waterfalls. Alpinum, Pac Sports, Alpinsport and ProMontana all organise sporting acitivites (see *Tour operators* under *Bled* and *Bohinj*).

## Vodni Park Bohinj

Opened in 2004, this new water park (Triglavska 17; tel: 04 577 0210; email: bohinj.vodnipark@siol.net; www.vodni-park-bohinj.si) has all the things that you

would expect from a water park, including spas, swimming pools and slides. This is a great place for families.
*Open: daily 09.00–21.00.*

## Kayaking and canoeing

Canoeing and kayaking are possible on lakes Bled and Bohinj, while kayaking also takes place on the upper Sava Bohinjka River. In addition tour operators organise excursions to the more challenging waters of the lower Sava Bohinjka, Radovna and Soča. Week-long kayaking courses (5–10 hours of tuition 13,200–24,000SIT) and guided kayak expeditions are also available.

## Canyoning

Canyoning is the navigation of riverbeds and waterfalls by jumping, swimming and using climbing ropes and can be done at a variety of levels from beginner to advanced (8,400–13,200SIT for a single trip). It centres on the Mostnica Canyon between Stara Fužina and the Voje Valley.

## Paragliding and tandem paragliding

Paragliding is a great way to experience the Julian Alps. You can take a tandem flight with an experienced instructor–pilot, take beginner's lessons or join a five-day certificate course. Flights typically take off from Vogar or Vogel. Trial flights cost 13,200–18,000SIT, tandem flights 15,600–20,880SIT, courses 60,000–84,000SIT.

## Golf

The 18-hole King's Course near Bled (Kidričeva 10c; tel: 04 537 7711; fax: 04 537 7722; email: info@golf.bled.si; www.golf.bled.si) is probably the finest golf course in the country and enjoys a stunning setting that gives any course in Europe a run for its money. The set-up here is getting increasingly slick with a resident professional and a revamp of the clubhouse to include a posh restaurant and some luxurious rooms. Golfers can also play the nine-hole Lake Golf Course.

## Rafting

Navigating white-water in a six-to-eight person rubber raft is an exhilarating experience. Rafting (4,800–6,000SIT for a single trip) generally takes place on the Sava Bohinjka and the Sava Dolinka, with rapids from grade one (gentle) to four (quite ferocious). Water levels on the Sava Bohinjka are often too low to raft in July and August.

## Fishing

Anglers can try their luck on Lake Bohinj (March–September) and on the Sava Bohinjka River (April–October). Fishing is by permit only and these are issued for one to seven days.

## Walking

There are myriad choices in the natural oasis of the Triglav National Park. The best option is to pick up a map at the tourist office in Bled or Bohinj and then set out.

Many low-level trails are suitable for all, but be sure to take local advice on more tricky options as the weather can close in very quickly in these parts.

## Cycling and mountain-biking

Bikes can be rented from tour operators in either Bohinj or Bled and at many hotels. Lakeside cycling is an easy and fun way of getting around, but conditions in the surrounding mountains and hills are much more challenging. More experienced mountain-bikers can check out the forested paths that weave their way through the valley and upwards towards the mountain summits. Bicycle rental and guided trips (one day 3,600–8,400SIT) are both available.

## Mountain hiking and climbing

Mountain hiking is one of the biggest draw-cards for visitors to Bled and Bohinj, many of whom want to scale the lofty heights of Triglav. Not for novice climbers, the ascent and descent of Triglav are tricky and hiring the services of a local and

### TACKLING TRIGLAV

Climbing Triglav is something that every Slovene is meant to do at least once in their life. Corner a handful of Slovenes, though, and you will be lucky if half have been to the summit of this 2,864m monster, and this is not just through apathy. Climbing Triglav is no picnic as it is more than twice the height of Ben Nevis (1,344m), the UK's highest peak, although none of the ascents starts at sea level. Any reasonably fit adult should be able to manage the climb, but before attempting an ascent it is essential to prepare yourself properly and to carry the right gear. A good head for heights is also an advantage, as the sinewy ridge on the approach to the summit is not for the faint-hearted. Hiring the services of a local guide is a good idea. The reward for careful preparation and physical exertion, though, is the bounty of sweeping views of the Julian Alps and Italy on one side and the Karavanke and Austria on the other, while Slovenia unfurls all around.

Slovenia's highest peak has inspired a sense of awe for centuries, with early Slav settlers believing that the imposing limestone mountain was home to a powerful three-headed deity. Today the mountain, which has been protected as a national park since 1981, is revered for its beauty (not the supernatural power that inhabits it) and takes pride of place on the Slovenian flag.

Most people take two days to tackle the summit – to which there are around two-dozen routes – and stay overnight in one of many mountain huts. Most huts open from June–September and offer basic and hearty Slovenian food, with accommodation costing around 1,800SIT per person.

Dramatic and forbidding, the northern approaches involve an ascent of the mountain's steep 1,200m north face and are definitely not for beginners. The southern approaches offer somewhat gentler routes, with those tackling Triglav for the first time frequently starting near Bohinj.

The quickest route to the summit is from the Sport Hotel in Rudno Polje experienced guide is recommended (ask at the TIC or check with a local tour operator). You should not hike in or climb any of Slovenia's mountains alone or without the proper equipment and safety gear.

The best-known climbing sites in Bohinj are just below the Bellevue Hotel in Ribčev Laz and at Pod Skalco, Bitnje and Bohinjska Bela. The Julian Alps provide a myriad climbing opportunities, with over 200 routes catering to everyone from the beginner to the more experienced climber. The Pod Skalco and Bellevue sites are popular with beginners and a range of courses take place here. There is also a climbing wall at the Pod Voglom Hotel for you to hone your skills. Again it is sensible to engage the services of a local guide for tougher ascents.

## Hydrospeed

This is basically body-boarding on the Sava, but with a wetsuit to keep you warm and help protect against the bumps (6,000SIT).

(1,345m above sea level), 18km southwest of Lake Bled. Rudno Polje can be reached by car, or by a daily bus that departs Bled at 08.25. From Rudno Polje the summit lies about six hours away, with many climbers opting to stay in the 53-bed Vodnikov Dom na Velem Polju mountain hut (approximately three hours away) or the 62-bed Dom Planika pod Triglavom (around five hours away). Slovene teenagers frequently complete the ascent and descent from Rudno Polje to the summit in a single day, but this is a difficult feat for even the fittest person and is definitely not recommended for the inexperienced.

A more popular route takes you from the Zlatorog Hotel in Bohinj to the summit via Slap Savica (Savica Falls), Komarča Crag, Črno Jezero (Black Lake), Veliko Triglavsko jezero (Great Lake), Zeleno Jezero (Yellow Lake), the Hribarice Plateau (2,358m) and the Dolič Saddle (2,164m). From Bohinj the summit is at least six to seven hours away, with the last hour traversing some fairly challenging terrain including rocks and a cliff face – where steel pegs acting as footholds and fixed cables assist with the final push to the top – and, quite often, snow.

There are three mountain huts on the way – the Dom Planika pod Triglavom, the 104-bed Koča pri Triglavskih Jezerih (four hours from Bohinj) and the 60-bed Tržaška Koča na Doliču (five hours from Bohinj). An alternative and longer route takes hikers from the village of Stara Fužina through the Planica Viševnik meadows to the Koča pri Triglavskih Jezerih hut.

The information given in this box is not a comprehensive guide to climbing Triglav. Before any summit attempt it is important to get local advice or to seek the services of a guide. It is also a good idea to purchase a detailed map and one of the books written about hiking in the Julian Alps (see *Appendix 3*). The Mountain Club PD Ljubljana–Matica (Miklošičeva 17; tel: 01 231 2645; email: matica@planid.org; www.planid.org/PD/Lj-Ma/Maja/en/Index.htm) can provide information about guides and mountain huts.

## Horseriding

The Mrcina Ranč Horseriding Centre (Studor; tel: 041 790 297; www.impel-bohinj.si/horseback_riding.htm. 3,400–3,800SIT for one hour trip) offers a variety of courses which allow visitors to ride their Icelandic horses, from an oval riding track for beginners to country riding, riding camps and even horse-sledding in the winter. One-hour excursions take you to the Devil's Bridge in Stara Fužina, while three-day trips explore the Pokljuka Plateau. They also operate a riding school. More unusual are their 'adrenalin tours', which combine riding with either canyoning or tandem paragliding.

## Alpine skiing

There is a simple and short ski run at Straža Bled (Rečiška 2; tel: 04 578 0512) on the southwest flank of Lake Bled. It operates during the day and evening when there is enough snow (often until early April). A ski lift ferries you up, but blink and you will miss the descent. There are nice views here and if you are a beginner or are just short of time it is not a bad option. There are a number of ski resorts around the Bohinj Valley including Kobla (Cesta na Ravne 7, Bohinjska Bistrica; tel: 04 574 7100; email: kobla@siol.net; www.bohinj.si/kobla), Vogel (Bohinj's main resort, with 38km of pistes; Ukanc 6; tel: 04 572 4236; email: vogel@bohinj.si; www.bohinj.si/vogel) and Soriška Planina (Selca 86, Selca; tel: 04 511 7835; email: alpmetal@krajnik.net), which have much more impressive facilities and a number of decent runs. The ski slopes in the Bohinj area cater to everyone from the beginner to the advanced skier. Instruction is also available in snowboarding, carving and telemark skiing.

## Cross-country skiing

Myriad trails in Vogel, the Pokljuka Plateau and Rudno Polje host the Cross-Country Skiing World Cup each year, and over 60km of well-maintained trails are open to visitors. One popular trail links Bohinjska Bistrica to Ribčev Laz.

## Ice-skating

In winter part of Lake Bohinj near Pod Skalco is given over to an artificial ice rink. Skate hire is available.

## DAY TRIPS AROUND BLED AND BOHINJ
### Begunje

The alpine village of Begunje, which lies just northeast of Bled and Radovljica, stakes various claims to fame including its Elan sports factory and one of Slovenia's most influential and popular folk groups, the Avsenik Brothers (www.avsenik-sp.si). It has also had a voluntary fire department for more than 100 years and was the birthplace of Anton Bonaventura Jeglič, who was the bishop of Ljubljana from 1898 to 1930 and is still remembered by Slovenes as a man who championed the national cause.

It is Begunje's sights that draw non-Slovenes to the town. These include the ruins of the medieval **Kamen Grad** (Kamen Castle), which dates from the 12th century. Limited funding has reined in dreams of restoring the castle to its former state, altough the Roman Tower has been renovated and the castle remains an impressive sight against the backdrop of the Julian Alps. On June 25 each year the castle comes alive with medieval re-enactments, archery tournaments and a large bonfire, as the residents of Begunje celebrate National Day.

The 14th-century **Begunje Mansion**, which was reconstructed in the 17th century and served as a Gestapo prison during World War II, is another notable sight (in the gardens you can find two of Jože Plečnik's structures – the Murka and Jožamurka sheds). Others are the **Church of St Urh** (constructed and modified from the 15th to 18th centuries) and the simple, white **Cerkev Sv Petra** (Church of St Peter), where many believe that a healing breeze is blown from a nearby hole.

## Vrba

Fans of France Prešeren can make the pilgrimage to the village of Vrba, a short drive northeast of Bled. The house where he was born was converted into a museum just before the onset of World War II. It is not as illuminating as the Prešeren House in Kranj; in many ways it is more interesting as an example of 19th-century Gorenjska architecture and furnishings than as a testament to the great man.

## KRANJSKA GORA

It is easy to see why the playground of Kranjska Gora, perched on the border between three countries in a stunning location at the foot of the Julian Alps, has become so popular. In winter it is a fully fledged winter-sports resort – Slovenia's largest – offering skiing, ski jumping, tobogganing, cross-country skiing, snowboarding and a base for exploring the Julian Alps. When the snow finally melts the sweeping slopes and sky-crunching peaks are the perfect oasis for walking, hiking and climbing. The Old-World charm of this small village has definitely been lost in a scramble of hotels, restaurants, bars and even casinos, as well as, of course, the web of ski slopes and lifts, but if it all gets too much just turn your eyes skywards and the epic beauty of the mountains soon helps you forget the rest.

The first written mentions of Kranjska Gora go back to the 14th century, but it was never really a major population centre due to the difficult terrain and the harsh winters. During World War I Russian prisoners of war were brought into the region to help forge a track through the untamed mountains (see *Over the Vršič Pass to Primorska*), but even today this elevated through-road can be shut by snow and avalanche threats as late as mid-May. There seems to be no stopping Kranjska Gora's rise and rise today, though: as the borders around it have dissolved with Slovenia's accession to the EU it has recently branched out into snowboarding, and a brand-new four-star hotel opened at the end of 2003. A round of the Ski Jumping World Cup is also held every year at nearby Planica, a long wild weekend of high-quality sport and wanton socialising excess that has taken a hallowed place on the calendar for many Slovenes.

### Getting there

Motorists travelling to Kranjska Gora from Primorska should be aware that the Vršič Pass can be closed from the first heavy snowfalls until late May.

Regular buses run to Kranjska Gora from Bled (1 hour 25 minutes), Radovljica (1 hour 25 minutes) and Ljubljana ($2^1/_2$ hours). In July and August buses also link the resort to Bovec ($1^3/_4$ hours).

## Tour operators

**Globtour** Borovška 90; tel: 04 582 0200; fax: 04 588 1979; email: globtour-kr.gora@g-kabel.si
**Julijana** Borovška 61; tel: 04 588 1325; email: julijana@siol.net; www.sednjek.si
**Skipass Travel** Borovška 95; tel: 04 582 1000; fax: 04 582 1014; email: skipass-travel@g-kabel.si; www.skipasstravel.si

## Where to stay

Staff at Kranjska Gora's tourist offices and tour operators will help you find private accommodation. Rooms cost 2,500–4,500SIT per person depending on the season and the grading of the property. Apartments sleeping two people start at 6,720SIT.

**Hotel Kompas** (156 rooms) Borovška 100; tel: 04 588 1661; fax: 04 588 1176; email: info@hoteli-kompas.si; www.hoteli-kompas.si. Despite recent renovations and its modern sauna, steam room, pool and spa treatments the Kompas still feels old-fashioned. Book a mountain-facing room and enjoy the spectacular views from your balcony. If you are travelling on a budget consider staying in the two-star annex. Singles 11,280–22,800SIT, doubles 15,360–38,400SIT, annex singles 8,600–12,480SIT, annex doubles 9,600–17,280SIT.

**Grand Hotel Prisank** (110 rooms) Borovška 93; tel: 04 588 4477; fax: 04 588 4479; email: info@htp-gorenjka.si; www.htp-gorenjka.si. Kranjska Gora's newest and pinkest hotel has modern rooms, yet still has a resort-hotel ambience. Singles 11,200SIT, doubles 16,000SIT, apartment 7,800–9,000SIT (sleeping 2–5 people).

**Hotel Larix** (115 rooms) Borovška 99; tel: 04 588 4100; fax: 04 588 4479; email: info@htp-gorenjka.si; www.htp-gorenjka.si. Renovated in 2002 the rooms are bright and clean. The wellness centre has a sauna, pool, steam room, solarium and a variety of spa treatments. Singles 11,200SIT, doubles 16,000SIT.

**Hotel Kotnik** (15 rooms) Borovška 75; tel: 04 588 1564; fax: 04 588 1859; email: kotnik@siol.net. Pleasant, small and bright yellow hotel at the heart of town. Good-sized if unremarkable rooms. Singles 9,000–12,160SIT, doubles 13,400–18,240SIT.

**Hotel Lek** (80 rooms) Vršiška 38; tel: 04 588 1520; fax: 04 588 1343; email: recepcija@hotel-lek.si; www.hotel-lek.si. Modern hotel with pool, sauna, tennis courts and stylish rooms. Doubles 16,200–38,600SIT, singles 11,600–22,800SIT.

**Hotel Alpina** (105 rooms) Vitranška 12; tel: 04 588 1761; fax: 04 588 1341; email: info@hotel-alpina.si; www.hotel-alpina.si. Newly renovated hotel with a sauna and steam room. Guests can also use the pool at Hotel Kompas free of charge. Singles 9,600–18,000SIT, doubles: 12,000–26,400SIT.

**Vila Triglav** (6 rooms) Ivana Krivca 6; tel: 04 588 1478; email: vilatriglav@g-kabel.si; www.rozle-gm.si. 2km out of town near Jasna Lake, with sauna, Jacuzzi, pool and fitness room. Singles 11,000–15,200SIT, doubles 18,000 –26,400SIT.

**Youth Hostel Borkar** (37 rooms) Borovška 71; tel: 031 536 288; fax: 04 588 1439; email: hostelborka@email.si. This HI-affiliated hostel has 80 beds in twin and triple rooms, a central location and a cheap and cheerful pizzeria. 4,500SIT per person.

**Camping Špik** Jezerci 21, Gozd Martuljek; tel: 04 588 0120; fax: 04 588 0115; email: hotel.spik@petrol.si. 4km east of Kranjska Gora, the campsite has an outdoor pool, children's playground, artificial climbing wall and courts for beach volleyball and tennis. 1,500–2,100SIT per person.

## Where to eat
**Gostilna Cvitar** Borovška 83; tel: 04 588 3600. Welcoming tavern in the centre of town serving Slovenian food and wines. There is also accommodation for up to 20.
**Gostilna Pri Martinu** Borovška 61; tel: 04 582 0300. The modern conservatory and terrace to the rear with views of the mountains compensate for the decidedly average food and brusque service. Soups are a good option as are the specials on the first page of the menu. The *gostilna* also has rooms.
**Donna** Koroška 16; tel: 04 588 5800. Good service and Mediterranean-influenced dishes make this classically styled restaurant a good choice.
**Hotel Kotnik** (see *Where to stay*). The hotel has two good restaurants, one serving pizza and the other grilled meat dishes.

## Entertainment and nightlife
**Cocktail Club Manhattan** Grand Hotel Prisank, Borovška 93; tel: 04 588 4477. Lounge bar meets Texan desert, with oversized fossils as décor, truly bizarre. This basement bar also has two pool tables, cocktails and a Wurlitzer jukebox playing wonderfully misnamed tunes like 'Even better than the real thin', and 'Number of the best'.
**Papa Joe Razor** Borovška 83; tel: 04 588 1526. Good food and 05.00 opening hours make this late night bar-restaurant a big hit.
**HIT Casino** Vršiška 23; tel: 04 458 8250; www.hit.si. South of the town centre and just across the Pišnica River, the casino is open 24 hours. If gambling isn't your thing then the bars and cabaret offer alternative entertainment. Strictly over 18s, with passport or national identity required for entry. A monthly guide to events at the Casino can be picked up around town.
**Casino Larix** Borovška 99; tel: 04 588 4100. Smaller and centrally located casino attached to the Hotel Larix.

## Practicalities
You can find banks, ATMs, shops, supermarkets, post office, bars and cafés on Borovška.

**Kranjska Gora Tourist Office** Borovška 99a; tel: 04 588 5020; fax: 04 588 5021; email: info@kranjska-gora.si; www.kranjska-gora.si. A useful source of information, the tourist office can also help you find private accommodation.
**Tourist Information Centre** Tičarjeva 2; tel: 04 588 1768; fax: 04 588 1125; email: tic@krnajska-gora.si; www.kranjska-gora.si.
**Post office** Borovška 92. Open Mon–Fri 08.00–19.00, Sat 08.00–12.00.

## What to see
### Liznjekova Hiša (Liznjek House)
This 18th-century house (Borovška 63; tel: 04 588 1999) in the preserved old quarter of town provides an insight into life before Kranjska Gora emerged as a

major tourist resort. It may have been the home of a wealthy local landowner but the chimney-less black kitchen and some other period features are typical of Gorenjska, and the museum is a decent wet-weather option. *Open: Tue–Fri 10.00–17.00, Sat–Sun 10.00–16.00 May–Oct and Dec–Mar. 500SIT, concessions 300SIT*

## Cerkev Marijinega Vnebovzetja (Church of the Assumption)

Like many of the other churches in the Gorenjska region, the parish church, at Borovška 78, has evolved over time, with different aspects added through the centuries. Local literature claims that there has been a church in the town since the 14th century, although the building that stands today started life in 1510. The addition of St Joseph's Chapel in 1758 expanded the northern end of the church, while the construction of the choir in 1837 united the church and its tower. The last renovation also brought a further chapel and Gothic windows. Towards the end of the 19th century the church acquired neo-Gothic altars and the ceiling frescos were repainted.

A recent restoration programme has seen the church returned to its 19th-century splendour. The vaulted ceiling of the nave, part of the original 16th-century structure, is one of the most impressive in Gorenjska and it is well worth tearing yourself away from the mountains to have a good look. The church is also home to two Gothic sculptures that many locals date back to the late 15th century.

## Activities
### Skiing and snowboarding

The massif around Kranjska Gora, with around 30km of pistes and 40km of cross-country courses, is one big winter-sports playground during the months when snow conditions are good, usually from December to early March, though the season can last a bit longer depending on the weather. Facilities are improving every year, with new ski lifts and floodlights for night skiing recently added, and a new hotel in late 2003. There are myriad ski slopes in and around Kranjska Gora with plenty of choices for everyone from tentative beginners looking to learn the ropes with the help of the numerous instructors in the resort, right through to experienced skiers seeking an adrenaline-pumping challenge on the Ruteč and Zelenci. The slopes include both downhill and slalom options. Snowboarding has also come of age in Kranjska Gora over the last few years.

**Kranjska Gora Ski Centre** Borovška 103; tel: 04 588 1414; fax: 04 588 1181; www.rtc-zicnice-kranjskagora.si. The ski centre sells ski passes valid from 2 hours to 10 days. Adult/child passes cost 15,000/10,000SIT, 22,000/15,000SIT, 41,000/28,000SIT, 129,000/87,000SIT for two hours, one day, one week; 49,500/31,000SIT for 10-day passes. Discounts are available on some passes for those over 55.

**Intersport Bernik** Borovška 88a; tel: 04 588 1470. This jack-of-all-trades offers everything from bike hire, quad-biking, walking and paintball to skiing and ski equipment hire. They also have a ski school and a winter ice-skating rink, and let apartments.

**Gorenjska Ski School** Borovška 99; tel: 04 588 4492. Ski school offering equipment hire.

**ASK Kranjska Gora Ski School** Borovška 99a; tel: 04 588 5302; email: sola@ask-kg.com; www.ask-kg.com. Tuition for cross-country skiing, alpine skiing and snowboarding is given on a group or individual basis. Group courses with two hours of lessons each day cost 6,750–18,250SIT for 1–6 days. Private lessons cost 6,000/9,600SIT for one/two people. Discounts for children.
**Sport Point** Borovška 93a; tel: 04 588 4883. Great shop renting skis, sledges, ski boots, ice skates and mountain-bikes. It also has a good coffee shop.

## Walking

The walking options around Kranjska Gora are almost endless, from one- hour low-level walks around the fringes of the resort, through to epic adventures over precipitous ridges to the lakes of Bohinj and Bled or serious ascents of the voluminous peaks that shoot like rockets above. Mike Newbury's book *A Guide to Walks & Scrambles in the Julian Alps Based on Kranjska Gora* (see *Appendix 3*) features a number of routes. On a clear day the easy stroll to Jasna Lake, 2km to the south of Kranjska Gora, is unforgettable as this impossibly blue lake shimmers with the Julian Alps as a dramatic backdrop. A statue of Zlatorog is on hand to provide perfect tourist photo opportunities.

## Climbing

The local men have held a reputation for centuries as first-class walking guides and the art is still very much in evidence in the resort today. There is a tempting range of testing peaks to choose from including Jalovec (2,645m), Prisank (2,547m), Razor (2,601m) and Škrlatica (2,740m). You can also reach the summit of Triglav from Mojstrana, 13km west of Kranjska Gora.

## Spas and swimming pools

When the weather conspires against outdoor activities, or if you just feel like it after a limb-bursting day on the slopes, a number of hotels including the Larix, Kompas, Lek and Alpina offer heated indoor swimming pools and more specialised spa services. Non-residents can generally pay to use the facilities.

## Special events
### Ski Jumping World Championships

Planica, a village close to Kranjska Gora, lays claim to be the home of ski jumping and the sport has come home to roost with a round of the World Championships now held in February or March every year on the site of the first-ever World Championships in 1972. Fittingly the 100m barrier was conquered here in 1936 and the 200m barrier was smashed in 1994 by the Slovenian teenager Primož Peterka on the giant ski jump that was built in the 1960s. The World Championships are a major sporting event and many Slovenes also use it as the perfect excuse to spend a few days immersed in the restaurants and bars of the packed resort of Kranjska Gora.

## OVER THE VRŠIČ PASS TO PRIMORSKA

The vertiginous route up from Kranjska Gora over the Vršič Pass to Primorska is one of the most dramatic mountain passes, and certainly the highest in Slovenia, a stunning experience whether you are walking, cycling (poor you) or driving. The route sweeps up in a flurry of winding turns and improbable ascents, rushing onwards through the harsh rock and ice. Hundreds of Russian prisoners of war died to forge this road and even today the extremities of this landscape are demonstrated as it is often closed for much of the winter, not reopening until late spring. The route is easy to follow and each turn is numbered with a marker.

Many people do not set aside enough time for exploring the Vršič Pass properly, choosing instead to use it as a scenic route down into Primorska and on to the coast, though if you do this you are missing out on a lot so try to squeeze in at least a long day with your own transport (local buses are very limited). **Jasna Jezero** (Lake Jasna) is just beyond Kranjska Gora and worth visiting before you push on to the **Ruska Kapelica** (Russian Chapel, turn No 8) dedicated to the fallen Russian soldiers of World War I, most of whom perished as a result of landslides. Further up the road is a cemetery for some of them (turn No 21), before you continue on to Vršič and the highest point on the road at 1,611m, where you have to pay to park.

From Vršič the road starts to curl south in search of the Adriatic, but if you have time you can take a while and tackle some of the hiking trails that lead off from here (there is a mountain hut on Vršič itself). At turn No 49 you can stop and follow a path to the source of the mighty Soča River, which you will become very well acquainted with if you are planning to spend any time in Primorska. The river lies around 2km from the road. Now you are in Primorska proper. The descent is through the Trenta Valley with the adventure-sports oases of Bovec and Kobarid awaiting to the south.

# Primorska

If Slovenia really is, to borrow the increasingly used cliché, 'Europe in Miniature', then Primorska is surely Slovenia in miniature. The smorgasbord of scenery ranges from the sweeping mountains of its northern Julian Alps fringes, right down the verdant Soča Valley to the harsh Karst and finally to the Adriatic Sea. This is Slovenia's only region with a coastline, although in this book we have  given its coastal strip a chapter (*The Slovenian Adriatic*) of its own. After a morning skiing or climbing in the Alps you can be savouring a fresh seafood lunch by the Adriatic within a couple of hours and this makes Primorska a popular destination for all kinds of visitors, from those looking to ski or fling themselves off a bridge on a bungee jump, to those just wanting to relax with a glass of wine in the bucolic escape of Goriška Brda. The food here is a joy as the climate is perfect for growing various varieties of fruit and vegetables, with plump olives, sturdy red wines and flavoursome tomatoes, the latter somewhat of a rarity in many European supermarkets these days.

## BOVEC

In the northern corner of Primorska is a town that was profiting from rural package tourism until the implosion of Yugoslavia in 1991. There followed a disastrous earthquake in 1998 which destroyed many of its buildings, though thankfully it did not take the life of any of its inhabitants. In the summer of 2004 the region was hit once again by a serious earthquake. Rather than succumbing to these blows, Bovec has picked itself up and engineered a remarkable re-emergence as a world-class adventure-sports playground and today the outlook is looking rosier. Bovec enjoys a stunning location set just to the south of the Julian Alps in the upper Soča Valley near the eponymous river renowned for its vivid emerald colour. This world of craggy peaks, wild waters and equally wild weather may today be an oasis for adrenaline junkies, but in World War I it was a living and dying hell for a million soldiers who perished on the Soča Front. On a wet day when incessant cold rain hampers many activities Bovec can be a pretty miserable place, but as soon as there is a gap in the clouds out come the rafts, canoes, skis and mountain-bikes.

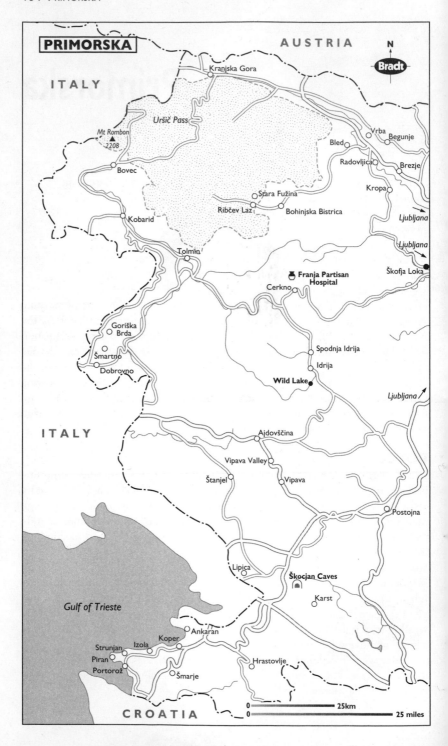

*Above* Town of Izola on the Slovenian coast

*Below* Overview of Piran from the Old Town Walls

*Above* Cruising on the Ljubljanica

*Right* Strolling by the banks of the Ljubljanica in Ljubljana's Old Town

*Below* Dragon Bridge, Ljubljana

## Getting there

Bovec is accessible by bus from Ljubljana (3³/₄ hours), Nova Gorica (1¹/₄ hours), Tolmin (50 minutes), Kobarid (30 minutes) and, in July and August, Kranjska Gora (1³/₄ hours). Buses stop near the Letni Vrt Restaurant on Trg Golobarskih Žrtev.

## Getting around

Most of the activity specialists in Bovec offer bicycle hire with half-day rental starting at around 2,160SIT, up to five-day rentals from 12,000SIT (see *Extreme-sports operators*).

## Tour operators

**Avrigo** Trg Golobarskih Žrtev 47; tel: 05 384 1150; fax: 05 384 1151; email: avrigotours.bovec@avrigo.si. Arrange private accommodation.

**Gotour Bovec** Trg Golobarskih Žrtev 50; tel: 05 389 6366; fax: 05 389 6368; email:gotour.bovec@siol.net. Arrange private accommodation.

## Where to stay

Private rooms are generally easy to find; simply look for the *sobe* or *zimmer frei* signs in the quiet Brdo area of town and on Rupa, which runs past Bovec's hotels. Alternatively the tourist office and the tour operators listed above will help you book a room.

**Hotel Kanin** (125 rooms) Ledina 9; tel: 05 388 6021; fax: 05 388 6081; email: hoteli.bovec@siol.net. Feels like an American motel, but with stunning views from the private balconies. There is also a good-sized swimming pool, a sauna and a small fitness room. Beware the hordes of marauding children in the corridors. Singles 10,800–14,800SIT, doubles 16,800–24,800SIT.

**Alp Hotel** (103 rooms) Trg Golobarskih Žrtev 48; tel: 05 388 6040; fax: 05 389 6387; email: hotelalp1@siol.net; www.alp-chandler.si. British owned and run three-star hotel with friendly service and good-sized rooms. Singles 8,000–10,700SIT, doubles 12,200–17,600SIT.

**Apartments Kaninska Vas** Kaninska Vas 7; tel: 05 388 6811; fax: 05 389 5588; email: tusi@siol.net; www.tusi.si. Fifty apartments in 3 blocks just 400m from the centre of town and sleeping 2–6 people. All with private kitchens, bathrooms and satellite TV. Some with balconies. 6,800–17,600SIT.

**Kajak Kamp Toni** Vodenca 1; tel: 05 389 6454; email: kajakkamptoni@siol.net. Located at the confluence of the Soča and Koritnica rivers, with space for 50 tents and 20 caravans. Kamp Toni is on the spot where the Germans launched their gas bombs in their front-busting assault during World War I. 1,800–2,200SIT.

**Kamp Liza** Vodenca 4; tel: 05 389 6370/6073; email: campliza@siol.net; www.slotravel.net/kamp-liza. Also near the confluence of the Soča and Koritnica, with space for 45 tents. 1,600SIT per person.

**Kamp Polovnik** Ledina 8; tel: 05 388 6090. Small campsite just 500m from the centre of town. 1,500–2,000SIT per person.

## Where to eat

**Gostišče Martinov Hram** Trg Golobarskih Žrtev 27; tel: 05 388 6214. Recently refurbished restaurant with a pleasant outdoor terrace. Soups, salads and pastas are perfect for a light meal. Fish, grilled meats and Balkan specialities also feature on the extensive menu. **Gostilna Sovdat** Trg Golobarskih Žrtev 24; tel: 05 388 6027. Slovenian dishes in more intimate surrounds.

**Restaurant Stari Kovač** Rupa 3; tel: 05 384 1700; fax: 05 384 1705; email: stari_kovac@hotmail.com; www.starikovac.com. Small inn serving delicious wood-fired pizza in its restaurant, terrace or summer garden. They also have 3 well-equipped apartments sleeping 2–8 people.

**Letni Vrt** Trg Golobarskih Žrtev 12; tel: 05 389 6384. Centrally located restaurant serving pizzas, fresh trout and grills. The restaurant is more atmospheric in the summer when its ornate garden is open.

## Entertainment and nightlife

**Plec Café** Trg Golobarskih Žrtev 18. Open daily until 01.00 this café-bar has pool tables and a garden.

**Pink Panther Bar** Kaninska Vas 7; tel: 031 588 854. Lively bar close to the Kaninska Vas Apartments, open until 01.00.

## Practicalities

You will find supermarkets, outdoor-clothing shops, banks and a pharmacy on Trg Golobarskih Žrtev.

**Tourist Information Centre** Trg Golobarskih Žrtev 8; tel: 05 384 1919; fax: 05 384 1915; email: info.lto@bovec.si; www.bovec.si or www.bovec.net. Open: daily 09.00–20.00 Jul–Aug, Mon–Fri 09.00–17.00 Jan–Sep, Sat 09.00–12.00 and 16.00–18.00, Sun 09.00–12.00 Sep–Dec.

**Post office** Trg Golobarskih Žrtev 9. Open Mon–Fri 08.00–09.30, 10.00–15.30 and 16.00–18.00, Sat 08.00–12.00.

## What to see

### War museums

While Kobarid's first-rate war museum is rightly regarded as giving the most comprehensive insight into the fighting on the Soča Front, there are three small private museums in Bovec that are, if anything, even more poignant as they have been put together by locals in their own homes. All three are worth visiting and are truly unique.

The **Museum of the 4th Bosnia Herzegovina Regiment** (Brdo 53; tel: 05 388 6577. Miloš Domevšček, by arrangement) was compiled by the grandson of a Bosnian soldier who fought for the Austro–Hungarians. He started collecting artefacts from the battlefields surrounding Bovec in 1997 after taking an interest in the old sepia image of his grandfather that hung in the family home, and by 2001 he had gathered enough to open a modest collection. Today the two-room museum is awash with old rifles, grenades and pieces of kit, with some unusual items such as an STD medicine pack with instructions in nine languages. The array of Slovenian beer bottles dropped by the troops on their way to the lines harks back to the days when there were over 100 brewers in Slovenia. There are also rooms for rent in the house for those wanting to stay with the colourful owner, though he only speaks Slovene and German.

Other collections include the **Museum of the 87th Regiment** (Kot 48; tel: 05 388 6249. Ivo Ivančič, by arrangement) and **A Farewell to Arms** (Klanc 1; tel: 05 388 6259. Sašo Prochazka, by arrangement).

## The lines outside Bovec

Anyone wanting to get a real feel for the war should head back north from Bovec to the section of the lines that has been opened up as an outdoor museum. Here you can walk amongst the old trenches and ramble around an old Austro-Hungarian position complete with a cramped officers' quarters, fire holes and original barbed wire. The shell crater on the summit brings back the harsh reality of what happened here, a stark contrast with the beauty of the Soča River which rushes past below.

## THE SOČA FRONT

The Soča (Isonzo in Italian) Front was the scene of some of the most savage and brutal warfare ever fought. Looking at the hulking, mist-shrouded peaks and sweeping snow-ravaged ridges high above the Soča River today it is hard to imagine that anyone could fight a war in this terrain, and it was the weather and terrain that often proved as vicious an enemy as the opposing army. The front, stretching all the way from Mt Rombon in the north down towards the Adriatic coast in the south, opened in May 1915 as Italy declared war on the Central Powers. Soon barbed wire had been strewn, trenches forged and heavy guns heaved into position as industrialised warfare came to Primorska. Much of the war was spent with the Italians launching offensive after offensive, which the Austro-Hungarian forces managed to repel, with little territory actually captured after the initial flush of Italian success.

The picture changed inexorably in October 1917 as the Italians went from dreams of further gains to being shoved right back across the plains of Friuli during the 'Twelfth Offensive'. The spark came from the German units who had been brought in to bolster the Austro–Hungarians. They dreamed up the 'Kobarid Breakthrough' which brought a new tactic – the *blitzkrieg* or 'lightning war'. Accompanying the usual heavy artillery onslaught came the use of gas as the Germans wiped out the opposing lines just north of Bovec in minutes. The Central Powers seized the opportunity and rushed into a rapid advance and soon the Italians were in full retreat, a disorganised scramble vividly captured by Hemingway in his *Farewell to Arms* (Hemingway served as an ambulance driver and was wounded during the fighting).

The Italians had been vanquished from Primorska but by the end of the war around a million men had lost their lives in the region's mountains and many of their skeletons still lie hidden amongst the rock and ice. The tactics of the *blitzkrieg* that were pioneered during the Kobarid Offensive were to be felt by many European nations during World War II and its spectacular success was not lost on one young German soldier at Kobarid, Erwin Rommel.

Continue on towards the Predel Pass and you will come to the sturdy Kluže Fortress right by the road. This was a crucial hub for the Austro–Hungarians and today it is open as a free museum. If you plan ahead and ask at the tourist information office in Bovec you can time your visit to coincide with performances by the *1313 Troop*, a group of local amateurs who dress up in original consumes and put on a show that recalls the days of company 1313, so-called as they were allocated a 1,313m-high ridge during the war. The performance is in a hotchpotch of German, Slovene and Croatian, reflecting the varied ethnic mix of the Central Powers troops, but it still gives English-speaking visitors an insight into those dark days. If you are feeling sorry for yourself on a wet and chilly day spare a thought for the World War I soldiers and cast your eyes across the road to the precipitous rock walls and the rudimentary metal stairs that the men had to haul themselves up to get to their positions.

## Adventure activities

The area around Bovec could have been sculpted with activity holidays in mind, with an almost endless list of possibilities for those willing to get stuck in. An increasing number of operators in the UK and Germany are starting to offer niche adventure breaks, but it is usually cheaper to organise things in Slovenia for yourself – easy enough to do but you may want to call a few days ahead to make sure that there are spaces and equipment. Note that all rafters and kayakers wanting to go out on the Soča by themselves need to get a permit, which can be purchased from the Bovec tourist office. As adventure tourism takes off the network of operators (see the following *Extreme-sports operators* section) is growing and overlapping so you may find yourself booking a kayak trip through the people you have just rafted with, but with the actual trip run by another operator, or vice versa. As competition grows prices are becoming flexible so look out for flyers offering good deals and ask around. Also keep an eye open for adrenaline packages that allow you to tackle three or four activities in one packed day if you are short of time. Safety is a real concern on the wild Soča River after a number of fatalities in recent years – the general rule of thumb is that if the locally trained Slovenian guides are not venturing out then you would be wise to follow suit.

### Kayaking

The Soča River is perfect for white-water kayaking (in the stubby short kayaks rather than the longer and slimmer sea kayaks). At any time there are challenging stretches to tackle for experienced kayakers, but after heavy rain the Soča really comes into its own and soon has less hardy paddlers scurrying upstream for respite. Kayak trips and one-to-five-day kayak courses are readily available. Courses 12,000–57,000SIT, kayak trip 8,400SIT.

### Canyoning

The idea of hauling your way up through the gushing waterfalls and rocky pools of Učja, Sušec or Mlinarica may not seem too appealing, but this fun sport is open to any fit adult. You will be kitted out with a life jacket and helmet, and safety standards are generally high. 8,500SIT.

## Hydrospeed

This is an adventure sport that is not as well known as its rafting or kayaking cousins, but if anything it gets you far closer to the water. Kitted out with a wetsuit, helmet, flippers and flotation board, you hurl yourself into the waters for an unforgettable adrenaline rush. 7,000–8,500SIT.

## Pot-holing

Slovenia is a world-class pot-holing destination and Bovec makes a good base for tackling the caves of the Kanin and Rombon lake basins. Descents are possible to depths of 1.5km, but conditions can change rapidly so local advice should always be sought; it is also advisable to go with a local operator who has detailed knowledge of the caves.

## Tandem paragliding

Tandem paragliding from the lofty heights of Mangart and Kanin is one of Slovenia's most exhilarating experiences, a genuinely unforgettable adventure that has people raving for the rest of their lives about the views from the Julian Alps right down to the Gulf of Trieste. A tandem flight takes around 25 minutes and costs 20,000SIT with Alpe Šport Vančar (see *Extreme-sports operators*).

## Mountain-biking

The sport is still in its infancy in Slovenia, but Outdoor Freaks (see *Extreme- sports operators*) in Bovec now has a first-rate stock of bikes and the experience to tailor some excellent trips into the surrounding mountains, as well as ad hoc tours that depend on the weather and track conditions. A new permanent track is set to open on the slopes of Kanin in time for the summer season in 2005. Hire 1,000SIT per hour, 3,500SIT per day.

## Skiing

The main ski fields, with the highest slopes in Slovenia at up to 2,220m, are on the slopes of Mt Kanin, where good ski conditions start in December and can linger right on into late May. The ATC Kanin ski resort (Dvor 43; tel: 05 389 6310; fax: 05 388 6930; email: kanin@siol.net) boasts over 9km of sledding tracks and a ski school, while passes allow skiers to use slopes that extend into Italy and Austria. Ski guides will also take skiers on tours into the neighbouring Krnica Valley. The four-person cable cars (open: 08.00–16.00) that transport skiers to the upper ski station operate in July and August, providing a great way for walkers and mountain-bikers to reach the higher altitudes (1,900/2,500SIT single/return). Group tuition costs 6,600–16,000SIT for six to 20 hours over two to six days. Private tuition is also available.

## Other winter sports

Snowboarding and other types of skiing, such as cross-country and telemark, are also starting to take a hold on Kanin and these activities can be organised through ATC Kanin (see *Skiing* above). Sledging, snow-rafting and ice-climbing are also becoming increasingly popular (see *Extreme-sports operators*).

## Walking and hiking

In summer the Kanin cable car is the most obvious way to open up the views quickly. From the terminus there are myriad options. One of the most popular walks is to the Boka Waterfall, widely regarded as the most powerful and impressive in Slovenia, while myriad trails climb Mt Kanin, Mt Rombon and various peaks. As with any high-altitude hiking it is advisable to hire the services of a qualified guide, who will accompany you on trips that last a day through to a week – seek advice at the tourist office or from one of the extreme-sports tour operators.

## White-water rafting

The Soča River, usually rated as grade three to four, is a serious white-water rafting river and should not be treated lightly. Rafts and other gear can be hired, but only experienced visitors should even consider going unaccompanied as there are real dangers, as has been demonstrated by recent fatalities. Going out with one of the increasing number of local operators is the safest and often the most fun option as they look after you for the whole trip (usually one to two hours on the river) and the guides know the river well – if they do not consider conditions suitable they will adapt their plans and choose another point of entry. Mini-rafts for two (known locally as 'outsiders') are also available. 4,800–9,600SIT for a 1–2-hour trip depending on how long it lasts and for how many people.

## Bungee jumping

Flinging yourself off a bridge with only a rubber band for company is a relatively new phenomenon to Slovenia. From April to October there are regular jumps from the 55m Solkan Bridge, a long way down to the mighty Soča. 8,400SIT.

## Extreme-sports operators

**Outdoor Freaks** Trg Golobarskih Žrtev; tel: 041 553 675; email; mac72attack@yahoo.com; www.freakoutdoor.com. Offer mountain-biking, mountain-bike rental, rafting, kayaking, tubing, hydrospeed, canyoning, and guides for those with their own equipment.

**Soča Rafting Sports Centre** Trg Golobarskih Žrtev; tel; 05 389 6200; fax: 05 389 6202; email: soca.rafting@arctur.si; www.socarafting.si. Offering rafting trips, canyoning, a kayak school, kayaking, canoeing, hydrospeed, caving and mountain-biking. In winter they run a ski and snowboard school, rent skis and organise tobogganing. The centre also arranges accommodation and excursions.

**Sport Mix** Trg Golobarskih Žrtev 18; tel: 05 389 6160; fax: 05 389 6161; email: traft@siol.net; www.sportmix.traftbovec.si. Arrange rafting, mini-rafting, canyoning and kayak tuition, as well as bicycle and scooter rental.

**Alpe Šport Vančar** Golobarskih Žrtev 20 trg; tel: 05 389 6350; fax: 05 389 6351; email: info@bovecsport.com; www.bovecsport.com. Organise rafting, mini-rafting, kayak lessons, hydrospeed, canyoning, tandem paragliding and winter sledding.

**Avantura** Tel: 041 718 317; email: bovecavantura@hotmail.com. With tandem paragliding, tandem parachute jumps, caving, canyoning and summer tobogganing. In winter they offer tobogganing, ski touring and ice-climbing.

**Bovec Rafting Team** Mala Vas 106; tel: 05 388 6128; fax: 05 389 6374; email:
bovec.rafting.team@siol.net; www.brt-ha.si. Kayak school, rafting, hydrospeed,
canyoning, cycling tours, bike and equipment hire, mountain guides and free-climbing
school. Snow-rafting in the winter months.
**Sport Activ** Brdo 7; tel: 05 388 6585. Rafting, canyoning, free climbing, snowboarding
and mountain-bike rental.
**Top Extreme Rafting** Trg Golobarskih Žrtev 19; tel: 041 620 636; email: info@top.si;
www.top.si. Offer bungee jumping, hydrospeed, kayaking, rafting, mini-rafting,
canyoning and mountain-biking.
**Sport Extreme** Tel: 05 389 6196; fax: 05 389 6197; email: sport-extreme@siol.net.
Arrange water sports, provide a guide service and organise dog-sled rides for children.
Sport Extreme also offers tourist-agency services.

# KOBARID

Immortalised by Ernest Hemingway in his epic *Farewell to Arms* Kobarid is a
modest town in the Soča Valley whose name is inexorably bound up with World
War I and the horrors of the savage Soča Front (see *The Soča Front* box). These
days it is a sleepy, unassuming and charming little place without the worst
elements of other tourist resorts like Bovec and Kranjska Gora, with a quiet main
square, some of the best seafood restaurants in the country and a fold of tree-clad
hills on all sides. The war, though, is never far away and visitors looking to delve
into its history will not be disappointed with the world-class Kobarid War
Museum and a ramble of military positions to explore in the surrounding forests.
There are also a number of private war museums in Kobarid. Today it is food that
makes Kobarid famous, with Slovenes, Italians and Austrians making regular
sojourns to this culinary mecca.

## History

Although World War I is the period most associated with this modest Soča Valley
town, human settlement in the region actually dates back to at least the Iron Age;
however, the first written mention of Kobarid, as Canoretum, was only made in
1184. Roman artefacts have been found dotted around the town and the remains
of a Roman fort have also been discovered on the hillsides above. Evidence of its
rich history is still being unearthed on the hills surrounding Kobarid and especially
at *Tonocov Grad* (Tonocov Castle), the site of a number of fortifications down the
centuries. After World War I the Italians occupied Kobarid, the Slovene language
was banned and the linden tree in Kobarid's main square, a national symbol of
Slovenia, was torn down. In World War II Kobarid once again rose to prominence
when partisans established the Kobarid Republic in defiance of the German
occupation of Yugoslavia.

## Getting there

Regular buses link Kobarid with Nova Gorica (45 minutes), Bovec (30 minutes)
and Tolmin (20 minutes), while less frequent services from Ljubljana (3 hours),
Cerkno (1¹/₂ hours) and Idrija (1 hour 50 minutes) also stop at the town.

## Where to stay

**Hotel Hvala** Trg Svobode 1; tel: 05 389 9300; fax: 05 388 5322; email: topli.val@siol.net; www.topli-val-sp.si. Welcoming four-star hotel run by the Hvala family. Guestrooms are light and spacious with attractive design touches. The hotel also boasts one of Slovenia's finest restaurants, the Topli Val, and a Finnish sauna. Singles 11,280–13,800SIT, doubles 15,360–20,400SIT.

**Restavracija Kotlar** Trg Svobode 11; tel: 05 389 1110; fax: 05 389 1112; email: kotlar.restavracija@siol.net; www.kotlar-sp.si. Stylish and understated double rooms with a small indoor pool, Turkish bath and solarium.

**Kamp Koren** Drežniške Ravne 33; tel: 05 389 1311; email: lidija.koren@siol.net. Well-equipped campsite with a laundry and bar, located just beneath the Napoleon Bridge, 500m north of Kobarid. Space for 40 tents. 1,200–1,800SIT per person.

## Where to eat

**Restaurant Topli Val** Trg Svobode 1; tel: 05 389 9300. With a culinary tradition spanning three decades the Hvala family has earned itself a well-deserved reputation for first-rate seafood. This is definitely the place for a splurge with exquisite sea bass and tunafish tartar, lobster and mouth-watering fish platters for two. Knowledgeable staff are on hand to help you choose the perfect wine to accompany your meal.

**Kotlar** Trg Svobode 11; tel: 05 389 1110. Whilst the food at the Kotlar may not quite match that served at the Topli Val, it is very good indeed. The restaurant has been serving simple fish dishes for over a decade. Creative touches include the likes of scallops encased in cheese. Freshwater trout with potatoes and spinach is a more traditional local speciality.

**Hiša Franko** Staro Selo 1; tel: 05 389 4120; www.hisafranko.com. Another excellent and creative restaurant that manages to serve up the likes of sushi as well as traditional Slovenian dishes. Much younger and funkier feeling than Kobarid's other dining options. Chic and modern rooms are also available for 18,200–21,600SIT.

**Gostilna Breza** Mučeniška 17; tel: 05 389 0040. Traditional Slovenian food is on offer in this popular and unpretentious eatery.

## Entertainment and nightlife

**Bar Pri Gotarju** Krilanova 3; tel: 05 388 5473. Kobarid's liveliest bar attracts a young crowd with its cheap draught beer (Union and Laško) and funky music. The interior of the bar itself is smoky and nothing special, but the outdoor terrace is a pleasant enough place to sit on a warm night.

## Practicalities

**Tourist information** Head to the Kobarid War Museum where friendly and helpful staff will give you literature and advice. They can also put you in touch with local guides.

**Internet access** Bar Cinca Mama at Trg Svobode 10 has a single internet terminal and charges 100/250/500SIT for 10/30/60 minutes.

**Post office** Trg Svobode 2. Open: Mon–Fri 08.00–09.30, 10.30–15.30 and 16.00–18.00, Sat 08.00–12.00.

**Nova KMB Banka** Trg Svobode 2. Open: Mon–Fri 08.00–18.00, Sat 08.00–12.00.

## What to see
### Kobarid War Museum
The excellence of the Kobarid War Museum (Gregorčičeva 10; tel: 05 389 0000; fax: 05 389 0002; email: info@kobariski-muzej.si; www.kobariski-muzej.si. Open: Mon–Fri 09.00–18.00, Sat–Sun 09.00–19.00. 800SIT) was recognised by a Council of Europe award in 1993. Opened in 1990 just as Yugoslavia was about to descend into its own bout of savagery the museum calmly and thoughtfully explores a range of aspects of the Soča Front, from the grim realities of the front line to the sufferings in the military hospitals further back, all without being over-emotional or judgemental. The highlight is the excellent section on the Kobarid Breakthrough.

### Cerkev Sv Antona (Church of St Anthony)
Haunting the slopes above the town is a legacy of Italian fascism and a poignant tribute to the Italians fallen during World War I. The harsh columned ossuary that surrounds the Church of St Anthony was commissioned by Mussolini in the 1930s during the Italian occupation and the remains of over 7,000 Italians lie here. The main staircase is dedicated to the unknown soldiers, while the names of the others are sculpted into the walls that encircle the church.

### World War I walking tour
Delving into the hills where thousands of Italian troops manned their positions before being wiped out by the Kobarid Breakthrough is an excellent way of getting a real feel for what happened. Pick up the free Kobarid Historical Walk leaflet from the Kobarid War Museum. Do not be fooled by the fact that it is only 5km as the crow flies or by promises that it is an easy walk, as in reality this circular walk will take you a good three hours if you want to take in everything, and when it rains the slippery, steep paths and trenches can be hazardous and energy-sapping. It is well worth the effort, though, both for the military history and the sweeping views of the Soča Valley opened up en route.

As you have already covered stop No 1 of the walk in the museum, and there is little to see at the old Roman settlement of Gradič, it is perhaps best to start from the **Italian Charnel House** (stop No 3). Although the path is waymarked (a splotch of paint – the symbol of the War Museum) it can be tricky to follow and you may end up having to double back to correct wrong turnings, so keep your wits about you. The trek north to **Tonocov Grad** (Tonocov Castle) takes you through some dense forest and over a gurgling stream before circling back on a steep ascent to the 'castle'. There is little to actually see in what has been a fortification since the Stone Age, with attempts to preserve the site currently blocking access. The crude pulley system that is being used to transport equipment up the hillside harks back to World War I when the Italians fortified the slopes in the same manner.

From Tonocov retrace your steps and cut right along the walkway, following the wooden handrail that leads to the **Italian third line**, which meanders down the hillside in search of the Šoca below. A series of bunkers and cleared trenches precedes a set of steep concrete stairs down to the road. Take care when crossing and rejoining the path to the left as cars scream around what is essentially a blind bend. On the final approach to the Šoca are a litter of front-line positions where your imagination may start to run away with you, especially on a gloomy windswept day. The crossing of the Šoca is quite dramatic, on a 52m swing bridge that was only completed in 1998, though it is on the exact site of its predecessor where troops crossed in World War I. If the water is too high (check with walkers coming the other way) and you do not want to get wet then there is little point in making the excursion up to the **Slap Kozjak** (Kozjak Waterfall) as it is virtually impossible to negotiate the last section of the path without having to plunge into the water. A steep path marked only in Italian and Slovene scrambles up the hillside back by the bridge. This was the site of a machine-gun position and the observation deck provides a great view of the Šoca thundering past. The walk back towards Kobarid is the least interesting section, except for the Napoleon Bridge, where the French emperor's forces once crossed, though the original was destroyed at the start of World War I by retreating Austrian soldiers. Follow the road and you will soon be back in Kobarid with an appetite that only a Šoca Valley trout can satiate.

## TOLMIN

There is little reason to visit the administrative hub of Tolmin itself, 16km from Kobarid. However, Športni Turizem Maja (Padlih borcev 1; tel: 05 381 0060; fax: 05 381 0061; email: maya.sport@siol.net; www.maya-bn.si) offer kayaking, whitewater rafting, hydrospeed, canyoning and mini-rafting in the Soča Valley. Their land-based activity programmes include cycling, hiking, caving and free climbing. Maja also provide accommodation in a HI- affiliated youth hostel.

Tolmin can be reached by bus from Bovec (50 minutes) or Kobarid (20 minutes).

## GORIŠKA BRDA

This corner of Slovenia, surrounded and heavily influenced by Italy on three sides, is one of the country's great travel secrets. Few British or American visitors to the country are aware of this Slovenian Tuscany, which is less than an hour's drive from Kobarid and easily accessible from the coastal resorts (via Solkan), but a sprinkling of Italian and German gastronomes are already in on the secret. Turning west across the Soča River from the main Bovec-to- Nova Gorica road at Plave, the road soon starts to climb and the landscape changes. Forests wrap themselves around the rolling Mediterranean hills and streams gurgle down the ridges as the Italian plains of Friuli unfurl in the distance. Soon you will be dawdling amongst sprawling vineyard-covered slopes, cherry and peach orchards and tiny villages clad in orange roof tiles, most topped by bleached white churches. With crisp Alpine winds from the north to add flavour and milder Mediterranean breezes to enhance body this is perfect wine-growing country and many of the country's most famous wine producers such as Movia and Simčič are based here. Keep your passport handy if you are driving around as it is all too easy to find yourself, by mistake, at one of the five minor border crossings into Italy.

# Where to stay

The Goriška Brda region provides a real opportunity for a get-away-from-it- all rural retreat. Accommodation is available on tourist farms, in *gostilnas* and in private rooms. Owners will often advertise the fact that they have rooms to let; otherwise the TIC in Dobrovo will be able to help you organise accommodation.

**Bužinel** Medana 16; tel: 05 304 5082; fax: 05 395 9155; email: sobe@gostilna-buzinel.si; www.gostilna-buzinel.si. This wine-cellar-cum-restaurant in Medana has light and modern guestrooms in nearby Pleŝivo, 1.5km from Medana.

**Tourist Farm Breg** Breg pri Golem Brdu 3; tel: 05 304 2555. Singles 5,000SIT, doubles 10,000SIT. Accommodation in a typical farmhouse on the western outskirts of the Goriška Brda region. Serving traditional Hungarian- and Italian-influenced Slovenian food such as goulash, white polenta and *pršut*.

**Tourist Farm Kline** Medana 20; tel/fax: 05 395 9408; email: klinec-medana@s5.net. Wine cellar with modern rooms in annex across the street.

# Where to eat

Roadside *gostilnas* serving traditional cuisine are a good option, as are the restaurants in Dobrovo and Šmartno listed below.

**Vinoteka Brda** Grajska 10, Dobrovo; tel: 031 342 369; fax: 05 395 9211; email: info@vinotekabrda.si; www.vinotekabrda.si. *Pršut* and cheese are always on hand to accompany a seemingly endless list of top-quality wines in this vinoteka brda located in the cellar of Dobrovo Castle. If you call ahead more substantial meals can be arranged. The owner can also help you select wines to take home. Wines on sale range from cheap and cheerful efforts through to Simčič Duet at over 8,000SIT a bottle.

**Grad Dobrovo (Dobrovo Castle)** Grajska 10. The restaurant accompanies its fine wines with smooth service and high-quality cuisine. Tempting starters include homemade salami, while mains include the likes of veal in Gorgonzola and cream sauce or a seafood platter of squid, sea bass and mussels. Desserts are equally mouthwatering.

**Turn Šmartno** 62; tel: 05 304 1311. An atmospheric place to try the local cuisine, which is, not surprisingly, strongly influenced by Italy with gnocchi, pasta and polenta (white not yellow) featuring heavily.

# Practicalities

**Tourist Information Centre** Trg 25 Mama, Dobrovo; tel: 05 395 9594; fax: 05 395 9595; email: obcina.brda@guest.arnes.si. Open: Mon–Thu 08.00–16.00.

# What to see
## The Brda wine road

Over the last few years the local authorities have started to invest in tourism and you can pick up a couple of leaflets at the tourist office in the town of Dobrovo, one outlining the highlights in the various villages and towns and the other pointing out the bountiful vineyards, *gostilnas* and restaurants that await your custom. Calling ahead is always a good idea when visiting a vineyard, especially if you want to eat there as well, but in season you can just pop in and you will usually be welcomed with open arms and furnished with a free sample. It is considered polite to buy at least a bottle – given the high quality in the region this should not be too much of a problem. Just look out for the signs that point off from the main roads heralding the various local producers. Wine tourism here is on the up, as evidenced by the extensions and outhouses being built as local families look to add dining rooms and accommodation to their vineyards.

Despite its small size Goriška Brda accounts for over 10% of all Slovenian wine production, with the split 60/40 in favour of white wines. There are high-quality whites and reds, but the general rule of thumb is that you will get a better quality of white for your money. The actual volume of wine production has dipped over the last decade; this is not a sign of decline in the local industry but rather a reflection of the damage caused by mass production in the 1950s and 1960s and also of the current drive for quality over quantity. Over the last decade or so modern equipment has been brought in to refine production, but things often remain on a pleasingly low scale with pesticide use and artificial input far less prevalent than in many wine-producing countries. Some of the most established grapes are rebula, merlot, beli pinot and pinot blanc.

### Dobrovo Grad (Dobrovo Castle)

Just a couple of hundred metres on from the tourist information centre in Dobrovo, at Grajska cesta 10, is the rectangular Dobrovo Castle, which was built on the foundations of an earlier fortification at the start of the 17th century. Today it is home to a modest museum and art gallery, with various temporary exhibitions. The real reason to come here is to eat and drink, as there is an excellent restaurant inside the castle itself and a first-rate *vinoteka* in the bowels of the castle (see *Where to eat*).

### Šmartno

Of all the cute villages that grace the Brda region little Šmartno is perhaps the most appealing. The majority of Šmartno's fortified walls are still intact with its several hundred residents managing to rebuild their homes in their original styles after a serious earthquake in the 1960s. The 16th-century Turn Tower now houses a restaurant and café (see *Where to eat*).

The residents of Šmartno are proud of their village's historical importance, and another sight worth visiting is the biggest parish church in Brda, the **Cerkev Sv Martin** (Church of St Martin), whose enormous belltower started life as a watchtower, part of the fortifications. The interior of the church is a bit faded, although the frescos by Slovenian artist Tone Kralj are worth looking at. Šmartno also has a handful of traditional stone buildings, identified by plaques on their doors, including the Gothic house whose late- Gothic portal today leads to the cellar. The 19th-century renovations saw the expansion of the living space and the addition of a *gunk* (balcony), typical of the Brda region.

### IDRIJA

From the Soča Valley most travellers make a beeline for Primorska's Karst and coastline, but if you follow suit you will miss out on the Idrija region and the winding rivers and gorges that made ideal terrain for partisan resistance during World War II.

Mention Idrija to most Slovenes and they will immediately think of two things: mercury and lace. This town of 6,000 inhabitants was once a buzzing hub of mercury production, the second largest in the world after Almaden in Spain; and intricate lace produced by local women is still a much-sought-after handicraft. While Idrija today has a somewhat subdued feel, largely thanks to the closure of the last of its mercury mines in 1995, it makes a good base for exploring the region, especially if you want to splash out and stay at the Kendov Dvorec, one of Slovenia's finest hotels. Unlike many former mining towns around Europe, Idrija's economy is still flourishing these days with local companies now churning out automobile parts for global customers, and almost zero unemployment.

## History
According to legend mercury was first discovered in 1490 by a local who scraped off some of the highly toxic metal when cleaning a tub in a stream, supposedly on the spot where the Church of the Holy Trinity now stands. Eighteen years later came the discovery of cinnabar. Idrija then grew as one of the richest mercury towns in Europe, with a maze of around 700km of shafts dug to a depth of 400m. The mine even functioned through two world wars and during the German occupation when a third of the workers joined the partisans. By the 1970s the mine was one of the most modern in the world, with safety standards that the early miners could only have dreamt of, but it became a victim of environmental awareness as the trend turned against the use of mercury and the price dropped rapidly from US$800 to US$80 a flask. The mine was closed temporarily in 1976 as a result and although it reopened in the 1980s the writing was on the wall and it was wound up and completely closed in 1995.

While the men of Idrija toiled in the darkness of the mineshafts that spread their tentacles beneath the town, the women began to make snow-white lace as a way of supplementing the low wages that their menfolk brought home from the mine. Today the tradition of lacemaking is kept alive by Idrija's older generation, with some younger women learning this skilled art at the town's dedicated lacemaking school.

## Getting there
You can drive to Idrija from Ljubljana, Škofja Loka or Nova Gorica in an hour or less, and from Tomlin in 45 minutes. Frequent buses also run to Idrija from Cerkno (25 minutes), Tolmin (1 hour), Ljubljana (1¼ hours), Bovec (1½ hours) and Kobarid (2 hours).

## Tour operators
**Kompas** Lapajnetova 37; tel: 05 372 2700. Also organises private rooms for 5,000SIT per person.

## Where to stay
**Kendov Dvorec** Na Griču 2, Spodnja Idrija; tel: 05 372 5100; fax: 05 375 6475; email: kendov-dvorec@s5.net; www.kendov-dvorec.com. Sublime five-star hotel that does everything with panache. Gloriously luxurious rooms (which are cheaper than you might

expect), great food and smooth service make this one of Slovenia's finest hotels and well worth the expense. Singles 18,000–32,500SIT, doubles 23,000–46,000SIT.

**Gostišče Barbara** Kosovelova 3; tel/fax: 05 377 1162; email: joze.medle@siol.net. Decent rooms with a prime location above the mine museum. Singles 10,500SIT, doubles 17,000SIT. Book ahead as there are only six rooms.

**Kmetija Želinc** (15 rooms) Staža 8, Zelin; tel: 05 372 4020; fax: 05 372 4021; email: kmetija.zelinc@iname.com; www.zelinc.com. If you have your own transport this farmhouse located by the Idrijca River is an excellent place to stay and eat. You can also indulge in a spot of fishing or take a dip in the outdoor pool. Choose from rooms in a 500-year-old farmhouse or in a more modern building. Singles 5,200SIT, doubles 10,400SIT.

**Dijaški Dom Nikolaj Pirnat** IX Korpusa 6; tel: 05 377 1052. This student dormitory cum summer youth hostel has 300 beds. 3,500SIT per person.

## Where to eat

**Kendov Dvorec** (see *Where to stay*). A restaurant as decadent as the hotel with an ever-changing menu backed up by myriad Slovenian wines. Dine and be treated like a king, a real indulgence.

**Gostilna Mlinar** Žirovska 4, Spodnji Idrija; tel: 05 377 6316. Welcoming *gostilna* serving delicious *žlikrofi* – a local speciality comprising homemade pasta stuffed with potatoes, herbs and a small amount of bacon, served with meat or cheese. Also good fish and game dishes.

**Gostilna Kos** Tomšičeva 4; tel: 05 372 2030. Unfussy *gostilna* serving tasty pork dishes and homemade *žlikrofi*. The menu is small, so you know your food is fresh.

**Gostilna pri Škafarju** Sv Barbare 9; tel: 05 377 3240. Centrally located restaurant, popular with tourists, serving *žlikrofi*, other regional specialities and pizza.

**Mercator** Lapajnetova 45. If you are just desperately in search of that elusive cheap snack, the friendly staff behind the deli counter will make you a sandwich.

## Buying lace

While the small shop within Gewerkenegg Castle (see *What to see*) sells lace there are a number of bigger outlets on Mestni trg. One of the best places to buy local lace products is the Galerija Idrijske Čipke (Mestni trg 17), which also has an outlet in Ljubljana (Gornji trg). Idrija's young girls are all still introduced to lacemaking at school and there is also a dedicated Lace School (Prelovčeva 2), with its own shop, in the town.

## Practicalities

**Tourist Information Centre** Lapajnetova 7; tel/fax: 05 377 3898. Open: daily 09.00–18.00 Jul–Aug, 09.00–16.00 Sep–Jun.

**Nova KMB Banka** Lapajnetova 43. Open: Mon–Fri 07.30–18.00, Sat 07.30–12.00.

**Post office** Lapajnetova 3. Open: Mon–Fri 08.00–19.00, Sat 08.00–12.00.

**Čuk** Rožna 4, Idrija; tel: 05 372 2760. Mountain-bike rental.

## What to see
### Antonijev Rov (Anthony's Mine Shaft)

Kosovelova 3; tel/fax: 05 377 1142. Tours: Mon–Fri 10.00 and 16.00, Sat, Sun and holidays 10.00, 15.00 and 16.00. Groups must book in advance. 1,000SIT. Roll call was at 04.00 when you were briefed on the day's work and given a number from the 'death clock' (failure to return it indicated that you were trapped below, in serious trouble). Then with only your normal clothes on and no head protection you delved down into the netherworld of one of Europe's oldest mines. This was the scene for many of the workers who toiled in Idrija's mines, but thankfully today at the museum things are a little more relaxed: although the clock says 04.00 the first tour actually starts at 10.00 and you have both an overcoat and a hard hat, not to mention a torch-wielding guide.

The tours take in a good section of the mine, which manages to tread a fine line between providing safe access for tourists and retaining many of its original features. It starts with a 20-minute video, which illuminates both the mine and the history of the town. Models of miners through the ages give a sense of what life was like. There is even a small chapel, reputed to be the only one in Slovenia not funded by the Church as it was crafted by the miners themselves. It features an image of St Barbara, the patron saint of miners. The trail delves down to a depth of 100m and passes blind shafts, backfilled areas and ore transporters. Fortunately these days you do not have to conquer the 1,000 steps up and down that the miners had to, and you are soon back safely above ground.

### Echoes of Idrija's mining past
The history of Idrija's days as mining hub litter the town and its surrounds. Other sights worth visiting include **Frančiškov jašek** (Frančiška's Shaft), the **Rudarska Hiša** (Idrija Miner's House), the **Kamšt waterwheel** and the **Klavže water dams**.

The entrance building to Frančiška's Shaft is another of Idrija's prized technical museums (contact the Town Museum; tel: 05 372 6600 for entry), this one capturing the history of the town through a display of restored machinery that was recovered from the mine. The **Idrija Miner's House** (contact the Town Museum) is a typical 19th-century wooden dwelling built to cater for the large number of miners. Due to the lie of the land around Idrija it is built into the hillside and clearly intended to house as many workers as possible, normally around 16. Although it looks quite spacious from the outside the cramped reality was that most families had just two beds for themselves and however many kids they had, so drawers and straw beds were brought into play.

The two-century-old Kamšt (key available from Vodnikova 22, or from the Town Museum; 300SIT; see listing below) meanwhile conveys the sheer scale of the mercury operation as this is the largest wooden waterwheel in Europe with a diameter of 13.5m, a gargantuan feat of engineering that harnessed the local water to produce a surge of power for the works underground. Further upstream, about 20km from Idrija, are the Klavže, the huge dams, known locally as the 'Slovenian Pyramids'. Completed in 1770, these were used to build up water pressure and then fire logs downstream for use at the mercury mines in Idrija.

### Grad Gewerkenegg in Mestni Muzej (Gewerkenegg Castle and Town Museum)
The austere-looking Gewerkenegg Castle (Prelovčeva 9; tel: 05 372 6600; fax: 05 377 3580) is one of the few castles in Slovenia that was never presided over by

feudal lords, as it was built by the mercury industry and served as both a fortified store and administrative offices and, of course, as the director's residence. Painstaking reconstruction work since the 1980s has brought it back into shape and earned it a *European Technical Museum of the Year* award in 1997.

The castle also houses a municipal history museum. If you have already been down the Anthony Mine the mining section may not hold your interest for too long, though it certainly goes into the subject of mercury in much greater detail. The municipal section is, however, fascinating, tracing the history of the town; its 'Milestones of the 20th Century' exhibition was opened in 2003. World War I is touched upon before the period of Italian rule between the wars is explored, with exhibits including signs proclaiming that the Slovene language was banned. The World War II period, when Idrija was occupied by first the Italians and then the Germans, and was central to Slovenia's strong partisan resistance, is also explored in detail.

A strikingly huge hammer and sickle, which originally hung proudly above the mine shaft, is now hung low to symbolise the fall of Yugoslav socialism. Look out for the series of photos from the Idrija Lace School, which demonstrate Idrija's ability to flourish regardless of the political climate. Photographs taken inside the school show portraits of Emperor Franz Josef – and later Mussolini – hanging in the classrooms, before Yugoslav hardman Tito usurped the Italian dictator. For lovers of lace the museum also houses a display of the intricate work of the local women, who traditionally took up the art to supplement their husbands' meagre income from the mine. The most interesting display is a huge piece of work that was meant for Tito's wife, but never received as the political climate changed yet again.

Nearby there is also a small and less slick display covering the Pavla Partisan Hospital, which treated more of the World War II wounded (an estimated 1,678) than its Franja sibling (see *Cerkno*). The simple displays show the bravery and determination of Dr Pavla Jerina (who still lives in Idrija today) and her colleagues, with one photo showing her with Dr Franja, who was a close friend. *Open: daily 09.00–18.00. 500SIT, concessions 300SIT.*

### Partizanska Tiskarna (Partisan Printing Workshop)

If Slovenia's partisan movement has caught your imagination then you might also want to check out the Partisan Printing Workshop. Here you can delve back in time to World War II and the highly dangerous production of a newspaper promoting resistance against Nazi occupation – the only such production in wartime Europe. Daily tours at 09.00 and 16.00 from April–October help bring this small workshop alive. Hidden in the hills the museum is, by design, hard to find, so contact the Town Museum (tel: 05 372 6600) who will provide directions.

### Divje Jezero (Wild Lake)

Anyone expecting a sweeping expanse of water will be sorely disappointed by what on the surface is little more than a pond. The real interest lies below in the mysterious creation of this lake, which despite its small appearance emits a continual stream of water. Hidden deep beneath the surface a network of caves snakes away to an elusive source. The Wild Lake has become something of a holy grail for Slovene cavers and divers; headstones around the lake, the most recent from December 2001, demonstrate the dangers of delving below the emerald veneer. So far 87m of the cave system has been mapped with the rest of the hidden depths (estimated to be around 120m) sure to tempt others into risking their lives in future, though you would be well advised not to be one of them. A trail of small wooden boards outlines local flora and fauna on the path around the lake. The trail was designed to be circular, though at times the far side is submerged in water and you have to double back and cross the bridge to access the other side of the lake. Look out as you cross for the gushing Jezernica River below; fittingly for its bijou source lake, the Jezernica is the shortest river in the country. If you have more time you can walk to the lake from Idrija by following a 'Science and Discovery Path', also known as the 'Rake', alongside a narrow water channel.

## AROUND IDRIJA
### Cerkno
Cerkno is an unassuming town on the main road between the Soča Valley and Idrija, but it is home to two important museums and the Cerkno Hills are good for walking. If you visit during spring you might also be lucky enough to see the 'Laufarji' men dressed from head to foot in hay like walking scarecrows. Wintertime visitors come to ski.

### Getting there
Buses run to Cerkno from Idrija (35 minutes), Ljubljana (1¼ hours), Tolmin (1½ hours), Kobarid (1¾–2¼ hours) and Bovec (2½–3 hours).

### Where to stay and eat
**Hotel Cerkno** Sedejev trg 8; tel: 05 374 3400; fax: 05 374 3433; email: hotel.cerkno@siol.net; www.hotel-cerkno.si. Large faceless hotel popular with skiers and coach parties. Redeeming features include a good-sized indoor swimming pool, sports hall, tennis courts and sauna. The hotel also issues ski passes. Singles 10,000–15,100SIT, doubles 16,300–26,400SIT

**Gačnik v Logu** tel: 05 372 4005. This *gostilna* and pension has an incredibly long menu. The salads and pastas are of a decent standard, with tasty karst noodles and *žlikrofi*. The 9 en-suite double rooms are also a pleasant accommodation option.

**Tourist Farm Grapar** Planina pri Cerknem 47; tel: 05 372 4117; email: kmetija.grapar@email.si; www.kmetija-grapar.com. Modern rooms combined with warm hospitality and the opportunity to sample traditional foods make this a good option if you have a bicycle or car. Planina is 5km from Cerkno on the road to Škofja Loka.

### Practicalities
Cerkno doesn't have a dedicated tourist office, but the staff at the Hotel Cerkno (see *Where to stay and eat*) will be happy to provide you with information and literature. There is a bank and a mini market on Glavni trg at the base of the road that leads you to the museum.

## What to see
### Cerkljanski Muzej (Cerkno Museum)

No-one quite seems to have decided whether the recently reopened Cerkno Museum (Bevkova 12; tel: 05 372 3180. Open: Tue–Sun 10.00–13.00 and 14.00–18.00. 300SIT, concessions 200SIT) is home to the oldest musical instrument in the world or to some prehistoric artefact that just happens to have a few holes through it. Either way it is worth having a look, not least because the museum also houses exhibits on the local Laufarija carnival including masks worn by participants.

### Partizanska Bolnišica Franja (Franja Partisan Hospital)

This former partisan hospital (Dolenji Novaki pri Cerknem; tel: 05 372 3180. Open: daily 09.00–18.00 Apr–Oct, 09.00–16.00 Mar, Oct and Nov, weekends 09.00–16.00 Dec–Feb. 700SIT) in the Pasica Gorge, north of Cerkno, is one of the most fascinating war museums in Europe. It is a testament to the determination of the local people to overcome Italian fascism and then Nazi suppression that they were willing to risk life and limb to tend to the local partisans, along with the Austrian, Polish, French, British and American combatants, who were treated at the main hospital. The only way to avoid the brutal attentions of the occupiers was to wedge the straggle of hospital buildings high up the rugged gorge, an amazing feat considering construction had to be clandestine and everything had to be brought in and out through the hostile terrain that formed a natural barrier against attack. A system of bunkers and mines helped nature repel two German attacks, in April 1944 and March 1945.

The hospital (named after Dr Franja Bojc Bidovec, its most renowned director) opened as a museum straight after the war. You can see that little has changed with many of the original artefacts, including stretchers, bunks, posters of Tito, an X-ray machine and, chillingly, the stark operating table and accompanying surgical instruments, left intact. You can walk through the various wards, kitchen, washroom and isolation room, though at the time of writing the upper shelter and burial ground were off limits after a landslide, a vivid reminder of the dangers and difficulties in working in this terrain. Despite the rudimentary conditions the hospital's record was impressive with only 52 of the 522 badly injured patients who were brought here succumbing to their injuries. Given the steep ascents and slippery rock steps on the 15-minute trail from the car park, disabled access is not possible. To get to the hospital just follow the plentiful signs from Cerkno.

## Activities around Idrija and Cerkno
### Skiing

In winter the road from Cerkno to the Partisan Hospital continues to climb on to the Cerkno ski field, not exactly world-class skiing but, if you are in the area, worth trying out. The **Cerkno Ski Centre** (Sedejev trg 8; tel: 05 374 3400; fax: 05 374 3433; email: hotel.cerkno@siol.net; www.hotel-cerkno.si), 10km from Cerkno, offers decent conditions for downhill skiing with pistes up to 1,300m. The centre also has a ski school, rents equipment and has a variety of chair and ski lifts. If there is not enough snow there is even a snowmaking machine. The **Vojsko Ski**

**Centre** (tel: 05 374 2100/374 2035), 12km outside of Idrija, is on a mountain plateau that is great for cross-country skiing. There are also cross-country runs at the **Javornik Ski Centre** (Lome; tel: 05 377 7544).

## Cycling

**Čuk** Rožna 4, Idrija; tel: 05 372 2760; fax: 05 372 2762. This company rents mountain-bikes and accessories and also organises guided tours in the region around Idrija and Cerkno.

## Hiking

Hiking in the *Cerkljansko Hribovje* (Cerkno Hills) is a popular local pastime. An English-language walking map is available from the Hotel Cerkno and its eight walks include a hike to the Franja Partisan Hospital.

## VIPAVA VALLEY

One of Slovenia's most famous wine regions is well set-up for receiving visitors and it is also easy to get here over the hills from Idrija and Cerkno, by the fast road from Nova Gorica and also from the coastal resorts. The first wine co-operative in Slovenia was founded here in 1894, though some locals reckon that wine was savoured here as early as Roman times. Getting around the small towns and villages is only really practical if you have a car. The scenery is dramatic, with the Karst starting to rise to the south and heavily wooded hills to the north, with the verdant valley in between awash with vineyards. White wines have traditionally been the mainstay of the valley, but in recent years local producers have ventured into red wine with some considerable success (though try telling that to the Goriška Brda connoisseurs who insist that their reds are always the finest in Primorska).

There are numerous producers and the local tourist office has put together a guide to local vineyards that are open to visitors. Look out for *vinska klet* signs, though calling ahead is always advisable.

Vipava Valley also has some worthwhile sights. The town of **Vipava** enjoys a dramatic location and is overlooked by a ruined castle. The castle was once owned by the powerful Lantheiri family and their 18th-century baroque mansion still sits in town, with the **Cerkev Sv Štefan** (Church of St Stephen), built in the same century, a further testament to the golden era before it became today's charmingly sleepy town.

In the hills above Vipava is **Zemono Dvorec** (Zemono Palace; Zemono; tel: 05 368 7007; fax: 05 366 5440. Open: Mon–Fri 12.00–19.00, Sat 09.00–14.00), a Renaissance mansion now reincarnated with an epicurean oasis, Gostilna Pri Lojzetu (Open: Wed–Sun noon–midnight), which draws in gastronomes from all over Slovenia and further afield. Other places worth dropping into are the largest settlement in the valley, **Ajdovščina**, with its Roman history; **Log**, with its 18th-century Nazarene frescos; and **Vipavski Križ**, a tiny village that stands on the foundations of a prehistoric predecessor and is now a protected cultural monument in its own right.

**Ajdovščina Tourist Information Centre** Lokarjev drevored 8b; tel: 05 366 3900; email: tic.ajdovscina@siol.net. Open: Mon–Fri 09.00–17.00, Sat 10.00–14.00.

### VISITING A VIPAVA VALLEY VINEYARD

The Tilia (Linden Tree) vineyard (Potoče 41, Kukanje, 5623 Dobravlje; tel/fax: 05 364 6683; email: tilia@lemut.net) is run by a friendly English-speaking couple, Matjaž and Melita Lemut. Their three young children ensure that the 6ha vineyard is one of the few in Europe where the largest stretch of vines is accompanied by a playground. After a tour through the modern but charmingly small-scale winemaking equipment (the total annual production has never been more than 30,000 litres since the vineyard started bottling in 1996), Matjaž will guide you down to his cosy cellar for the serious business of tasting.

There will usually be some homemade bread and cheese, maybe with some walnut oil for dipping, to accompany the wines – if you are looking for something more substantial call ahead and they can rustle up a wholesome meal or even get in a local chef.

Tilia specialises in young wines and we sampled an excellent fruity pinot grigio (*sivi pinot* in Slovene) and a passable chardonnay. The sauvignon blanc was quite complex given the young age of the vineyard and the dessert wine was of such quality that it was being served in the five-star Kendov Dvorec Hotel in Idrija when we ate there. In total over 50% of the wines are exported, more through a network of personal contacts than through importers, to Austria, Croatia, Sweden, Switzerland and Denmark. Matjaž even produces a wine for Alan Ducasse in New York that sells at US$150 for half a bottle – you can pick it up here for a few euros!

Vipava may be renowned for its reds and while Tilia's merlot is not their greatest product, their stab at cabernet sauvignon has an impressive body, with smoky overtones. Matjaž's hospitality and *joie de vivre* can be addictive so make sure to peel yourself away after buying a few bottles before he wheels out the 'cheeky young brandy' that is one of his new pet projects. Another development may soon see a couple of rooms opened up so that you can indulge without worrying about who will drive you back to your hotel.

## KRAS (THE KARST)

The Karst straddles Primorska and the western edge of neighbouring Notranjska, dividing Slovenia's alpine north from the Adriatic in a flurry of rugged limestone. The region gave the world the geological term Karst, and it is an epic land where rivers simply disappear, vast caverns delve deep into the bowels of the earth and hidden waterways rush below. Dotted around the wooded hillsides are pretty orange-roofed towns and villages, many of them offering views south towards the Adriatic.

### Škocjanske Jama (Škocjan Caves)

The only downside of visiting the Škocjan Caves (tel: 05 763 2840; fax: 05 793 2844; email: psi.info@psi.gov.si; www.park-skocjanske-jame.si) is that most of the other caves that you visit around the world afterwards will pale in comparison. This

UNESCO World Heritage-listed marvel is a truly remarkable place and is well worth the trip no matter how little time you have in Slovenia. If Hollywood producers could get their hands on this unique landscape it would make a perfect setting for a *Lord of the Rings*-style epic. The first written mention of the caves came in the 2nd century BC and there is evidence of Iron-Age religious ceremonies at the site, but they were never fully explored until the 19th century. Before you delve underground on a guided tour – the only way to access the caves unless you are on a scientific research project – go up to the lookout point, which is signposted from the visitor's centre. From this lofty vantage point the scale of Škocjan becomes clear as the Reka River is swallowed into the abyss below, not to reappear for another 34km across the border in Italy.

The Škocjan Caves were formed over millions of years by the corrosive actions of the Reka River, which helped create today's subterranean world. This is a constantly changing landscape and the complex is still being actively studied and surveyed by speleologists today. The myriad karstic features include small and large caves, stalagmites and stalactites, with the caves also home to rare and endangered species of bat as well as stone martens and spiders. Water levels vary throughout the year and other seasonal variations include the striking ice stalactites that can be found in winter.

### Škocjan Caves tour

The 1¹/₂-hour tour (daily 10.00 and 13.00 with an additional tour at 15.00 on Sun Jan–Mar and Nov–Dec, 10.00, 13.00 and 15.30 Apr–May and Oct, 10.00, 11.30, 13.00, 14.00, 15.00, 16,00 and 17.00 Jun–Sep. 2,000SIT. Available in English, Slovene, German and Italian) begins with a ten-minute hike to the entrance, through an artificial tunnel. The park authorities have mercifully resisted the temptation to jazz things up and the 2km main trail is a narrow and simple one with no frills – the caves speak for themselves. You will see a network of other paths that snake tantalisingly in and around the Reka, but these are off-limits for tourists.

First up on the walk is the **Silent Cave**, where some of the largest and most impressive stalactites and stalagmites that you are ever likely to see combine to conjure up a scene that the guides aptly call 'paradise'. The trail moves on and groups tend to stretch out as stragglers attempt to take photos, which has been recently banned by the park authorities. The next section is even more dramatic as the vastness of the **Great Hall** unfurls like something from a science fiction movie, a huge space over 100m wide with a ceiling hanging around 30m overhead. You do not need any tacky soundtrack as the rumble of the Reka beckons from its nearby gorge.

For vertigo sufferers the next part can be an ordeal as a dimly lit path descends through the Tolkienesque netherworld of the **Murmuring Cave** and then crosses the narrow Cerkvenik Bridge over the Hankejev Kanal, which looks like something out of an *Indiana Jones* movie, though it is sturdy enough and was rebuilt in 2003. If you can bear to peer over, the views of the Reka bursting through the cavern are stunning. The path follows the Reka for a while before it snakes back around past the **Gours**, a series of rock pools, a kind of small-scale version of Pamukkale in Turkey – if you are lucky after heavy rain there may be some water in them – and then emerges at the vast opening of the **Schmidl Hall** that used to be the main entrance to the caves. A walkway leads around to a funicular that spirits you back up to the path below the visitors centre – if you did not have a chance to look over the caves from the viewpoint you can do so now. There is a modest café and *gostilna* at the visitor's centre. Plans have been mooted to open up a few hotel rooms for those wanting to stay overnight near the caves, though they will have to get past UNESCO first.

## Exploring the Karst

During World War II the Karst was the centre of fierce partisan resistance and during the savage German revenge attacks whole villages were burned down and their inhabitants sent off to concentration camps. In a sense the area has not really recovered, with only state aid, European funding and the promise of tourism providing hope of a renaissance. The Karst is renowned, though, for its culinary produce with the most famous exports being *pršut*, richly flavoured ham (similar to Spanish *jamon serrano* or Italian *proscuitto*) that is dried by the bitter *Burja* winds, and the robust Teran red wine. Spending a few days rolling between the various beautiful chocolate-box hill towns, enjoying snatched glimpses of the Adriatic, the Italian Alps and the Vipava Valley, washed down with *pršut* and Teran, is one of the most enjoyable experiences Slovenia has to offer.

## Lipica

The chances are that you will have heard of Lipica's most famous residents, the graceful white Lipizzaner horses, which attract hordes of visitors to this small Karst town each year. The name of the horses, Lipizzaner, is derived from the name Lipica which translates into English as a small linden tree. Dating back to 1580, today Lipica's stud farm extends over 300ha of fields. If you are not content to merely watch the horses on the guided tour then you can have riding lessons, take a horse- drawn carriage ride or hire a horse to explore the surrounding countryside. If it is raining when you visit the stud farm, then you can always ride in the indoor arena. Try to time your visit to coincide with one of the intricate displays of the Classic Riding School – call ahead.

### Getting there

There are no public transport services to Lipica. A taxi from Sežana costs from 1,500SIT. Sežana can be reached from Ljubljana by either train ($1^1/_2$–2 hours) or bus ($1^3/_4$–2 hours).

### Where to stay

**Hotel Maestoso** Tel: 05 739 1580; www.lipica.org. Situated at the heart of the stud farm with recently renovated and well-equipped rooms, an indoor pool, sauna, casino, restaurant and conference centre. Singles 13,600–18,000SIT, doubles 17,600–23,000SIT, suite 28,000–33,500SIT.
**Hotel Klub** Tel: 05 739 1580; fax: 05 734 6373; www.lipica.org. Also located within the grounds of the stud farm and with a fitness centre, sauna, bar, restaurant and club rooms. Singles 7,100–13,560SIT, doubles 14,000–19,000SIT.

## Entertainment and nightlife

**Grand Casino Lipica** Lipica 5; tel: 05 731 0600; email: marketing.lipica@casino.si; www.casino.si/lipica. If you do not feel you have spent enough money already then head to this swish casino with slot machines, poker tables, blackjack and roulette. Open nightly until 03.00/04.00.

## What to see
### Kobilarna Lipica (Lipica Stud Farm)

The timetable for events at the Lipica Stud Farm (Lipica 5; tel: 05 739 1580; fax: 05 734 6370; email: lipica@siol.net; www.lipica.org) is complicated and subject to change. Tours of the stud farm (1,400SIT) are available daily throughout the year at 13.00, 14.00 and 15.00, with additional tours at weekends and in the peak season. Riding presentations (2,800SIT) take place at 15.00 on Fridays and Sundays and at noon Wednesdays and Thursdays from April to October. There are additional 15.00 shows on Tuesdays from May to October. Call ahead to check these times.

Many people are surprised to learn that you can find the world-famous Lipizzaner horses outside of Vienna, although the Karst village of Lipica has been the proud home to a Lipizzaner stud farm for over four centuries. It was established by the Austrian archduke of Vienna in 1580, after experts informed him that the Karst provided all the necessary conditions for a successful stud farm, making Lipizzaners one of the oldest breeds of horse in the world. Kobilarna Lipica remained the property of the Viennese court until the end of World War I.

The brilliant white Lipizzaner horses (which are actually grey or black when they are born), which were once trained to manoeuvre during battle, now entertain visitors from across Slovenia and all over the world. Perhaps ironically the horses originally trained for conflict were relocated during time of war – moving to Hungary on three occasions during the Napoleonic Wars and then to Vienna in World War I. The horses were threatened once again during World War II when they were seized by the Germans, with only a small number ever returned.

Lipizzaner horses are very distinctive – broad, muscular and standing around 1.6m tall. Apparently walking on the Karst also gives them very hard hooves. They have a gracious gait, thick and silky tails and manes. The characteristic whiteness that people associate with the horses develops over time, so a dazzling white Lipizzaner is at least six years old.

There is more to keep you occupied at Lipica, though, than just its magnificent horses. Countryside trails around the village are good for walkers and cyclists, while the golf course and tennis courts provide other ways to keep fit. Adults staying in one of Lipica's hotels can also find plenty to keep them occupied in the Grand Casino while visitors over 12 years old can take riding lessons. Lessons last 50 minutes and cost 3,500SIT (group lesson), or 4,800SIT (individual instruction). Dressage tuition costs 13,000SIT, while a four-person horse-drawn carriage ride costs 4,500/8,500SIT for 30 minutes/one hour.

## Štanjel

This stunning little Karst town is a real find, the sort of place that no-one you know will ever have been to and that everyone will want to visit when you tell them about it. Wrapped across a vine-clad hillside is an orange-roofed hill town, complete with its own castle and church, art galleries and places to stay. All around are expansive views of Slovenia and Italy, something not lost on man throughout the centuries: as far back as Roman times there was a fort on the site. On the third Sunday of every month a small but lively market fills up the main square as you enter through the town gate. Everything is on sale here from bottles of sturdy Teran wine and massive jars of local honey, right through to all sorts of Yugoslav-era paraphernalia and even leftovers from the two world wars including bullets, helmets and (when we visited) a set of British-army-issue dungarees.

## Where to stay
**Štanjel 29** Tel: 05 734 6283. Jože Švagelj has an apartment for 4 people.
**Štanjel 18** Tel: 05 769 0150. Matjaž Hadalin has an apartment sleeping up to 4 people.
**Štanjel 29** Tel: 05 769 1007. Vesna and Marjan Černe have an apartment sleeping 2.
**Štanjel 6a** Tel: 05 769 0112; email: nassa.desella@siol.net. Jožef and Marija Švagelj have rooms.
**Kobdilj 5c** Tel: 05 769 0116. The Fratnik's have rooms.

## Where to eat and drink
**Stranarjev Hram** Štanjel 29. This small bar with an even smaller terrace located opposite the Mala Galerija is a great place to enjoy a drink.
**Okrepčevalnica** Grad Štanjel; tel: 05 769 0197. Café-bar located within the castle, serving snacks.
**Gostilna Zoro** Štanjel 42; tel: 05 769 0101

## Practicalities
**Tourist Information Centre** Tel: 05 769 0056; email: tic.stanjel@komen.si; www.komen.si. Open: Mon, Wed and Sat 11.00–16.00, Sun 14.00–17.00. Located up the stairs next to the castle.
**Post office** Štanjel 59a
There is a small **souvenir shop** housed in the old tower and you can buy honey from Jožef and Marija Švagelj (Štanjel 6a; tel: 05 769 0018).

## Elsewhere in the Karst
Other notable Karst attractions include **Hrastovlje**, a town that is home to the Church of the Holy Trinity, renowned for its frescos of the *Dance of Death*, which date back over 500 years and include some of the earliest examples of the Slavic Glagolithic script ever found. **Rihenberg Grad** (Rihenberg Castle), with a chequered history laced with Habsburgs, Slovene counts and Nazi troops is the largest and oldest castle in Primorska and its ramparts boast sweeping views out over the Karst.

# The Slovenian Adriatic

While neighbouring Croatia's sweeping 1,185-island-studded coastline tends to overshadow Slovenia's more modest 47km slice of the Adriatic – even many Slovenes head south to Croatia rather than to their own coast – there are plenty of reasons to swoop south, not least the idyllic Mediterranean climate and lifestyle. The Venetians from just across the water have left an architectural bounty from their years in charge with the old cores of the towns of Koper, Izola and – especially – Piran the highlight of a visit to Slovenia's coastline. Then there is Piran's young and brash sibling, Portorož, an unsubtle but fun beach resort with plenty of tacky trimmings. Given its location the Slovenian coastline unsurprisingly bears many similarities with Italy, a connection that manifests itself in the use of Italian, the seafood and the architecture which is the most visual legacy of the long period of Venetian rule.

Between the world wars the entire coast was occupied by Italy, and Mussolini's administration set about a process of Italianisation by banning the use of Slovene and its teaching in schools, as well as renaming streets and bringing in Italian settlers. 'Zone B' was handed to Yugoslavia after World War II and, although many Italians did choose to leave, the Italian community in coastal Slovenia is still vibrant; Italian words and accents can be heard all over and street signs are bilingual. Croatian influences emerge too, which is not too surprising as Slovenia shares its tiny corner of the Istrian peninsula with Croatia. The Slovenian Adriatic still feels very much at a crossroads and, sitting down to an al-fresco dinner in Piran, the bright lights of the Italian city of Trieste blink to the north while the shadowy hulk of Croatia looms just to the south. A border feud was still simmering between Slovenia and Croatia at the time of going to press with the Croatians at one point said to be threatening to cut off Slovenia's access to the open sea, which would be disastrous for the Slovenian port of Koper.

## KOPER

Many Slovenes dismiss the nearest the coast has to a city due to its unattractive port. It is easy to write it off as any approach reveals a welter of heavy industry and docklands, but delve beyond this and the shabbily attractive Venetian heart of Koper unfurls. Koper's glory days were during Venetian times when it took on a role as a major port. Koper slipped into decline under the Austro-Hungarians as

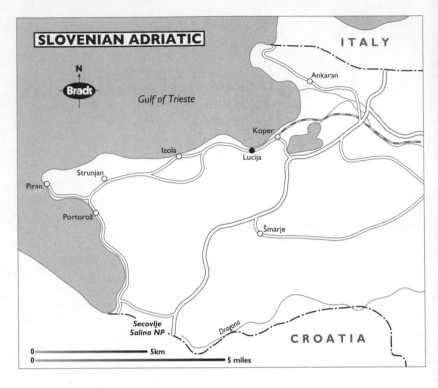

Trieste and Rijeka both took much of its trade away; somewhat ironically today the successful port thrives on business from Austria and Hungary. One problem for visitors is that the few restaurants and bars close early as most locals make a beeline for the coastal resorts or stay home.

## Getting there

Frequent buses run from Izola (15 minutes), Piran (30 minutes), Strunjan (20 minutes) and Portorož (25 minutes) on the coast to Koper. Services also run from Ljubljana (2¹/₄ hours), Postojna (1¹/₄ hours), Celje (3³/₄ hours), Maribor (5¹/₄ hours) and Murska Sobota (6¹/₄ hours). Train services are less frequent, but there are trains to/from Postojna (1¹/₂ hours) and to/from Ljubljana (2¹/₂ hours). Koper also has a marina that welcomes visiting yachts.

**Bus station** Kolodvorska 11; tel: 05 639 5269
**Railway station** Kolodvorska 11; tel: 05 639 5263
**Marina Koper** Kopališko nabrežje 5; tel: 05 662 6100; fax: 05 662 6161; email: info@marina-koper.si; www.marina-koper.si

## Getting around

**Altana Taxi** Tel: 041 852 145
**Big Red** Tel: 05 641 8310; www.slo-istra.com/aquamarine. This passenger boat runs along Slovenia's coast during the main tourist season, travelling between Piran, Bernardin,

Strunjan, Portorož, Izola, Koper and Ankaran. The fare from Koper is 600–2,300SIT depending on your final destination. Sailing frequencies and times vary.

## Tour operators
**Kompas** Pristaniška 17; tel: 05 627 2346; fax: 05 627 4135; email: kompas.koper@siol.net. Services include accommodation, car rental and onward travel.

## Where to stay
**Hotel Koper** (65 rooms) Pristaniška 3; tel: 05 610 0500; fax: 05 610 0594; email: koper@terme-catez.si; www.terme-catez.si. Koper's best hotel overlooks the sea on the fringe of the Old Town, with huge bedrooms and plush public areas. You can also use the gym, pool and spa facilities at the Aquapark Žusterna across the bay. Singles 12,900SIT, doubles 23,800–25,800SIT.

**Hotel Vodišek** (32 rooms) Kolodvorska 2; tel: 05 639 2468; fax: 05 639 3668; email: city@hotel-vodisek.com; www.hotel-vodisek.com. Rooms sleeping 1–4 people are simply furnished with wooden floors and white bedding. The hotel also has its own rustic restaurant. Singles from 9,600SIT, doubles from 14,300SIT, triples from 17,900SIT, quads from 21,000SIT.

**Garni Hotel Pristan** (18 rooms) Ferraska 30; tel: 05 614 4000; fax: 05 614 4040; email: hotel@luka-kp.si; www.pristan-koper.si. Newish hotel geared towards businesspeople with rooms and apartments. Singles 11,000–12,000SIT, doubles 16,800–18,000SIT, triples 21,600–23,400SIT, apartments 16,000–30,600SIT.

**Aquapark Hotel Žusterna** (117 rooms) Istrska 67; tel: 05 663 8000; fax: 05 663 8010; email: zusterna@terme-catez.si; www.terme-catez.si. Definitely one for families, this hotel has an impressive array of leisure facilities including indoor and outdoor swimming pools, gym, Roman-Irish baths and a fitness centre. Guest rooms are on the small side. Check for special offers. Singles 13,900SIT, doubles 24,800–28,800SIT.

**Dijaški Dom Koper** (380 beds) Cankarjeva 5; tel: 05 627 3250; fax: 05 627 3182; email: ddkoper@guest.arnes.si; www.d-dom.kp.edus.si. This large student dormitory transforms into an HI-affiliated youth hostel from mid-Jun–mid-Aug with affordable beds in triple rooms. 3,000SIT per person.

## Where to eat
Restaurants are thin on the ground in Koper's Old Town. Fast food comes in the form of the *bureks* on sale at Kidričeva 8.

**Istrska Klet Slavček** Župančičeva 39; tel: 05 627 6729. Old-World restaurant selling hearty Slovenian specialities. Try the bean and sausage soup, followed by Hungarian goulash or roast pork knuckle and washed down with wine from the vineyards near Koper.

**Skipper** Kopališko nabrežje 3; tel: 05 627 1750. Second-floor restaurant with terrace overlooking the marina. A lively atmosphere, fresh fish and tasty grills make this one of the best dining spots in town. Try the scampi soup or seafood salad.

**Market** Pristaniška (adjacent to Mercator). Stallholders sell fresh food Mon–Fri 07.00–20.00 and Sat 07.00–11.00.

**Mercator** centrally located stores include Prešernov trg 1, Pristaniška 2 and Titov trg 2. The latter is also open on Sunday mornings.

**Na stopničkah** Župančičeva 37. Deli that makes sandwiches and is also open on Sunday mornings.

## Entertainment and nightlife

If you are looking for a lively night out you won't find it in Koper's Old Town. Locals travel to the neighbouring resorts for nightlife. However, there are a number of pleasant venues for a quiet drink.

**Kavarna Kapitanija** Ukmarjev 8; tel: 05 626 1963. This mellow café near the marina has a large outdoor terrace.

**Lord Byron Pub** Repičeva 2. Welcoming British-style pub tucked away off Prešernov trg with Guinness, Caffreys, Staropramen and Tennents Super on draught.

If you are still looking for a party and don't mind leaving the Old Town then try Papas or Abar at Zeleni Park; the latter is open until 02.00. The Ogrlica Centre also has some late-night bars.

## Shopping

Koper's Old Town is a decent place to go shopping especially if you are hankering after a new pair of shoes, attractive jewellery or just like to window shop in galleries and boutiques. The best streets to indulge in a spot of retail therapy are Čevljarska and Kidričeva. Look out for:

**Atelije Galerija Art** Kidričeva 37; tel: 05 641 9510
**Galerija Žbona** Čevljarska 8; tel: 041 600 120; www.galerija-zbona.si. Ceramics, modern art and sculpture by contemporary Slovene artists.
**Atelje Terracota Umetnostna Obrt** Župančičeva 41a; tel: 05 627 1056. Terracotta animals and pots.

## Practicalities

**Tourist Information Centre** Pretorska palača, Titov trg 3; tel: 05 664 6403; fax: 05 664 6405; email: tic@koper.si; www.koper.si. Open: Mon–Sat 09.00–20.00, Sun 09.00–12.00 Jun–Aug, Mon–Fri 09.00–17.00, Sat 09.00–12.00 Sep–May.
**Banka Koper** Kidričeva 14. Open: Mon–Fri 08.00–12.00 and 15.00–17.00, Sat 08.00–12.00.
**Ljubljanska Banka** Pristaniška 43. Open: Mon–Fri 08.30–13.00 and 15.30–17.00.
**Volksbank** Pristaniška 45. Open: Mon–Fri 08.30–13.00 and 15.30–17.00.
**Post office** Muzeski trg 3. Open: Mon–Fri 08.00–19.00 and Sat 08.00–12.00.
**Pina** Kidričeva 43; tel: 05 627 8072. Arguably the best internet café outside of Ljubljana with high-speed connections, affordable prices and modern PCs with flat screens. Open: Mon–Fri 09.00–22.00.

## What to see
### Exploring the historic quarter
A good place to start a walking tour of Koper is in the central square, one of the few important public spaces in Slovenia to keep its socialist-era name of Titov trg. Head for the 36m campanile (Titov trg. Open: daily 09.30–13.30 and 16.00–18.00.

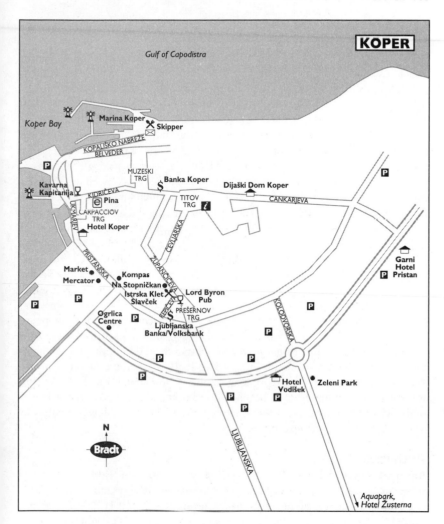

400SIT), which was modelled on the campanile across the water in Venice, for a bird's-eye view of the city and you will see the tight warren of streets that make up the Old Town stretching out below. The rather austere-looking **Stolnica Marija Vnebovzetja** (Cathedral of the Assumption) lies below the belltower. The square is also home to the 12th-century **Rotunda Janeza Krstnika** (Rotunda of John the Baptist) baptistery, which you will see if you look north. Elsewhere on Titov trg is the most dramatic building in Koper: the **Pretorska Palača** (Praetorian Palace). What used to be the home of the Venetian-era mayor now houses a tourist information centre and also functions as a cultural hub with temporary exhibitions and shows. At the opposite end of the square is the well-preserved **Loža** (Loggia), which dates back to the 15th century. The Loggia Café is now housed within the loggia, offering a unique experience as you sip your *bela kava* amidst the hub of Venetian Koper and admire the square. Upstairs is a modest art gallery, **Galerija Loža** (Titov trg 1; tel: 05 673 2689. Open: Tue–Sat 15.00–22.00, Sun 20.00–22.00. 400SIT).

Head east out of Titov trg on to Kidričeva, a narrow pedestrianised thoroughfare which has connected the square to the Adriatic for centuries. You will soon come to the **Pokrajinski Muzej** (Koper Regional Museum; Palača Belgramoni, Kidričeva 19; tel: 05 663 3570; fax: 05 663 3571. Open: Mon–Fri 08.00–13.00 and 18.00–20.00, Sat 08.00–13.00 Jun–Aug, Mon–Fri 08.00–15.00, Sat 08.00–13.00 Sep–May. 350SIT) at No 19 on the left, which is housed in the 16th-century Belgramoni Palace. Inside you will find a variety of exhibits, including a copy of the *Dance of Death* that you may already have seen in the Karst in Hrastovlje. Continue along Kidričeva and you will soon come upon two medieval houses at Nos 31 and 33, with raised painted timbered upper levels, unlike anything else that you will find on the coast. Opposite on the right is the **Palača Totto** (Totto Palace) sporting the unmistakable Venetian lion, symbol of the Divine Republic. Further down are a trio of disused churches, indicative of a city whose Old Town definitely needs a major refurbishment. At No 29 is the simple façade of the 16th-century **Cerkev Sv Nikolaj** (Church of St Nicholas), with the 18th-century **Cerkev Sv Trojice** (Church of the Holy Trinity) at No 23. If you want to take a minute to check your emails and have a coffee then pop into Pina at No 43, probably the best internet café on the coast (see *Practicalities*).

Kidričeva soon opens out into the expanse of Carpacciov trg with its shops and cafés. Look out for the Roman well and also the Column of St Justin, the latter commemorating the part Koper played in fighting the Turks during the landmark tussle against the Ottomans in 1571 at the Battle of Lepanto. From here the Adriatic beckons and there is a long walkway just across the Belveder (the waterfront road) with plenty of benches to relax on and take in the sun. A branch of the Mercator supermarket chain is located just behind the walkway if you want to grab a drink or rustle up a picnic.

## Activities
**Aquapark Žusterna** Istrska 67; tel: 05 663 8000; fax: 05 663 8010; email: zusterna@terme-catez.si; www.terme-catez.si. Open to non-residents this is a great place to indulge in a spot of pampering. A 30-minute massage costs 4,500SIT, use of the gym 1,500SIT and two hours' use of the swimming pools 1,100–1,550SIT depending on the day of the week.

## IZOLA
Most visitors make a beeline south for Piran, but consider at least stopping off for lunch in Izola, 5km to the south of Koper, as it offers some of the finest seafood in Slovenia from its own fishing fleet. The most dramatic approach to the town is from the south, as Izola rears up from the sea like a mini-Piran and proudly shows off its Venetian-style architecture – approach from the north and you may well want to skip past the hulking dry dock that welcomes you. The Romans and the Venetians have both played their part in Izola's history, while these days tourism is increasingly shaping the town, as Izola smartens itself up in an attempt to win much-needed visitors. The whole seafront is currently being revamped and May 2004 saw a new and alternative film festival arrive in Izola, which focused on films

made by African, Asian, Latin American and eastern European producers. This event combined film with outdoor screenings on Manziolli trg, camping and even Bollywood projections on the beach. The four-day event is set to be repeated at the end of May each year and will be ticketed. For more information contact Izola Cinema; email: info@isolacinema.org; www.isolacinema.org.

## Getting there
Coastal buses connect Portorož (10 minutes), Strunjan (10 minutes), Koper (15 minutes) and Piran (20 minutes) with impressive frequency. More limited services run to and from Ljubljana ($2^{1}/_{2}$ hours), Celje (4 hours), Maribor ($5^{1}/_{2}$ hours) and Murska Sobota ($6^{1}/_{2}$ hours).

**Big Red** Tel: 05 641 8310; www.slo-istra.com/aquamarine. This passenger boat runs along Slovenia's coast during the main tourist season travelling between Piran, Bernardin, Strunjan, Portorož, Izola, Koper and Ankaran. The fare from Izola is 800–1,400SIT depending on your final destination. Sailing frequencies and times vary. The *Prince of Venice* also calls here from Venice (see *Getting There and Away* in *Chapter 2*).

## Tour operators
**Bele Skale** Cankarjev drevored 2; tel: 05 640 3555; fax: 05 641 8200; email: beleskale@siol.net; www.beleskale.si. Centrally located tourist agency that organises private accommodation, car and bicycle rental.
**Turist Biro Simonov Zaliv** Morova 6a; tel: 05 660 3100; fax: 05 641 8402; email: simonov.zaliv@htp-simonov-zaliv.si; www.htp-simonov-zaliv.si. A couple of streets back from the Marina behind the Delfin Hotel. Arranges accommodation and a range of sporting activities.

## Where to stay
**Hotel Marina** Veliki trg 11; tel: 05 660 4100; fax: 05 660 4410; email: marina@belvedere.si; www.belvedere.si. Located at the heart of the Old Town, this hotel has decent rooms with minibars, satellite TV and air conditioning. The health spa offers a choice of Jacuzzi, sauna, massage and thalassotherapy. Singles 11,000–18,200SIT, doubles 12,800–20,600SIT.
**Hotel Delfin** Tomažičeva 10; tel: 05 660 7000; fax: 05 660 7420; email: delfin.recepcija@siol.net. Large waterfront hotel geared towards tour groups and located 1km from town. Singles from 12,000SIT, doubles from 18,000SIT.
**Hotel Belvedere** Dobrava 1a; tel: 05 660 5100; fax: 05 660 5171; email: belvedere@belvedere.si; www.belvedere.si. Standard 3-star hotel with good-value apartments (if you are planning to stay for at least 3 nights) sleeping 2–3 people. Singles 11,400–19,200SIT, doubles 12,100–21,300SIT, apartments 7,700SIT–19,000SIT.
**Kamp Belvedere** Dobrava 1a; tel: 05 660 5100; fax: 05 660 5171; email: belvedere@belvedere.si; www.belvedere.si. Adjacent to the Belvedere Hotel, 3km from town on a hill overlooking the Bay of Trieste, this campsite has a capacity for 500 tents. Reservations not accepted. 1,000–1,880SIT per person.
**Campsite Jadranka** Pole 8; tel: 05 640 2300; fax: 05 641 8358; email: freetimedoo@siol.net. Beachfront campsite 1km east of the Old Town. 1,000–1,800SIT.

## Where to eat

**Parangal** Sončo nabrežje 20; tel: 05 641 7440. This deservedly popular restaurant offers excellent fish and has a terrace that spreads out along the waterfront. The 'first class' fish platter cannot be beaten, although there is a slightly cheaper option using 'second class' seafood.

**Gostilna Ribič** Veliki trg 3; tel: 05 41 8313. Held in equal esteem to Parangal by the locals. The car park that sits between this fish restaurant and the sea can be off-putting for visitors.

## Entertainment and nightlife

**Gavioli** Located amidst Izola's industrial zone and only open weekends, Gavioli is Izola's more exclusive club. 2,500–4,000SIT.

## Practicalities

**Tourist Information Centre** Sončno nabrežje 4; tel: 05 640 1050; fax: 05 640 1052; email: tic.izola@izola.si; www.sigov.si/izola. Limited tourist information, but can help you find private accommodation.

**Post office** Cankarjev drevored 1. Open: Mon–Fri 08.00–19.00, Sat 08.00–12.00.

**Banka Koper** Drevored 1 Maja 5. Open: Mon–Fri 08.30–12.00 and 15.00–17.00, Sat 08.30–12.00.

**A Banka** Pittonijeva 1. Open: Mon–Fri 08.00–12.00 and 16.00–18.00, Sat 09.00–12.00.

**Izola Hospital** Polje 5; tel: 05 660 6000

## What to see

There are few real sights in Izola with the fun being in just lazing away the afternoon in one of the seafood restaurants, wandering around the small web of Venetian streets and dawdling around the coast. Attractions as such include the **Cerkev Sv Mavricija** (Church of St Maurus) whose belltower rises high above the town and the **Besenghi degli Ughi Palace**, where you can hear the efforts of local music students and admire the fine stuccowork on the façade. The local authorities have dabbled with renovating the waterfront past the marina with a landscaped park, but turn the corner and a concrete pier at the town's main beach lies cracked in two. One positive move has been to tempt Slovene artists into Izola with cheap rents and the Old Town now has a sprinkling of little studios where you can pick up some truly unique works as well as slightly cheesy images of the coastal towns. A tourist train is on hand to whisk you around.

## Activities

The **Sub-net Diving School** (Simonov zaliv; tel: 041 620 042; email: izola@sub-net.si; www.sub-net.si) offers a variety of courses, including PADI, and dives. Explore a shipwreck or Slovenia's only marine reserve. They also rent dive equipment and have another centre in Piran. Prices start at 5,500SIT for a guided dive from the shore.

## PIRAN

Piran is by far the most attractive town on Slovenia's bijou coastline, the sort of oasis that you cannot pull yourself away from and where you will end up wanting to buy a house. You will not be alone as property prices are accelerating in the Old Town as the city's young people are nudged out to nearby Lucija – EU accession has hastened this move as in the first few months of membership around a dozen Old Town dwellings were snapped up as holiday homes. Piran sits dramatically on its own peninsula with the Adriatic lapping all around, while Trieste is clearly visible to the north and Croatia to the south. Preserved as a national monument its narrow, cobbled streets hark back to the days of the mighty Venetian Republic, which gave Piran many of its most elaborate and attractive buildings. Sitting today on the waterfront at sunset, savouring fresh seafood and a chilled glass of locally produced Malvazija wine, with the lights of Trieste twinkling to the north and the shadowy hulk of Croatia looming to the south, Piran is a truly magical place to be.

## History

While the Venetian legacy is the most striking, the name Piran probably comes from the Greek word 'pyr', meaning fire, when the extremities of Piran were illuminated to ward off passing ships. Early in its history, both the Romans and the Slavs breezed through Piran before La Serenissima wrapped itself around the town in the 13th century and held on to it for the best part of five centuries. Under the Austro–Hungarians in the 19th century Piran sprawled out along the coast towards Portorož but these days development has moved inland and the hills in the hinterland are awash with holiday homes, though the central core remains intact and protected. Between the world wars Piran was firmly under Italian rule and a wave of settlers flocked in to bolster the fascist attempts to Italianise the town by banning the use of the Slovene language and its teaching in schools. Although some Italians did flee when Piran was handed to Yugoslavia there is still a lively Italian community today with no fewer than four Italian elementary schools. Sadly some of Piran's older buildings are in a sorry state as few businesses or residents can manage to make the sums add up when it comes to renovating them and sticking to the strict preservation rules at the same time; something that passing visitors do not need to worry about as it only adds to the charm of the town.

## Getting there

Regular buses connect Piran to Portorož (5 minutes), Strunjan (10 minutes), Izola (20 minutes), Koper (30 minutes), Postojna (1³/₄ hours), Ljubljana (2³/₄ hours), Celje (4¹/₄ hours), Maribor (5³/₄ hours) and Murska Sobota (6³/₄ hours).

Amazingly tourists are allowed to park on Tartinijev trg (see *A walking tour*); if there are no spaces you will be directed to the public car park at Formače near Bernardin, from where you can either walk (15–20 minutes) or hop on a free shuttle bus.

## Getting around

**Big Red** Tel: 05 641 8310; www.slo-istra.com/aquamarine. This passenger boat runs along Slovenia's coast during the main tourist season travelling between Piran, Bernardin, Strunjan, Portorož, Izola, Koper and Ankaran. The fare from Piran is 500–1,800SIT depending on your final destination. Sailing frequencies and times vary. The *Prince of Venice* also stops at Piran (see *Getting There and Away* in *Chapter 2*).

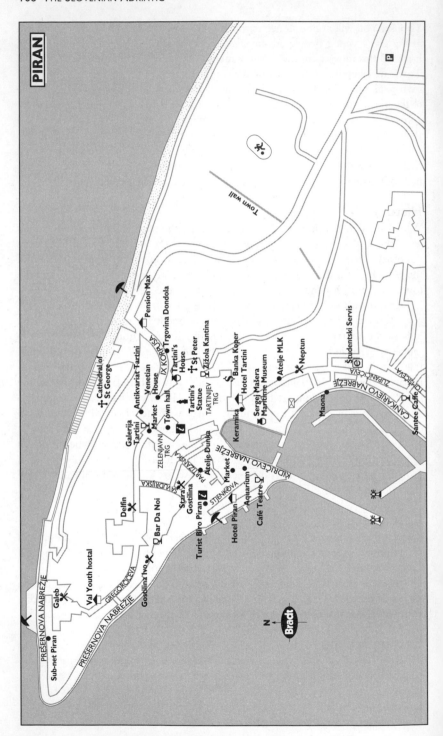

**Taxi Piran** Tel: 05 673 0700
**Taxi Jani** Tel: 05 625 0258. This company also has minibuses.

## Tour operators

**Turist Biro Piran** Tomažičeva 3; tel: 05 673 2509; fax: 05 673 2507; email:
info@tuirsbiro-ag.si; www.turistbiro-ag.si
**Maona** Cankarjevo nabrežje 7; tel: 05 673 0220; fax: 05 673 4519; email:
maona@siol.net; www.maona.si

## Where to stay

**Hotel Piran** (78 rooms) Stjenkova 1; tel: 05 676 2100; fax: 05 676 2520; email:
marketing@hoteli-piran.si; www.hoteli-piran.si. Welcoming hotel on the seafront. Modern
rooms have a minibar and satellite TV. Try to book a sea-facing room with a balcony. The
hotel also has some car parking spaces. Singles 11,000–18,800SIT, doubles 17,200–28,400SIT.
**Tartini Hotel** Tartinijev trg 15; tel: 05 671 1666; fax: 05 671 1601; email: info@hotel-
tartini-piran.com; www.hotel-tartini-piran.com. Stylish modern hotel with individual
rooms. Although they do not have the sea views of the Hotel Piran, square-view rooms
have an appeal of their own. Singles 9,400–15,100SIT, doubles 7,000–12,200SIT,
apartments 26,900–40,500SIT.
**Pension Max** IX Korpusa; tel: 041 692 928; email: info@maxhotel-piran.com;
www.maxhotel-piran.com. Friendly and welcoming pension on the way up to the Stolna
Cerkev Sv Jurija (Cathedral of St George). Singles 12,000SIT, doubles 14,400SIT.
**Val Youth Hostel and Garni Hotel** (22 rooms) Gregorčičeva 38a; tel: 05 673 2555;
fax: 05 673 2556; email: yhostel.val@siol.net; www.hostel-val.com. Simple two–four
bedded rooms with shared bathroom facilities on each floor. 4,800– 5,740SIT per person.
**Hotel Barbara Fiesa** (44 rooms) Fiesa 68; tel: 05 617 9000; fax: 05 617 9010; email:
hotel.barbara@siol.net; www.rlv.si/fiesa. Singles 8,500–11,100SIT, doubles
13,000–18,200SIT. Located in nearby Fiesa the hotel offers good-value rooms with sea
views and balconies. Four of the rooms sleep 4 people.
**Avtokamp Fiesa** Tel: 05 674 6230. This Fiesa campsite is very busy in July and August.
1,600–2,200SIT per person.

## Where to eat

Most locals avoid the flurry of tourist-orientated seafood restaurants dotted along
the waterfront. In these you pay more and also run the risk of sacrificing quality.
These waterfront restaurants do, though, offer great views out across the Adriatic.

**Neptun** Župančičeva 7; tel: 05 673 4111. Ask any local where the best place to eat
seafood is and they will send you here. An intimate dining space and good service form
part of the appeal, but the winning ingredient is excellent food. The gnocchi with cheese
and shrimps is to die for. The only things Neptun doesn't have are sea views and a terrace.
**Galeb** Pusterla 5; tel: 05 673 3225. Another local favourite. In the summer the restaurant
spills out on to the waterfront terrace. Serves seafood specialities and grills.
**Gostilna Ivo** Gregorčičeva 3; tel: 05 673 2233. As good as it gets on the waterfront strip.
This unfussy seafood trattoria-style set-up does the likes of grilled squid and sea bass well,
with a generous platter for two also available.

**Stara Gostilna** Savudrijska 2; tel: 040 640 240. Tasty grills, fresh fish and friendly staff make Stara a good option.
**Delfin** Kosovelova 4; tel: 05 673 2448. Another fish restaurant favoured by locals, just off Trg 1 Maja.

## Entertainment and nightlife

**Café Teatre Piran** *The* place to see and be seen in Piran. Great café-bar with a polished wooden interior, mellow music and great sea views from the terrace. The only downside is the seriously dodgy Guinness. Housed in Piran's bright yellow theatre, you cannot miss it.
**Bar Da Noi** Another waterfront bar with friendly staff and a good-sized garden. The music can be a bit iffy though.
**Zižola Kantina** Tartinijev trg 10. Tiny bolthole with a terrace overlooking the main square. Blink and you miss it.
**News Café** Obala 4f, Bernardin; tel: 05 674 1004. Good food – including breakfast, open sandwiches, gnocchi, pasta and enormous salads – and regular live music all make the walk here worth the effort (if you are not staying in Bernardin). Decent cocktail list and range of beers too in a huge venue. Just follow the sea around the coast from Piran in the direction of Portorož. Open until 02.00.
**Santeé Caffe** Župančičeva 18; tel: 041 258 087. Bright and modern café-bar selling tasty ice-cream.
**Galerija Tartini** Zelenjavni trg 10. Stylish café-cum-art gallery that spills out onto the square in the warmer months.

## Shopping

**Atelje Dunka** Partizanska 2; tel: 05 673 0501. Contemporary ceramics including funky vases and statues of cats made in the onsite workshop.
**Antikvariat Tartini** IX Korpusa 5; tel: 031 751 224. Great little shop selling antiques and bric-a-brac. They even had a bust of Tito last time we were there.
**Atelje MLK** Župančičeva 3; tel: 041 578 924. Sells handmade glass and contemporary paintings.
**Keramika** Cankarjevo nabrežje 1. Wide range of ceramics including artistic tiles.
**Trgovina Dondola** IX Korpusa 18. Handmade ceramics geared towards a tourist market.
**Tourist Market** You can pick up cheap jewellery, prints of Piran and other seaside souvenirs at this small market on Kidričevo nabrežje outside the aquarium.
**Food** For fresh food head to the market on Zelenjavni trg. On the square you will find a fishmonger, mini market, bakery and a pharmacy. If these are closed there is a **Mercator** at Levstikova 5.

## Practicalities

**Tourist Information Centre** Tartinijev trg 2; tel: 05 673 0220; fax: 05 673 0221; email: ticpi@Portoroz.si; www.portoroz.si. Open: Mon–Fri 09.00–16.00, Sat 09.00–12.00 Sep–Jun, daily: 09.00–13.00 and 15.00–21.00 Jul–Aug.
**Post office** Leninova 1. Open: Mon–Fri 08.00–19.00, Sat 08.00–12.00.
**Banka Koper** Tartinijev trg 13. Piran's most central bank. Open: Mon–Fri 08.30–12.00 and 15.00–17.00, Sat 08.30–12.00.

**Študentski Servis** Županičičeva 14; tel: 05 671 0020. Visitors are allowed to use the internet facilities at Piran's student centre. The service is free for young Slovenes, but you may have to pay a small charge depending on who is on duty. The first time we went it was free, but next time we paid 300SIT for an hour.

## What to see
### A walking tour
A good place to start is on the remaining stretch of the Town Walls high above Piran, at their most impressive at sunrise or sunset, as the town glows in oranges and reds with the Adriatic spreading out all around. To get to the walls walk up past **Stolna Cerkev Sv Jurija** (Cathedral of St George) and follow the road up the hill. Cut left through what looks like someone's garden, just before you get to the walls, and a staircase takes you up on to the well-preserved stretch. On a clear day the Italian Alps are plainly visible and you get a bird's-eye view of Piran – here you can appreciate just how tightly woven its medieval town plan, or lack of it, is.

From the walls, if you fancy relaxing at the beach, turn right as you walk back towards the Cathedral of St George's Church, currently blighted by scaffolding. Follow the path that curls around the coast to the small resort of Fiesa 1km away, a real summer playground that gets packed when the mercury rises. Otherwise go into the church and have a look at the sculpture of George himself slaying the dragon. Now head back down the hill to Tartinijev trg, once actually part of the town's harbour, but now Piran's showpiece square and the hub of local life. It is a real shame that, despite the solid attempt by the local authorities to cut traffic in the Old Town, this striking square is still blighted by parked cars. Dominating the centre of the square is a statue by the Venetian sculptor Antonio dal Zotto of Giuseppe Tartini, the locally born composer who gives the square its name. The **Cerkev Sv Petra** (Church of St Peter) has stood on the square since the 13th century, though it has been revamped in various styles over the centuries.

The 19th-century **Mestna Hiša** (Town Hall) stands to the right on the site of the old Venetian loggia with the civic, Slovenian and European Union flags all flying proudly over the square. Perhaps the most attractive building in the whole square is the ruby-red **Benečanka** (Venetian House), which dates back to the 15th century and is still in pretty good shape. Look out for the Venetian lion and the inscription 'lassa pur dir', which translates as 'let them talk', said to be a reference to the love-struck man who commissioned the house as a testimony to his love for a local girl. Apparently, he wanted to show he was not afraid of local gossips.

### Tartinijeva Hiša (Tartini's House)
The house where Piran's most famous son was born (Kajuhova 12; tel: 05 663 3570. Open: daily 11.00–12.00 and 17.00–18.00 Sep–May, 09.00–12.00 and 18.00–21.00 Jun–Aug. 250SIT) now houses the Giuseppe Tartini Memorial Room, dedicated to the renowned composer. Tartini was cherished by Slovenes throughout the country; although he was born in what comprises present-day Slovenia, his family was Italian. Exhibits on display include Tartini's death mask, one of his violins and some of his original scores. The museum was opened in 1991.

## GIUSEPPE TARTINI

The great composer was born in Piran on April 8 1692, in the house that is now a museum dedicated to him and his work. His father, a merchant who later became involved in the local salt trade, came to Piran from his native Florence and married his mother, a woman from Piran, in 1685. There is some evidence that Tartini showed his musical talent at an early stage in his life, but one of the most important violinists of the 18th century was almost lost to music after he flirted with life in Naples running a martial arts school, an art he had learned during his time at the University of Padua, where he was studying law. Padua was also a crucial period in Tartini's love life as he met Elisabetta Premazore when he was still a teenager and married her in the city in 1710.

From Padua his life took an ecclesiastical turn as he moved to Assisi to join the Franciscan brotherhood where he devoted much of his time to music. As his reputation grew he ventured further afield, playing regularly in Assisi's surrounds and also in Ancona, before moving to Venice with his wife in 1715. Tartini quickly established himself as one of the most renowned performers in Italy and when he was not composing and teaching others, he was devoted to travelling to and performing in Milan, Bologna and Naples. After a two-year period being feted and productive in Prague Tartini settled back in his beloved Padua where he spent the rest of his life. His performances around the country were severely limited after a minor stroke and he died in Padua in 1770, a year after his wife, with a requiem being held in the city in his honour. Today Tartini is remembered as not only a great violinist, but also as a composer and musical theorist. Tartini left a more immediate legacy in the expertly trained graduates from the violin school he ran in Padua.

### Pomorski Muzej Sergej Mašera (Sergej Mašera Maritime Museum)

Housed in the 19th-century **Gabrielli Palača** (Gabrielli Palace), located on the waterfront, the maritime museum (Cankarjevo nabrežje 3; tel: 05 671 0040; fax: 05 671 0050; email: muzej@pommuz-pi.si; www2.arnes.si/guest/kppomm/index.htm. Open: Tue–Sun 09.00–12.00 and 15.00–18.00. 800SIT, concessions 700SIT) has exhibits based around seafaring, maritime routes, trade and salt making. Highlights include the shipbuilding display and intricate model ships. Remember to seek out the museum's sailing ship *Galeb* which is moored in Piran harbour.

### Akvarij (Aquarium)

Piran's modest Aquarium (Kidričevo Nabrežje 4; tel: 05 673 2572; fax: 05 674 7242. Open: daily 10.00–12.00 and 14.00–19.00 mid-Mar–mid-Jun, Sep–mid-Oct, 09.00–22.00 mid-Jun–Aug. 500SIT, concessions 300SIT) may not be the biggest or most high-tech of its kind in the world, but it does have a good selection of local marine life and is a good option for a rainy day, especially for those with children in tow.

## Activities
### Boat tours
**Salinarka** (tel: 031 653 682) run boat tours to the saltpans and Salt Museum at Sečovlje. The charge of 2,600SIT for adults and 1,000SIT for children includes all entrance fees. They also pick up from Bernardin and Portorož.

### Diving
**Sub-net Piran** Prešernova nabrežje 24; tel: 05 673 2218; email: info@sub-net.si; www.sub-net.si (see *Izola* entry).

# PORTOROŽ
The reality of Portorož may be bit more prosaic than the 'port of roses' moniker suggests. In summer this can be some people's idea of hell as thousands of tourists descend to cram into the large hotels and squash together on the congested beaches. To be fair to Portorož, though, it is trying to clean up its old socialist-era image with refurbished hotels, numerous 'wellness centres' and a choice of new bars and restaurants that overcome the nightmare of the old-fashioned hotel buffet. Portorož these days is a fun place to put your feet up and relax for a few days. It also makes a good base for exploring the coast and striking out into Croatia.

## Getting there
### By car
The main thoroughfare in Portorož, Obala, which runs along the seafront, is full of parking spaces, the majority of which are pay and display. There are also secure car parks near the Hotel Metropol and Hotel Palace.

### By sea
**Portorož Marina** (Solinarjev 8; tel: 05 676 1100; fax: 05 676 1210; email: reception@marinap.si; www.marinap.si) has over 1,000 berths and welcomes visiting yachts. Facilities are good and include hotel accommodation, restaurants, supermarket, laundry, car rental, yacht charter and equipment, clothing and most other supplies that you might need. There is also the possibility of day returns to Venice by catamaran.

### By bus
Buses serve Portorož from Piran (5 minutes), Strunjan (5 minutes), Izola (10 minutes), Koper (25 minutes), Postojna ($1^3/_4$ hours), Ljubljana ($2^3/_4$ hours), Celje (4 hours 20 minutes), Maribor (6 hours) and Murska Sobota ($7^1/_2$ hours).

### On foot/by bicycle
A pleasant 40-minute walk that curls around the bay takes you from Piran to Portorož. If you have a bike the journey will be even quicker.

## Getting around
**Atlas Express** Obala 55; tel: 05 674 6772. Offer bicycle and scooter hire for 2–24 hours. Bikes 1,900–5,300SIT, scooters 4,600–10,500SIT. You must be over 18 and have a valid driving licence to hire a scooter.

**Taxi Portorož** Tel: 05 674 5555
**Big Red** Tel: 05 641 8310; www.slo-istra.com/aquamarine. This passenger boat runs along Slovenia's coast during the main tourist season, travelling between Piran, Bernardin, Strunjan, Portorož, Izola, Koper and Ankaran. The fare from Portorož is 400–2,000SIT depending on your final destination. Sailing frequencies and times vary, so check the timetable on the main pier or at the tourist information centre.

## Tour operators

Portorož is overflowing with tourist agencies who arrange private accommodation. Those listed below are clustered together on Obala.

**Kompas** Obala 41; tel: 05 617 8000; fax: 05 674 7258; email: kompa.turizem.Portoroz.si
**Maona** Obala 55; tel: 05 674 0363; fax: 05 674 6423; email: maona@siol.net www.maona.si
**Top Line** Obala 55; tel: 05 674 7161; fax: 05 674 7029; email: top.line@siol.net; www.topline.si
**Atals Express** Obala 55; tel: 05 674 6772; fax: 05 674 8820; email: atlas.portoroz@siol.net
**Turist biro** Obala 57; tel: 05 674 1055; fax: 05 674 1056; email: info@turistbiro-ag.si; www.turistbiro-ag.si

## Where to stay

**Hotel Riviera** (183 rooms) Obala 33; tel: 05 692 3333; fax: 05 692 3180; email: booking@hoteli-morje.si; www.hoteli-morje.si. Everything about this hotel is stylish from the lobby to its cocktail bar and wellness centre offering Thai massage. Large bedrooms are modern and comfortable and the hotel also has three heated seawater swimming pools and one of the best breakfast buffets in Slovenia. Singles 82,000–138,000SIT, doubles 110,000–186,000SIT, suites 150,000–390,000SIT.
**Hotel Slovenija** (160 rooms) Obala 33; email: booking@hoteli-morje.si; www.hoteli-morje.si. The Riviera's sister hotel has modern and comfortable rooms with balconies, cable TV and minibars. For a real treat ask for a room with a waterbed. Guests also have direct access to the Riviera's swimming pools and spa centre. Singles 82,000–138,000SIT, doubles 110,000–186,000SIT, suites 150,000–390,000SIT.
**Grand Hotel Metropol** (104 rooms) Obala 77; tel: 05 690 1000; fax: 05 690 1900; email: sales@metropolgroup.si; www.metropolgroup.si. Despite its luxurious rooms, five-star rating and impressive list of facilities including its own casino, this immense concrete hotel may not be to everyone's taste. Singles 22,000–29,500SIT, doubles 33,000–45,000SIT, suites 50,000–65,500SIT.
**Hotel Roža** (111 rooms) Obala 77; tel: 05 690 2000; fax: 05 690 2900; email: sales@metropolgroup.si; www.metropolgroup.si. The poorer sister of the Grand Hotel Metropol has good-sized rooms with balconies and sea views. Guests can use all the facilities at the other hotel. Singles 14,500–19,500SIT, doubles 21,500–29,500SIT.
**Kamp Lucija** Seča 204; tel: 05 690 6000; fax: 05 690 6900. Campsite offering water sports, mini-golf and other sports facilities. With onsite entertainment, a restaurant and a shop. 1,700–2,500SIT per person.

# Where to eat

There are myriad dining options in Portorož which are unashamedly geared towards tourists. This means that you can often get an inexpensive set-price meal, but the food is rarely outstanding.

**Restavracija Zlato Sidro** Obala 55; tel: 05 674 5074. A stone staircase adorned with an imitation Venetian lion leads you to the restaurant's raised and secluded terrace. Away from the bustle on the main street, this is the spot in Portorož for a romantic meal. Good seafood makes up for the cheesy music and plastic furniture.

**Pizzeria Figarola** Obala 14a; tel: 05 674 2200. A light air-conditioned interior and good pizzas make this one of Portorož's most popular restaurants. If you don't fancy a pizza then they also serve tasty pasta dishes and large salads.

**Restavracija Gregory** Obala 14a; tel: 05 674 2200. Located to the rear of Figarola with a typical menu of fish and grills. The food is good though. For children there is the cheekily named 'McDonald's Gregory Burger'.

**Mercator** Obala 53. Central branch of the omnipresent supermarket chain.

# Entertainment and nightlife

**Mystica** Hotel Riviera. This raised terrace with stylish furniture and loungers is one of the best locations for a drink on a summer's night. Choose from the extensive list of cocktails, but make sure you get there before it closes at 22.00.

**Paprika Pub** Obala 20a. Live music, a sleek interior and tree-fringed terrace overlooking Portorož make this new bar a popular spot.

**News Café** (see *Piran* listing)

**Avditorij Portorož** Senčna pot 12; tel: 05 676 6700; www.avditorij.si. Keep a lookout for performances in the auditorium's open-air amphitheatre.

**Grand Casino Portorož** Obala 75a; tel: 05 676 0373; www.casino.si. Late-night gambling and entertainment.

# Practicalities

**Tourist Information Centre** Obala 16; tel: 05 674 0231; fax: 05 674 8261; email: ticpo@portoroz.si; www.portoroz.si. Open: daily: 09.00–17.00 Sep–Jun, 09.00–13.00 and 15.00–21.00 Jul–Aug.

**Banka Koper** Obala 33. Open: Mon–Fri 08.00–12.00 and 15.00–17.00, Sat 08.30–12.00.

**Post office** K Stari 1. Open: Mon–Fri 08.00–19.00, Sat 08.00–12.00.

# What to see

As a purpose-built resort, a visit to Portorož is not about what to see and more about relaxing and participating in the many activities on offer. Nearby Sečovlje with its saltpans and unique flora and fauna is definitely worth a visit.

## Sečovlje Salina Nature Park

Just 3km from Portorož, on Slovenia's southwestern border with Croatia, is a unique nature park covering 6.5km². The Sečovlje saltpans (tel: 05 672 1330; email: kpss@soline.si; http://.kpss.soline.si) are divided into two parts, Lera in the north and Fontanigge in the south, by the Grande–Drinica Channel. In Lera salt is still being harvested from the pans, whilst this process was abandoned in Fontanigge back in the 1960s. Today the southern part is home to the **Muzej Solinarstva** (Museum of Salt Making; tel: 05 671 0040. Open: daily 09.00–13.00 and 14.00–19.00. 500SIT), where you can still see traditional salt-harvesting methods that date back to the 14th century. Both Lera and Fontanigge are open to the public and can be explored on foot or by bicycle along well-marked routes.

The salt production alone did not earn Sečovlje the status of a nature park, which it was awarded in 2001: its distinctive and diverse fauna and flora also played a role. Shallow water with high levels of salinity, the salt-production process itself and the Mediterranean climate all combine to create the ecological conditions necessary to support a diverse and thriving fauna and flora. Sečovlje has an abundance of salt-loving plants and is home to more than 270 species of birds. The pans are an ornithologist's dream in the spring and autumn when migrating birds stop off en route to or returning from Africa or the rest of Europe. Look out for the three species of heron that have been spotted at the nature park throughout the year, the Little Egret, the Great White Egret and the Grey Heron.

## BORDER BOTHER

Take a wrong turning on the Slovenian Adriatic and you may well end up in Croatia, which is not necessarily a bad thing as it has plenty to offer. Croatia's majority stake of the Istrian peninsula tempts not just visitors as Slovenia has been locked in a dispute over where the border lies since the two countries became independent back in 1991. The crux of the issue is that Slovenia wants to at least secure its present coastline and guarantee its access to the open sea, while Croatia wants to assert its own coastal rights and solidify its dominance of this stretch of the Adriatic. The argument has been widened into the practicalities of the Dragonja River, which marks much of the border and has confused the issue by changing its course. This wrangle and other similar squabbles along the border keep rearing up and then slipping back down the agenda when both countries draw bad press from it and the only thing that you will probably notice are the flash new Slovenia Policija speedboats that prance proudly up and down Slovenia's coast in a clear statement that these are firmly Slovenian territorial waters.

This ongoing problem stems from the fact that prior to 1991 there was no distinct Croatian or Slovenian territorial sea, just one uniform area belonging to Yugoslavia, which gave all of the federation's member states uniform access to international waters. Along with the independence of both countries, came the question of how to divide the former Yugoslav territorial seas between them and to ensure that Slovenia continued to have access to international waters.

## EXPLORING THE HINTERLAND

While most visitors rumble up and down the busy coast road the hinterland of Slovenia's slice of the Istrian peninsula is worth visiting on a day trip or as an alternative route to save any backtracking through the coastal resorts. You will need your own wheels, though, as public transport is infrequent at best. Following the highway north from Koper you will gain altitude quickly and soon be peering down on Koper and the Adriatic with the Karst rising to the northwest. The main road here continues all the way to Croatia, but you should fork off after 15 minutes at the turn marked Šmarje. This quiet hilltop village has a Partisan Monument, with the names of local men who died fighting the Nazis, and the modest Church of the Virgin Mary. Circle back down the main road and take the right turn for Korte, a charming hamlet that boasts sweeping views of the surrounding hilltop villages and the green vine-covered slopes. Look out also for the vinska klet signs that are sprinkled around the hills – you can often arrange tastings or at the very least secure a bottle of the local produce from the various wine houses.

Although they are both part of the Sečovlje Salinas Nature Park, Lera and Fontanigge are not connected by land and have separate entrances. To access Fontanigge by land you have to cross the Slovenian border check-point and then turn right before you reach the check-point on the Croatian border. Both Lera and Fontanigge can also be reached by boat with Solinarka (tel: 05 677 2383; email: altair@siol.net. Pick-up from Bernardin 09.15, Portorož 09.30 or Piran 09.45, in July and August. 2,500SIT). If you don't make it to the saltpans, the shop on the ground floor of the **Benečanke Hiša** (Venetian House; Tartinijev trg 10) in Piran sells products made from the salt harvested there.

## Activities and excursions
### Boat trips
**Burja Tours** End of the main pier; tel: 041 621 678; email: franjo@burja.com; www.burja.com. This company offers a variety of excursions on board a modern boat including a trip to Poreč, a fish picnic and sunset cruises. They also pick up in Koper, Izola and Piran.
**Aquamarine** Tel: 05 641 8301; fax: 05 640 0188; email: aquamarine@siol.net; www.slo-istra.com/aquamarine. Run trips from Bernardin harbour.

### Indulge
**Wai Thai Wellness Centre** Hotel Riviera, Obala 33; tel: 05 692 3333; www.hoteli-morje.si. Treat yourself to a Thai massage, facial or an oriental honey wrap in the Riviera Hotel's luxurious spa. The centre's signature Wai Thai Massage costs 11,500SIT for 80 minutes.
**Hanna** Obala 26; tel: 05 677 0500; www.hannabeauty.com. This beauty salon also offers a variety of massages, facials and beauty treatments.
**Terme Palace** Obala 43; tel: 05 696 9010; www.hoteli-palace.si. The Hoteli Palace's

modern thermal pools, thalassotherapy centre, massage and a wellness centre are all great places to treat yourself.

### Panoramic flights

A range of excellent-value panoramic flights are available from Portorož Airport (Sečovlje 19; tel: 05 672 2525; fax: 05 672 2530; email: info@portoroz-airport.si): an eight-minute tour of the bay costs 3,500SIT, 15- or 30-minute flights over the Istrian coast 5,800SIT and 10,500SIT respectively. For a real treat see Slovenia's magnificent mountains from the air with a one-hour-and-40-minute flight over Bovec, Triglav, Bohinj, Bled and Lesce for 35,000SIT.

### Yacht charter

Round up nine fellow travellers and hire a yacht for the day (**Adriatic Yacht Charter** tel: 05 674 6501 after 16.00) and split the 114,000SIT (€475) charge between you.

### Swimming

If you don't fancy plunging into the sea then most of the hotels will also let you use their pools for a fee, although these are usually full of salt water too. Two hours at the Riviera Hotel will cost you 1,000–1,250SIT. If you want to rent a towel and robe then you will need a deposit of 2,500SIT.

*Postojna cave formations*

# Notranjska

The world-famous caves at Postojna, Predjama Castle and Lake Cerknica aside, much of southerly Notranjska is still very undiscovered and economically much undeveloped. In Notranjska's west the Karst landscape of Primorska continues with its landmark caves and disappearing rivers and lakes. To the east, though, it is a very different story as the vast forests of Slovenia's southern  flank take over. This is no post-Sunday lunch country park jaunt as amidst the pitch-black forests bears, lynx and wolves still run wild. If Hollywood is looking for a venue for shooting a follow-up to the *Blair Witch Project* they could not pick anywhere more dramatic or spooky. This unheralded region does have one major claim to fame – the locals here insist that Notranjska was the birthplace of skiing in Europe, a sport they say was born on the Bloke Plateau.

## POSTOJNSKA JAMA (POSTOJNA CAVES)

Slovenia's largest cave complex, and Europe's most visited, is certainly no secret and on a packed high-season day it feels like all of the 30 million tourists who have visited the caves over the years are there at once. It is easy to recoil at the concrete hotel that blights the entrance, the rip-off car parking and toilet charges, as well as the factory-like processing of tourists, but the two-million-year-old caves themselves make up for it all for most visitors. A good plan, though, is to come here first for the wow factor and then hop across to the Škocjan Caves (see *Primorska*), which most people find even more dramatic. For those slightly squeamish with heights or the infirm the Postojna Caves are much more manageable with solid concrete paths, few steep ascents and most of the distance covered by train.

**Postojna Caves** Jamska 30; tel: 05 700 0100; fax: 05 700 0130; email: info@postojnska-jama.si; www.postojnska-jama.si. Tour times: Mon–Fri 10.00, 12.00, 14.00, Sat, Sun and holidays 10.00, 12.00, 14.00, 16.00 Jan–Mar, Nov–Dec. Daily 10.00, 12.00, 14.00, 16.00 Apr and Oct. Daily at hourly intervals between 09.00 and 18.00 May–Sep. Various single and combination ticket options. The most expensive ticket gives entrance to Postojna Caves, Proteus Vivarium, Predjama Castle and Predjama Cave 4,790SIT/3,190SIT/2,790SIT adults/students/children.

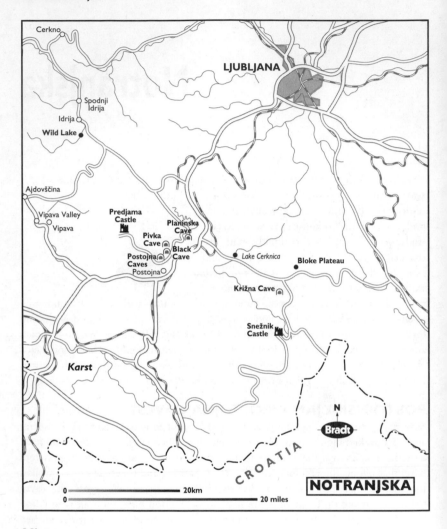

## History

Like most of the caves in Slovenia's Karst region the Postojna Caves are millions of years old. The huge 21.5km-long cave complex has been known to man for centuries (the first recorded human visit to the caves was in 1213), but it was not until the 19th century that they were extensively explored after lighting was installed and the first pathways were constructed in 1818. By the 1820s the first guidebook to the caves had appeared. The Habsburg Prince Ferdinand is said to have been one of the first tourists to delve into the caves and millions have followed ever since.

Mankind's abuse of this delicate ecosystem began as soon as it was discovered, with the earliest visitors blackening the formations nearest to the entrance with torchlight and carving their names on fragile stalagmites. In 1824 this mistreatment began in earnest with the staging of the first event ever held – a dance – in the modern-day **Kongresna Dvorana** (Congress Room). The first organised tour arrived in 1936 and the opening of the Vienna–Ljubljana–Trieste railway in 1857 saw the number of people visiting the Postojna Caves rise dramatically. With scant regard to conservation the caves' first railroad was constructed in 1872. Further lighting was installed in 1884 and gas-powered locomotives began operating on the caves' railway track in 1914 (in 1959 these were replaced by electric trains which preserve the air quality more effectively).

Other damage inflicted upon the caves was largely dictated by the political climate of the time and they have been used as bunkers, hideouts and for storage. During World War II the Germans even amassed fuel in the caves; a stockpile that brought devastating destruction to some areas when the opposing partisan forces set it alight. These days the tourist operation is slick and efficient and, in a bid to protect the caves, the transit of the masses of people, who, understandably, want to visit one of Slovenia's most spectacular attractions is carefully managed. The only way to see the caves is on a tour, where the paths must be adhered to and the taking of photographs is not allowed (although many visitors flaunt this rule).

## Formation

Experts estimate that the formation of the Postojna Caves dates back over four million years, with the River Pivka eroding the limestone rock to create a system of caverns. Tectonic movements facilitated the river in its work and allowed it to penetrate the caves at deeper and deeper depths. As a result the caves have three distinctive levels, with the river continuing to flow and cut its way through the rock at the lowest. Scientists believe that the oldest limestone formations first began some 40,000–100,000 years ago; sadly many of these have now dried out and are falling apart, while the larger stalagmites and stalactites on display today are believed to date back a mere 8,000 years. These other-worldly creations are formed by rainwater as it seeps through the limestone and brings deposits with it, that very slowly, drip by drip, settle on the tip of the ever-growing stalagmites or stalactites. Occurring at a rate of less than 1mm every ten years this growth is invisible to the human eye, but is given away by the splashing droplets of rain and moist surfaces. Take time to notice the slightly different colours of the formations in Postojna Caves. These variations are caused by the presence of minerals and chemicals in the rainwater, as well as the quantity of rainwater permeating the stone – the whitest structures are the most 'pure'.

## The tour

The only way to see the caves unless you are on a scientific research trip is to go on the $1^1/_4$-hour guided tour, which allows a bit of walking between two train trips. Take a look at the Pivka River below the tourist complex as it disappears into the caves, later to resurface as the Ljubljanica which flows through the Slovenian capital. The tour starts with a stampede towards the entrance where the cute toytown trains await. Do not be fooled by their innocuous appearance, though, as they rattle off downhill for 2km at a fair rate and if you pop your head up for a closer look at the stalactites you are risking serious injury. The line (laid in 1872) skirts myriad stalactites and stalagmites on a narrow route in. On arrival at the foot of **Velika Gora** (Great Mountain) the hordes are divided up by language and

## THE KARST'S HUMAN FISH

Some 200 living species have been discovered in Postojna Caves, with their most famous resident being the 'human fish' or *proteus anguinus* – a species found only in Slovenia's Dinaric Karst. These little candyfloss-pink salamanders have human-like skin, although it has no pigment in it, and can live to a ripe old age of 100 years, spending their entire lives blind with no need for sight in their entirely dark native habitat.

Known by Slovenes as *mocherils* (a word that has emerged from the phrase 'that which burrows into wetness'), *proteus anguinus* is believed to be the only amphibian that lives in caves and is the largest of the cave dwelling species. Adults can grow to be some 25–30cm long, are thin and snake-like with a flat tail that aids swimming. They also have two pairs of legs: the front ones, located just below their heads, have three digits and the hind ones, near the tail fin, bizarrely have just two. Other peculiarities are its ability to breathe inside and outside of the water. It does this through three pairs of bright red gills that are located at the back of its head, rudimentary lungs and even through their skin! Scientists have also discovered fundamental differences between the human fish and other amphibians, as *proteus anguinus* does not finish the process of metamorphosis, instead reaching its sexual maturity as a larva (but between 16 and 18 years old) – a phenomenon that science terms neoteny. Today knowledge of the *proteus anguinus* remains limited so it is no surprise that for centuries the local people spoke of mysterious small dragons being found in pools near the region's myriad caves.

### Proteus Vivarium (Human Fish Museum)

Open: Mon–Fri 10.00–15.00, Sat, Sun and holidays 10.00–16.00 Jan–Mar, Nov–Dec, daily 10.00–16.00 Apr and Oct, daily 09.00–18.00 May–Sep. Tours take around 45 minutes, starting at 10 minutes past the hour with the last tour an hour before closing. 1,000SIT, students 700SIT and children 600SIT. The Postojna Caves' most famous resident, the 'human fish' or *proteus anguinus*, is a species that is found only in the Slovenian Karst. On your cave tour the only chance you get to see it is in a brightly lit pool, but here you can learn much more about it and other cave flora and fauna in a new visitor's centre dedicated to speleobiology (the scientific study of life underground). As well as exhibits there is also a multimedia show.

trooped off for their 1.5km walk, starting with a stroll up Great Mountain itself and then a wander through the galleries and caverns that house a variety of sizes and shapes of stalactites, stalagmites and pillars, many with nicknames such as Spaghetti.

The trail then drops down to the sturdy Russian Bridge, built by prisoners of war in World War I, that leads through to the aptly named Beautiful Cave before entering the Winter Hall where the Brilliant and Diamond formations have become the rather phallic symbol of the caves. There is much less description of the formations than in Škocjan and you are also whisked through at a fair pace. The

*Above* Celje Castle, Štajerska
*Right* Postojna Caves, Notranjska
*Below* Predjama Castle, Notranjska

*Above* Typical Štajerska church
*Right* Cycling, Logarska Dolina, Štajerska
*Below* Otočec Castle, Dolenjska

walking section ends – after having paid a visit to some captive *proteus anguinus* (human fish – see *The Karst's Human Fish* box) – in the **Koncertna Dvorana** (Concert Hall), a voluminous space that is used for concerts, although a tacky souvenir stand, that is meant to keep you occupied while you wait for the trains out, somewhat ruins the ambience.

## Getting there
Buses and trains call at Postojna town, with buses from Ajdovščina (45 minutes), Koper ($1^1/4$ hours), Ljubljana (1 hour), Nova Gorica (1 hour 20 minutes), Piran ($1^3/4$ hours) and Maribor ($4^1/2$ hours). Trains arrive from Ljubljana (1 hour 20 minutes) and Koper ($1^1/2$ hours). From Postojna you can walk to the caves, 1.5km from the centre of town, or get a taxi (see *Getting around*).

## Getting around
### By taxi
**Vladimir Bezek** Tel: 05 726 3002
**Eki Alilovski** Tel: 040 217 169

## Where to stay
**Hotel Jama** Jamska 28; tel: 05 728 2400; fax: 05 700 0130; email: hoteli-turizem@siol.net. The only hotel at the caves is a dingy establishment catering to tourist groups. Plans have been mooted for a major renovation. Singles 8,000–10,000SIT, doubles 12,000–16,000SIT.

## Where to eat
Whichever of Jamska's cafés or restaurants you choose to eat at you can guarantee that it will be expensive (770SIT for a humble burger or 450SIT for a can of Coke) and usually disappointing, so take your own food and enjoy a picnic in the sunshine. If you are staying at Hotel Jama it has a passable restaurant, but if you have a car you would be better off finding a countryside *gostilna* instead.

## Practicalities
**Tourist Information Centre** Jamska 30; tel: 05 700 0100; fax: 05 700 0130; email: info@postojnska-jama.si; www.postojnska-jama.si. The tourist centre has a list of accommodation, restaurants and bars in the Postojna area, as well as general information about the caves. They can help you book private accommodation, though getting there may be difficult if you do not have your own transport. The TIC also has three internet kiosks, with perhaps the most expensive internet access in Slovenia. 400SIT/700SIT/1,100SIT/1,300SIT 15/30/45/60 minutes.
There is a Banka Koper ATM next to the Proteus Vivarium.

## POSTOJNA TOWN
If you have your own wheels, or your cave tour finishes early enough to allow you to catch a bus out of Postojna, it is a good idea to leave, as with many more interesting places – such as Slovenia's coastal towns or the villages of the Karst – within striking distance the unattractive town of Postojna is not really worth spending the night in.

## Getting there

Buses and tours call at Postojna town, with buses from Ajdovščina (45 minutes), Koper ($1^1/_4$ hours), Ljubljana (1 hour), Nova Gorica (1 hour 20 minutes), Piran ($1^3/_4$ hours) and Maribor ($4^1/_2$ hours). Trains arrive from Ljubljana (1 hour 20 minutes) and Koper ($1^1/_2$ hours).

## Getting around

### Taxi

**Vladimir Bezek** Tel: 05 726 3002
**Eki Alilovski** Tel: 040 217 169

## Tour operators

**Kompas** Titov trg 2; tel: 05 726 4281; fax: 05 726 5251; info@kompas-postojna.si. Booking private accommodation.

## Where to stay

**Hotel Kras** Tržaška 1; tel: 05 726 4071; fax: 05 726 4225; email: hotel.kras@siol.net. Postojna's centrally located hotel has seen better days. It also has its own restaurant and pizzeria. Singles from 7,400SIT, doubles from 10,500SIT.

**Hudičevec** Razdrto 1, Hruševje; tel: 05 703 0300; fax: 05 703 0320; email: hudicevec@siol.net; www.hudicevec.com. Pleasant tourist farm 8km from Postojna with doubles, quads and an apartment sleeping 6. 3,840SIT per person.

**Kamp Pivka Jama** Veliki Otok 50; tel: 05 726 5382; email: avtokamp.pivka.jama@siol.net. Camping and bungalows with an on-site restaurant 4km northwest of Postojna. Camping 2,000SIT, bungalows 13,000–19,000SIT.

## Where to eat

**Minutka** Ljubljanska 14; tel: 05 726 5720. Decent and large pizzas cooked in a wood-fired oven.

**Restavracija Jadran** Titov trg 1; tel: 05 720 3900. Housed in a large white building on Postojna's central square, this restaurant serves good grills and fish dishes, with seating inside and on its outdoor terrace.

**Sladoledni Vrt** Titov trg 3. This outdoor ice-cream parlour in the main square is a good place to grab a drink, cake or a toasted sandwich.

**Restavracija Milena** Hruševje 4, Hruševje; tel: 05 756 1063. Located 8km from the caves, this charming restaurant offers typical dishes from Slovenia as well as wines from the Karst and Vipava Valley.

## Entertainment and nightlife

You will find bars on Ljubljanska and Tržaška. Cankarjeva, which runs parallel to Ljubljanska, has a cluster of café-bars including Kafe bar Teatre at No 1 and Okrepčevalnica Postojna at No 6.

## Practicalities

**Tourist Information Centre** Titova; tel: 05 720 1610; email: td.tic.postojna@siol.net. Open: 10.00–21.00 Jun–Sep. Situated in a kiosk near the Hotel Kras.

## OTHER CAVES

The area around Postojna is awash with caves, underground rivers and other various Karst peculiarities. None is as geared to the needs of tourists as Postojna, though, which is not necessarily a bad thing for adventurous visitors prepared to don some boots and do without the luxuries of electric lighting. Conditions and access vary greatly, although the caves are generally becoming easier to visit as interest grows. **Otoška Jama** (Otoška Cave) is less than 2km from Postojna on the road to Predjama Castle. This cave was once linked to the Pivka River, and hence to Postojna, but is now dry. Check at the Postojna TIC to arrange access – note that there are no electric lights. A short distance north of Postojna you will find two caves in close proximity: **Pivka Jama** (Pivka Cave) and **Črna Jama** (Black Cave). These caves, like Postojna Caves, were formed by the Pivka River and have a variety of wet and dry sections. Tours: daily 09.00, 13.00 and 15.00 Jun–Sep ($1^1/2$ hours). Booking ahead is essential (ask at the Postojna TIC).

On the road to Lake Cerknica is **Planinska Jama** (Planinska Cave; tel: 041 338 696), where the Pivka and Rak rivers meet, the largest wet cave in Slovenia. This is a challenging cave complex where access very much depends on water levels and only experienced cavers should head here.

## PREDJAMSKI GRAD (PREDJAMA CASTLE)

One of the most striking castles in Europe, never mind Slovenia, stands out proudly from the rugged hillside 10km west of the Postojna Caves. The tourist operation at the 700-year-old castle is stepping up a gear and there are now medieval pageants, with combination tickets sold in conjunction with the Postojna Caves and guided tours. As you approach through the car park look at the tree to the left, which is said to be the spot where Slovenia's answer to Robin Hood was finally buried after years of robbing the rich to give to the poor. In reality it appears Erasmus Lueger may have been more a Rob Roy than the Robin Hood of children's stories; a romantic, but ruthless, rogue who proved a thorn in the side for more than just the region's various competing ruling elites. While his castle lay under siege he took full advantage of the porous local landscape and sneaked in and out through an underground cave. You cannot help, though, feeling sorry for a man who met his maker as he was thumped by a cannonball while he sat on the place where even folk heroes have to go sometimes.

After you pass the ticket kiosk the drama of the castle really unfolds as it stands high above, hanging impossibly from the sheer cliff face. Look out to the right for the jousting arena that has been re-created complete with a royal box for the very popular re-enactments as well as the catapult that all-too-vividly demonstrates how the besieging forces used to attack Predjama. You can just buy a ticket and use the information booklet to navigate your own way around the castle, but a guided tour is a better option as the tall stories of its most famous resident are often more interesting than what is actually on show.

**Predjama Castle** Tel: 05 751 6015; fax: 05 751 5260. Open: Mon–Fri 10.00–16.00, Sat–Sun 10.00–17.00 Jan–Feb, Nov–Dec, daily 10.00–17.00 Mar–Apr and Oct, 09.00–18.00 May and 09.00–19.00 Jun–Sep. 1,000SIT, students 700SIT, children 600SIT.

# PREDJAMA CAVE

If you have not yet had your fill of caves then you can pop beneath the castle and explore the cave that used to provide a lifeline for Erasmus Lueger, on a 45-minute tour. Rubber boots are available for hire just after the main ticket desk for the castle, but if you have a sturdy pair of shoes that you do not mind getting wet ask the guide as they may be fine. You will however need a torch as there are few frills in this dark lair. The four-level cave was formed by the action of Lokva River which still runs through it. On the second level down, look out for the graffiti that has been left over the centuries by various visitors, while the fourth level down is the active section where the Lokva is continuing its mysterious work. The waters from Predjama eventually snake their way out again in the fertile Vipava Valley. Experienced cavers can delve down deeper than the normal guided excursion.

**Predjama Cave** Tel: 05 751 6015; fax: 05 751 5260. Tours: 11.00, 13.00, 15.00, 17.00 May–Sep, Oct and Apr by appointment. There are no tours from Nov to Mar when bats hibernate in the cave. Entrance to the castle and cave 1,690SIT, students 1,100SIT, children 950SIT.

## Where to eat

**Gostilna Požar** Predjama 2; tel: 05 751 5252. The only restaurant at Predjama Castle is worth visiting if you can get a seat on the outdoor terrace where the views make up for any inadequacies in the food. Busy days at the height of season are a bit of a scrum.

# LAKE CERKNICA

Slovenia's largest lake does not exist for much of the year. The vast freshwater lake that spreads south of the town of Cerknica, just off the Ljubljana–Koper motorway, vanishes completely in the summer as its waters evaporate and seep down into the Karst caverns and underground channels below. Cerknica has always been a source of amazement for man and over the centuries the local people have tried, unsuccessfully, to drain the lake to make agricultural land and prevent flooding, or to trap it for irrigation. A greater understanding of the machinations of the disappearing lake came with Baron Janez Vajkard Valvasor (see page 40) whose seminal work won him a fellowship of the Royal Society in London. Of the lake Valvasor proclaimed: 'There is no lake as remarkable in Europe or in any other of the three corners of the world.'

Today the lake still retains much of its mystery, whether you visit when the lake unfurls for miles and canoeists, swimmers, anglers and boaters flock to its shores, or when the water vanishes leaving a dried-up moonscape, or even in the depths of winter when sheets of ice form in the shallow waters as ice skaters take full advantage.

To appreciate the scale of the meandering lake you can either drive or cycle around the unsealed roads that are raised above the waters. En route there are soaring birds of prey, ducks and butterflies which are part of the 2,000 animal and plant species that live in and around the impermanent lake. From the unspectacular town of Cerknica head down the 2km road to Dolenje Jezero, which sometimes lies right on the edge of the lake. The **Muzej Jezerski Hram**

## BLOKE INVENTS SKIING

Ask around Notranjska and most people will proudly tell you that this is where skiing in Europe was first pioneered. For centuries the local people have used the rudimentary wooden 'bloke skis' for cross-country skiing on the frozen Karst expanse of the Bloke Plateau. The skis used here, mainly fashioned from birch or beech trees, are much shorter and broader than Nordic skis, but the skiing techniques employed are virtually the same and cross-country skiing is still popular here today.

(Lake Cerknica Museum; tel: 01 709 4053; email: jezerski.hram@siol.net; www.jezerski-hram.si) here delves deeper into Slovenia's most intriguing lake. There are guided tours of the museum (Open by appointment for groups of seven or more – with tours in Slovene, English, German or Italian) that last just over an hour, as well as a multivision show. If the museum is closed the adjacent bar will probably still be open and this is a good place to grab a drink and some advice. There is also a relief map by the bar outside that gives a good idea of the layout of the lake – fittingly it has dried up and cracked in the middle. Continue on from Dolenje Jezero and you will soon be on the unsealed section of road with the lake on either side. The village of Otok, 'island' in Slovene, as the name suggests is right in the heart of the lake. From here you can circle back up through Gorenje Jezero to Grahovo where you can rejoin the main Cerknica to Dolenjska road.

### Getting there
Buses from Ljubljana (1¼ hours) stop in Cerknica. The lake is located 2.5km south of the town.

### Where to stay
**Telič Vilma** Brestova 9; tel: 01 709 7090; fax: 01 709 7092; email: drago.telic@siol.net. This pleasant B&B located 500m east of the town centre has two rooms that offer good views of the lake. Singles 4,700SIT, doubles 6,900SIT.

### Practicalities
**Tourist Information Centre** Cesta 4 maja 51; tel: 01 709 3636; email: tdrustvo@volja.net. Open: Mon–Fri 07.30–15.00. Staff at the TIC can help you find private accommodation.

## KRIŽNA JAMA (KRIŽNA CAVE)
A 10km drive south of Lake Cerknica is the Križna Cave, which offers the unique chance to cruise through a cave complex aboard a rubber raft, admiring the stalactites and stalagmites from an unusual vantage point. Cave bears used to haunt the many underground lakes and these days their legacy is thousands of fossilised remains. The caves were not fully explored until the 1920s and today visitors are welcome to venture into one of the least known – amongst tourists anyway – of

the cave systems in Slovenia. There are a number of tours available whether you want to walk in or paddle in, though options are limited after heavy rainfall when the water level surges throughout the network of caves.

**Guided Tours** Bloska Polica 7; tel: 041 632 153; email: krizna_jama@yahoo.com; www.kovinoplastika.si/gsk/krizna-jama. Troha Alojz will guide you through the cave. One-hour visits to the dry part of the cave with a boat ride on the first lake cost 1,100SIT, concessions 550SIT (minimum charge 3,000SIT). Four-hour tours to Kalvarija cost 14,000/18,000/22,000SIT for 2/3/4 people.

## SNEŽNIK GRAD (SNEŽNIK CASTLE)

Continue just over 5km south from Križna towards the Croatian border and you come to Snežnik Castle (Kozarišče 67; tel: 01 705 7814. Open: Wed–Fri 10.00–12.00 and 15.00–18.00, Sat–Sun 10.00–18.00 Apr–Oct. 700SIT) This ornate Renaissance creation lies across a charming little bridge. Inside many of the 19th-century furnishings remain. From the castle it is possible to head off for a spot of trekking in the wilds of the Snežnik Plateau, though mind the bears (seriously).

# Dolenjska and Bela Krajina

Dolenjska is the region that stretches east from Notranjska skirting the Croatian border at first to the south and then to the east. This is a land of rolling hills that is laden with history in the form of old castles and monasteries. Dolenjska is also intrinsically linked to the development of the Slovene language. When Primož Trubar laid the foundations of the language back in the 16th  century, it was based upon the dialect spoken by the inhabitants of Dolenjska. There is the city of Novo Mesto, well worth visiting, a sprinkling of health spas (or *termes*) and the Kolpa and Krka rivers. Tagged on to the southeastern fringe of Dolenjska is tiny Bela Krajina. The temptation is to just lump them together as a 'Greater Dolenjska', but that would not be doing justice to Bela Krajina, culturally distinct and a vibrant part of the country where folk music is far more than just another concert.

## KOČEVJE AND KOČEVSKI ROG

This protected oasis is one of the wildest parts of Europe, never mind Slovenia. Here when you are trampling through the heavily wooded slopes you are as likely to see a bear as you are anyone else. There is much more to Kočevski rog, though, than its rugged beauty, and the wider Kočevje area has a fascinating

### CVIČEK

One of Dolenjska's most popular tipples is definitely an acquired taste, one that a large number of Slovenes throughout the country seem to have developed. The signature wine of the region, *Cviček*, is a blend of red and white grapes with a dry acidic flavour and a low alcohol content (usually around 10%). A washed-out ruby colour, it is distinctly different in both its appearance and taste to rosé wine. Locals extol the virtues of this unique beverage, claming that it is light and refreshing, yet lively (this refers to the acidic aftertaste), which might explain why it is consumed in such substantial quantities. *Cviček* is traditionally a cheap wine, which goes well with cold meats like *pršut*. For your first taste try the Matinčič brand, which is usually dependable.

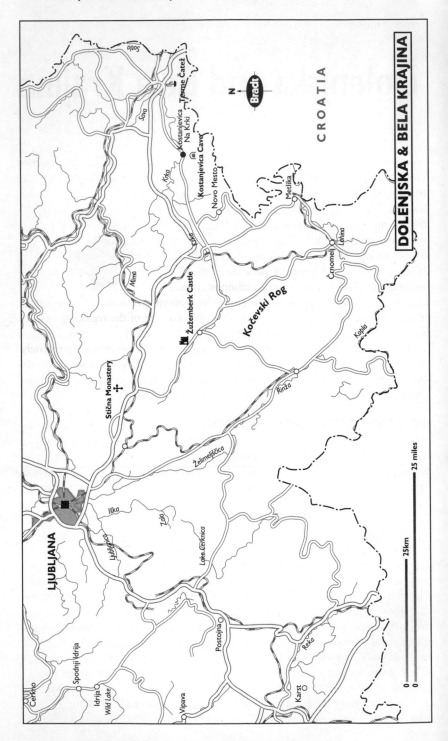

history. During the Middle Ages the region was populated by a group of peasants who had emigrated south from present day Germany. Over the centuries the inhabitants of Kočevje's villages developed their own distinct culture, dialect and identity, which, while it was influenced by the land that they inhabited, remained essentially German. The advent of World War II brought Italian occupation, under the control of Nazi Germany, to the Kočevje area and Hitler ordered the Kočevje Germans to relocate to Slovenia's German-occupied territory. There they were offered estates and homes from which Slovenes had been forcibly removed and packed off to Serbia, Germany and elsewhere in Europe.

At the end of the war some of the Kočevje Germans returned to their former residences, however they too chose, or were forced, to leave and the wider area of Kočevski rog became an off-limits military area. The Yugoslav army then set about constructing a system of intricate, and allegedly nuclear-proof, underground shelters, in order to safeguard Slovenia's communist leadership in the event of another war (ask at the tourist office for information about guided tours). Those moving in the higher echelons of Yugoslavia's socialist regime were also given exclusive access to the natural park of Kočevski rog, and it became a popular hunting and holiday destination amongst officials. One of the most tragic consequences of the militarisation of the wider Kočevje area and the establishment of an exclusive playground, was the destruction of much of the region's heritage, with villages and more than 40 churches razed to the ground.

An even more sinister event occurred in the area of Kočevski rog immediately after the war, when those troops who had been fighting against Tito's partisans during the conflict were prevented from escaping into Austria and sent back to Yugoslavia by British forces. Some historians estimate that up to 12,000 former members of the Home Guard were slaughtered by the communist authorities in the woods of Kočevski rog. The dead were then unceremoniously dumped into mass graves, which were in turn blown-up in a bid to eradicate any evidence of this evil act. While he was never formerly implicated, many believe that the massacre occurred at the request, or at least with the approval of, Tito. The relatives of the dead were also prevented from visiting the site until Slovenia secured its independence in 1991. Today a small church commemorates the thousands of men that died even though the war had already ended.

Returning to the dark days of World War II, visiting Kočevski rog it is easy to see why it was such a perfect hideaway for partisan forces, including the famous *Baza 20* (Base 20), from where hundreds of partisans once ran their operations, with Tito himself even visiting. It may not be as well preserved as the Partizanska Bolnišica Franja (Franja Partisan Hospital) near Cerkno, but it is nonetheless dramatic as your mind conjures up images of the partisans risking life and limb to resist their Nazi occupiers. Today the site is a national monument, though many of the original buildings have long since disappeared and the ones that remain are not in good condition. Considering the importance of Base 20 this is nothing short of a scandal, though given the shift in the political climate away from Yugoslav socialism perhaps not too surprising.

There are two small partisan hospitals in the Kočevski rog that you can visit, Jelendol and Zgornji Hrastnik. Jelendol, just north of Base 20, opened in 1943 and went on to treat 330 patients, saving the lives of an impressive 309 of these. The bodies of the 21 people who died lie in a nearby graveyard. Zgornji Hrastnik, to the south of Base 20, also accepted its first patients in 1943 and unlike many of the Kočevski rog wartime hospitals it was not dug into a dark hollow, but instead built in an elevated position. Of the 400 wounded who were treated 69 died, with a small cemetery nearby a poignant reminder. To visit the memorial rooms at the hospitals you will have to arrange it in advance with the tourist office in Novo Mesto.

### Getting there

Kočevje can be reached by bus from Ljubljana ($1^1/2$ hours) and Novo Mesto. Base 20 is 8km from Dolenjske Toplice (see next listing) – heading south for 1km you will come to the mountain road, which has a car park located 7km along it. From the car park Base 20 is a 15–20-minute walk.

### Practicalities

**Tourist Office** Trg zbora odposlancev 72; tel: 01 893 1460. Open: daily 07.00–19.00 Apr–Aug, Mon–Fri 08.00–15.00 Sep–Mar.

### What to see

**Pokrajinski Muzej Kočevje** (Kočevje Regional Museum) Prešernova 11; tel: 01 895 5114; fax: 01 895 0305; www.pmk-kocevje.si. Open: Mon–Tue 09.00–12.00, Thu–Sat 09.00–12.00 and 16.00–18.00. An exhibition of the life, history and culture of Kočevje's former German population.

## DOLENJSKE TOPLICE

If Base 20 has left you feeling emotionally drained then 8km away to the east is one of Slovenia's most popular spa complexes, a perfect stop-off if you are heading further east to Novo Mesto. Unlike some of the country's more modern spa towns, Dolenjske Toplice has a touch of class with some 19th-century buildings dating from the days when the stressed-out citizens of Vienna would have sought refuge here. Today the therapeutic treatments are worth travelling for and the town also makes a good base for exploring the Kočevje area on foot or by bike.

### Getting there

Regular buses run from Novo Mesto (20 minutes) to Dolenjske Toplice. There is also a daily bus from Ljubljana ($1^1/2$ hours), which leaves at 07.10 (08.15 on Sundays).

### Tour operators

**K2M** Pionirska 3; tel/fax: 07 306 6830; email: info@k2m.si; www.k2m.si. This tourist agency located near the tourist office can arrange accommodation, kayaking, rafting and eight-day guided cycling trips. It also rents out bicycles.

### Practicalities

**Tourist office** Zdraviliški trg 8; tel: 07 384 5188; fax: 07 384 5191; email: tic.dtoplice@volja.net. Open: Mon–Fri 10.00–17.00, Sat 10.00–12.00 and 15.00–18.00, Sun 10.00–12.00.

**Post office** Zdraviliški trg 3. Open: Mon–Fri 10.00–12.00 and 15.00–18.00, Sat 10.00–12.00.
**Nova Ljubljanksa Banka** Zdraviliški trg 8. Open: Mon–Fri 08.00–12.00 and 15.00–17.00.

## What to do

The indoor and outdoor pools at Dolenjske Toplice's lagoon (tel: 07 391 9400; fax: 07 306 5662; email: booking.dolenjske@krka-zdravilisca.si; www.krka-zdravilisca.si/si/dolenjske) come complete with underwater massages, waterfalls and water jets. In addition to its therapeutic waters the *terme* also offers a combination of dry and wet heat in its Oasis Centre, while a unique facility is the Japanese sweat bath (a hot pool and waterfall heated to 40°C). If you are feeling brave you can even take a traditional Finnish sauna on the spa's nudist terrace. Shiatsu massage, reflexology, aromatherapy massage and hot-stone therapy are also on offer in the Aura Centre.

## NOVO MESTO

The largest city in Dolenjska has a booming economy, with a major Renault factory, the national flagship pharmaceutical company, Krka, and a number of other industrial companies providing plenty of employment. All the more sad then that many of the historical buildings that crowd the old centre are in a shabby state and the Old Town is all too often choked with traffic. Still, when the traffic congestion eases and you troop into town across the Krka River, which curves around the Old Town in a looping horseshoe, Novo Mesto can be one of the most attractive cities in Slovenia. Evidence of human settlement here dates back as far as the Bronze Age, but it was not until the 14th century that Novo Mesto first became a city.

### Getting there

Buses run to Novo Mesto from Otočec (15 minutes), Dolenjske Toplice (20 minutes), Ljubljana (1 hour) and Brežice (1 hour 10 minutes). The city is also connected by train to Črnomelj (1 hour), Metlika (1$^{1}/_{4}$ hours) and Ljubljana (1$^{3}/_{4}$ hours).

**Bus station** Topliška 1; tel: 07 332 1123
**Railway station** Kolodvorska 1; tel: 07 298 2100

### Tour operators

**Globtour** Rozmanova 19; tel: 07 337 4022; email: globtour.novomesto@globtour.si
**Kompas** Novi trg 10; tel: 07 393 1520; email: kompas.nm@siol.net
**Robinson** Glavni trg 1; tel: 07 338 2800; fax: 07 338 2810; email: robinson@siol.net; www.robinson-sp.si

### Where to stay

**Hotel Krka** (53 rooms) Novi trg 1; tel: 07 394 2112; fax: 07 331 3000; email: dolenjske.t@krka-zdravilrsca.si; www.krka-zdravilisca.si. Fairly standard business hotel which doesn't quite match up to its 4 stars, but it is in a hard-to-beat location. Singles 17,000SIT, doubles 26,000SIT, suites 35,000SIT.

**Gostilna Pri Belokranjcu** (13 rooms) Kandijska 63; tel: 07 302 8444; fax: 07 302 8445; email: gostilna.pri.belokranjcu@insert.si; www.pribelokranjcu-vp.si. Located around 1km from Novo Mesto's Old Town on the main road heading west, this welcoming *gostilna* has light and simply furnished rooms and serves regional fare in its restaurant. Singles 7,400SIT, doubles 11,200SIT.

**Apartmaji-Sobe Ravbar** (2 rooms, 5 apartments) Smrečnimova 15–17; tel: 07 373 0680; fax: 07 373 0681; email: uros.ravbar@siol.net; www.ravbar.net. Friendly family-run guesthouse close to the centre of town, with tidy rooms and apartments that sleep 2–6 people. Singles 4,000–6,500SIT, doubles 6,000–9,200SIT, triples 7,500–12,900SIT, apartments 8,500–18,000SIT.

## Where to eat

**Restavracija Breg** Cvelbarjeva 9; tel: 07 332 1269. Old Town restaurant with a summer garden serving traditional Dolenjska dishes.

**Kvarna Tratnik** Glavni trg 11; tel: 07 497 5079. Centrally located café-cum-pizzeria.

**Pizzerija and Spaghettarija Don Bobi** Kandijska 14; tel: 07 338 2400. Popular pizzeria 10 minutes' walk from the Old Town (cross the Kandijski Bridge and head west).

**Gostišče Dežmar** Ljubljanska 65; tel: 07 337 9300. Offering Slovenian and regional specialities including venison and freshwater fish dishes. Located a short distance out of town, follow the road east from the railway station. Dežmar also has accommodation for up to 6 people.

## Entertainment and nightlife

The bars on Glavni and Novi trg are a little jaded, but good fun nonetheless.

**Bar Boter** Kandijska 9; tel: 041 213 466. During the warmer months the riverside terrace offers great views back across to the Old Town – well worth the short walk. Open on Fri and Sat until 01.00.

**Kulturni Centre Janeza Trdine** (Cultural Centre Janez Trdina) Novi trg 5; tel: 07 393 0390; fax: 07 393 0392; email: info@kulturnicenter.com; www.kulturnicenter.com. Has a programme of theatre, concerts and exhibitions. The Cultural Centre actually has two locations, the one on Novi trg and the Dom Kulture (House of Culture) hall on Prešernov trg. The latter is also a cinematic venue.

**Planet Tuš** Topliška 2; tel: 07 373 7480; email: info@planet-tus.com; www.planet-tus.com/novomesto. Multi-screen cinema and supermarket complex just west of Šmihelski Bridge (on the south side of the Krka River).

## Practicalities

**Tourist Information Centre** Novi trg 6; tel: 07 393 9263; fax: 07 332 2512; email: tic@novomesto.si; www.novomesto.si. Helps arrange accommodation and offers bicycle hire.

**Post office** Novi trg 7. Open: Mon–Fri 07.00–20.00, Sat 07.00–13.00.

**Banka Koper** Novi trg 5

**SKB Banka** Novi trg 3 and Glavni trg 10

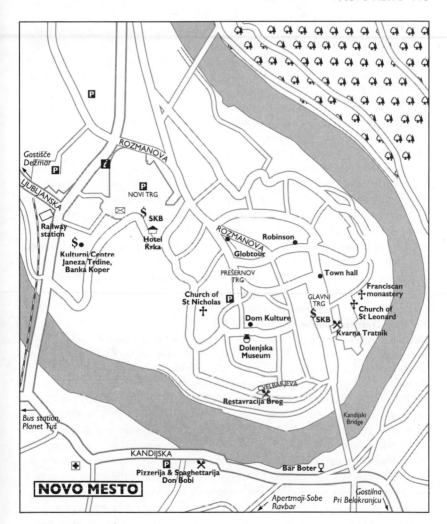

# What to see
## A walking tour

A good place to start a walking tour of Novo Mesto is at the grey **Mestna Hiša** (Town Hall), whose façade has recently been given a revamp. Look behind it and you will come across the pale yellow **Cerkev Sv Lenarta** (Church of St Leonard), which was built by Franciscan monks from Bosnia, though the exterior on show today is from the 19th century. To the church's left is the **Frančiškanski Samostan** (Franciscan Monastery). If you fancy taking a break in a café head back to Glavni trg, though if the traffic is busy you may not want to bother given the congestion and pollution.

The next stop on the tour is the **Dolenjski Muzej** (Dolenjska Museum; Muzejska 7; tel: 07 373 1130; fax: 07 373 1112; email: dolenjski.muzej@guest.arnes.si; www.dolmuzej.com), which is easily identified by the decommissioned guns that sit outside it. Inside are various artefacts from as far back as the Bronze Age as well as leftovers from the days when Celtic tribes breezed through the region. *Open: Tue–Fri 08.00–17.00, Sat 10.00–17.00, Sun 10.00–13.00 Apr–Oct, Tue–Fri 08.00–16.00, Sat 09.00–13.00 and Sun 09.00–12.00 Nov–Mar. 600SIT.*

Moving on from the museum, further up the hill you come to the **Cerkev Sv Nikolaja** (Church of St Nicholas), which is a bit of an architectural hotchpotch. A unique design feature is the altar that is built at a right angle to the main body of the church. Look out for traces of baroque and Gothic architecture and the painting of St Nicholas himself by Italian master Tinoretto. Novo Mesto looks at its best from the other side of the Krka River so head for the bridge over the river by the train station to see a sweep of the Old Town. On the way look for the old section of town walls that still stand. Turn left once you have crossed the river away from the new shopping mall and follow Kandijska – the Old Town will keep peeking through the buildings and vegetation. After ten minutes you will come to Bar Boter (see *Entertainment and nightlife*) so if you are thirsty pause for a drink before heading back across the **Kandijski Most** (Kandijski Bridge) to Glavni trg and the town hall.

## BACK TOWARDS LJUBLJANA

If you are short on time then you can back up towards Ljubljana by rail or road. If you have your own wheels then make sure to stop off at **Žužemberk Grad** (Žužemberk Castle; Občina Žužemberk, Grajska trg 33; tel: 07 388 5180. 1,000SIT) and then **Stična Samostan** (Stična Monastery; tel: 01 787 7100; fax: 01 787 7570). The former is a chunky castle overlooking the Krka River that has never really recovered from being savaged during World War II. You still get some idea of its grand scale from its remaining towers and in summer it is a great place to be when outdoor concerts are held here. However, until the local authorities get serious about the refurbishment then the castle will not really look its best again. Stična, meanwhile, like Pleterje further to the east is one of the oldest monasteries in Slovenia, dating back to the 12th century. If it looks more like a fortress than a monastery it is due to sturdy defences that were necessary to keep out the Ottomans. The monastery has taken on various design features over the centuries with Baroque, Gothic, Renaissance and Romanesque all woven into the structure. Although you can visit the religious museum, which is spread across two floors, the refectory and the library, as well as Abbey Church, this is no fusty old museum as around a dozen monks still live and pray on site.

## ABBEYS AND CASTLES EAST OF NOVO MESTO

East of Novo Mesto, Dolenjska still manages to squeeze in a flurry of castles and health spas, as well as a monastery, before the Croatian border, which is now connected by motorway to Novo Mesto and on to Ljubljana.

### Otočec Grad (Otočec Castle)

This castle on its own island just outside Novo Mesto is home to one of the most famous hotels in Slovenia. The rumbling express road above can be a bit of a pain, but it really is a special place as the castle rests in the midst of the Krka River surrounded by a park, with a cheaper hotel on one bank and a campsite on the other. Wherever you are staying, or if you just want to visit on a day trip, you can meander around the small islet watching the swans and ducks vying for attention with the rowing boats that the Hotel Grad rents out. The castle may look like an original Renaissance building, but most of it is actually the result of post World War II reconstruction. The castle's room rates may be a bit much for many travellers, but the restaurant is very reasonable with four courses for 3,700SIT.

## Where to stay

**Hotel Grad** (34 rooms) Tel: 07 307 5700; fax: 07 307 5420; email: booking.otocec@krka-zdravilisca.si; www.krka-zdravilisca.si. Period rooms and an undeniably romantic location hold a certain appeal. Unfortunately neither the accommodation nor the service is what you might expect from a five-star hotel, and some of the rooms are starting to look a little tatty, but it does still have bags of atmosphere. Singles 24,500–26,500SIT, doubles 34,300–37,800SIT.

**Hotel Šport** (160 beds) Grajska 2; tel: 07 307 5165; fax: 07 307 5167; email: booking.otocec@krka-zdravilisca.si; www.krka-zdravilisca.si. Actually comprised of a hotel, motel and self-catering bungalows, the Šport is a more affordable option than the castle itself, although the resort-style hotel can't even begin to match the romance of Hotel Grad. Sports facilities include tennis courts and an aerobics studio. Singles 12,050–16,950SIT, doubles 20,100–28,000SIT.

**Kamp Otočec** Grajska 2; tel: 07 307 5165; email: booking.otocec@krka-zdravilisca.si; www.krka-zdravilisca.si. Seasonal campsite with 60 spaces located around 300m east of the castle (just follow the signposts). 600SIT per person.

## Activities

A map detailing hiking trails and cycle paths is available from either of the hotels at Otočec. There are also horseriding stables at Struga Castle, which is a 20-minute walk from Otočec past the camping ground.

## Šmarješke Toplice

Only 5km from Otočec is this decent health spa (tel: 07 307 3230; fax: 07 307 3107; email: marketing.smarjeske@krka-zdravilisca.si; www.krka-zdravilisca.si) also handy for Novo Mesto. In addition to its pools Šmarješke Toplice offers a diverse range of health treatments in its new Vitarij Centre – including a complete relaxation programme based around the four elements (air, water, earth and fire) that incorporates aromatherapy, body wraps, venotonic baths (using thermal water, sea salt and herbal extracts), personalised cardiovascular training programmes, relaxation methods, colonic irrigation and cryomassage (using ice).

## Where to stay

**Na Dobravi Apartmaji** (15 flats) Tel: 07 384 3400; fax: 07 307 3107; email: booking.smarjeske@krka-zdravilisca.si; www.krka-zdravilisca.si. These modern apartments sleeping 4 or 5 people with private kitchens are located 1km from the Šmarješke Toplice.

There is also an onsite fitness centre, sauna, solarium and Jacuzzi. 4-person apartments 15,000–18,000SIT, 5-person apartments 18,000–20,000SIT.

**Krka (I and II)** Šmarješke Toplice Health Resort; tel: 07 384 3400; fax: 07 307 3107; email: booking.smarjeske@krka-zdravilisca.si; www.krka-zdravilisca.si. Pleasant enough rooms, some with balconies. Singles from 15,000SIT, doubles from 24,000SIT.
**Šmarjeta** Šmarješke Toplice Health Resort; tel: 07 384 3400; fax: 07 307 3107; email: booking.smarjeske@krka-zdravilisca.si; www.krka-zdravilisca.si. Built in the early 1990s the Šmarjeta is a more modern alternative to the Krka Hotel. Singles from 16,000SIT, doubles from 27,000SIT.

## Samostan Pleterje (Pleterje Monastery)

Set in the rolling hills of Dolenjska with white robed monks flitting behind the sturdy walls Pleterje Monastery (Drča 1, Šentjernej; tel: 07 308 1225; email: katuzija.pleterje@siol.net) is an intriguing place to visit. You can visit the shop and take in the multivision show – call ahead – but you cannot delve into the inner sanctum, which just adds to the mystery and appeal of Pleterje. There is an hour-long walk that meanders through the forest around the exterior wall, offering tantalising glimpses into the monastery and taking in the vineyards and orchards. The monastery's shop sells its famous wines and brandies, the most interesting being the pear brandy that comes complete with a real pear inside – they slip the bottle around when the pear is hazelnut-sized and when it matures they snip it off and add the brandy. You will probably find this on sale at Ljubljana's airport if you don't want to drag around a bottle from the monastery for the rest of your trip.

## Kostanjevica Na Krki

Blink and you will miss Slovenia's smallest town. It may not really be deserving of the term town as it is only really two streets and has a population that would pack into one of the houses, but it makes for a good day trip, especially if you combine it with a visit the nearby cave. The town straddles the Krka River with a sprinkling of things to see and do, including visiting a brace of Gothic churches, the former **Cistercijanski Samostan** (Cistercian Monastery) and the **Galerija Božidar Jakac** (Božidar Jakac Gallery; Grajska 45; tel: 07 498 7333; fax: 07 498 7335; email: info@galerija-bj.si; www.galerija-bj.si. Open: Tue–Sun 09.00–18.00 Apr–Oct, Tue–Sun 09.00–16.00 Nov–Mar. 600SIT, concessions 300SIT), with its eclectic display of works on various media, some of them culled from Jakac's days as a partisan. Other Slovene artists also get a look in with a surprisingly extensive collection given the small size of the town.

### Practicalities

**Tourist office** Talcev 20; tel: 07 498 7108. The tourist office was closed during our last visit in June 2004 due to lack of funds, a situation the locals were hoping would be resolved soon.

## Kostanjeviška Jama (Kostanjevica Cave)

It may not be as impressive as the caves that you will see in Notranjska and Primorska, but this small cave (Grajska 25; tel: 07 498 7542; email:

gregor.cuk@siol.net; http://www.users.volja.net/kjknk), which penetrates 20m underground, is one of the most accessible in Slovenia. Illuminated trails take in some interesting shapes that have been affectionately named the Teddy Bear, Santa Claus, the Rainbow, Christ and the Sabre. There is also a smattering of wildlife inside the cave including horseshoe bats. *Tours: 10.00, 12.00, 14.00, 16.00 and 18.00 weekends and holidays, mid-Apr–Jun and Sep–Oct, daily 10.00, 12.00, 14.00, 16.00 and 18.00 Jul–Aug. 1,000SIT, students 600SIT, children 300SIT.*

## Terme Čatež

Terme Čatež (Topliška 35; tel: 07 493 5000; fax: 07 493 5520; email: info@terme.catez.si; www.terme-catez.si) lays a fair claim to being the most impressive thermal spa in the country. If you are looking to relax for a few days or to indulge in some serious pampering then head here. Slovenia's largest spa resort boasts a range of therapeutic and leisure facilities from Finnish saunas, Turkish baths and Jacuzzis through to myriad indoor and outdoor thermal pools with a total surface area of 13,000m², some heated to 36°C and others specifically geared up for children, with water slides, waves and a slow river ride under waterfalls. The highlight for many visitors is the Irish–Roman baths. For 7,200SIT you and a loved one, or a travelling companion for that matter, can forget about reality for two hours and enter spa heaven. Although it is fairly private (there are never more than six people using the facilities at any one time), the experience may not be for the prudish as it all takes place in your birthday suit (you can cover up with a toga between stations). The session includes an aromatherapy scrub and massage after you plunge into a variety of hot and cold pools and saunas. A pleasant touch takes the form of a glass of bubbly, or a fruit elixir, in a Jacuzzi before your massage and then it all finishes with a half-hour sleep on an airbed. Thermal pools are not Čatež's only attraction – you can also play golf and tennis, take a boat out or fish in the Sava River, go horseriding or try your hand at archery.

### Where to stay

**Hotel Terme** (150 rooms) Topliška 35; tel: 07 493 5000; fax: 07 496 2721; email: terme.catez@terme.si; www.terme-catez.si. The fitness studio, health and beauty spa and swimming pools (both indoor and outdoor) geared towards adults make this hotel a winner with singles and couples. Large modern guestrooms have minibars, satellite TV, balconies and baths. If you are planning to stay in Čatež for a couple of days the half- or full-board options are a good idea. Keeping with the tradition of health spas in Slovenia, Čatež also has its own health centre and offers a variety of therapeutic programmes, which incorporate the thermal water. Singles 23,400–25,000SIT, doubles 31,800–35,800SIT.
**Hotel Toplice** (131 rooms) Topliška 35; tel: 07 493 5023; fax: 07 493 6700; email: toplice@terme-catez.si; www.terme-catez.si. The indoor thermal pool complex or Winter Thermal Riviera, is attached to the Hotel Toplice; as such the hotel tends to attract families. Rooms are modern and comfortable. Singles 21,600–23,800SIT, doubles 28,200–32,600SIT.
**Zdravilišče** Topliška 35; tel: 07 493 5022; fax: 07 493 5009; email: zdravilisce@terme-catez.si; www.terme-catez.si. Geared towards those suffering from ill health, or mobility

difficulties, this hotel has a nursing department whose staff work around the clock. Singles 12,900–13,200SIT, doubles 21,200–21,800SIT.

**Apartment Village and Camping** Topliška 35; tel: 07 493 6000; fax: 07 496 2229; email: camp@terme-catez.si; www.terme-catez.si. Modern apartments sleeping 3–5 people, with kitchens, two bedrooms and a parking space. Just make sure you remember which of the 400 apartments is yours. The campsite has space for tents, camper vans and caravans. Each pitch has an electricity supply. Apartments 22,000–24,000SIT. Camping 2,880–3,120SIT per person. Ask for special rates for longer stays in apartments.

## Mokrice Castle and Golf Course

Right on the edge of the Croatian border on the main Novo Mesto to Zagreb road is this luxury hotel (Rajec 4, Jesenice na Dolenjskem; tel: 07 457 4240; fax: 07 495 7007; email: mokrice@terme-catez.si; www.terme-catez.si) which is housed in a medieval castle that once stood guard against the Ottomans. Mokrice comes complete with an 18-hole golf course that boasts some spectacular holes, especially the tenth which swings back down the hill towards the castle itself.

Guestrooms at Mokrice are large and furnished in period style – the suites in the turret are something to behold with huge round beds and tables big enough to hold a board meeting. Guests get free use of the facilities at Terme Čatež, as they are owned by the same people. Singles 23,990–26,600SIT, doubles 29,990–34,200SIT, suites 59,900–68,200SIT.

## BELA KRAJINA

The 'White March', named after its silver birch trees, is one of Slovenia's smallest but most rewarding regions, as in this southeastern corner many of the folk traditions and cultures that have been lost elsewhere have been cherished and preserved and the locals are only too keen to share them with interested visitors. This is border country as Bela Krajina sits atop a ridge that basically separates Slovenia from Croatia and you are never more than a few miles from the Croatian border. The local tourist association has teamed up with neighbouring Dolenjska to offer a numbered trail of key towns, villages and attractions. This is especially useful in Bela Krajina as tourism is in its embryonic stages, so make sure to pick up a leaflet at the tourist offices in Metlika or Črnomelj in Bela Krajina, or in Novo Mesto in Dolenjska. Also make sure to check with the same offices for a list of current events to ensure you do not miss any of the cultural shows and festivals – the village of Adlešiči is particularly well known for regular cultural events such as concerts using traditional instruments like the lute and tamburica, instruments also used commonly across the border in Croatia. The tourist offices in Metlika and Črnomelj tend to co-ordinate the local attractions and can fill you in on where to pick up keys for churches and also on current opening hours as these can be fluid in these laid back parts of the country. Taking a car or renting a bike is the best way to explore Bela Krajina and the tourist offices in both Metlika and Črnomelj can usually arrange bicycle hire.

## METLIKA

Though it plays second fiddle in size to its great rival Črnomelj to the south, Metlika is a much more appealing place to visit with a compact Old Town hidden inside the less appealing outskirts. The local tourist office is very helpful and should be your first port of call – as well as dishing out as many brochures as you can handle and myriad words of advice they have also been known to furnish visitors with the odd fresh local strawberry. If you can time your visit here to coincide with the three-day wine festival that swings through Metlika in late May all the better.

## History
Metlika's history is long and eclectic with evidence of Stone-Age settlement before the Romans fortified the town. Later it became a key bulwark against the Ottomans and was attacked 19 times and sacked more than once before they were finally sent on their way. In the 20th century Metlika paid heavily for backing the partisans when its Italian occupiers razed many buildings to the ground. Metlika has always been a survivor, though, and it has managed to pick itself back up and celebrate its rich history through a range of festivals and cultural events. The economy moved from agriculture before World War II into viniculture and textiles (such as the successful Komet underwear manufacturer) and workers now come in daily from all over Bela Krajina, Dolenjska and Croatia.

## Getting there
Buses from Črnomelj (20 minutes), Novo Mesto (50 minutes) and Ljubljana (1³/₄ hours) stop at Metlika, as do trains from the same places – Črnomelj (20 minutes), Novo Mesto (1 hour) and Ljubljana (2¹/₂ hours).

## Where to stay
Private accommodation can be arranged at the TIC.
**Hotel Bela Krajina** (24 rooms) Cesta Bratstva in Enotnosti 28; tel: 07 305 8123; fax: 07 363 5281. Metlika's only hotel is just a couple of minutes' walk from the Old Town. The rooms are a little on the tatty side. Singles from 4,000SIT, doubles from 7,000SIT.
**Kamp Primostek** Tel: 07 305 8123; email: gostinstvo.sodec@siol.net. Riverside campsite 2km from Metlika with enough camping spaces for 300 people and accommodation in log cabins for up to 40. It has a restaurant with outdoor terrace. Camping 1,200SIT per person, cabins 2,000–2,500SIT per person.
**Kamp Podzemelj ob Kolpi** Tel: 07 306 9572; email: gostinstvo-turizem@gtm-metlika.si. Larger campsite around 7km from the centre of Metlika, only easily accessible if you have your own car or a bike. 1,500SIT per person.

## Where to eat
**Pri Bartusu** Mestni trg 6. Centrally located restaurant overlooking the Cerkev Sv Nikolaja (Church of St Nicholas).
**Pizzerija Lipa** Cesta Bratstva in Enotnosti 83; tel: 07 363 5130. Good pizza with all the usual suspects on the menu.
**Gostilna Budački** Ulica Belokranjskega odreda 14; tel: 07 363 5200. Filling and tasty Slovenian dishes are the order of the day at this pleasant *gostilna* 500m south of the Old Town.

## METLIKA WINE

The Metlika Wine Co-operative began production back in 1909 and is still at the backbone of the industry today. From its very modest beginnings it now boasts 25ha of vineyards as well as pooling the production of its members who cover much of Bela Krajina's 700ha of vineyards. While they do produce the Zdravica red, reputed to have health-giving properties, the excellent Modra Frankinja red and a passable rizling, chardonnay, a champagne-style sparkling wine and a dessert wine, their most renowned product is the Metliška Črnina, a red unique to Bela Krajina that you should try at least once during your visit. The co-operative has looked on enviously as Cviček across in Dolenjska has grown and grown in popularity and been given special status by the EU. In recent years the popularity of Bela Krajina's wines has also been rising, and the co-operative now has an outlet in Ljubljana. It has also branched out into food products. The Metliška Črnina varies from 10.5–11.5% alcohol content with a full body and dry finish and it goes particularly well with local game.

## Practicalities

**Tourist Information Centre** Mestni trg 1; tel: 07 363 5470; fax: 07 363 5471; email: tdvigred.metlika@siol.net; www.metlika.si. Open: Mon–Fri 08.00–15.30, Sat 09.00–12.00 Jun–Oct, Mon 08.00–17.00, Tue–Sat 08.00–14.00 Nov–May.

**Nova Ljubljanksa Bank** Trg Svobode 7. Open: Mon–Fri 08.00–12.00 and 15.00–17.00.

## What to see
### Metliški Grad in Belokranjski Muzej (Metlika Castle and Bela Krajina Museum)

Metliški Grad (Metlika Castle; Trg Svobode 4; tel: 07 306 3370; fax: 07 305 8177; email: belokranjski.muzej@guest.arnes.si. Open: Mon–Sat 09.00–17.00, Sun 09.00–12.00. 500 SIT, concessions 300–400SIT) and its courtyard, rebuilt in the 18th century, are home to weddings, a gallery, summer concerts, a viniculture collection and also the excellent Belokranjski Muzej (Bela Krajina Museum). The museum offers a 15-minute video on the history of Bela Krajina and its towns, villages and churches, before you enter the main exhibits which cover its history from prehistoric times right through to the end of World War II. It starts with the bounty from local archaeological digs which includes tools, bracelets and vases, before moving on through Roman times, local arts and crafts, including a fine collection of the brightly coloured wooden Easter eggs for which the region is famous. The World War II exhibits are fascinating with photographs of active partisan brigades in Bela Krajina as well as various weapons and pieces of kit.

### Slovenski Gasilski Muzej (Fire Brigade Museum)
The locals are very proud of the fact that the first-ever fire brigade in Slovenia was formed in Bela Krajina in 1869, so proud in fact that they opened this

museum (Trg Svobode 5; tel: 07 305 8697. Open: Mon–Sat 09.00–13.00, Sun 09.00–12.00. Free) in two buildings close to the castle in 1969 to commemorate the fact. If you are visiting the castle anyway the museum is worth seeing as entry is free and you can learn about the history of the fire services in Bela Krajina complete with uniforms, photos and even disused fire engines, as well as some very early models consisting of a wooden cart with a couple of water barrels slung on the back.

## Trg Svobode
Sprouting out of the middle of the square is a small park that is dominated by a grenade-sporting partisan – nothing unusual for a Slovenian town – but next to the heroic fighter is a bust of Tito, much more of a rarity as he has been deposed in most villages and towns across the country. This perhaps reflects the rich ethnic mix of Bela Krajina, itself a rarity in homogenous Slovenia, as Slovenes, Croats and Serbs all share this border region. Look out also for the trio of busts that commemorate the local dead from World War II when Črnomelj was briefly the capital of the independent Slovenian state.

## Mestni trg
Just a short walk along past the tourist office from Svobode trg is Mestni trg, a pleasant public space that is dominated by the **Cerkev Sv Nikolaja** (Church of St Nicholas), built in the 18th century on the site of a church that was burned to the ground in 1705. The model was Križanke's Church of St Mary in Ljubljana so if you are headed back to the capital you can compare the two when you get there.

## Kolpa River
Just a few kilometres outside Metlika is the Kolpa River, the place to be in summer as it is renowned as the warmest river in Slovenia, perfect for swimming, canoeing or just lazing by its banks. Good places to take a dip include Primostek and Podzemelj. The river is also easily accessible to the south near Črnomelj.

## Tri Fare Rosalnice (Three Parishes of Rosaline)
Just outside of Metlika are three impressive gothic churches, a trio of pilgrimage churches that sit dramatically together inside the same walls. It is still unclear as to why and exactly when the three churches were built on the site; what is clear is that the site has been an important pilgrimage venue for centuries, at least as far back as the 13th century when it was mentioned in print for the first time and that they later fell under the ownership of the Teutonic Knights.

The **Žalostna Matere Božja** (Church of our Lady of the Sorrows), with its buttressed exterior, is reckoned to be the oldest, though today's incarnation owes much to 17th- and 18th-century makeovers. Look out for the particularly elaborate late baroque altar and pulpit. The middle building, the **Cerkev Glej Človeka** (Ecce homo), is a church dedicated to Ecce homo meaning 'Behold the Man' and features an octagonal interior, while the **Lurške Matere Božje** (Church of our Lady of Lourdes) was mentioned by Valvasor (see page 40) in the 17th century,

**METLIKA'S WINE ROAD**
Bela Krajina's tourist office has recently put together a wine road map that covers the vineyards in the north of the region. You risk a fate worse than death if you try to order a Cviček here as there is a great rivalry between the Dolenjska wine and Bela Krajina's finest Metliška Črnina. You can just tour around looking for the wine cellars (vinska klet) using the trail handed out by the tourist offices in Bela Krajina or even get them to call ahead for you and arrange a tasting programme.

though the church's graffiti dates it at least as far back as 1565. The conversion from a single to triple vane was not made until the 19th century. Easter is a good time to be here for the Way of the Cross procession. Another important event is St Bartholomew's Day on August 24.

### Walking and Mirna Gora
Bela Krajina is an excellent area for walking with a surfeit of unspoilt rolling hills. Mirna Gora is the highest peak in the region and you can see most of Bela Krajina from up here as well as a swathe of Croatia. Before World War II there was a Franciscan church up here, but it was burned down by the Italians, though there have been recent attempts to bring it back to life. The trail up through the birch trees is a great way to spend an afternoon and there is also a mountain hut on Mirna Gora, as well as a restaurant and picnic area. Pick up the leaflet from the tourist office in Metlika which details four walks, from 3.5km to 10.5km, around the slopes and forests.

## ČRNOMELJ
Metlika's big rival, also bigger in population, makes much of the fact that, unlike its northern upstart, it never succumbed to the Ottomans. It enjoys a strategic and scenic position between the bends of the Dobličica and Lahinja rivers. Today, though, it looks far shabbier than Metlika with crumbling footpaths and façades, though it is worth visiting given its equally interesting history. Local archaeological digs suggest that settlement dates back as far as the early Iron Age and there is also evidence that the Romans occupied the area, before it received its municipal charter at the same time as Metlika in the 15th century. Sturdy fortifications and a moat, which was only filled in the 19th century, kept out the Turks. The Italians, however, did succeed in taking the town during World War II and after their capitulation the partisans took over. In spring each year the town comes alive with the **Jurjevanje** (St George's Day) celebrations (see *St George's Day Festival* box).

### Getting there
Buses run to Črnomelj from Metlika (20 minutes), Novo Mesto (40 minutes) and Ljubljana ($2^1/4$ hours), as do trains from Metlika (20 minutes), Ljubljana ($2^1/4$–$2^3/4$ hours) and Novo Mesto (45 minutes).

# Where to stay

**Gostilna Müller** (4 rooms) Ločka 6; tel: 07 356 7200; www.gostilna-muller.si. Offering rooms with air conditioning, minibars and satellite TV. Singles 5,500SIT, doubles 10,000SIT.

**Hotel Lahinja** Koldovorska 60; tel: 07 306 1650; fax: 07 306 1640; email: hotel.lahinja@volja.net. Uninspiring and faded hotel. Some rooms have shared facilities. Doubles without/with bathrooms 7,000–13,200SIT/12,000–18,000SIT.

# Where to eat

**Gostilna Müller** Ločka 6; tel: 07 356 7200. Popular eatery with outdoor terrace and vast interior dining space. Rich creamy sauces are the order of the day; try the Bela Krajina *žlikrofi* or the gnocchi with boletus mushrooms and cream. Disappointingly its nightclub is currently only open to large pre-booked groups.

**Gostilna Skubič** Pod Lipo 4. The restaurant's rear terrace overlooking the river is the nicest setting for a meal in town. Hearty grills and some fish dishes feature on the menu.

**Mercator** Kolodvorska 39

# Practicalities

**Tourist Information Centre** Trg Svobode 3; tel: 07 306 1100; email: turizem@crnomelj.si; www.crnomelj.si. Open: Mon–Fri 07.30–15.30, Sat 09.00–12.00.

**Post office** Koldovorska 30. Open: Mon–Fri 07.00–19.00, Sat 07.00–12.00.

**Dolenjska Banka** Trg Svobode 2

**Ljubljanska Banka** Pod lipo 4a

# What to see

**Črnomaljski Grad** (Črnomelj Castle), built originally in the 12th century, may look a bit tatty and need a revamp these days but this was once the grand headquarters of the Teutonic Knights in the area. Here you will find the local tourist information centre and a modest museum with some images of the town

## ST GEORGE'S DAY FESTIVAL

The popular St George's Day, or *Jurjevanje*, cultural and folk festival was first held in Črnomelj in 1964 and despite the saint's name its origins go back to much earlier days when the local people thanked their Slavic deities for the arrival of spring. This day used to be celebrated in many other parts of Slovenia, but it has long since been forgotten, only to live on in culturally vibrant Bela Krajina. Many of the traditions surrounding the festival, such as the dunking of *Zeleni Jurij* (Green George), a young lad clad from head to toe in birch tree leaves and branches, in the Lahinja River may have vanished, but each year bonfires are still lit on the eve of St George's Day and people still get dressed up in the traditional stark white costumes to perform folk songs and resurrect their ancient dance, the Kolo. Another highlight is the procession of Green George from house to house.

through the ages. The expansive fresco of the eponymous saint beckons you towards the **Cerkev Sv Petra** (Church of St Peter), but there is not much to see inside this baroque place of worship. The **Cerkev Sv Duha** (Church of the Holy Spirit) is crying out for a decent refurbishment. If you want to sample or buy some of the local wines the best place to head is to the **Črnomaljska Klet** wine information centre (Ulica Mirana Jarca 2; tel. 07 306 1100 near the castle and tourist office).

# Štajerska and Prekmurje

*Ljubljančani* often like to make fun of Štajerska, dismissing it as one big industrial farm, but Slovenia's largest region does actually have plenty to offer, from two impressive cities, Maribor and Celje, and what is arguably the most attractive town in Slovenia, Ptuj, through to castles and parks and, of course, perhaps the country's finest beer, Laško. Spas are big here too with thermal water spurting out of the ground and people frolicking in it everywhere you look. You would be well advised to join them in a region where the stresses and strains caused by your hard sightseeing can so easily be erased by relaxing in a spa. Another highlight of the Štajerska region is Logarska Dolina, a stunning valley eulogised as the 'Jewel of the Alps' that brings all Slovenes out in a proud smile when you mention it. Then there is Prekmurje, a picturesque region of rolling hills, hearty cuisine and sturdy castles that is heavily influenced by Hungary across the border, which is as distinct from the rest of Štajerska as Bela Krajina is from Dolenjska.

## MARIBOR

Maribor is not the sort of place to accept the 'second city' tag lying down. Impressively located on the banks of the Drava River with the waters sweeping past an extensively pedestrianised Old Town, Maribor may not be as populous as Ljubljana, but this vibrant city is laden with things to do and see. In summer when the Lent Festival buzzes through and the city comes to a virtual standstill, as its residents indulge in the myriad shows and a jug or two of Laško, this is the place to be. Maribor is a bit of a playground all year round: in winter the slopes of the nearby Pohorje Massif beckon with everything from beginner runs through to World Cup standard thrills, while in summer the river and the Pohorje are obvious places to relax for a while.

### History

Archaeological finds dating back as far as 2400BC suggest that Slovenia's second city has been inhabited for almost 4,500 years. Copper-Age settlers, Illyrians, Celts, Romans and Huns all number amongst the city's former residents, however it only really began to flourish in the middle of the 13th century when Maribor (or Marchburg as it was known then – later becoming Markburg) was first mentioned in historical documents. This recognition also prompted the

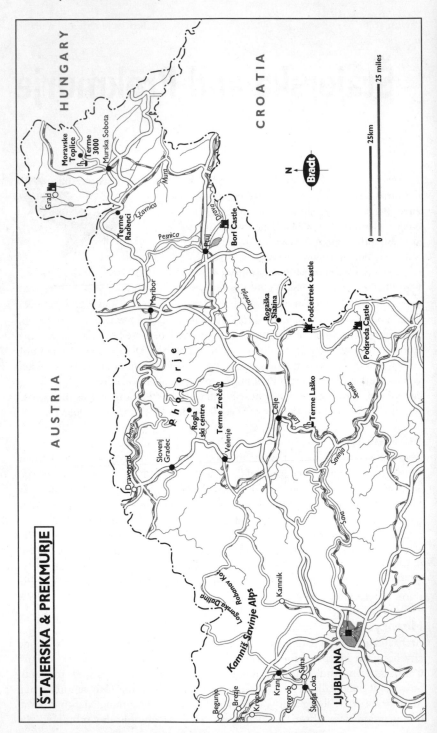

ŠTAJERSKA & PREKMURJE

townspeople to erect a defensive city wall, which was 2km in length and marked the boundary of the present-day Old Town, and four defence towers to stave off Turkish attacks. The 15th century was blighted by ethnic cleansing, when the large and influential Jewish population was banished from the town. A similar fate was to greet the protestant minority in 1600 when the Catholic Church ordered their removal.

Mother Nature succeeded where the Ottomans failed and in the late 17th century around a third of Maribor's population was wiped out by the plague; she has in fact devastated the city on numerous occasions, with fires in 1513, 1601, 1648 and 1699. The next defining events in the city's history include brief periods of French occupation (1805 and 1809) and the construction of the Vienna–Trieste railway (completed in 1857), which was accompanied by a surge of industrial development. Maribor continued to prosper and emerged from World War I relatively unscathed and with a strong textile industry. Its fortunes during World War II were in stark contrast to the earlier conflict, when industry in occupied Maribor came to a standstill and Allied air raids all but demolished parts of the city. In the post-war years Maribor has made an impressive recovery and while recent years have seen its industrial output decline, the city is fighting back by establishing itself as a centre for tourism and other services.

## Getting there
Regular trains from Ptuj (45 minutes), Celje (1 hour) and Laško (1¼ hours) stop at Maribor. There are also direct services from Ljubljana (1¾–2½ hours), Murska Sobota (2 hours), Postojna (3 hours 20 minutes) and Koper (4–5 hours). Daily international trains from Venice, Trieste, Zagreb, Vienna, Graz and Budapest also come to the city. Buses from Ptuj (30 minutes), Murska Sobota (1¼ hours), Celje (1 hour 20 minutes) and Ljubljana (3 hours) also serve Slovenia's second city.

**Railway station** Partizanska 50; tel: 02 292 2100. The station has self-service left-luggage lockers at 400SIT for 24 hours. If you lose the key you will have to fork out 5,000SIT to replace it. There is also an ATM and information point at the station.
**Bus Station** Mlinska 1; tel: 080 1116

## Getting around
### By bus
A comprehensive and easy-to-follow bus map can be obtained from the tourist information centre with almost all of the city's 20 services running through the centre of Maribor. Lines are colour coded and destinations correspond with those on the city map.

### By taxi
There are taxi ranks at Trg Svobode, the railway station, Partizanska and Heroja Bračiča.

## Tour operators
**Kompas** Trg Svobode 1; tel: 02 252 5718

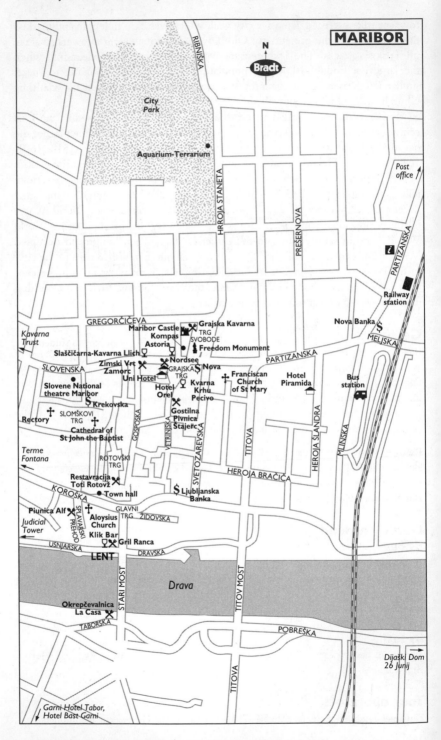

MARIBOR

N

Bradt

City Park

Aquarium-Terrarium

RIBNIŠKA

HEROJA STANETA

PREŠERNOVA

PARTIZANSKA

Post office

Railway station

GREGORČIČEVA

Maribor Castle          Grajska Kavarna
Kompas          TRG
Astoria          SVOBODE
                         Freedom Monument

Kavarna Trust

Slaščičarna-Kavarna Llich

Zimski Vrt          Nordsee
Zamorc          GRAJSKA          Nova
Uni Hotel          TRG

SLOVENSKA

Nova Banka

MELJSKA

PARTIZANSKA

Hotel Piramida

Bus station

Slovene National theatre Maribor

Krekovska

Hotel Orel          Kvarna Krhu Pecivo          Franciscan Church of St Mary

Rectory          SLOMŠKOVI TRG
Cathedral of St John the Baptist

Gostilna Pivnica Štajerc

GOSPOSKA

VETRINJSKA

SVETO ZAREVSKA

TITOVA

HEROJA ŠLANDRA

MLINSKA

Terme Fontana

ROTOVŠKI TRG

Restavracija Toti Rotovž
Town hall

HEROJA BRAČIČA

KOROŠKA

Ljubljanska Banka

Piunica Alf
Judicial Tower

Aloysius Church          GLAVNI TRG          ŽIDOVSKA

SPLAVARSKI PREHOD

Klik Bar

Gril Ranca

USNJARSKA          DRAVSKA

LENT

STARI MOST

Drava

TITOV MOST

POBREŠKA

Okrepčevalnica La Casa

TABORSKA

Dijaški Dom 26 Junij

TITOVA

Garni Hotel Tabor, Hotel Bast Garni

## Where to stay

Some of the best accommodation options in Maribor are in Maribor Pohorje, just a ten-minute drive from the city. Details are listed in the Maribor Pohorje section.

**Hotel Orel** (140 rooms) Grajski trg 3a; tel: 02 250 6700; fax: 02 251 8497; email: orel@termemb.si; www.termemb.si. This above-average three-star hotel has well-equipped rooms and a very central location. Guests have free use of many of the recreational facilities at Terme Fontana west of the city centre. Singles 11,500–14,200SIT, doubles 14,000–20,200SIT, apartments 22,300–28,000SIT.

**Hotel Piramida** (76 rooms) Heroja Šlandra 10; tel: 02 234 4400; fax: 02 234 4360; email: piramida@termemb.si; www.termemb.si. Centrally located seven-storey business hotel. Good-sized rooms have minibars, satellite TV and private bathrooms. Five minutes from the main railway station. Guests here can also use many of the facilities at Terme Fontana free of charge. Singles 17,000–21,100SIT, doubles 21,100–30,700SIT.

**Uni Hotel** (10 rooms) Grajski trg 3a; tel: 02 250 6700; fax: 02 251 8497; email: uni.hotel@termemb.si. Very centrally located hostel, which is generally used for long-term stays by students. Casual visitors can stay here but due to the high demand reservations are recommended. 3,800SIT per person.

**Dijaški Dom 26 Junij** Železnikova 12; tel/fax: 02 480 1710; email: vojteh.stefanciosa@guest.arnes.si; http://www.maribor.uni-mb.si/26junij/html/index.html. Maribor's other youth hostel doubles up as student dormitories and is only open in July and for the first three weeks of August. Located 3km from the centre, the hostel can be reached by bus 3, which takes you within 300m. 2,300–3,000SIT per person.

**Garni Hotel Tabor** (44 rooms) Heroja Zidanška 18; tel: 02 421 6410; fax: 02 421 6440; email: hoteltabor@podhostnik.si; www.hoteltabor.podhosnik.si. Pleasant medium-sized and family-owned hotel, with modern and stylish rooms, located 10-minutes' walk from the south bank of the Drava River and 15 minutes' walk from the Old Town. The hotel also has private parking and its own restaurant. Singles 8,160SIT, doubles 12,720SIT, triples 16,560SIT, quads 21,360SIT.

**Hotel Bajt Garni** Radvanjska 106; tel/fax: 02 332 7650; email: info@hotel-bajt.com; www.hotel-bajt.com. Family-run hotel located in the suburb of Nova Vas, just south of the city centre, with simple, but stylish rooms. Singles 7,968–9,240SIT, doubles 10,896–13,392SIT, triples 17,946SIT.

## Where to eat

**Gostilna and Pivnica Štajerc** Vetrinjska 30; tel: 02 234 4234. Great beer hall and restaurant serving schnitzels, fried chicken and a variety of Hungarian-influenced goulashes. Read the menu carefully because one of the stews is made from horsemeat. A jug of their own recipe beer, the eponymous Štajerc, is also a must. The well-shaded terrace is great on sunny days.

**Gril Ranca** Dravska 10; tel: 02 252 5500. On a balmy summer's evening the terrace of this waterfront restaurant is a great place to eat. Enjoy grilled meats amidst the hustle and bustle of the neighbouring café-bars.

**Restavracija Toti Rotovž** Rotovški trg 9; tel: 02 228 7650. Upscale restaurant in a 16th-century dwelling at the heart of Maribor's Old Town. The eclectic menu offers everything from Thai, Japanese and Mexican dishes to more traditional Slovene flavours. There is also dancing in the cellar on Friday and Saturday evenings.

**Pivnica Alf** Splavarski prehod 6; tel: 02 251 4844. This beer hall tucked down a narrow street off Koroška sells hearty and affordable food as well as a variety of pizzas.

**Okrepčevalnica La Casa** Taborska 12; tel: 02 332 1482. Located on the south side of the Drava just beyond the Stari Most (Old Bridge) this great little eatery serving Spanish-, Greek- and Slovene-influenced meals is cheap and popular with students. There are also great views across the river to the Old Town from the outdoor terrace, and you really feel like you have escaped the hustle and bustle of the city above.

**Pri Treh Ribnikih** Ribniška 9; tel: 02 234 4170. Historic restaurant with a stunning brick-vaulted wine cellar and leafy terrace in the heart of Maribor's city park. Immaculate service and good food come at a price.

**Zimski Vrt Zamorc** Gosposka 30; tel: 02 251 2717. Pleasant restaurant with a wide selection of dishes. Try the shrimps with mushrooms and rice.

**Nordsee** Slovenska 1; tel: 02 252 5212. Serving cheap and cheerful seafood Scandinavian style. This is also a good place to grab a sandwich.

## Entertainment and nightlife

Maribor is overflowing with lively café-bars and the city takes on a Parisian feel as the locals move on to the streets during the warmer months. Poštna south of the cathedral is particularly charming.

**Grajska Kavarna** Grajski trg 2. On a sunny day the café that spills out on to the square from the castle has a hard-to-beat location, especially if the monthly organic market is open. Admire the 15th-century fortifications and watch life pass by in this central square as you sip a *bela kava*.

**Astoria** Slovenska 2; tel: 02 251 5250. On the fringe of Grajski trg this café is a great place for people watching.

**Kavarna Krhu Pecivo** Grajski trg 6; tel: 02 251 4842. Grab a snack in this café immediately behind the statue of St Florian, protector of firemen and wine.

**Kavarna Trust** Gosposvetska 84; tel: 02 235 0126. Heading west on the street that continues on from Slovenska you will arrive at this popular student haunt. The café also has a nightclub that is open daily until 03.00, however some residents are trying to rein in the opening hours.

**Slaščičarna-Kavarna Ilich** Slovenska 6; tel: 02 250 2408. Frequented by locals who reckon this café has the best ice-cream in Maribor.

**Casino Maribor** Glavni trg 1. Housed in an attractive building in the centre of town the casino has gaming machines on the ground level and Black Jack and Roulette on the first floor for more serious gamblers. The casino also has a decent restaurant and its own bar 'Clip Bar' with a terrace overlooking the Drava. Gaming rooms open daily until 02.00; the bar and restaurant close at 23.00.

**Slovensko Narodno Gledališče Maribor/SNG Maribor** (Slovene National Theatre Maribor) Slovenska 27; tel: 02 250 6100; fax: 02 252 1207; email: sng.maribor@sng-mb.si; www.sng-mb.si. Maribor's National Theatre actually comprises three buildings, with the first auditorium and former casino dating from 1851. The oldest part of the theatre boasts an attractive neo-classical façade and an ornate concert hall. The new buildings date from 1979 94. As well as hosting a packed annual calendar of theatrical, operatic and musical performances the theatre is also the hub of the annual Borštnik Festival – a fortnight of top-quality dramatisations – held in mid–late October.

## Practicalities
### Tourist Information Centre
The TIC (Partizanska 47; tel: 02 234 6600; fax: 02 234 6613; email: zzt@maribor.si; www.maribor-tourism.si. Open: Mon–Fri 09.00–18.00, Sat 09.00–13.00) is located five minutes' walk from Maribor's historic core and opposite the railway station. Friendly staff dish out tourist leaflets and can help you find accommodation. They can also arrange tourist guides, but need advance notice of this. If you speak German you might be able to join a tour that has already been organised.

### Post offices
Partizanska 1. Open: Mon–Fri 08.00–19.00 and Sat 08.00–12.00.
Partizanska 54. Open: Mon–Fri 07.00–19.00, Sat 07.00–18.00, Sun 08.00–12.00.

### Internet
**Kiber Kavarna-Cyber Café** Kneza koclja 9; tel: 02 229 4022. Centrally located internet café just east of Glavni trg.
**Klik Bar** Dravska 10. One of a handful of café-bars situated on the north bank of the Drava, immediately west of the Stari Most, with free internet access.

### Banking
**Ljubljanska Banka** Vetrinjska 2
**Krekovska Banka** Slomškov trg 18
**Nova Banka** Trg Svobode 6 and Partizanska 42

## Shopping
**Kiosks** selling bread, cakes, ice-cream and meat are concentrated at the beginning of Partizanska between Trg Svobode and Prešernova.
**Mercator** can be found at Glavni trg 10 and Partizanksa 7.
**Mladinska Kinga** Partizanksa 8, Vetrinjska and Gospoka.
**Abruni Gallery** Ventrinjska 5; tel: 02 252 6473. Great for window shopping or shelling out on works by contemporary Slovene and African artists.
**Galerija Dum** Židovska 10. Another gallery showcasing modern work by Slovene painters.
**Vinag Wine Cellar** Trg Svobode 3; tel: 02 220 8111; www.vinag.si. If you don't have time to explore the vineyards around Maribor, you could do worse than visit Vinag in the centre of town. Your tour will take you into the cellar where 5.5 million litres of wine are stored in huge wooden barrels, and even larger steel barrels. The cellar fell victim to thirsty German troops during World War II, and today the oldest wine in their collection dates back to 1946. Apparently a bottle of this vintage will set you back around 1,680,000SIT (€7,000). There are around 30 types of far more affordable wines for sale in the shop upstairs including White Riesling, Chardonnay, Pinot Grigo, Sauvignon Blanc and three varieties of sparkling Penina Royal. Around 90% of the wine produced by Vinag is white, and this is reflected in the bottles on sale.

## What to see
### A walking tour

Maribor is easy to get around on foot and a good place to start is across the Drava River on the opposite side to the Old Town where you can see how the historic core shapes up with its orange roof tiles. Cross **Stari Most** (Old Bridge) and you will be in Lent. Head down on the left-hand side of the bridge and you will soon be amongst the busy bars and cafés of this lively part of town. As you walk west you will come across a building smothered with a tentacle of vines. Unusually for the Maribor region these are red wine grapes and even more unusually they are reputed to be the oldest vines in the world (as recognised by the *Guinness Book of Records*), having grown here for almost 500 years. When they are harvested only 20 litres of wine are produced and it is precious stuff indeed, retailing at around 16,800SIT (€70) for a 20cl bottle. If you are a visiting dignitary you may be in with a better chance of snaffling some as the Pope is amongst the luminaries to have been given a bottle as a unique souvenir of the city.

Looking west along the river you will see the **Sodni Stolp** (Judicial Tower), one of four towers that hark back to the days when the city's walls stood strong. Turn north now and you will pass **Alojzijeva Cerkev** (Aloysius Church) and come out in Glavni trg, one of the city's most important squares. The striking **Kužno Znamenje** (Plague Memorial) in the middle dazzles with its gold. One of the most notorious visitors to the **Mestna Hiša** (Town Hall) was Adolf Hitler, who stood on the balcony in 1941 and claimed Maribor for the Third Reich.

Duck under the arch and you will be in Rotovški trg where a pavement café is open in the warmer months if you are getting thirsty. Head a block further north and you will be in Slomškov trg, a leafy square that is dominated by the city's vast cathedral. The **Cerkev Sv Janez Krstnik** (Cathedral of St John the Baptist) is an architecture student's dream. The Romanesque base has been added to over the ages, as the city's wealthier citizens tried to keep up with all the new fads with baroque, rococo, Renaissance and neo-classical styles all on show. Other majestic buildings that front the square include the headquarters of Maribor University – the **Rektorat** (Rectory) – the main office of the city's postal service and the **Slovensko Narodno Gledališče** (Slovene National Theatre).

Head back east now towards another of the city's main squares, Grajski trg, home to **Mariborska Grad** (Maribor Castle), which looks more like a palace. Have a look at the **Frančiškanska Cerkev Sv Marija** (Franciscan Church of St Mary) to the southeast, the red-brick one, whose construction is the subject of a bizarre local urban myth. It is said that local women who had sinned were asked to donate two bricks each and if you imagine how many bricks are in this voluminous building then that is a lot of sinning for a place of Maribor's modest size! If you want to indulge a bit yourself continue slightly further north to Trg Svobode where the **Vinag Wine Cellar** awaits with 5.5 million litres of wine, of which 90% is white. A more sobering sight outside is the haunting dark sphere, cruelly named 'Kojak' by some of the city's youth who use it as a meeting point, which is the **Freedom Monument** at the heart of Freedom Square (*svobode* means freedom). On it are images of 167 locals who were executed by the occupying

Germans during World War II and equally touching is the inscribed letter at its base of a partisan's parting note to his wife and family before he was shot.

If you want to escape the centre for a while just go a few blocks further north and you will come to the **City Park**, which is a haven with plenty of space for strolling around and taking it easy away from the bustle.

## Alojzijeva Cerkev (Aloysius Church)

Constructed in 1769 this late baroque church is the design of local architect Johannes Fuchs. Its most notable features include attractive rococo railings and ornate colonnades on the main altar. A more unusual aspect of the church are the panoramas of Celje, Ptuj and Maribor that can be found in the altar painting, where St Maximilian is depicted in Celje, St Viktorin in Ptuj and St Aloysius himself in Maribor.

## Kužno Znamenje (Plague Memorial)

Around a third of Maribor's citizens were wiped out as the plague ravaged the city in the 17th century. The immense gratitude that the survivors felt when the disease finally left the city, led them to erect the Kužno Znamenje in 1681, a memorial that took the form of a column topped by a figure of the Virgin Mary. The monument that visitors see today is an 18th-century structure, the work of Jožef Štraub who, using a degree of artistic licence, added the six saints that surround the virgin mother.

## Mestna Hiša (Town Hall)

This late Gothic structure dates from 1515, but was re-mastered in an Italian-Renaissance style in 1565 – the balcony was also added at this time. On the front of the building you will be able to spot Maribor's coat of arms and an unusual onion-dome topped tower, while inside the baroque wedding hall is also worth seeking out. During the 19th century the authorities, somewhat misguidedly, gave the town hall a makeover and it gained a late classicist appearance; fortunately it was restored to its 16th-century appearance in the 1950s.

## Cerkev Sv Janez Krstnik (Cathedral of St John the Baptist)

This former church acquired its cathedral status back in 1859 when Bishop Anton Martin Slomšek (after whom Slomškov trg is named) moved the seat of the diocese to Maribor. Almost 250 years later the Slovene bishop is on his way to becoming the country's first modern saint. Like France Prešeren, Slomšek was a powerful force in terms of the preservation of Slovenian literature and culture during the 19th century. The bishop's most celebrated acts are, as already mentioned, the transference of the see of the bishopric to Maribor from Styria, at a time when German nationalism dominated life in Slovenia, and his establishment of the Mohorjeva Society. The latter was a publishing house, which Slomšek used to promote both Catholicism and the development of Slovenian literature in general. Works produced by Slovenia's oldest surviving publishing house found their way into the majority of Slovenian homes in the early 20th century, with over 90,000 subscribers by 1914, a fact made more impressive when you consider that it occurred against a backdrop of growing German nationalism.

Dating from the 12th century the **stolnica** (cathedral) (Slomškov trg 21; tel: 02 251 8432) was originally constructed in Romanesque style and gained its present-day Gothic appearance in the 14th and 15th centuries, with the belltower being added in 1623. Mother Nature changed the appearance of the cathedral in the late 18th century when the campanile was reduced from its lofty 76m to its present-day 57m as a result of the destruction inflicted upon it by a bolt of lightning – fortunately this shortened version still makes a good vantage point from which to survey the Old Town. Inside the cathedral visitors can admire the choir benches whose 18th-century reliefs depict the life of St John the Baptist, a replica of Ruben's *Descent from the Cross* and stained-glass windows illustrating the work of Bishop Slomšek. The cathedral is particularly atmospheric during one of the frequent organ recitals. *Belltower open: 09.00–18.00. Free.*

### Mariborska Grad in Pokrajinski Muzej (Maribor Castle and Provincial Museum)

Like many of the historic buildings in Maribor's Old Town, the 15th-century castle (Grajska 2; tel: 02 228 3551; fax: 02 252 7777; email: info@pmuzej-mb.si; www.pmuzej-mb.si) exhibits a number of architectural styles including its medieval fortifications, flamboyant rococo staircase and the baroque Loretska Chapel. Today the castle is but a mere shadow of its former self – city planners gradually removed three defensive towers, the main portal and its gate during the 19th century – and most of the castle's rooms are occupied by exhibits of the **Pokrajinski Muzej** (Provincial Museum). English-language handouts guide you through the museum's ethnological and archaeological collections – exhibits of traditional costume, gemstones, apothecary and church artefacts. For many visitors the most interesting displays are those covering the town's history and culture. As you walk around look out for the wonderfully outsized ceiling frescos in the first-floor Knight's Hall – Johan Glebler's 1763 depiction of clashes between Christian and Turkish forces. *Open: Tue–Sat 09.00–17.00, Sun 10.00–14.00 Apr–Dec. 500SIT.*

### Frančiškanska Cerkev Sv Marija (Franciscan Church of St Mary)

Constructed at the turn of the 20th century according to the plans of Viennese architect Richard Jordan, the Franciscan Church of St Mary stands on the spot of a former convent and 18th-century church. The austere structure that stands today is covered entirely in red bricks, which locals claimed were transported here by women wishing to receive atonement for two sins (each is said to have carried two bricks).

### Maribor Mestni Park (Maribor City Park)

Located just north of the city centre, on Tomšičeva, you will find this 5ha green oasis. First landscaped between 1872 and 1896 the present-day park is home to three fish ponds, colourful flowerbeds, ornate fountains, a children's playground and a maze of footpaths. In the warmer months musicians play from the pavilion, while the *akvarij-terarij* (aquarium-terrarium) is a useful distraction for those travelling with kids on a rainy day. For most the real reason to visit the park is to scale the Piramida, a 386m hill that offers good panoramas over the city and the Pohorje Mountains.

**LENT FESTIVAL**
During the 17-day-long Lent Festival, which usually starts on the third Friday in June, Maribor becomes one big cultural and party oasis. A temporary stage is pushed out onto the Drava and numerous venues spring up to cater for the flush of theatre performances and concerts that ripple through the city as fireworks crackle overhead. Just mention the Lent Festival to any local and their faces will light up and so will yours if you are lucky enough to be in town.

### Akvarij-Terarij (Aquarium-Terrarium)

The older aquarium (tel: 02 251 2295; email: akvarij-terarij@florina.si; www.florina.si/akvarij-terarij/index.html) dating from 1953 is home to more than 100 species of fish including brightly coloured tropical fish, piranhas and those indigenous to Slovenia's Adriatic coast. The more modern terrarium houses a large number of amphibians, insects and reptiles including a rattle-snake, cobra, python and boa constrictor, turtles, crocodiles and lizards.
*Open: Mon–Sat 08.00–19.00, Sun 09.00–12.00 and 14.00–19.00. 550SIT.*

### Terme Fontana

The emphasis at this terme (Koroška 172; tel: 02 234 4100; fax: 02 234 4114; email: fontana@termemb.si; www.termemb.si) is firmly on health and rehabilitation, with a diagnostic centre and treatments ranging from massage and acupuncture to personal fitness programmes and magnetic therapy. For the more casual user, though, Fontana also has indoor and outdoor thermal pools, underwater massage jets and Jacuzzis heated to temperatures between 33°C and 37°C. Fontana also has a fitness centre, saunas, a steam bath, solariums and massage programmes.

## MARIBOR POHORJE

It may not boast the skyscraping peaks of the Julian Alps, but the Pohorje is a pleasure-filled playground for all sorts of activities right on the edge of the city. Here you can head off for a spot of skiing or mountain-biking, paintballing or horseriding. The Pohorje makes a useful alternative base if you love your skiing or walking as it is still easy to get into town by bus or taxi. Leafy suburbia up here gives way to World Cup-run ski slopes and a multitude of things to do.

### Getting there

Bus 6 runs between the centre of Maribor and the Pohorje at frequent intervals.

### Where to stay

There is plenty of accommodation available in the Pohorje offering everything from basic hostel-style accommodation to five-star luxury, mountainside ski lodges and private rooms.

**Habakuk** (131 rooms and 9 apartments) Pohorska 59; tel: 02 300 8100; fax: 02 300 8128; email: habakuk@termemb.si; www.termemb.si. If your budget will stretch to a five-star hotel then stay here at one of Slovenia's best hotels. Indoor and outdoor thermal pools and whirlpools with a water temperature that hovers around 33°C, sauna, Turkish bath, fitness centre, squash courts and a variety of spa treatments are the hotel's biggest lure. Out of season (spring and early summer) you may well have all these things to yourself. Well-equipped guestrooms are large and comfortable. Singles 26,600–32,500SIT, doubles 35,600–46,800SIT, suites 48,200–53,600SIT (32,300–35,500SIT single use), apartments 55,400–60,200SIT.

**Bellevue** Na slemenu 35; tel: 02 220 8841; fax: 02 220 8849; email: info.scp@sc-pohorje.si; www.pohorje.org. This former hotel now functions as one of Slovenia's best-located youth hostels, standing 1,050m above sea level next to the upper cable car station on the Maribor Pohorje. As well as magnificent views the hostel offers 186 beds, around a third of which have private showers and toilets; the rest have shared facilities. The hostel's bar and restaurant are great places to meet fellow travellers and Slovenes, especially during the ski season. Winter walks, tobogganing and discos also feature on the hostel's seasonal entertainment programme.

**Apartments Martin** Hočko Pohorje 103; tel: 02 220 8841; email: info.scp@sc-pohorje.si; www.pohorje.org. Ski lodges split into two apartments on the ski slopes close to the upper cable car station. Simple chalet-style bedrooms sleep 2–4 in doubles, twins and bunks. For larger groups two of the lodges have basement apartments accommodating up to 15 people. 22,800–33,600SIT/27,600–38,400SIT sleeping 6–7/12–15.

**Hotel Areh** Lobnica 62; tel: 02 220 8841; fax: 02 220 8849; email: info.scp@sc-pohorje.si; www.pohorje.org. 3- and 4-bed rooms are available in this ski lodge located at the Areh peak summit. The hotel also has its own restaurant and hires out ski equipment. Half-board 7,600–9,600SIT per person.

**Mekina** Grizoldova 31; tel: 02 613 1604; fax: 02 614 2255; email: mekina@volja.net; http://www.users.volja.net/mekina. Five-minutes' walk from the Habakuk Hotel rooms in this welcoming pension are clean and comfortable. Singles 7,200SIT, doubles 9,600SIT, triples 14,400SIT.

**Villa Divji Petelin** Pohorska 41; tel: 02 614 0153; fax: 02 614 0154; email: divji.petelin@siol.net; www.divjipetelin.com. Offering bed and breakfast in simply decorated, but stylish and comfortable rooms. The villa also has private parking and serves food. Singles 7,000SIT, doubles 12,000SIT, triples 16,000SIT.

## Activities
### Skiing
The main reason to visit Maribor Pohorje in season is to ski. This is one of the country's biggest ski resorts, which boasts 63km of ski slopes that are well served by a cable car and ski lifts, with a large variety of runs that lend themselves to all levels of skier, from the beginner to the advanced. The Pohorje also has its own ski and snowboard schools. For two days each January Maribor Pohorje plays host to the Women's Alpine Skiing World Cup. One of its more unusual features is the fact that 7km of the ski slope are illuminated at night, allowing you to experience night skiing. For more information contact **Športni Centre Pohorje** (Pohorska 60; tel: 02 603 6553; fax: 02 603 6565; www.pohorje.org).

### Adrenaline Park Pohorje
When the ski season is over activities offered by the Adrenaline Park Pohorje (tel: 02 220 8841; fax: 02 220 8849; email: info.park@sc-pohorje.si; www.pohorje.org) take over the region. Visitors can choose from a range of activities.

## High ropes course

This is basically an obstacle course that takes place 8m above the ground. Challenges include crossing from one high platform to another as you walk across narrow ropes, tackling the elevated rope climbing wall and swinging on a series of suspended tyres. The course is located on Trikotna jasa and is accessible on foot or by chair lift. A four-hour programme costs 8,400SIT; combine this with summer sledding or paintball for 10,100SIT.

## Downhill mountain-biking

The Pohorje's challenging downhill track is open all year round and descends 500m from the starting point at Bolfenk. Only for experienced mountain-bikers and those with specially adjusted bikes. Helmets and body armour are also a must.

## Summer sledding

Sledding in the Pohorje is not just confined to winter and in the summer months a 5km track takes you from the top of Bellevuc's cable car station back to the base – descending 725m in total. Be warned this is not for the faint-hearted as the sleds can go as fast as 50km/h. 2,160SIT per hour. Alternatively you can take a two-hour trip from Trikotna jasa into the valley for 2,880SIT.

## Paintball

Adrenaline-pumping simulated warfare takes place in the summer season at an altitude of 580m (near the High Ropes Course). The aim of the game is to capture the opposing team's flag, while preventing yours from being captured by them. The only snag is that if you are 'killed', or rather struck by a high-speed paintball as it is propelled from another player's gun, then you are out. Still there is always the next game. 2,400–3,600SIT for two hours depending on group size.

## Walking

For those who like to take their exercise at a more leisurely pace the Pohorje's hills, which have a variety of marked trails, are great for rambling in. A good mountain map is also essential to keep you on the right track. Routes include walks to the **Slap Šumik** (Šumik Waterfall), **Črno Jezero** (Black Lake) and the virgin forest Pragozd. The Rozika forest trail, which begins next to the Bellevue Hostel to the Church of St Bolfenk and offers some stunning views. The Areh Hotel is another good place to begin an exploration of the Pohorje's walking paths.

# ZREČE AND ROGLA
## Getting there

The easiest way to reach both Rogla and Zreče is by car. From Murska Sobota or Maribor head southwest towards Ljubljana and Celje for 30km, taking the Slovenske Konjice exit and from there following the road to Zreče and then Rogla. From Ptuj head for Kidričevo, Slovenska Bistrica and continue southeast to Slovenske Konjice before travelling on to Zreče and/or Rogla.

## Getting around

Regular buses connect the terme to the ski centre.

## Terme Zreče

About 17km away from the ski slopes you will find a modern health spa with five swimming pools whose healing thermal waters are naturally heated to temperatures of 26°C to 35°C. Zreče also has a fitness centre, Turkish bath and dry saunas. Accommodation is provided in the Dobrava Hotel or self-catering villas from 8,500SIT per person.

## Rogla Olympic and Ski Centre

One of Slovenia's premier ski resorts the Rogla Olympic and Ski Centre offers skiing, snowboarding and telemark skiing on 12km of downhill pistes and 18km of cross-country tracks; snow-making machines ensure that there is always enough snow for the winter sports to take place. Only 2km of the pistes are classified as easy, but those with some skiing experience can take advantage of advanced lessons in the ski school. After a hard day on the slopes why not go for a ride in a snowmobile, or take a scenic helicopter tour. Skiing competitions, night skiing and full equipment hire are also offered.

The Olympic Centre itself has a large sports hall with badminton, tennis, volleyball, squash, handball and basketball courts, as well as a swimming pool, massage and sauna facilities and a fitness centre. Outside there is a football pitch, running track and courts for tennis, basketball and handball. Accommodation is available in the resort's Planina and Rogla hotels or self-catering bungalows from 6,800SIT per person.

For more information about the Rogla Olympic and Ski Centre and Terme Zreče contact owners Unior (Cesta na Roglo 15, Zreče; tel: 03 757 6000; fax: 03 757 2446; email: turizem@unior.si; www.unior.si).

## VELENJE

A thoroughly modern city that grew up around the coal industry, Velenje is an interesting, if not exactly attractive, place to visit. It is also home to Gorenje, one of the most successful Slovenian companies, which exports kitchen appliances around the world. Its original name of Titovo Velenje came when it was 'born' in 1959. During the heyday of Yugoslav socialism a city in each of the sectors that made up Yugoslavia was adorned with the Tito moniker, and was held up as a successful example of socialism. In Slovenia this honour was bestowed upon Velenje. The two main reasons to visit are to see the brace of interesting museums: the **Muzej Premogovništva Slovenije** (The Coal Mining Museum of Slovenia) and **Velenjski Grad in Pokrajinski Muzej** (Velenje Castle and Regional Museum).

### Getting there

Velenje can be reached by bus from Slovenj Gradec (40 minutes), Celje (45 minutes), Dravograd (1 hour) and Ljubljana (1³/₄ hours). Trains from Celje also stop in Velenje (50 minutes).

### Where to stay

Velenje can easily be visited in a single day and there is nothing in the town that really merits an overnight stay.

# What to see
## Muzej Premogovništva Slovenije (Coal Mining Museum of Slovenia)
The mine that was once the driving force of the town is not the all-encompassing giant it once was, though the onsite museum (Stari Jašek–Koroška cesta; tel: 03 587 0997; fax: 03 587 0997; email: peter.pusnik@rlv.si; www.rlv.si/muzej/eng) is well worth visiting all the same. The museum allows an actual tour of sections of the mine, which takes $1^1/_2$ hours. Following the path of the first shaft sunk into the mine in 1887, the tour takes you past fairly realistic models of miners hacking out the lignite as the chamber fills with wailing sirens and the clanging of the mechanised shaft and work tools. A presentation covers the issues of environmental pollution and the decline of Slovenia's coal mining industry. If your time in the pit has made you peckish then you can also visit the canteen and eat like a real miner. Located 1.5km from the centre of town in Škale.
*Open: daily 09.30–17.00. 1,800SIT.*

## Velenjski Grad in Pokrajinski Muzej (Velenje Castle and Regional Museum)
Dating from the 13th century, the present-day castle (Ljubljanska 54; tel: 03 898 2630; fax: 03 898 2640; www.muzej.velenje.org) owes its appearance largely to additions that were made 300 years later. Today visitors can explore the castle's keep with its vaulted cellar, defensive walls and round tower. The museum exhibits are, however, the real reason to visit. Nine permanent collections include baroque artwork taken from the **Cerkev Sv Jurij** (Church of St George) in Škale, more than 1,000 artefacts from Africa and 20th-century paintings by various Slovene artists, as well as the unique reconstructions of a 1930s inn and an early 20th-century general store. The shop and inn are not just stuffy museum pieces and visitors are invited to quench their thirst or purchase souvenirs.
*Open: Tue–Sun 09.00–17.00. 400SIT.*

# CELJE
Trawling through the heavy industry on the outskirts of Celje, your first instinct may be to leave again, especially if you are thrown into the maelstrom of the local traffic system with honking horns, frenetic junctions and one-way streets. Endure beyond the morass, though, and one of Slovenia's most attractive and historic Old Towns awaits, whose green and hilly surrounds offer plenty of opportunities to escape the traffic and industry. Celje is not yet firmly on the tourist trail so you will probably have it largely to yourself.

## History
Celje has a long history, with archaeological finds suggesting settlement here dates as far back as the Iron Age. After this time Celje was settled by the Celts then the Romans, the latter elevating it to the status of a town in the 1st century AD under the name Claudia Celeia. Barbarian raids 400 years later saw the end of Roman rule and left Celje in ruins. It took another 600 years for Celje to recover its former prominence and by the 15th century it had become an important and powerful administrative, economic and urban centre under the counts of Celje, who later

became dukes. This was Celje's golden age when the dukedom was the strongest in this part of Europe and it is a period that many locals still fondly hark back to. The achievement of the counts is also recognised in the Slovenian national coat of arms, where you will find three yellow stars that came from the emblem of the Dukes of Celje. This mighty feudal dynasty came to an abrupt end when the last duke, Count Ulrich II, was murdered in 1456 and the city has been playing catch up ever since.

## Getting there
Buses run to Celje from Ljubljana (1¹/₂ hours), Maribor (1¹/₂ hours), Ptuj (2 hours) and Murska Sobota (2¹/₄–2¹/₂ hours). Trains from Laško (10 minutes), Velenje (50 minutes), Rogaška Slatina (45 minutes–1 hour), Maribor (45 minutes–1 hour), Ptuj (1 hour) and Ljubljana (1–1¹/₂ hours) also stop there.

**Railway station** Krekov trg 1
**Bus station** Aškerčeva

## Getting around
There is a taxi rank on Krekov trg near the Hotel Evropa. You can also call taxis on the following numbers:

**Radio Taxi** Tel: 03 554 2200
**Avto-Taxi** Tel: 041 630 624
**State Express** Tel: 040 611 335

## Tour operators
**Kompas** Glavni trg; tel: 03 428 0308
**Globtour** Razlagova 1; tel: 03 544 2511

## Where to stay
**Hotel Evropa** Krekov trg 4; tel: 03 426 900; fax: 03 426 9620; email: hotel.evropa@siol.net; www.hotel.evropa.si. This friendly three-star is centrally located near the train station and has bright and modern rooms with showers. Even with the windows closed some of the rooms get a lot of noise from the street and the nearby church bell. Singles 9,700SIT, doubles 13,000SIT.
**Štorman** (45 rooms) Mariborska 3; tel: 03 426 0426; fax: 03 426 0395; email: recepcija.storman@siol.net; www.gostilne-hotel-storman.com. Nine-storey business hotel close to the bus station. Singles 9,150SIT, doubles 13,950SIT, triples 16,350SIT.
**Turška Mačka** (26 rooms) Gledališka 7; tel: 03 548 4611; fax: 03 544 2908; email: info@majolka.si; www.majolka.si. Like the hotel itself the rooms are small, but clean. Singles 6,500SIT, doubles 10,300SIT.
**Hotel Astor** (30 rooms) Ljubljanska 39; tel: 03 545 2018; fax: 03 545 1401; email: merx@merx-gt.si; www.astor-hotel.net. The outdoor swimming pool, private garage and pleasant location near the Savinja River almost make up for the 15-minute walk to Celje's Old Town. Singles 7,770SIT, doubles 11,990SIT, triples 14,625SIT.
**Dijaški Dom** Ljubljanska 21; tel: 03 426 6600; fax: 03 426 6621. Student dorm providing cheap accommodation for visitors in July and August. Ten minutes' walk from the tourist office. From 2,800SIT per person.

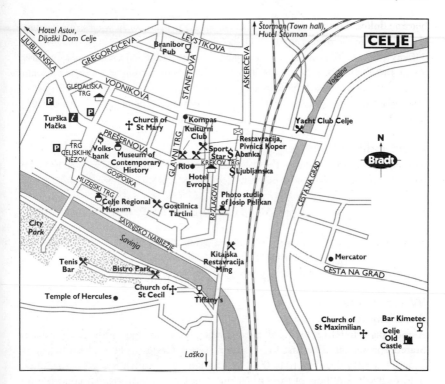

## Where to eat

**Restavracija and Pivnica Koper** Prešernova 2. It may not be the tastiest food you will ever eat, but the pasta, pizzas and grilled-meat dishes are good value; a small pizza costs from just 770SIT. Despite its official address the entrance is on Gubečeva. There is also a small terrace.

**Gostilnica Tartini** Glavni trg 12. One of Celje's best-located restaurants serves pretty standard fare in the form of pasta, pizza and salads, but is housed in an attractive building and looks out over the equally striking square.

**Bistro Park** Maistrova 2. If you are intending to explore the handful of attractions in Breg then you could do worse than eat here. Located next to the City Park the shaded terrace has views of the Savinja River and Old Town – a rarity in Celje. Whilst the location is great the food is fairly average.

**Kitajska Restavracija Ming** XIV Divizije 14; tel: 03 548 588. If you find yourself hankering after Chinese food this spacious restaurant makes a decent stab at Chinese cuisine.

**Rio** Prešerenova 1. Shop selling a wide selection of food and drinks.

**Mercator** Cesta na Grad 31. This mini market might just fit the bill after a sweaty walk to the old castle.

## Entertainment and nightlife

**Sport Star** Prešernova 2. Celje's most stylish and popular bar attracts a young crowd.

**Kulturni Club** Galvni trg 8. Lively café-bar housed in an ornate art nouveau building with a dark wood interior and outdoor terrace.

**Yacht Club Celje** Teharska 2. Not as salubrious as the name might suggest, this local bar situated close to the river is popular with locals.
**Tiffany's** Breg 6. This bar full of local character has a pool table and a small outdoor terrace.
**Tenis Bar** Mestni Park. Not just for tennis players, this unimposing bar next to the tennis courts is pleasantly situated in the leafy town park.
**Branibor Pub** Satnetova 27; tel: 03 492 4144. Open late every night 01.00–02.30 with regular live music performance, this is one of Celje's most popular bars.

## Practicalities

**Tourist Information Centre** Trg Celjskih Knezov 9; tel: 03 492 5080. Open: Mon–Fri 09.00–17.00, Sat 09.00–13.00 Nov–Mar, Mon–Fri 08.00–18.00, Sat–Sun 11.00–17.00 Apr–Oct.
**Post office** Krekov trg 9. Open: Mon–Fri 07.00–20.00, Sat 07.00–13.00. There is an ATM outside.
**Volksbank** Celjskih Knezav trg 1. Open Mon–Fri 08.30–16.30.
**Abanka** Krekov trg 7. Open: Mon–Fri 08.30–12.00 and 14.30–17.00.
**Ljubljanska Banka** Krekov trg 4. Open: Mon–Fri 08.30–12.00 and 14.30–17.00.

## What to see
### A walking tour

A good place to start is by Hotel Evropa where you can enjoy a fortifying *bela kava* before you set off. The first sight is **Stari Grad Celje** (Celje Old Castle; open: daily 09.00–21.00 summer, 10.00–17.00 winter; free) which is a good 45-minute trek, so if you are short of time or feeling a bit lazy you can catch a taxi from the rank by the hotel. If you are on foot from Krekov trg turn to the right of the railway station and follow the tracks to the underpass, which leads to a bridge over the Savinja River. Once across the bridge leave the road and take the footpath to the right along the riverbank before descending and taking the pedestrian crossing over Cesta na Grad. After the small sports stadium a short cut leads up through the forest – only take this if you are covered up and have some insect repellent as the bugs are ferocious. Either way your final approach to the castle will be back on the winding Cesta na Grad with good views of Slovenia's largest castle.

Originally constructed at the beginning of the 13th century, the castle that visitors see today has undergone a series of changes under its various residents and more recently faced years of decline. The castle wall and northern defence tower were added at the end of the 13th century, while the 14th century saw the lords of Žovnek (who later became the counts and then the dukes of Celje) mould the interior of the fortress to residential quarters, the dukes also added the four-storied Frederick's Tower. Other defining events include the 1348 earthquake, a 15th-century extension of the living space and the enlargement of the wall the following century. As the power of the dukes of Celje declined and the castle lost its strategic position it was abandoned and fell into ruin by the 17th century. Over the last decade serious attempts have been made to restore parts of the immense fortress, which has suffered a barrage of looting down the years – including the pilfering of the roof and the best stones for construction elsewhere and its exploitation as a quarry – and today it is just slowly returning to its former glory. Standing on the solid ramparts staring out over the hills and the city you can conjure up the days when the Dukes of Celje were masters of all they surveyed. There is also a Children's Gallery (Stari Grad Celje; tel: 041 615 274; open: daily 10.00–18.00) in the castle, a tourist information point and a pub called Hermanova Krčma (tel: 031 227 353), although you shouldn't count on either of the latter two places being open.

If you are thirsty after the steep ascent to the castle then check out Bar Kimetec, located on the road that branches away to the left as you near the castle; a wooden carving of a man holding a jug of Laško beer will help you find the way. If you want to come back down to continue the tour then just retrace your steps or if the walk has whetted your appetite for a spot of hiking there are a number of options from up here (see *Activities*, page 226). Cross the bridge back over the river and take the underpass before breaking right to take a quick look at **Cerkev Sv Maksimiljana** (Church of St Maximilian), built on a site where some sources claim Bishop Maximilian was beheaded in the 2nd century.

From here walk back to Krekov trg and take Razlagova past the defence tower and water tower, before you come out by the river. From here go over the bridge to your right and head up the welter of stairs to the **Cerkev Sv Cecilije** (Church of St Cecila). Nearby is a throwback to Roman times with the reconstructed **Heraklejev Tempelj** (Temple of Hercules). Head back down through the leafy **Mestni Park** (City Park), a favourite drinking venue for the city's waylaid youth, and cross the footbridge to the stretch of grass that harbours a preserved stretch of the Old Town walls as well as a bundle of Roman remnants. One street inside the Old Town is Muzejski trg with its choice of museums before you end up on Trg Celjskih Knezov where you will find the tourist information centre. Turn right on to pedestrianised Prešernova and follow it along towards Krekov trg. On the way you will come across the **Cerkev Sv Marije** (Church of St Mary), which no longer houses the bones of the dukes of Celje, but is still worth sticking your head in. Cut right before you get to Krekov trg and you will end up in Glavni trg, the city's finest square, which is home to a plague pillar and a charming collage of 18th- and 19th-century buildings, as well as a sprinkling of cafés for you to relax in and reward yourself with a drink.

## Museums and galleries
### Pokrajinski Muzej Celje (Celje Regional Museum)
Muzejski trg 1; tel: 03 428 0950; fax: 03 428 0966; email: info@pokmuz-ce.si; www.pokmuz-ce.si.
The Dukes of Celje are crucial to the city's history and this exhibition space delves into their story – a rather gruesome array of skulls that is on display is said to have been those of the famed dukes, an interesting way to treat the city's finest. Other things to look out for are rooms done in various architectural styles, such as art nouveau and baroque, as well as the Celje Ceiling, a lavish mural that depicts images from Roman and Greek mythology.
*Open: Tue–Sun 10.00–18.00 Mar–Oct.*

### Muzej Novejše Zgodovine Celje (Celje Museum of Modern History)
Prešernova 17; tel: 03 428 6410; fax: 03 428 6411; email: mnzc@guest.arnes.si; www.muzej-nz-ce.si.

If you want to follow the story of Celje down the ages, well since the beginning of the 20th century at least, this is the place to come and fittingly the exhibits are housed in the old town hall. Opened in 1963 the museum's permanent collection includes artefacts that illuminate the history of dentistry in Slovenia, workmen's tools, weapons used by soldiers in World War II, enamel kitchenware (this has been produced at the EMO Enamel Factory since 1894) and even weighing scales. For visitors letters saying farewell to their loved ones written by those imprisoned in Stari Pisker during the Nazi occupation of the city, may be of more interest. Another highlight is a mock-up of an old street renovated to look like 20th-century Celje with typical shops of the time. Elsewhere postcards and posters illuminate changes that have occurred in Celje and Štajerska during the course of the 20th century. Incorporated into the museum is the children's museum Herman's Den – the only museum in Slovenia designed for kids.
*Open: Tue–Fri 10.00–18.00, Sat 09.00–12.00, Sun 14.00–18.00. 500SIT, concessions 300SIT.*

### The Photo Studio of Josip Pelikan
Razlagova 5; tel: 03 548 5891.
In a separate building you will find what is arguably the Museum of Contemporary History's most interesting collection: Josip Pelikan's photographs of Celje. The Celje-born photographer's images include studio shots, landscapes, photographs of the city's industry sector and people relaxing in nearby termes, all of which combine to give a pictorial history of the city and its environs between 1919 and 1977.
*Open: Tue–Fri 10.00–14.00, Sat 09.00–12.00, Sun 14.00–18.00.*

## Activities
The verdant hills that surround Celje are a great place for walking. A handful of easy walks are signposted from the castle end of Cesta na Grad and should take you between 1½ and 2½ hours. These include a 2-hour hike to Tovsti Vrh at 834m, a 2-hour walk to Grmada at 718m and a 1½-hour trail to Celjska Koča at 651m. The insects in the woods can be ferocious in spring and summer so remember to bring your insect repellent. It is also important to take the usual walking safety precautions.

## LAŠKO
Just 11km from Celje, Laško is popular with day trippers. Laško first appeared in written documents in 1227 as a market town, however archaeologists believe that humans settled in the area centuries before, including the Celts and the Romans. Laško's important trading role diminished under the Austro–Hungarians and it didn't regain its town status until its 700th anniversary in 1927. Today much of the town's architecture is modern and largely unattractive with few tourist sights. Instead visitors are lured here by its spa and the beer that is produced by the very popular Laško brewery.

### Getting there
Trains from Celje (10 minutes) and Maribor (1¼ hours) stop at Laško.

## Where to eat
**Restavracija Špica** Trg Svobode 7; tel: 03 734 3330. With trout, grilled meats and around 30 different pizza toppings Špica caters to all tastes.
**Pačnik Tavern** Aškerčev trg 10; tel: 03 573 0452. Welcoming tavern serving regional cuisine and wine.
**Kmetijska Zadruga** Kidričeva 2. Outlet for local farmers selling organic meat, fish and other farm produce.

## Practicalities
**Tourist Information Centre** Trg Svobode 8; tel: 03 733 8950; fax: 03 733 8956; email: turisticno.drustvo.lasko@siol.net; www.turisticnodrustvo-lasko.si

## What to see
### Pivovarna Laško (Laško Brewery)
Laško (Trubarjeva 28; tel: 03 734 8000; fax: 03 573 1817; email: info@pivo-lasko.si; www.pivo-lasko.si. Group tours by appointment) have been brewing beer since 1825 and they have recently bought stakes in their main rival Union to become Slovenia's leading beer producer (see *Beer Battles* box in *Chapter 3*). The company's best-known brand is the blond Zlatorog, which is available in bottles or on draught in almost every bar in the country. Other products include Temno Laško (dark beer), Lahko Laško (light beer), Zlatorog Club, Pils and Roler (see *Beer Battles* box in *Chapter 3*).

### Terme Laško
The spa at Laško (Zdraviliška 4; tel: 03 734 5111; fax: 03 734 5298; email: tajnistvo@zdravilisce-lasko.si; www.zdravilisce-lasko.si) is becoming as big a business as the brewery these days with ambitious plans for extensions and new hotels. At present the spa offers everything from therapeutic spring waters at temperatures of 32°C to 35°C, medical consultation and rehabilitation to aerobics and relaxation classes. The treatments offered in its wellness centre including hot- and cold-stone therapies, facials and body massages are a real highlight. Terme Laško also has an impressively large sauna centre with a range of dry and wet rooms. If you can't bear to drag yourself away then accommodation is available in the terme's 210-bed hotel.

## LOGARSKA DOLINA
When Austrians cross the border to come and enjoy your mountain scenery it has to be a sign that you have something special. Logarska Dolina, or 'Logger's Valley', is indeed special; a stunning glaciated valley where the green meadows give way to papier-mâché mountains that loom improbably into the heavens above. The views are sublime and rival any stretch of mountain scenery in Europe, but there is a lot more to do in Logarska Dolina than just ogle at the landscape as facilities are well set up so you can get in and about it all. All of Logarska Dolina is a protected park (www.logarska-dolina.si) and entrance to it is controlled through a gate, where a 1,000SIT charge is levied on cars (payable each time you leave and re-enter). Two kilometres further on the scenery really opens

up as you approach an information kiosk that has a good map of the area and can also dish out plenty of literature. This is where you will find the Plesnik Hotel, *the* place to stay and eat within the valley.

## Getting there

Reaching Logarska Dolina on public transport is not that easy, especially outside of the main tourist season. Most buses will take you as far as Gornji Grad from where there is one daily service to Mozirje (45 minutes). Buses to Gornji Grad come from Ljubljana (1 hour and 50 minutes) and Kamnik (1 hour). It is also possible to reach the settlements of Solčava, Ljubno ob Savinji and Luče from Velenje and Celje, but services are irregular and you would be well advised to ask locally before setting out.

## Where to stay

**Hotel Plesnik and Vila Palenk** (32+11 rooms) Logarska Dolina 10; tel: 03 839 2300; fax: 03 839 2312; email: hotel.plesnik@siol.net; www.plesnik.si. This oasis feels a world away from big-city life. The main building is a comfortable retreat with a swimming pool and sauna in the basement – though be aware that a lot of guests choose to dispense with their clothes in the pool, sauna and on the sun beds. The Vila Palenk to the back is run by the same people, with very cosy rooms where you can burn your own log fire and relax on your balcony. The views from the valley-facing rooms in the main hotel are, however, more impressive. Whether you are staying or not a meal here is worth it too, though try to avoid weekends in summer when weddings can take over. Hotel singles 17,800–18,800SIT, hotel doubles 27,600–29,600SIT, vila singles 14,800SIT, vila doubles 23,600SIT.

**Plesnik Tourist Farm** (5 rooms) Logarska Dolina 13; tel: 03 838 9006. More affordable accommodation 200m from the Plesnik Hotel. 4,400SIT per person.

**Na Razpotju** (10 rooms) Logarska Dolina 14; tel: 03 839 1650. Attractive guesthouse with balconied rooms, just 300m from the Plesnik Hotel. Singles 9,900SIT, doubles 15,800SIT.

**Juvanija Tourist Farm** (10 beds) Logarska Dolina 8; tel: 03 838 9080. 5,280SIT per person.

**Lenar Tourist Farm** (9 beds) Logarska Dolina 10; tel: 03 838 9006; email: logarska@siol.net. 4,080SIT per person.

## Where to eat

**Hotel Plesnik** Logarska Dolina 10; tel: 03 839 2300. The hotel's restaurant is undoubtedly the best place to dine in the valley. In the summer months the best seats are on the outside terrace, however similar views of the valley can be had from the windows. The fixed-price menu, which most diners opt for, is surprisingly good value at around 2,500SIT per person and is decent. For a real treat splash out on the à la carte dishes and choose a more expensive bottle of wine from their sizeable list.

**Rinka Inn** Logarska Dolina 15; tel: 03 838 9036. Much further up the valley on the way to Rinka Waterfall, this *gostilna* is a popular weekend lunch venue for Slovene families.

**Na Razpotju** Logarska Dolina 14; tel: 03 839 1650. The guesthouse terrace is a pleasant place for a relaxed and informal meal. Look out for the spit-roast pork.

## Practicalities
**Tourist Information Centre** Logarska Dolina 9; tel: 03 838 9040; fax: 03 838 9003; email: logarksa.dolina@siol.net; www.logarska-dolina.si. Located in a hut at the foot of the driveway leading to the Plesnik Hotel. Open: daily 09.00–13.00 May–Oct. Out of season the staff at the hotel will help you.

## Activities
Logarska Dolina has many outdoor activities to help you really enjoy and discover one of Slovenia's most stunning landscapes. Activities can be arranged at the tourist information centre; if this is closed ask at your accommodation.

### Mountain-biking
One of the best ways to explore the 7km expanse of the valley is to hire a bike, however Logarska Dolina has quite a steep incline and is certainly not a place to practise if you have never ridden a bike before. There are plenty of trails for those looking to strike out independently, however you can also embark on guided tours. As a guide rental costs 600SIT an hour, or 2,400SIT a day, although your hotel or pension may let you use a bike for free.

### Walking and hiking
Hiking up to the **Rinka Slap** (Rinka Waterfall) is easy enough, but if you want to tackle any of the 2,000m-plus peaks around here make sure you have all the necessary gear and a good map, as well as letting someone know your intended route. If you are looking for a more leisurely experience there is a sprinkling of *gostilnas* and cafés dotted around the valley, which are especially good on weekends. If you like your rambling to be more social then you can join a guided tour; this is charged according to the size of the group with a minimum charge of 8,400SIT for up to ten people.

### Other activities
The extensive list of activities that you can book at the tourist office, which take place in or around the valley itself, also include horseriding (3,120SIT for a one-hour guided tour), tandem paragliding (8,400SIT per hour), rock climbing (3,600SIT for two hours), archery (2,400SIT) and kayaking or rafting (both 5,760SIT). More leisurely pursuits are available in the form of a horse-drawn carriage ride (5,400SIT per hour), ride in a hay cart (1,200SIT per hour), a dip in the Plesnik's pool (1,920SIT, free for guests) or five minutes in their solarium (1,920SIT).

## ROBANOV KOT AND MATKOV KOT
If you are staying for a few days and have your own wheels you can travel through to the neighbouring valleys of Robanov Kot or Matkov Kot. These are much less developed than Logarska, and while maybe not quite as attractive they are still stunning.

## PTUJ
Ptuj is the most complete historical town in Slovenia, a rhapsody of well-preserved medieval, Romanesque, Gothic and Renaissance architectural styles that is still

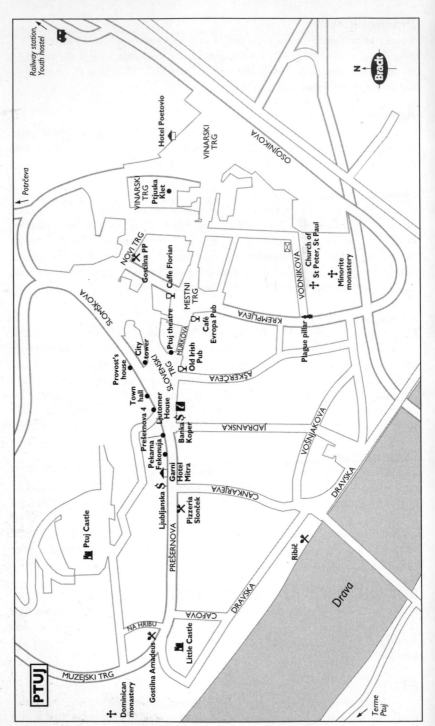

*Above* Palace Hotel at Portorož, on the Slovenian coast
*Right* Celica Hostel, Ljubljana
*Below* Črnomelj Old Town, Bela Krajina

*Above* Glavni trg, Maribor, Štajerska
*Right* Ptuj Old Town, Štajerska
*Below* Festival masks in Ptuj, Štajerska

built around a medieval plan which feels far removed from the modern world. Stretching out across the Drava River with its castle dominating the Old Town above, Ptuj invites comparisons with Prague, though things are on a much more compact and manageable scale. Strolling through the town often feels like leafing through the musty pages of a historical novel, and standing on the castle ramparts looking over the Drava River most visitors instantly fall in love with Ptuj, even though few can pronounce it (try saying 'putuy' with your lips pursed and you will come close enough). Ptuj really should be one of Europe's most-visited towns, but thanks to a lack of awareness that is accompanied by a serious lack of accommodation in high season it has not yet become too crowded, though there are some big plans for more hotels and the turning of the dammed section of the Drava that forms Ptuj Lake into a leisure park.

## History

Ptuj's rich history flits through a period when the Mithraic cult was dominant in the area. Roman times were also important for Ptuj as the river port of Poetovio, when it was the largest Roman settlement in Slovenia. Centuries later Ptuj's landmark castle served as a bulwark against the Turks and also held off the attentions of the Hungarians. Ptuj lost its role as Štajerska's most important town when the railway arrived in its rival Maribor in the 19th century, which is good news for today's tourists as the lack of industrial development has aided the preservation of this architectural gem.

## Getting there

Frequent bus services connect Ptuj to Maribor (30 minutes) and Ljubljana (3¹/₂ hours). Trains from Maribor (45 minutes–1 hour), Celje (1 hour), Murska Sobota (50 minutes–1 hour 10 minutes) and Ljubljana (2–3 hours) also stop in Ptuj.

**Railway station** Osojnikova 2; tel: 02 292 5702
**Bus station** Osojnikova 11; tel: 02 771 1491

## Where to stay

**Garni Hotel Mitra** (23 rooms) Prešerenova 6; tel: 02 787 7455; fax: 02 787 8889; email: info@hotel-mitra-fm.si; www.hotelptuj.com. Located right at the heart of Ptuj's Old Town the hotel has been welcoming visitors since 1870. Spacious rooms and traditionally styled public spaces all add to the hotel's charm. If you have your own car, the only bugbear will be the absence of parking spaces. The car park by the castle is free. Singles 9,600SIT, doubles 14,400SIT, apartments 18,000SIT.
**Youth Hostel** (55 beds) Osojnikova 9; tel: 02 780 5540; fax: 02 779 2181. This centrally located hostel is just 250m from the bus station and 500m from the train station has 2–6 bed rooms. From 3,500SIT per person.
**Terme Ptuj** Pot v toplice 9; tel: 02 782 7821; fax: 02 783 7771; email: info@terme-ptuj.si; www.terme-ptuj.si. You can stay in bungalows and apartments sleeping up to 6, or camp at the terme, a 20-minute walk from the Old Town. Apartments 9,400–20,900SIT, bungalows 8,700–13,400SIT per person, camping 2,400SIT per person.

**Hotel Poetovio** (29 rooms) Vinarski trg 5; tel: 02 779 8201; fax: 02 779 8231. A step down from the Garni Hotel Mitra, with acceptable rooms. Singles 6,500SIT, doubles 9,000SIT.

## Where to eat

**Café Evropa Pub** Mestni trg 1. The menu comes in the form of a newspaper – like the News Café in Bernardin – and features a wide range of alcoholic beverages as well as cheap and tasty pizzas. Stick with the *malo* (small) size pizzas unless you are sharing. When the pizzeria closes this becomes one of the town's most popular bars.
**Gostilna PP** Novi trg 2; tel: 02 749 0622. Inexpensive set lunches cost from 790SIT. The Sunday buffet brunch is also very popular with locals. However in terms of quality and taste, you get what you pay for.
**Ribič** Dravska 9; tel: 02 749 0635. If you eat out only once in Ptuj make it here. Smooth service, great fresh fish and seafood, as well as unique serving touches like soup served in a hard bread roll make the bill easier to stomach. There is no English menu, but the waiting staff will happily help out and tell you about the daily specials. If the weather is good the terrace next to the Drava is an unbeatable setting.
**Gostilna Amadeus** Prešerenova 36; tel: 02 771 7051. Another decent dining option serving good-quality Slovenian dishes at more affordable prices than Ribič.
**Pekarna Fekonja** Prešerenova 4. Bakery with fresh bread.
**Pizzerija Slonček** Prešerenova 19; tel: 02 776 1311. Standard but cheap pizzas.

## Entertainment and nightlife

Ptuj's historic core is bursting with café-bars with the biggest concentrations running along Prešerenova to Murkova and then onto Mestni trg.

**Café Evropa Pub** Mestni trg 1 (see *Where to eat*)
**Old Irish Pub** Murkova 5. Draught Guinness, a vaulted brick ceiling, friendly staff and a small terrace are all part of the winning formula.
**Ptuj Grad** (Ptuj Castle); tel: 02 748 0260. If you are seeking more cerebral entertainment, there are frequent performances at the castle.
**Gledališče Ptuj** (Ptuj Theatre) Slovenski trg 13; tel: 02 749 3250. Check the board outside for the performance schedule.
**Bar Caffe Florian** Mestni trg. Popular spot with outside tables and watched over protectively by the statue of St Florian, patron saint of fire and firemen.

## Practicalities

**Tourist Information Centre** Slovenski trg 14; tel: 02 771 5691; fax: 02 771 0175; email: info@ptuj-tourism.si; www.ptuj-tourism.si. Open: Mon–Fri 09.00–18.00 and Sat 09.00–12.00.
**Post office** Vodnikova 2. Open: Mon–Fri 08.00–19.00, Sat 08.00–13.00.
**Banka Koper** Slovenski trg 3
**Ljubljanska Banka** Prešerenova 6
**Hospital** Potrčeva 23; tel: 02 771 5511
**Health Centre** Potrčeva 19a; tel: 02 771 2511
**Emergency dentist** Potrčeva 19a; tel: 02 771 2511

# What to see
## Grad Ptuj and Pokrajinski Muzej Ptuj (Ptuj Castle and Ptuj Regional Museum)

The 12th-century Ptuj Castle came under state ownership at the end of World War II after a chequered history which, at one point, saw it presided over by a Scottish family, the Leslies, from 1656 through to 1802 (see the family coat of arms on the first floor). Today the first thing that you will notice when you visit the castle is the sweeping view over the Old Town and the Drava River. You can explore the regional museum on your own, but it does not cost much more, and it is infinitely more interesting, to book yourself on to a guided tour in advance – they are in very high demand and you are unlikely to be able to just turn up and join one.

The first stop on the guided tour is the armoury, where weapons dating from the late 14th century to the end of World War II are displayed behind glass cabinets. This surprisingly contemporary space is more interesting for its architectural detail; one of the preserved stone walls dates from the 12th century when curators think it was probably a stable, while the Romanesque window and vaulted ceiling suggests that this room was later used as a residential space. The rest of the ground floor is home to a smorgasbord of costumes and furniture, largely dating from the 16th to the 19th centuries. A narrow medieval turret leads up to the first floor, which functions as one large gallery. If you are on a self-guided visit take time to really explore this level of the castle. Highlights of the building itself include the colonnades that overlook the courtyard and the baroque Festival Hall – dating from the 17th century and renovated in 2002 this is a particularly atmospheric place to watch a performance (see *Entertainment and nightlife*). This room is worth visiting to see the huge collection of Turkerie portraits. The exotic ladies in them are not really as dainty as they may at first look as these paintings were shockingly risqué at the time with underwear hinted at and suggestive use of fruit. The largest painting is of a harem, which is particularly daring when you consider that it dates back to the 17th century.

Other highlights in the museum's collection include the 'soft Gothic' statues from the early 15th century and the collection of modern art by celebrated Slovene artist France Mihelič. Meanwhile the salon, Chinese salon and ladies' salon are interesting as the proprietors have endeavoured to restore their 18th-century appearance. Also look out for the colourful displays showing masks and costumes from the local Kurentovanje Festival (see box), which are part of the ethnological collection. Worth checking out as well is the separate musical section, which delves into the instruments found from local digs, including a Roman flute from the 2nd century that the curators reckon may be the oldest in existence. This interactive space which was renovated in 2003 is especially appealing to children; music comes on to accompany the displays as you walk around and you can even have a go on the snare drum if your skills are up to it.

A small café operates within the castle with a few tables outside in summer if you are thirsty after your drumming.

**Ptuj Castle** Open: Daily 09.00–17.00 mid Oct–Apr, 09.00–18.00 May–mid Oct, with extended opening hours at weekends in Jul and Aug 09.00–20.00. Guided tour 800SIT, concessions 600SIT, entrance only 600SIT.

**KURENTOVANJE FESTIVAL**
The Kurentovanje is one of Slovenia's most vibrant and alluring festivals, taking hold of the town every year in the run up to Shrove Tuesday. The festival originates from early Slavic times when it emerged as a ritual designed to fend off winter and its evil spirits. The most colourful part of the action is when the local men dress in extravagant costumes with masks to become 'kurents' – the demons coming from the other side – who you cannot miss as they rollick around rattling their cow bells. Their handmade costumes feature massive feathery headgear and scary masks top off the outfits. At the height of the festival over 300 young men can be heard hollering around the town trying to win the favour of local maidens, who traditionally throw handkerchiefs to show their approval, though apparently in recent years the tradition has moved on with G-strings replacing handkerchiefs on more than one occasion. Look out for the other character at the head of the processions, who is one of the devils that the festival is trying to chase out of town.

### A walking tour

Strolling around Ptuj could not be easier as the tourist office issues a good map and most of the main attractions have a multi-lingual information board, including English, with a paragraph on each stop to make things easier. A good place to start a walking tour of Ptuj is from the castle itself as you can easily make out the layout of the town as it unfolds below and plan out your route.

First up just below the castle ramparts (take Na Hribu) is the **Dominikanski Samostan** (Dominican Monastery; Muzejski trg 1; tel: 02 787 9230. Open: daily 09.00–17.00 Oct–May, 09.00–18.00 Jun and Sep, Mon–Fri 09.00–18.00, Sat–Sun 09.00–20.00 Jul–Aug. 600SIT, concessions 300SIT), which rests in a small park below the castle to the right when you are facing the river. A glass screen leads through to a fine collection of Mithraic Shrines that were unearthed in and around Ptuj at Spodnja Hajdina. From here head downhill and you will be near the river on Dravska; strike out for the footbridge and continue on past the Ribič Restaurant and you will come to Minoritski, site of a **Minoritski Samostan** (Minorite Monastery). The **Cerkev Sv Petra in Pavla** (Church of Sts Peter and Paul) was mauled in an Allied air attack during World War II and is only now being rebuilt.

As you head up back towards the castle and away from the river up Krempljeva look out for the plague pillar, a gleaming gold image of Mary and Jesus. You are now in the heart of the Old Town and soon you will spill out into Mestni trg, which is home to a couple of interesting buildings and a smattering of bars. Take a look at the **Mestna Hiša** (Town Hall) on the right, a relative newcomer for Ptuj as it was only added at the start of the 20th century.

Follow Murkova up the hill and you are now in Slovenski trg, a pretty square with a triangular ramble of cobbles forming an island in the middle. The brightly coloured façade to the right is **Gledališče Ptuj** (Ptuj Theatre), which demonstrates Ptuj's cultural vibrancy by playing host to cutting-edge theatre rather than sticking with safer classics. Dominating the square above is the **Mestni Stolp** (City Tower).

Lurking behind is the **Cerkev Sv Jurija** (Church of St George). The lump of stone outside is a 2BC chunky Roman leftover, which looks a bit faded especially as it is exposed to the elements here. It depicts scenes from the *Orpheus* story, but it has other stories to tell as it was once also used for public beatings. Other notable buildings in the square include the **Ljutomer Hiša** (Ljutomer House), the Provost's House and the former town hall. Take Prešernova ulica, one of Ptuj's prettiest streets and also home to the oldest building in Ptuj at No 4; if you want a break take a seat at one of the sprinkling of cafés in this street, before wrapping up the tour with a stop at the **Mali Grad** (Little Castle).

### Terme Ptuj

There are plans to build a new hotel at Terme Ptuj (Pot v toplice 9; tel: 02 782 7821; fax: 02 783 7771; email: info@terme-ptuj.si; www.terme-ptuj.si) as the town develops as a tourist destination, but for now this is just a good place to come and relax. It is only a ten-minute walk from town across the Drava and is perfect for soothing limbs aching after tackling Ptuj's Old Town. An all-day ticket to the thermal complex costs 2,000SIT and an evening ticket 1,600SIT.

### Ptujska Gora (Ptuj Mountain)

From Ptuj Castle on a clear day you can easily make out the Ptuj Mountain and the **Cerkev Sv Marija** (Church of St Mary) which lie 13km across the Drava. One of Slovenia's most important churches, Cerkev Sv Marija serves as the main pilgrimage church for the Štajerska region and attracts pilgrims from all over Slovenia. In fact, in terms of Catholic pilgrimage, Ptujska Gora comes second only to Brezje in Gorenjska. As you approach look out for the plague pillar that was erected to mark the drastic epidemics of the 17th century. A church has stood on the mountain since the 14th century. The walls are buttressed and the interior comprises three aisles. One of the highlights is the relief of the Virgin Mary herself, which is famous because it depicts people from diverse economic and cultural backgrounds all seeking refuge under the Madonna's coat.

### HALOZE WINES

To the south of Ptuj are the Haloze Hills, which produce a range of excellent wines. If you are short of time in Ptuj you will find the Ptjuska Klet (Ptuj Wine Cellar; Vinarski trg 1; tel: 02 787 9810; fax: 02 787 9813; email: tanja.vinkler@perutnina.si; www.haloze.com), where you can go on an hour-long tour (booking in advance is essential) and explore the wine cellars, watch a video and then, of course, try some of the produce including Riesling, Chardonnay, Muscat and Pinot Noir. The wine vats themselves are huge (around 3.5 million litres of wine is stored here) and the cellars are all the more atmospheric for their minimal lighting. Look out for the old hidden storage area, which has fine wines dating back as far as 1917 that are housed in a fortified section designed to keep out the attentions of the German occupiers in World War II.

## ŠTAJERSKA CASTLES
### Borl Grad (Borl Castle)

A frontier castle located 12km from Ptuj in Haloze (follow the road for Zavrč), Borl Grad (email: info@borl.org; www.borl.org) dates back to the turn of the 12th century when Frederick of Ptuj lived here, although the castle belonged to King Bela IV of Hungary. Some sources suggest that settlement on the sight of today's impressive castle dates back as far as Neolithic times and over the centuries various masters have presided over this strategic hillock overlooking the Drava River, including the Romans and the Hungarians. Borl has had its fair share of setbacks including a devastating earthquake in the 16th century and a fire in the 18th, but one of its darkest periods came during World War II when it was used as a staging post for Nazi victims en route to the concentration camps. From the end of the war until 1948 the castle lay empty, then became a refugee camp before being partially renovated in the early 1950s. Further renovation saw the addition of a restaurant and the castle was transformed into a hotel, however years of underinvestment and the collapse of the access bridge across the Drava River saw this close in 1981. Since 1994 various artistic programmes have been taking place within the castle, however like many of Slovenia's castles Borl Castle still requires a lot of renovation work.

### Podčetrtek Grad (Podčetrtek Castle)

In the border village of Podčetrtek, 15km from Rogaška Slatina, you will find one of many eye-catching Slovenian castles. The 12th-century fortification draws the eye with its impressive shape dominating a strategic position, though this time there is not actually that much to see when you head for a closer look. Damage sustained in the 1974 earthquake and years of neglect have left the castle in a sorry state and while you can easily walk up to it (as countless passers-by do) the castle is not actually open to the public.

### Podsreda Grad (Podsreda Castle)

Located in the Kozjanski Park (Podsreda 45; tel: 03 800 7100; fax: 03 800 7108; email: kozjanski-park@kp.gov.si) at Podsreda some 20km southwest of Podčetrtek Castle, this Romanesque castle dates back to the beginning of the 13th century, although much of its present-day incarnation is the result of careful restoration work. Its main attractions are the small chapel and defence tower, both frequently held up as some of the best examples of Romanesque architecture in Slovenia. It is possible to visit alone or as part of a guided tour and while the exhibition of Rogaška glass is nothing special, the collection of prints dedicated to the Štajerska region are interesting enough.
*Open: Tue–Sun 10.00–18.00 Oct–Apr. 500SIT, concessions 350SIT.*

## TERME RADENCI

Right on the edge of Prekmurje at Radenci, and very close to the border with Austria, is one of Slovenia's most famous spas, the source of the 'three hearts' mineral water that you will see all over the country. Radenci (ZdravilIško naselje 12; tel: 02 520 1000; fax: 02 520 2723; email: prodaja.zdravilisce@radenska.si;

www.radenska-zdravilisce.si) has been a popular spa resort since the 19th century and is said to have been a favourite retreat of Emperor Franz Ferdinand amongst others. The spa operation is becoming increasingly slick here with prices in euros and everything available from a three-hour play in the pools for 1,600SIT right through to a seven-day detox and slimming programme. You can just turn up and use the pools with that three-hour ticket, though remember to bring a towel as they do not hire them out and you will have to beg nicely to scrounge one from a member of staff. Inside there is a 25m swimming pool that is cool enough to lane-swim in, and a more relaxed fun pool that includes a water-jet system that grabs unsuspecting bathers and deposits them outside where steam rises from the hot pool. There are lots of nooks and crannies here with bubbling Jacuzzis and water sprays as well as sun loungers. Radenci also has a smaller outdoor pool that attracts mainly adults and is an oasis of calm on a busy summer day when hordes of children descend on the complex. For real spa addicts there is even an onsite museum to fill you in on the history of this impressive spa.

## PREKMURJE

This tiny enclave of northeastern Slovenia, so named as it lies 'beyond' the strategic Mura River, is one of the most distinctive parts of the country and many travellers find it one of the most enjoyable to visit. Historically Prekmurje is the region of Slovenia that has been most influenced by Hungary. Even today the area of Lendava is home to a constitutionally recognised Hungarian minority, here the children learn Hungarian at school and anyone who wants to join the civil service must be fluent in both Slovene and Hungarian. Around 6,000 Hungarians live in and around Lendava and their national tongue is the region's official second language. This Hungarian minority also has a sufficiently powerful vote to return one MP to the Slovenian parliament (there are a total of 90 seats). Today's picture of ethnic harmony couldn't be further removed from that of less than a century ago when during the Hungarian rule in Prekmurje the Slovene language was actively subjugated. World War I saw Prekmurje become part of the new Yugoslavia, yet this small corner of Slovenia found itself subjected to Hungarian oppression once again during Hungarian occupation in 1941.

It is easy to say that Prekmurje is the Hungarian part of Slovenia given its proximity to Hungary, the similarities in much of its architecture, cuisine (goulash is one of the most popular dishes) and crafts, but this does not give the whole picture. Little Prekmurje, a land of fertile plains, vineyards and rolling hills is neither entirely Slovenian nor Hungarian – for example even under Hungarian rule many people still spoke Slovene and today while most locals are happy to be Slovene they are still proud of their Magyar traditions. The best way to explore it is just to get on a bike or in your car and meander around the country lanes, stopping off at any of the villages you find interesting. In many villages you will see more tractors and bicycles than cars and find a pace of life that is more 19th than 21st century. Drifting through the narrow lanes as the signature white storks set off from the field next to you and the little churches twinkle all around, Prekmurje manages to surprise many travellers and encourages many a repeat visit. With EU accession has come a drive for tourism with signs for *sobes*, restaurants and the like popping up all over the place and at least one British property speculator moving to snap up holiday homes in May 2004 in a region that lies supremely well located in the northeastern corner of Slovenia and bordered by Austria, Hungary and Croatia. Despite this strategic location Prekmurje was for a long time hindered by its geography – somewhat of a surprise when looking at a map as it occupies such a strategic position in central Europe. The map does not tell the whole story as Prekmurje was previously isolated from the south by the lack of a bridge over the Mura River and much of its terrain is awash with flooded pools and marshes. Over the centuries the list of the civilisations who have rattled through Prekmurje reads like a who's who of European history with the Illyrians, Celts, Romans, Slavs and the Hungarians all playing a part.

## MURSKA SOBOTA

It may be the largest town in Prekmurje, but the regional centre is not an instantly lovable place with a smattering of modern buildings and industrial developments blighting the few more promising districts. Nevertheless it is worth visiting the Town Park, a green lung that unusually for Slovenia refuses to hide its socialist-era past with an imposing war memorial complete with two howitzers, heroic soldiers and Cyrillic script. This monument commemorates the bravery of the Soviet soldiers who liberated the area at the end of World War II. Interestingly enough this is the only Soviet monument in Slovenia, and Prekmurje is the only area where the Soviet Red Army actually ventured into as a part of the Allied liberation operation at the end of the war. Head behind the monument to cross into the largest section of the park where a small pond leads on to **Grad Sobota** (Sobota Castle; Trubarjev drevored 4; tel: 02 527 1706; fax: 02 521 1155; email: pok.muzej@pok-muzej-ms.si; www.pok-muzej-ms.si. Open: Tue–Sat 10.00–17.00, Sun 10.00–13.00. 500SIT), which is home to **Pokrajinski Musej Murska Sobota** (the Regional Museum of Murska Sobota). The castle has its origins in the 16th century, though it was given a major Renaissance makeover and later opened as a museum in 1955. The well- presented first-floor display space was refurbished in 1997 and the museum these days does much more than tell the story of the town and its immediate surrounds, as it spills over into more general Prekmurje themes from prehistoric times right through to the early 21st century.

### Getting there

Buses from Radenci (15 minutes), Maribor (2 hours), Celje ($2^1/4$–$2^1/2$ hours) and Ljubljana (4 hours) all stop at Murska Sobota. Trains from Ptuj (50 minutes–1 hour and 10 minutes), Maribor ($1^1/4$ hours) and Ljubljana ($3^1/2$ hours) also call there.

### Where to stay

**Hotel Diana** (95 rooms) Slovenska 52; tel: 02 524 1200; fax: 02 532 1097. Fortunately the interior of the hotel is much nicer than its monstrous concrete exterior. Geared firmly towards business visitors, rooms are functional rather than luxurious. The hotel offers various dining choices including its popular pizzeria, and also has a fitness centre, pool tables, squash courts and its own thermal pool. At weekends the hotel's nightclub attracts Murska Sobota's younger citizens.

## Where to eat

**Hotel Diana** Slovenska 52; tel: 02 524 1200. The hotel's busy pizzeria serves decent pizzas.

**Mercator** Slovenska 40
For a quick snack join the locals queuing at the bustling bakeries and *slaščicarna* (ice-cream parlours) on Kodjeva.

## Practicalities

**Tourist Information Centre** Kiosk outside Slovenska 37; tel: 02 534 1130. Open: Mon–Fri 09.00–17.00, Sat 08.00–12.00.
**Ljubljanska Banka** Slovenska 41 and Trg zmage 7. Open: Mon–Fri 08.00–17.00.
**Banka Koper Slovenska 27** Open: Mon–Fri 08.00–16.00.
**Post office** Zmage trg 10. Open: Mon–Fri 07.00–19.00, Sat 07.00–13.00.

## Exploring Prekmurje

It's a good idea to seek local advice and pick up some literature at the new tourist information centre in Murska Sobota. Armed with a new tourist map of Prekmurje and the ever-increasing amount of flyers promoting restaurants, hotels and the like – most of them are in Slovene or German only – head out of the town and soon you will descend into the bucolic escape that is much of the region. Planning where to go is up to you and if you have time just venture out and see what you come across, but keep your passport handy as it is all too easy to wind up at an international border by mistake in these parts.

The flat Prekmurje plain is perfect for cycling. A collection of leaflets detailing seven waymarked cycling routes titled *Cycling Around Prekmurje* will help you in your exploration. The trails vary in length from 14km to 50km and are graded from easy to difficult. A 44km trail starts at the Lipa Hotel in Lendava and extends south to the forest of Murska Šuma and east to Kapca before returning to the starting point. We picked up our leaflets at the tourist information centre in Maribor, but the offices in Murska Sobota and Lendava (Kranjčeva 4; tel: 02 578 8390) should also be able to help you. The longest tour crosses into Hungary, so again you will need to remember to take your passport with you.

## GRAD

If you only have a day strike north from Murska Sobota for Grad, where Slovenia's largest baroque castle awaits. Dating from the early 13th century the castle's layout is noteworthy for its almost triangular shape. After decades of neglect – refurbishing a castle with a largely Hungarian heritage was not close to the top of the Yugoslav government's priority list – European Union money is finally helping to turn this sleeping giant around. For now only the ground floor has been revamped with a number of museum rooms now open to the public including a pottery, herbalist and the old kitchen, while on the second floor you can see the old living quarters which are now used for local weddings. Look out also for the scale model of how the castle may once again look and also for the helpful English-language signs, which help add a bit of background. There are usually guides on hand to give you

## TOURIST FARMS

Hotel accommodation in Slovenia tends to be concentrated in its big cities and towns. As a result most hotels cater to a business crowd and rooms are often scarce, expensive or very average. In many interesting historical locations like Kranj (the fourth-largest city in Slovenia) there is often just one hotel. Savvy visitors however are beginning to take advantage of private rooms in rural villages, or just outside main urban centres. This system of rural accommodation, or agritourism, in Slovenia is well organised and farm or agricultural properties offering tourist services are called tourist farms. Farm stays give guests the opportunity to visit some of Slovenia's most beautiful areas, experience real Slovenian hospitality, try traditional foods and get active in the countryside. Staying on a farm is also usually much cheaper than staying in a hotel. UK-based **Just Slovenia** (The Barns, Woodlands End, Mells, Frome, Somerset BA11 3QD; tel: 01373 814230; fax: 01373 813444; email: justslovenia@planos.co.uk; www.justslovenia.co.uk) can arrange farm stays before you leave for Slovenia, or when you are there. The Slovenian Tourist Board also produce a catalogue called *The Countryside: Tourist Farms* which gives contact details for The Association of Tourist Farms in Slovenia (www.sloveni-tourism.si/touristfarms) and its members.

There are tourist farms throughout Slovenia, but the majority are located in Gorenjska, in and around Triglav National Park with its stunning Julian Alps, and in the regions of Prekmurje, Dolenjska and Bela Krajina. Again many offer regional foods, so in Prekmurje you are in line for fiery goulash dishes and *gibinica*, the delightful dessert for which the region is renowned.

a quick tour for the princely sum of 350SIT. A variety of plans has been mooted for Grad and hopefully this vast place will soon ring with life once again.

From Grad you can head back east dodging storks, tractors and octogenarians on bicycles through vineyards and tiny villages accompanied by churches that lie within the Goriška Park.

## MORAVSKE TOPLICE AND AROUND

In the southeastern corner of Prekmurje you will find Lake Bukovnisko, a good place to relax on a sunny day, though your hire car will not thank you for rattling it down the last section of the unsealed road to the lake. From here dip down to the pretty village of Bogojina – there are many villages as charming as this, though none can boast as stunning a church by ubiquitous Slovene architect Jože Plečnik. Lying on the edge of fields in a sleepy village where the residents often call out a greeting as you pass, this dramatic edifice comes as something of a surprise.

Continue west on through Tesanovci, which has a flurry of local potteries, with the more commercial ones displaying signs on the main streets as you pass. Soon you will be at Moravske Toplice, just short of Murska Sobota, home to Terme 3000, one of the country's largest and most impressive spas. For an alternative afternoon there is also a golf club and if you really want to kick back there are hotels as well so you can spend a few days here and try some of the health treatments.

## TERME 3000

Sava Hotels recently took over the resort (Kranjceva 12; tel: 02 512 2200; fax: 02 548 1607; email: info@terme3000.si; www.terme3000.si) so no doubt big plans will now be afoot, but the facilities are already impressive. Here you can smell the sulphur as you approach and soon you will be bathed in the bubbling thermal waters. There are indoor and outdoor sections with lanes for swimming, Jacuzzis, sunbeds and even flumes if you fancy something a bit different – beware that although these are mainly for kids the green one is not for the faint-hearted as it plummets in a near-vertical drop.

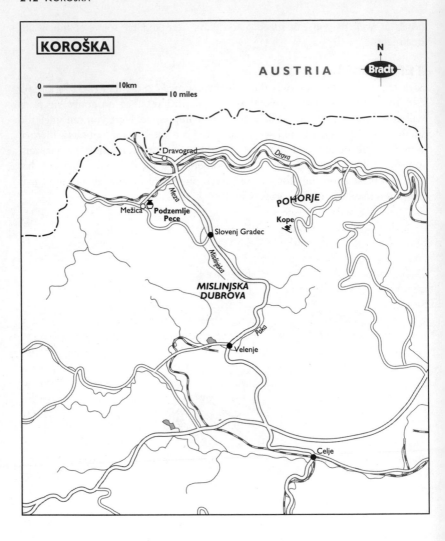

# Koroška

Historically Koroška (Carinthia), and Štajerska (Styria), have shared a regional identity with their Austrian neighbours – at one time a historic site near Klagenfurt (Celovec in Slovene) was the seat of the early Slovenian state of Carinthia (Carantania), and the modern day Austrian provinces of Carinthia and Styria both have sizeable Slovene minorities. This common heritage has given Slovenia's north western corner architecture and a way of life that is broadly similar to that in Kaernten (Steiremark) across the border. While it may closely resemble Austria, plucky little Koroška in Slovenia's north defiantly rejected the advances of its powerful neighbour after World War I when its citizens chose to be part of the Kingdom of Serbs, Croats and Slovenes instead of being absorbed by Austria. The choice of the people to the north of the Kobansko Hills to throw their lot in with Austria still rankles with many people in Koroška who feel passionately Slovene. Koroška also stood up to the might of the Yugoslav army in 1991 when they put up fierce resistance and hampered the army's attempts to secure the border posts with Austria. It may not quite have the drama of the mountainscapes to its west, but it offers easy access to the Pohorje Massif and is largely made up of rolling tree-shrouded hills that are bisected by the broad sweep of the Drava, Slovenia's second-longest river, which cuts through Koroška from west to east on its route to joining the even mightier Danube. The drive to or from Maribor is picturesque as the road follows the Drava with plenty of floating cafés and restaurants to rest at on your way, although the odd hydro-electric power station does detract from the ambience slightly. Cycling is also a good way to explore the smattering of small towns and villages en route, though the main highway can be busy and potentially dangerous for those on two wheels.

## SLOVENJ GRADEC

The largest town in Koroška is a pleasant enough place to spend a few days and is also a good base for exploring the region with convenient transport connections. Everything you are likely to need is on two streets in the old town: Meškova and Glavni trg, which run parallel to each other and are connected by Trg Svobode. A sprinkling of cafés, bars and restaurants dot all three in summer and there are also a number of worthwhile sights to cover even if you are desperate to get out

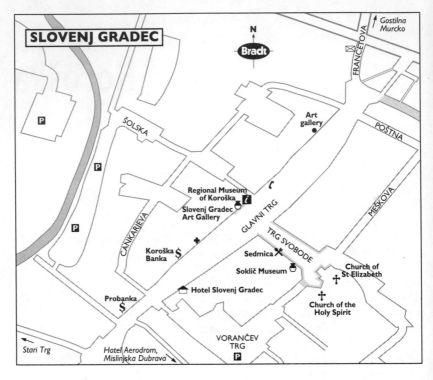

into the hills and explore. Winters can be bitter in these parts and not for nothing is Slovenj Gradec known as the coldest town in Slovenia. Slovenj Gradec's cultural scene does help liven up the darkest of days as this was the home of composer Hugo Wolf, the baroque painter Franc Strauss as well as today being home to a modern art gallery and a sprinkling of street sculptures. The town is keen to forge its links with the outside world and in 1989 it was bestowed the title of 'Peace Messenger City' by the United Nations. During the Balkan conflicts of the 1990s it was actively involved in the peace movement and in organising aid convoys into the region. Two days of festivities are given over to commemorate this honour and promote world peace each year – with the Peace Festival filling Glavni trg on October 23, and the town's residents also celebrating United Nations day on October 24.

## History

Like the rest of Koroška Slovenj Gradec has always been a town torn between different cultures and even today it feels both Germanic and Slovene. Evidence of civilisation extends as far back as Roman times when it was known as Colatio. During the days of the Ottomans Slovenj Gradec had to hold fast against their repeated attacks. While the Ottomans could not snuff out the town fire almost did in 1903, but slowly Slovenj Gradec staggered back to its feet. Under the communist regime Slovenj Gradec and Koroška often felt dismissed and ignored by Belgrade as being 'too German', but the upside is that heavy industrial development never really took hold here and you will struggle to find any building over a couple of storeys.

## Getting there
Slovenj Gradec is served by buses from Dravograd (20 minutes), Velenje (40 minutes) and Ljubljana ($2^1/_2$ hours).

## Where to stay
**Hotel Slovenj Gradec** Glavni trg 43; tel: 02 884 5285; email: vabo@siol.net. The town's most centrally located hotel has reasonably priced rooms, but offers standards to match the low prices. Singles 6,600SIT, doubles 12,000SIT, triples 16,500SIT, apartments 15,400SIT.

**Hotel Aerodrom** (12 rooms) Mislinkjska Dobrava 110, Šmartno pri Slovenj Gradec; tel: 02 885 0500; fax: 02 885 0522; email: hotel@aerodrom-sg.si; www.aerodrom-sg.si. You will find the best accommodation option in Slovenj Gradec at the Aerodrom (airstrip), a ten-minute drive south of the centre towards Velenje. This new hotel housed by the runway has its own restaurant and bar, as well as modern, spacious and high-tech rooms. The real winner though is its pleasant location amongst the forested hills that surround the city. If your budget won't stretch to four-star hotel prices they also have bungalows and a campsite. Singles 11,000SIT, doubles 18,000SIT, suites 25,000SIT.

## Where to eat
There are few central options for dining in the centre of town.

**Sedmica** Trg Svobode 7. Popular pizzeria with outdoor seating in the warmer months.
**Gostilna Murko** Francetova 24; tel: 02 883 8103. If you don't mind a short stroll (500m) then this tourist-orientated *gostilna* just north of the centre offers more traditional Slovenian cuisine.

## Practicalities
**Tourist Information Centre** Glavni trg 24; tel: 02 881 2116; fax: 02 881 2117; email: tic@slovenj-gradec.si; www.mesto-sg.si. Open: Mon–Fri 09.00–18.00, Sat–Sun 09.00–12.00.
**Post office** Francetova 1. Open: Mon–Fri 08.00–18.00, Sat 08.00–12.00.
**Probanka** Cankarjeva 1
**Koroška Banka** Glavni trg 30

## What to see
Housed in the old town hall are both the Regional Museum of Koroška and the Slovenj Gradec Art Gallery. In the same building on ground level is the tourist office so pop in there before you head upstairs if you want some more information on the town.

### Likovnih Umetnosti Slovenj Gradec (Slovenj Gradec Art Gallery)
On the first floor is the art gallery (Glavni trg 24; tel: 02 884 1283; fax: 02 882 2130; email: galerija@glu-sg.si; www.glu-sg.si), a Tardis-like space with a large

hall for temporary exhibitions added on to the back of the original Fine Arts Gallery that deals exclusively in modern art. It was first opened as part of an international arts exhibition in 1966. Of the permanent collections the work of Ljubljana-born abstract artist Bogdan Borčiç is perhaps the most interesting. Borčiç has taught in Ljubljana and Belgium and has held over 100 solo exhibitions around the world, but these days he calls Slovenj Gradec home. Outside the museum is another striking work, the strangely shaped *Venetian Horse* by Oskar Kogoj, a favourite meeting place for the town's youth.
*Open: Tue–Sun 09.00–18.00. 500SIT, concessions 300SIT.*

### Koroški Pokrajinski Muzej (Regional Museum of Koroška)

The Regional Museum (Glavni trg 24; tel: 02 884 2055) upstairs is by no means a high-tech or flashy experience, but for its simplicity it is worth having a look around. It focuses mainly on the fire in 1903 which devastated Slovenj Gradec on a Sunday morning while its citizens were at church. On display are old fire trucks and equipment with the most interesting exhibits the photos showing what the town looked like before and then after being engulfed by the flames. In 1992 the museum added an archaeological collection with many finds from Roman Colatio the highlights of a range of exhibits that also includes sections on the prehistoric, early Slavic and medieval periods. There are also regular temporary exhibitions such as those dedicated to Slovenj Gradec folk band Štirte Kovači (see box), but the museum, like all of the cultural attractions in Slovenj Gradec, is firmly in need of some investment to realise its full potential.
*Open: Tue–Sun 09.00–18.00. 400SIT, concessions 300SIT, free Sun.*

### Sokličev Muzej (Soklič Museum)

This private museum housed in the former residence of the town's priest (Trg Svobode 5; tel: 02 884 1505) is a real gem, however it faces an uncertain future as it needs serious investment to really function properly. There have been rumours that the bishop of Maribor is more than a little interested in acquiring the unique collection and shifting it off to Štajerska, with the museum reverting to its original function as clergy living quarters. Jakob Soklič was a great patron of the arts until his death in 1972 and his quarters house a stunning array of artefacts, sculptures and paintings from various periods, though a few of the paintings are of dubious quality and all too many are portraits of the local composer Hugo Wolf. There are a number of portraits of various bishops including one by Zoran Music, now one of Slovenia's most famous artists, who lived with his patron here in his early days. Other interesting things to look out for include a black-and-white photo of Soklič taking a stroll through town with a certain Tito and a scale model of the **Cerkev Sv Elizabeta** (Church of St Elizabeth). To get into the museum ask at the tourist office, who can also arrange a guided tour.

### Cerkev Sv Elizabeta (Church of St Elizabeth)

Slovenj Gradec, a town that has been torn between Protestantism and Catholicism over the centuries, today boasts no fewer than four churches. St Elizabeth's, in the heart of town on Trg Svobode, is the oldest building in Slovenj Gradec. The

**ŠTIRJE KOVAČI**

The 'Four Blacksmiths' were all, as the name suggests, blacksmiths from in and around Slovenj Gradec. They came together in 1954 and ever since have been churning out cheesy folk tunes to appreciative audiences in Slovenia and across the border in Austria and Germany. Their accordion ditties take over the airwaves on Slovenian radio stations on Sundays when families are having their traditional Sunday dinners. They have toured the world and can be heard in Slovenian outposts from Sydney to Cleveland.

church was refurbished at the start of the new millennium and is now back to something approaching its best. Look out for the Gothic ceiling and the baroque altar. On the right is a large tombstone, taken from the graveyard that used to rest on the site, which was once the family stone of a local protestant family before they decided to flee north. Above is a window that was dedicated to local painter Hugo Wolf by his mother. The painting behind the altar is by local baroque artist Franc Mihael Strauss – see if you can spot the image of the artist himself staring back at you. Strauss was no artistic pauper scraping two pennies together as when he painted this work his other role was as the mayor of the town. Behind the church look out for the small section of town walls that are all that is left of the original fortifications.

### Cerkev Sv Duha (Church of the Holy Spirit)
If the building is locked don't just walk away as you can still see inside one of the most interesting churches in Koroška. This 15th-century church's main attractions are the scenes of *The Passion of Christ* with the images on the archway showing a sobering depiction of the *Last Judgement*. All are baroque.

### Stari Trg
Just a short walk out of the centre of Slovenj Gradec is Stari trg, where settlement has been traced as far back as prehistoric times. This is the site of Colatio, the old Roman town that once stood on the important road north. Archaeological digs have unearthed a graveyard and numerous artefacts, from Roman coins right through to ceramics, though there is very little to actually see these days. Continue on from here and you can explore the Church of St Pancras, with its 17th-century defences.

### Mislinjska Dobrava
This adventure playground just to the south of Slovenj Gradec lies around the banks of the Mislinjska River with wooded slopes all around. It makes an alternative regional base to Slovenj Gradec with a funky hotel and campsite at the Slovenj Gradec Aerodrom (Mislinkjska Dobrava 110, Šmartno pri Slovenj Gradec; tel: 02 885 0500; fax: 02 8875 0510; email: info@aerodrom-sg.si; www.aerodrom-sg.si). The busy little flying club here offers scenic flights at very

reasonable rates with everything from ten-minute spins around the environs of the airfield through to more expansive trips south over the Pohorje. They are pretty flexible and can cater to most requests if you call ahead. A ten-minute trip costs 4,000–5,000SIT, 15 minutes 5,500–7,000SIT, 20 minutes 9,000–12,000SIT and one hour 12,000–15,000SIT (flights charged per person). If you want to travel further afield you can negotiate this with the pilots. The vicinity of the airport is also a great place to go horseriding, walking or cycling (though it is a good idea to seek advice from the TIC in Slovenj Gradec first) and explore the surrounding countryside, while the aerodrom's campsite has tennis courts. If you are feeling a little more sedentary the café/restaurant at the aerodrom is a good place to sit and watch the planes zip around.

## KOPE
Keen skiers may want to head off to the slopes at Kope (Glavni trg 41, Slovenj Gradec; tel: 02 882 2740; fax: 02 883 8806; email: info@kope@sc-pohorje.si), 16km from the centre of Slovenj Gradec, where there is often snow from November through to late spring. A variety of runs are geared towards both the beginner and the more experienced skier with the longest piste spanning 1,400m with a descent of 500m. In all the Kope ski centre has 8km of alpine ski runs – with around half of them pitched at the intermediate skier – and 15km of cross-country trails. Those who have never skied before can enrol with the ski school, while more experienced skiers can test their skills on the competition course. Equipment rental, snowboarding and night skiing are also offered. Outside of the winter the Pohorje mountain range is a great place for hiking. Accommodation is available.

### Getting there
Head south from Slovenj Gradec on the Velenje road. After 3km head east and you will find the ski centre at the end of the road another 13km away. Buses run from Slovenj Gradec to Kope when there is enough snow for skiing.

## DRAVOGRAD
As the name suggests this town rests on the banks of the lifeblood Drava River, where it meets the Meža and Mislinja rivers, in a strategic spot just across from the Austrian border. Many people speed through en route from Maribor to Logarska Dolina or Slovenj Gradec, but it is well worth stopping off to take a look at the town, not least to admire its location. The **castle** that gave the town the other half of its name is now in ruins, but you can take a look by an easy path up from town. There are two interesting churches to explore as well: the **Cerkev Sv Vida** (Church of St Vitus) and the **Cerkev Sv Janeza** (Church of St John). The former is a Romanesque church dating back to the 12th century, while the latter just outside of the town centre is baroque. A string of dwellings dating from the 17th to the early 19th centuries is also of interest, as are the dam of the Dravograd HEP and the marshland behind it; both of these are home to a large number of birds (some migratory) and unusual flora. Bird enthusiasts should keep their eyes peeled for sandpipers, egrets and various gulls.

## Getting there

Buses from Slovenj Gradec (20 minutes), Velenje (1 hour) and Ljubljana ($2^1/_2$ hours) run to Dravograd, as does the train from Maribor ($1^1/_2$ hours).

## Where to stay

**Hotel Hesper** (44 rooms) Koroška 48; tel: 02 878 4440; fax: 02 878 4443; email: info@hesper.si; www.hesper.si. Modern hotel that looks like a motel and has its own café-bar and restaurant. The décor in the bedrooms is a little busy, but they are comfortable and a good size. There are also apartments with their own kitchens that sleep up to 4 people. The hotel also has a pleasant restaurant. Singles 7,900SIT, doubles 11,500SIT, apartments 27,000SIT.

## Where to eat

**Gostilna Lovski Rog** Trg 4 julia 37; tel: 02 878 3288. Hearty Slovenian food.
**Restavracija Kaiser** Trg 4 julia 27; tel: 02 878 3104. Centrally located café-restaurant serving a variety of snacks and meals.
**Pizzeria Kapra** Meža 24; tel: 02 872 0236. Popular pizzeria located just south of the Drava on the road towards Slovenj Gradec.

## Practicalities

**Tourist Information Centre** Trg 4 julia 57; tel: 02 871 0285; email: info.dravograd@triera.net. Open: daily 09.00–18.00 May–Oct.
**Post office** Trg 4 julia 1
**Koroška Banka** Trg 4 julia 42

# PODZEMLJE PECE

Cycling down a mine shaft might sound like an unlikely activity, but that is exactly what is on offer here. The experience is unusual to say the least, but also a fun way of exploring the old lead and zinc mines in the north of Koroška under the Peca and Uršlja mountains. Lead has been mined here since Roman times and at one point there were over 800km of tunnels snaking beneath the surface. The tours run for 5km along the old routes taken by the ore transporters. You will have to book ahead and if you need a bike let them know as they will generally presume you have your own. All riders are given the necessary helmets and headlamps. Tours usually start from outside the Hotel Club Krnes in Črna na Koroškem. Non-cyclists can arrange two-hour walking tours of the Tourist Mine and Museum (tel: 02 870 0180; fax: 02 870 0165; email: rscm@sgn.net; www.podzemljepece.com. Open: Tue–Sun 09.00–17.00. Mine Tours 11.00 and 15.00 or by appointment) in the nearby town of Mežica, with a trip on an old mining train all part of the fun.

Many of the activities available in and around Logarska Dolina (see *Štajerska*) are also available from Črna na Koroškem in Koroška.

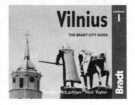

# Appendix 1

## LANGUAGE

The official language of the Republic of Slovenia is Slovene, a Slavic language that has a lot in common with the languages spoken by Slovenia's Croatian, Serbian, Bosnian and Montenegrin neighbours. Slovenes use a version of the Roman alphabet with 25 letters: a b c č d e f g h i j k l m n o p r s š t u v z ž. Many letters are pronounced as they are in English, but there are a number of key exceptions.

## Pronunciation
### Vowels

a – short pronunciation like 'a' in 'hat'

a – long pronunciation like 'a' in 'rather' (to confuse things it can also sound like the 'u' in 'hut'

e – short pronunciation like the 'e' in 'vet'

e – long pronunciation like the 'ea' in 'wear'

i – short pronunciation like the 'i' in 'pink'

i – long pronunciation like the 'ee' in 'seem'

o – short pronunciation like the 'o' in 'off'

o – long pronunciation like the 'aw' in 'paw'

u – like the 'oo' in 'foot'

### Consonants

c – like the 'ts' in 'rats'

d – like the 'd' in 'dog'

g – like the 'g' in 'gold'

j – like the 'y' in 'yacht'

l – like the 'l' in 'leak'

r – Slovenes roll the letter 'r', pronouncing it from the tip of their tongue, in the same way as the French and the Scots

v – can sound like the 'v' in 'vodka', but more often takes the form of the 'w' in 'water'

### Consonants with carons

č – like the 'ch' in 'chomp'

š – like the 'sh' in 'sham'

ž – like the 'su' in 'treasure'

## Basics

| | | | |
|---|---|---|---|
| hello | *zdravo* | here you are | *izvolite* |
| good day | *dober dan* | excuse me | *dovolite mi, prosim* |
| good morning | *dobro jutro* | sorry | *oprostite* |
| good evening | *dober večer* | Mr | *gospod* |
| goodbye | *nasvidenje* | Mrs | *gospa* |
| yes | *da/ja* | Miss | *gospodična* |
| no | *ne* | what | *kaj* |
| please | *prosim* | why | *zakaj* |
| thank you | *hvala* | when | *kdaj* |
| (very much) | *(lepa)* | who | *kdo* |

## Conversation

| | |
|---|---|
| How are you? | *Kako ste?* |
| Very well thank you | *zelo dobro hvala* |
| My name is ... | *Imenujem se ...* |
| What's your name? | *Kako vam je ime?* |
| I am English/Scottish/Welsh/Irish/ American/Canadian/Australian | *Sem Anglež/Škot/Valižan/Irec/ Američan/Kanadčan/Avstralec* |
| Where are you from? | *Od kod ste?* |

## Family

| | | | |
|---|---|---|---|
| aunt | *teta* | husband | *mož* |
| brother | *brat* | mother | *mama* |
| daughter | *hči* | sister | *sestra* |
| father | *oče* | son | *sin* |
| grandfather | *stari oče* | uncle | *stric* |
| grandmother | *stara mama* | wife | *žena* |

## Language

| | |
|---|---|
| Do you speak English? | *Ali govorite angleško?* |
| I don't speak Slovene | *Ne govorim slovensko* |
| Please speak more slowly | *Govorite počasneje prosim* |
| I understand | *razumem* |
| I don't understand | *ne razumem* |
| Please write it down | *Prosim zapišite* |
| How do you say ...? | *Kako rečete ...?* |

## Accommodation

| | | | |
|---|---|---|---|
| inn | *krčma/gostilna* | rooms available | *proste sobe* |
| pension | *s prenočišci* | towel | *brisača* |
| guesthouse | *gostišče* | room | *soba* |
| campsite | *kamping* | bed | *postelja* |
| youth hostel | *mladinsko prenočišče* | dorm bed | *skupna ležišča* |
| student dormitory | *študentski dom* | full board | *polni penzion* |

| | |
|---|---|
| half board | *polpenzion* |
| Can I see the room? | *Ali lahko vidim sobo?* |
| I have a reservation | *Imam rezervacijo* |
| Do you have a single/double room? | *Ali imate prosto enoposteljno/ dvoposteljno sobo?* |
| with a bath/shower | *s kadjo/prho* |
| Could you wake me at … ? | *Ali me lahko zbudite ob … ?* |
| I'd like a … | *Rad bi …* (male) *Rada bi …* (female) |
| How much is it per night/per person? | *Koliko stane na noč/po osebi?* |
| Is breakfast included? | *Ali je zajtrk vključen?* |

## Health and emergencies

| | | | |
|---|---|---|---|
| police | *policija* | hand | *roka* |
| hospital | *bolnišnica* | blood | *kri* |
| ambulance | *rešilec* | chest | *prsni koš* |
| chemist/pharmacy | *lekarna* | leg/foot | *noga* |
| dentist | *zobozdravnik* | head | *glava* |
| doctor | *doktor* | shoulder | *rama* |
| ache/pain | *bolečina* | stomach | *želodec* |
| arm | *laket* | | |

## Directions

| | | | |
|---|---|---|---|
| Where is the … ? | *Kje je … ?* | opposite | *nasproti* |
| turn left/right | *obrnite levo/desno* | here/there | *tu/tam* |
| near/far | *blizu/daleč* | north | *sever* |
| go straight ahead | *pojdite naravnost naprej* | south | *jug* |
| | | east | *vzhod* |
| behind | *zadaj* | west | *zahod* |
| in front of | *spredaj* | | |

## Driving/transport

| | | | |
|---|---|---|---|
| airport | *letališče* | garage | *mehanična delavnica* |
| aeroplane | *letalo* | petrol | *bencin* |
| bus | *avtobus* | petrol station | *bencinska črpalka* |
| train | *vlak* | motorway/highway | *avtocesta* |
| railway station | *železniška postaja* | road | *cesta* |
| platform | *peron* | puncture | *preluknjana zračnica/ avtomobilska guma* |
| bus station | *avtobusna postaja* | | |
| bus stop | *avtobusno postajališče* | map | *zemljevid* |
| timetable | *vozni red* | bicycle | *kolo* |
| car | *avto* | ferry | *trajekt* |
| A one-way ticket to . . . please | *Enosmerno vozovnico za … prosim* |
| A return ticket to . . . please | *Povratno vozovnico za … prosim* |
| Can I reserve a seat? | *Ali lahko rezerviram sedež?* |
| What time does the bus/train leave? | *Kdaj odpelje avtobus/vlak?* |
| Stop here please | *Ustavite tukaj prosim* |

## Signs

| | | | |
|---|---|---|---|
| entrance/exit | *vhod/izhod* | prohibited | *prepovedano* |
| open/closed | *odprto/zaprto* | (male/female) | *(moško/žensko)* |
| arrivals/depatures | *prihod/odhod* | toilets | *stranišče* |
| information | *informacije* | | |

## Places

| | | | |
|---|---|---|---|
| shop | *trgovina* | church | *cerkev* |
| (main/old/upper/ | *(glavni/stari/gornji/* | field | *polje* |
| town) square | *mestni) trg* | lake | *jezero* |
| garden | *vrt* | laundry | *pralnica* |
| street | *ulica* | market | *tržnica* |
| bridge | *most* | cave | *jama* |
| bank | *banka* | mountain | *gora* |
| bay | *morski zaliv* | hill | *hrib, grič* |
| village | *vas* | forest | *gozd* |
| fountain | *vodnjak* | museum | *muzej* |
| port | *pristanišče* | house | *hiša* |
| monastery | *samostan* | town hall | *mestna hiša* |
| waterfall | *slap* | shopping centre | *nakupovalni center* |
| fair | *sejem* | river | *reka* |
| school | *šola* | sea | *morje* |
| beach | *plaža* | tower | *stolp* |
| therapeutic spa | *toplice* | Old Town/City | *stari del mesta* |
| post office | *pošta* | town | *mesto* |
| valley | *dolina* | city | *veliko mesto* |
| castle | *grad* | cathedral | *stolnica* |
| centre | *središče* | island | *otok* |
| chapel | *kapelica* | | |

## Eating and drinking

| | |
|---|---|
| restaurant | *restavracija* |
| taverna | *gostilna* |
| good appetite | *dober tek* |

## Fish

| | | | |
|---|---|---|---|
| lobster | *jastog* | sole morski | *list* |
| mussels | *školjke* | fried fish | *ocvrta riba* |
| octopus | *hobotnica* | grilled fish | *riba na žaru* |
| shrimps | *škampi* | dorada | *orada* |
| squid | *lignji* | trout | *postrv* |
| sea bass | *brancin* | prawns | *rakci* |
| salmon | *losos* | tuna | *tuna* |

## Meat

| | | | |
|---|---|---|---|
| ham | *šunka* | goulash | *golaž* |
| sausage | *klobasa* | lamb | *jagnjetina* |
| beef | *govedina* | mixed grill | *meso na žaru* |
| chicken | *piščanec* | veal | *teletina* |
| pork | *svinjina* | rabbit | *zajec* |
| turkey | *puran* | foal | *žrebiček* |
| venison | *divjačina* | air-dried ham | *pršut* |

## Fruit and vegetables

| | | | |
|---|---|---|---|
| apple | *jabolko* | cucumber | *kumara* |
| pineapple | *ananas* | tomato | *paradižnik* |
| peach | *breskev* | cabbage | *zelje* |
| cherry | *češnja* | onions | *čebula* |
| grape | *grozdje* | garlic | *česen* |
| pear | *hruška* | beans | *fižol* |
| banana | *banana* | mushrooms | *gobe* |
| lemon | *limona* | peas | *grah* |
| watermelon | *lubenica* | carrots | *korenje* |
| raspberry | *malina* | pepper | *paprika* |
| apricot | *marelica* | spinach | *špinača* |
| melon | *melona* | courgette | *bučke* |
| plum | *sliva* | (black) olive | *(črne) olive* |
| orange | *pomaranča* | artichoke | *artičoke* |
| strawberry | *jagoda* | asparagus | *beluši* |
| (green/mixed) | *(zelena/mešana)* | basil | *bazilika* |
| salad | *solata* | ruccola | *rukola* |
| potato | *krompir* | | |

## Dessert

| | | | |
|---|---|---|---|
| ice-cream | *sladoled* | strudel | *štrudelj* |
| traditional | | cream cake/slice | *kremna rezina* |
| Prekmurje dessert | *gibanica* | | |
| traditional | | | |
| Slovenian cake | *potica* | | |

## Drinks

| | | | |
|---|---|---|---|
| beer | *pivo* | tea (with milk/ | *čaj (z mlekom/* |
| coffee | *kava* | lemon) | *z limono)* |
| milky coffee | *bela kava* | wine | *vino* |
| espresso with milk | *macchiato* | (white, red, rosé) | *(belo, črno, roze)* |
| fruit juice | *sok* | | |
| (mineral) water | *(mineralna) voda* | | |

## Miscellaneous

| | | | |
|---|---|---|---|
| bread | *kruh* | cheese | *sir* |
| egg | *jajce* | (sour) cream | *(kisla) smetana* |
| omelette | *omleta* | | |
| beef/mushroom/bean/vegetable/fish soup | | *goveja/fižolova/gobova/zelenjavna/ribja juha* | |

## Meals and useful words

| | | | |
|---|---|---|---|
| breakfast | *zajtrk* | cup | *skodelica* |
| lunch | *kosilo* | glass | *kozarec* |
| dinner | *večerja* | plate | *plošča* |
| boiled | *kuhano* | bowl | *skleda* |
| grilled | *na žaru* | knife | *nož* |
| fried | *ocvrto* | fork | *vilica* |
| roast | *pečenka* | spoon | *žlica* |
| baked | *pečen* | | |

## Useful words and phrases

| | | | |
|---|---|---|---|
| maybe | *mogoče* | big | *mala* |
| good | *dober* | small | *velika* |
| bad | *slab* | money | *denar* |
| the bill, please | | *račun prosim* | |
| Where is the toilet? | | *Kje je stranišče?* | |
| What's the time? | | *Koliko je ura?* | |
| How much does this cost? | | *Koliko stane?* | |
| not much | | *komaj da/ne veliko* | |
| you're welcome | | *prosim/ni za kaj* | |
| married | | *poročen/poročena* (male/female) | |

## Numbers

| | | | |
|---|---|---|---|
| 0 | *nič* | 15 | *petnajst* |
| 1 | *ena* | 16 | *šestnajst* |
| 2 | *dve* | 17 | *sedemnajst* |
| 3 | *tri* | 18 | *osemnajst* |
| 4 | *štiri* | 19 | *devetnajst* |
| 5 | *pet* | 20 | *dvajset* |
| 6 | *šest* | 30 | *trideset* |
| 7 | *sedem* | 40 | *štirideset* |
| 8 | *osem* | 50 | *petdeset* |
| 9 | *devet* | 60 | *šestdeset* |
| 10 | *deset* | 70 | *sedemdeset* |
| 11 | *enajst* | 80 | *osemdeset* |
| 12 | *dvanajst* | 90 | *devetdeset* |
| 13 | *trinajst* | 100 | *sto* |
| 14 | *štirinajst* | 1,000 | *tisoč* |

## Time, days and months

| | | | |
|---|---|---|---|
| What is the time? | *Koliko je ura?* | morning | *zjutraj* |
| It is ... | *Ura je ...* | noon | *poldan* |
| two o'clock | *dve* | afternoon | *popoldne* |
| nine o'clock | *devet* | evening | *večer* |
| eight thirty | *pol devetih* | night | *noč* |
| quarter to five | *tričetrt na pet* | January | *januar* |
| quarter past eleven | *enajst in četrt* | February | *februar* |
| Monday | *ponedeljek* | March | *marec* |
| Tuesday | *torek* | April | *april* |
| Wednesday | *sreda* | May | *maj* |
| Thursday | *četrtek* | June | *junij* |
| Friday | *petek* | July | *julij* |
| Saturday | *sobota* | August | *avgust* |
| Sunday | *nedelja* | September | *september* |
| day | *dan* | October | *oktober* |
| today | *danes* | November | *november* |
| yesterday | *včeraj* | December | *december* |
| tomorrow | *jutri* | | |

## Colours

| | | | |
|---|---|---|---|
| black | *črno* | green | *zeleno* |
| white | *belo* | blue | *modro* |
| red | *rdeče* | orange | *oranžno* |

*Dragon Bridge, Ljubljana*

# Appendix

## WHERE NEXT?

Given its central European location Slovenia makes a great gateway for visiting a number of European countries, whether on a day trip or as an extension to your holiday. You can even start your journey in one of the neighbouring countries and then venture into Slovenia with a network of budget airlines now plying routes all over Europe, making one-way flights cheaper than ever – see www.whichbudget.com for ideas. Slovenia's immediate neighbours are Austria, Croatia, Italy and Hungary, however we have focused on the two destinations most frequently added on to a visit to Slovenia: Croatia and Italy, with an emphasis on the former as it is not so well known.

## Croatia

Just over a decade ago Croatia, like Slovenia, was involved in a war of divorce from Yugoslavia. These days one of Europe's newest nations has emerged as an unspoilt destination that boasts a coastline studded with 1,185 islands, an idyllic Mediterranean climate, a string of stunning Venetian towns and excellent cuisine.

Croatia's embryonic tourist industry was decimated by the eruption of fighting in 1991 as the country struggled to gain independence from Yugoslavia. Images of the destruction made their way onto news bulletins across Europe, however the coastline escaped the worst ravages of war, with the fighting being concentrated largely in the hinterland; even here the most intense period of fighting was over by 1992. The conflict also staved off mass tourism, leaving mile upon mile of one of Europe's most dramatic littorals pleasantly devoid of the hordes. Today tourist numbers are back on the rise, but there is still plenty of opportunity to escape the crowds and enjoy a secluded experience.

Croatia's capital, Zagreb, is only two hours by train from Ljubljana, and is an easy day trip from much of Štajerska, Dolenjska and Bela Krajina. This cosmopolitan city impresses with its Old Town, lively nightlife, grand architecture, green spaces and excellent museums. The country's main appeal, though, lies further south with its expansive Adriatic seaboard. The region of Istria is just south of coastal Slovenia and has a well-developed tourist infrastructure, a vast coastline and myriad rural retreats offered by its hinterland, making it a great and easy area to escape to. The picturesque hill towns of Motovun, Grožnjan and Buje are highlights in an inland area that is currently enjoying favourable comparisons with Tuscany, albeit with far cheaper truffles and more affordable holiday homes.

The highlight of the Istrian coastline is undoubtedly Rovinj, a spectacular Italianate town strutting out atop a rocky outcrop in a collage of orange-tiled roofs and dreamy church spires. Rovinj was once under Italian control and a legacy remains, with many locals bilingual and a string of restaurants offering an array of Italian delights at very affordable prices. Over the last decade a colony of artists have also moved into Rovinj and the town now overflows with niche galleries, where the artists themselves are only too keen to talk about their work. Then there are the boutique shops where visitors can stock up on the fine local truffles, wine and other Epicurean treats.

Heading south again, Dalmatia largely escaped the Tito-era tourist development that impacted Istria and as a result many of its hotels, restaurants and bars operate on a pleasantly small scale. Here old Venetian villas and two-millennia-old Roman palaces still buzz with life. Dalmatia's most famous resort is Dubrovnik and with good reason. The much-eulogised 'Pearl of the Adriatic' is stunning, backed by steep limestone crags to the rear and fronted by the sublimely blue waters of the Adriatic. In between is a perfectly preserved city-state, encompassed within medieval walls that house a cocktail of baroque churches and palaces.

A great way to discover Croatia's rugged landscape is from the sea, with 1,185 offshore islands, over 30,000km$^2$ of coastal waters and around 50 marinas on offer. Add in the favourable winds and the idyllic weather from May through to September and it is no surprise that the country is rapidly establishing itself as a world-class sailing destination. Bill Gates, Bernie Ecclestone and Benetton are said to be amongst those now regularly cruising Croatian waters.

For a tranquil and rustic sailing experience the Kornati Islands are a perfect destination. George Bernard Shaw heaped praise on this truly unique landscape of barren stark white islands and crystal-clear waters when he gushed: 'On the last day of the Creation God desired to crown his work, and thus created the Kornati Islands out of tears, stars and breath.' Despite their beauty, for experienced sailors the Kornati Islands may not be challenging enough. If so consider either heading further north and trying out Istria with its resort-strewn coastline, or perhaps even better island-studded Dalmatia to the south, where local winds, such as the maestral and the yugo, can make life pretty interesting, as can the sudden summer thunderstorms. Buses from Istria run up and down the Dalmatian coastline.

Today a number of travel companies offer trips that take in both Slovenia and Croatia, usually with a mountain element in Slovenia and then a trip to the Croatian coast. Flying into Ljubljana you can easily organise this yourself, continuing south to Zagreb by rail or road and then on to the coast, perhaps flying back from Split with Croatia Airlines (www.croatiaairlines.hr) or Dubrovnik or Spat with British Airways (www.britishairways.com), making backtracking unnecessary. Travelling by bus or in your own car is the best way to get around Croatia, although the rail network has improved lately with a new express train from Zagreb to Split on the coast.

For more information on Croatia see the national tourist office on www.croatia.hr and *Croatia: The Bradt Travel Guide*.

## Italy

Crossing the border to Italy opens up a whole new range of possibilities. From the Slovenian coast the Italian city of Trieste, once part of the Austro-Hungarian Empire, is within easy driving distance or a short train journey away. It has a real gateway feel to it, sandwiched between east and west on a map of Europe that is rapidly changing. With borders opening up and a new direct rail link from Ljubljana to Venice it has now lost some of its strategic importance and it is increasingly being sidelined, which adds to the faded grandeur of many of its buildings. Trieste today has a real end-of-the-world feel, a city that legendary travel writer Jan Morris chose as the setting for her last book – the aptly titled *Meaning of Nowhere*.

It is also possible to catch a ferry from the Slovenian coastline to Venice (see *Getting There and Away* in *Chapter 2*) with day trips or longer stays possible. The treasures of Venice are well documented and arriving by sea is a great experience. This is an aquatic playground like no other with everyone, even the police, fire brigade and ambulance service, all travelling by canal. Venice is also connected by rail to Ljubljana.

From Venice and Trieste the comprehensive and good-value Italian rail network (www.trenitalia.com) beckons with the likes of Florence, Rome and Bologna only a journey away. For more information on Italy see the Italian Tourist Office website at www.enit.it.

## Austria and Hungary

It is possible to cross from Slovenia into Austria or Hungary and continue your travels there. Both countries have much to offer – for more information see www.austria-tourism.co.uk and www.hungarytourism.hu.

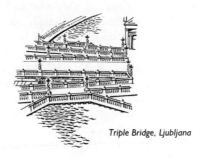

*Triple Bridge, Ljubljana*

# Appendix

## FURTHER READING
### Magazines and newspapers
#### Entertainment

*Ljubljana Calling* is a monthly listings magazine, which can be hard to find in its printed version but is available at some of the city's hotels.

*Ljubljana Life* is a quarterly magazine with plenty of tourist information and some longer articles. It is available at tourist information centres and hotels throughout the city.

#### News and current affairs

*Slovenia News* is a weekly colour magazine with features on personalities and cultural events. Look out for copies at TICs, cafés and hotels throughout the city.

*Slovenia Times* is an excellent English-language monthly newspaper that covers politics, the economy and also has occasional tourist supplements. Again this can be picked up at TICs and hotels.

## Books
### Architecture

Gooding, Mel and Music, Marko and Fiennes, Mark *National & University Library, Ljubljana, Slovenia, 1936–39, by Jože Plečnik (Architecture in Detail Series)* Phaidon Press, 1997. In-depth examination of what many consider to be Plečnik's finest architectural achievement.

Hrausky, Andrej and Koželj, Janez *Architectural Guide to Ljubljana: 100 Selected Buildings* Rokus, 2002. Insightful guide to Ljubljana's impressive architecture. Hard to buy outside Slovenia.

### Fiction

Bartol, Vladimir (translated by Michael Biggins) *Alamut* Scala House Press, 2005. Historical fiction, commonly regarded as the most popular book ever written by a Slovene. Set in 11th-century Iran, the book has parallels with the rise of fascism in the 20th century and the fundamentalist terrorism in the 21st.

Blatnik, Andrej *Skinswaps (Writing from an Unbound Europe)* Northwestern University Press, 1998. Sixteen short stories by the popular Slovene post-modern writer.

Debeljak, Ales *The City & the Child* White Pine Press, 1999. Anthology of contemporary poems by the popular Slovene poet.

Holton, Milne and Taufer, Veno (Translators) *Waterlings* Northwestern University Press, 2000. Six epic Slovenian poems about mythical water beings translated into English.

Jančar, Drago (translated by Michael Biggins) *Mocking Desire* Northwestern University Press, 1998. The story of a creative writing teacher who takes a job in New Orleans and who, as a Slovene in America, remains very much an outsider, a stranger who can't get used to the unfamiliar customs and people, most of whom have never heard of where he is from.

Mozetič, Brane *Butterflies* Meeting Eyes Bindery, 2004. Poetry anthology.

## History

Benderley, Jill and Craft, Ivan *Independent Slovenia* Palgrave Macmillan, 1997. In-depth study of Slovenia's political and economic development during the years following independence.

Benderley, Jill *Independent Slovenia: Origins, Movements, Prospects* Palgrave Macmillan, 1996. Decent introduction to Slovenia and the country's recent political and economic history.

Carmichael, Cathie and Gow, James *Slovenia & the Slovenes* Indiana University Press, 2001. Thorough examination of history, economics, politics and culture in 20th-century Slovenia.

Fink-Hafner, Danica and Robbins, John, R *Making a New Nation: Formation of Slovenia* Dartmouth, 1996. Examining the role of Slovenia in the Socialist Federal Republic of Yugoslavia and its emergence as an independent country.

Mrak, Mojmir and Rojec, Matja and Rojec, Marika (Editors) *Slovenia: From Yugoslavia to the European Union* World Bank, 2004. Weighty but informative read focusing on the reasons for the dissolution of Yugoslavia and Slovenia's political and economic development since 1991, including its integration into the EU.

Prunk, Janko *A Brief History of Slovenia: Historical background of the Republic of Slovenia* Zalozba Mihelac, 1994. Useful introduction to Slovenia and its history. Can be a little too general at times.

*War in Slovenia: From first 'attacks' on YPA to final victory over the Yugoslav Army* Ljubljana International Press Centre, 1991. Fascinating insight into Slovenia's ten-day war of independence with Yugoslavia. Limited availability.

## Mountaineering/hiking

Brown, Simon *Walking in the Julian Alps* Cicerone Press, 1993. Now something of a classic, a range of easy-to-follow walks for all levels of fitness and experience.

Collomb, Robin *Julian Alps Mountain Walking* West Col Productions, 1998. Giving details of more routes in the Julian Alps.

Mihelič, Tine *Mountaineering in Slovenia: The Julian Alps and Kamnik and Savinja Alps* Cordee, 2003. Comprehensive guide for those interested in tackling Slovenia's mountains.

Newbury, Mike *A Guide to Walks & Scrambles in the Julian Alps Based on Kranjska Gora* Zlatorog Publication, 2003. Excellent rambling guide with trails suitable for everyone from the novice to the experienced walker.

Robertson, David and Stewart, Sarah *Landscapes of Slovenia* Sunflower Books, London, 2003. Essentially a book for hikers, Robertson and Stewart also present six itineraries for exploration by car and highlight great picnic spots alongside their 41 main walking trails.

## Travel

McKelvie, Robin and Jenny *Ljubljana: The Bradt City Guide* Bradt Travel Guides, 2005

## Other

Dolenc, Milan *Lipizzaner: The Story of the Horses of Lipica* Control Data Publishing Co, 1986.

## Maps

**Geodetski Zavod Slovenije dd** (www.gzs-dd.si) produce the majority of maps to Slovenia. Their maps are available in hotels, TICs and bookstores in Slovenia. Bookstores and online retailers outside of Slovenia should also stock maps produced by Geodetski zavod Slovenije dd.

*Julian Alps (Walking Maps)* Freytag & Berndt 2000. Detailed walking maps.

**Kod & Kam** Trg Francoske Revolucije 7; tel: 01 200 2732. Stock a wide range of maps and road atlases.

## Websites

### Tourist information

**Ljubljana Tourism** www.ljubljana-tourism.si
**Slovenian Landmarks** www.burger.si
**Slovenia Tourism** www.slovenia.info

### General information

**State Portal of the Republic of Slovenia** http://www.e-uprava.gov.si/e-uprava/en/portal.euprava

### Local transport

**Avtobusna Postaja Ljubljana** (Ljubljana Bus Station) www.ap-ljubljana.si

### Daily newspapers

**Delo** www.delo.si
**Dnevnik** www.dnevnik.si
**Večer** www.vecer.si

### Business news

**Slovenia Business Week** www.gzs.si

### English-language news

**Republic of Slovenia Public Relations and Media Office** www.uvi.si/eng
**Sinfo** www.uvi.si/eng/slovenia/publications/sinfo
**Slovenia Bulletin** http://www.geocities.com/ljubljanalife/News.htm
**Slovenia Business Report** www.gvrevija.com
**Slovenia Magazine** www.zdruzenje-sim.si
**Slovenia News** www.uvi.si/eng/slovenia/publications/slovenia-news
**Slovenia Times** www.sloveniatimes.com

## Lifestyle and culture

**Ljubljana Calling** www.ljubljana-calling.com
**Ljubljana Digital Media Lab** www.ljudmila.org
**Ljubljana Life** www.geocities.com/ljubljanalife
**Slovenian Ministry of Culture** www.kultura.gov.si

## Gay and lesbian

**Slovenian Queer Resources Directory** www.ljudmila.org/siqrd

*Prešeren statue, Ljubljana*

# WIN £100 CASH!

## READER QUESTIONNAIRE

**Send in your completed questionnaire for the chance to win
£100 cash in our regular draw**

All respondents may order a Bradt guide at half the UK retail price – please
complete the order form overleaf.

*(Entries may be posted or faxed to us, or scanned and emailed.)*

We are interested in getting feedback from our readers to help us plan future Bradt
guides. Please complete this quick questionnaire and return it to us to enter into
our draw.

Have you used any other Bradt guides? If so, which titles? . . . . . . . . . . . . . . . . . .
. . . . . . . . . . . . . . . . . . . . . . . . . . . . . . . . . . . . . . . . . . . . . . . . . . . . . . . . . . . . . . . .
What other publishers' travel guides do you use regularly? . . . . . . . . . . . . . . . . . .
. . . . . . . . . . . . . . . . . . . . . . . . . . . . . . . . . . . . . . . . . . . . . . . . . . . . . . . . . . . . . . . .
Where did you buy this guidebook? . . . . . . . . . . . . . . . . . . . . . . . . . . . . . . . . . . . . .
What was the main purpose of your trip to Slovenia (or for what other reason did
you read our guide)? eg: holiday/business/charity etc.. . . . . . . . . . . . . . . . . . . . . . . .
. . . . . . . . . . . . . . . . . . . . . . . . . . . . . . . . . . . . . . . . . . . . . . . . . . . . . . . . . . . . . . . .
What other destinations would you like to see covered by a Bradt guide?
. . . . . . . . . . . . . . . . . . . . . . . . . . . . . . . . . . . . . . . . . . . . . . . . . . . . . . . . . . . . . . . .
Would you like to receive our catalogue/newsletters?

YES / NO (If yes, please complete details on reverse)

If yes – by post or email? . . . . . . . . . . . . . . . . . . . . . . . . . . . . . . . . . . . . . . . . . . . . .
Age (circle relevant category) 16–25     26 45     46–60     60+

Male/Female (delete as appropriate)

Home country . . . . . . . . . . . . . . . . . . . . . . . . . . . . . . . . . . . . . . . . . . . . . . . . . . . . . .
Please send us any comments about our guide to Slovenia or other Bradt Travel
Guides. . . . . . . . . . . . . . . . . . . . . . . . . . . . . . . . . . . . . . . . . . . . . . . . . . . . . . . . . . . . .
. . . . . . . . . . . . . . . . . . . . . . . . . . . . . . . . . . . . . . . . . . . . . . . . . . . . . . . . . . . . . . . .
. . . . . . . . . . . . . . . . . . . . . . . . . . . . . . . . . . . . . . . . . . . . . . . . . . . . . . . . . . . . . . . .
. . . . . . . . . . . . . . . . . . . . . . . . . . . . . . . . . . . . . . . . . . . . . . . . . . . . . . . . . . . . . . . .

## Bradt Travel Guides

23 High Street, Chalfont St Peter, Bucks SL9 9QE, UK
Telephone: +44 (0)1753 893444 Fax: +44 (0)1753 892333
Email: info@bradtguides.com
www.bradtguides.com

# CLAIM YOUR HALF-PRICE BRADT GUIDE!

## Order Form

To order your half-price copy of a Bradt guide, and to enter our prize draw to win £100 (see overleaf), please fill in the order form below, complete the questionnaire overleaf, and send it to Bradt Travel Guides by post, fax or email.

Please send me one copy of the following guide at half the UK retail price

| Title | Retail price | Half price |
|---|---|---|
| ... ........................................... | ........ | ....... |

Please send the following additional guides at full UK retail price

| No | Title | Retail price | Total |
|---|---|---|---|
| ... | ........................................ | ........ | ....... |
| ... | ........................................ | ........ | ....... |
| ... | ........................................ | ........ | ....... |

|  |  |
|---|---|
| Sub total | ....... |
| Post & packing | ....... |
| (£1 per book UK; £2 per book Europe; £3 per book rest of world) | |
| Total | ....... |

Name ........................................................

Address ........................................................

Tel ......................... Email ........................

☐ I enclose a cheque for £ ....... made payable to Bradt Travel Guides Ltd

☐ I would like to pay by credit card. Number: ........................

Expiry date: ... / ...    3-digit security code (on reverse of card) .....

☐ Please add my name to your catalogue mailing list.

Send your order on this form, with the completed questionnaire, to:

**Bradt Travel Guides/SLO**
23 High Street, Chalfont St Peter, Bucks SL9 9QE
Tel: +44 (0)1753 893444 Fax: +44 (0)1753 892333
Email: info@bradtguides.com
www.bradtguides.com

# Bradt Travel Guides

| | | | |
|---|---|---|---|
| Africa by Road | £13.95 | Kabul Mini Guide | £9.95 |
| Albania | £13.95 | Kenya | £14.95 |
| Amazon | £14.95 | Kiev City Guide | £7.95 |
| Antarctica: A Guide to the Wildlife | £14.95 | Latvia | £12.95 |
| The Arctic: A Guide to Coastal | | Lille City Guide | £5.95 |
| Wildlife | £14.95 | Lithuania | £12.95 |
| Armenia with Nagorno Karabagh | £13.95 | Ljubljana City Guide | £6.95 |
| Azores | £12.95 | London: In the Footsteps of | |
| Baghdad City Guide | £9.95 | the Famous | £10.95 |
| Baltic Capitals: Tallinn, Riga, | | Macedonia | £13.95 |
| Vilnius, Kaliningrad | £11.95 | Madagascar | £14.95 |
| Bosnia & Herzegovina | £13.95 | Madagascar Wildlife | £14.95 |
| Botswana: Okavango Delta, | | Malawi | £12.95 |
| Chobe, Northern Kalahari | £14.95 | Maldives | £12.95 |
| British Isles: Wildlife of Coastal | | Mali | £13.95 |
| Waters | £14.95 | Mauritius | £12.95 |
| Budapest City Guide | £7.95 | Mongolia | £14.95 |
| Cambodia | £11.95 | Montenegro | £12.95 |
| Cameroon | £13.95 | Mozambique | £12.95 |
| Canada: North – Yukon, Northwest | | Namibia | £14.95 |
| Territories | £13.95 | Nigeria | £14.95 |
| Canary Islands | £13.95 | North Cyprus | £12.95 |
| Cape Verde Islands | £12.95 | North Korea | £13.95 |
| Cayman Islands | £12.95 | Palestine with Jerusalem | £12.95 |
| Chile | £16.95 | Panama | £13.95 |
| Chile & Argentina: Trekking | | Paris, Lille & Brussels: Eurostar Cities | £11.95 |
| Guide | £12.95 | Peru & Bolivia: Backpacking & | |
| China: Yunnan Province | £13.95 | Trekking | £12.95 |
| Cork City Guide | £6.95 | Riga City Guide | £6.95 |
| Costa Rica | £13.99 | River Thames: In the | |
| Croatia | £12.95 | Footsteps of the Famous | £10.95 |
| Dubrovnik City Guide | £6.95 | Rwanda | £13.95 |
| East & Southern Africa: | | St Helena, Ascension, | |
| Backpacker's Manual | £14.95 | Tristan da Cunha | £14.95 |
| Eccentric America | £13.95 | Serbia | £13.95 |
| Eccentric Britain | £11.95 | Seychelles | £12.95 |
| Eccentric California | £13.99 | Singapore | £11.95 |
| Eccentric Edinburgh | £5.95 | Slovenia | £13.95 |
| Eccentric France | £12.95 | South Africa: Budget Travel Guide | £11.95 |
| Eccentric London | £12.95 | Southern African Wildlife | £18.95 |
| Eccentric Oxford | £5.95 | Sri Lanka | £12.95 |
| Ecuador, Peru & Bolivia: | | Sudan | £13.95 |
| Backpacker's Manual | £13.95 | Svalbard | £13.95 |
| Ecuador: Climbing & Hiking | £13.95 | Switzerland: Rail, Road, Lake | £12.95 |
| Eritrea | £12.95 | Tallinn City Guide | £6.95 |
| Estonia | £12.95 | Tanzania | £14.95 |
| Ethiopia | £13.95 | Tasmania | £12.95 |
| Falkland Islands | £13.95 | Tibet | £12.95 |
| Faroe Islands | £13.95 | Uganda | £13.95 |
| Gabon, São Tomé & Príncipe | £13.95 | Ukraine | £14.95 |
| Galápagos Wildlife | £14.95 | USA by Rail | £12.95 |
| Gambia, The | £12.95 | Venezuela | £14.95 |
| Georgia with Armenia | £13.95 | Your Child Abroad: A Travel | |
| Ghana | £13.95 | Health Guide | £9.95 |
| Iran | £12.95 | Zambia | £15.95 |
| Iraq | £14.95 | Zanzibar | £12.95 |

268

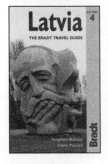

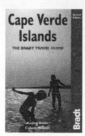

# NOTES

# NOTES

# Index